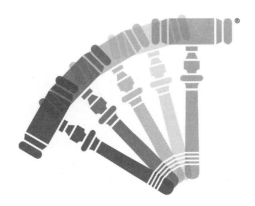

Casenote™ Legal Briefs

TORTS

Keyed to Courses Using

**Prosser, Wade and Schwartz's
Torts: Cases and Materials**

Eleventh Edition

by Schwartz, Kelly and Partlett

PUBLISHERS

76 Ninth Avenue, New York, NY 10011
http://lawschool.aspenpublishers.com

© 2006 Aspen Publishers, Inc.
a Wolters Kluwer business
http://lawschool.aspenpublishers.com

Printed in the United States of America.

ISBN 0-7355-5957-0
2 3 4 5 6 7 8 9 0

Format for the Casenote Legal Brief

Nature of Case: This section identifies the form of action (e.g., breach of contract, negligence, battery), the type of proceeding (e.g., demurrer, appeal from trial court's jury instructions) or the relief sought (e.g., damages, injunction, criminal sanctions).

Party ID: Quick identification of the relationship between the parties.

Fact Summary: This is included to refresh your memory and can be used as a quick reminder of the facts.

Rule of Law: Summarizes the general principle of law that the case illustrates. It may be used for instant recall of the court's holding and for classroom discussion or home review.

Facts: This section contains all relevant facts of the case, including the contentions of the parties and the lower court holdings. It is written in a logical order to give the student a clear understanding of the case. The plaintiff and defendant are identified by their proper names throughout and are always labeled with a (P) or (D).

Concurrence/Dissent: All concurrences and dissents are briefed whenever they are included by the casebook editor.

Analysis: This last paragraph gives you a broad understanding of where the case "fits in" with other cases in the section of the book and with the entire course. It is a hornbook-style discussion indicating whether the case is a majority or minority opinion and comparing the principal case with other cases in the casebook. It may also provide analysis from restatements, uniform codes, and law review articles. The analysis will prove to be invaluable to classroom discussion.

Palsgraf v. Long Island R.R. Co.

Injured bystander (P) v. Railroad company (D)

N.Y. Ct. App., 248 N.Y. 339, 162 N.E. 99 (1928).

NATURE OF CASE: Appeal from judgment affirming verdict for plaintiff seeking damages for personal injury.

FACT SUMMARY: Helen Palsgraf (P) was injured on R.R.'s (D) train platform when R.R.'s (D) guard helped a passenger aboard a moving train, causing his package to fall on the tracks. The package contained fireworks which exploded, creating a shock that tipped a scale onto Palsgraf (P).

🏛 RULE OF LAW
The risk reasonably to be perceived defines the duty to be obeyed.

FACTS: Helen Palsgraf (P) purchased a ticket to Rockaway Beach from R.R. (D) and was waiting on the train platform. As she waited, two men ran to catch a train that was pulling out from the platform. The first man jumped aboard, but the second man, who appeared as if he might fall, was helped aboard by the guard on the train who had kept the door open so they could jump aboard. A guard on the platform also helped by pushing him onto the train. The man was carrying a package wrapped in newspaper. In the process, the man dropped his package, which fell on the tracks. The package contained fireworks and exploded. The shock of the explosion was apparently of great enough strength to tip over some scales at the other end of the platform, which fell on Palsgraf (P) and injured her. A jury awarded her damages, and R.R. (D) appealed.

ISSUE: Does the risk reasonably to be perceived define the duty to be obeyed?

HOLDING AND DECISION: (Cardozo, C.J.) Yes. The risk reasonably to be perceived defines the duty to be obeyed. If there is no foreseeable hazard to the injured party as the result of a seemingly innocent act, the act does not become a tort because it happened to be a wrong as to another. If the wrong was not willful, the plaintiff must show that the act as to her had such great and apparent possibilities of danger as to entitle her to protection. Negligence in the abstract is not enough upon which to base liability. Negligence is a relative concept, evolving out of the common law doctrine of trespass on the case. To establish liability, the defendant must owe a legal duty of reasonable care to the injured party. A cause of action in tort will lie where harm,

though unintended, could have been averted or avoided by observance of such a duty. The scope of the duty is limited by the range of danger that a reasonable person could foresee. In this case, there was nothing to suggest from the appearance of the parcel or otherwise that the parcel contained fireworks. The guard could not reasonably have had any warning of a threat to Palsgraf (P), and R.R. (D) therefore cannot be held liable. Judgment is reversed in favor of R.R. (D).

DISSENT: (Andrews, J.) The concept that there is no negligence unless R.R. (D) owes a legal duty to take care as to Palsgraf (P) herself is too narrow. Everyone owes to the world at large the duty of refraining from those acts that may unreasonably threaten the safety of others. If the guard's action was negligent as to those nearby, it was also negligent as to those outside what might be termed the "danger zone." For Palsgraf (P) to recover, R.R.'s (D) negligence must have been the proximate cause of her injury, a question of fact for the jury.

▶ ANALYSIS
The majority defined the limit of the defendant's liability in terms of the danger that a reasonable person in defendant's situation would have perceived. The dissent argued that the limitation should not be placed on liability, but rather on damages. Judge Andrews suggested that only injuries that would not have happened but for R.R.'s (D) negligence should be compensable. Both the majority and dissent recognized the policy-driven need to limit liability for negligent acts, seeking, in the words of Judge Andrews, to define a framework "that will be practical and in keeping with the general understanding of mankind." The Restatement (Second) of Torts has accepted Judge Cardozo's view.

▬▬

Quicknotes

FORESEEABILITY A reasonable expectation that change is the probable result of certain acts or omissions.

NEGLIGENCE Conduct falling below the standard of care that a reasonable person would demonstrate under similar conditions.

PROXIMATE CAUSE The natural sequence of events without which an injury would not have been sustained.

▬▬

Issue: The issue is a concise question that brings out the essence of the opinion as it relates to the section of the casebook in which the case appears. Both substantive and procedural issues are included if relevant to the decision.

Holding and Decision: This section offers a clear and in-depth discussion of the rule of the case and the court's rationale. It is written in easy-to-understand language and answers the issues(s) presented by applying the law to the facts of the case. When relevant, it includes a thorough discussion of the exceptions to the case as listed by the court, any major cites to the other cases on point, and the names of the judges who wrote the decisions.

Quicknotes: Conveniently defines legal terms found in the case and summarizes the nature of any statutes, codes, or rules referred to in the text.

Aspen Publishers is proud to offer *Casenote Legal Briefs*—continuing thirty years of publishing America's best-selling legal briefs.

Casenote Legal Briefs are designed to help you save time when briefing assigned cases. Organized under convenient headings, they show you how to abstract the basic facts and holdings from the text of the actual opinions handed down by the courts. Used as part of a rigorous study regime, they can help you spend more time analyzing and critiquing points of law than on copying out bits and pieces of judicial opinions into your notebook or outline.

Casenote Legal Briefs should never be used as a substitute for assigned casebook readings. They work best when read as a follow-up to reviewing the underlying opinions themselves. Students who try to avoid reading and digesting the judicial opinions in their casebooks or on-line sources will end up shortchanging themselves in the long run. The ability to absorb, critique, and restate the dynamic and complex elements of case law decisions is crucial to your success in law school and beyond. It cannot be developed vicariously.

Casenote Legal Briefs represent but one of the many offerings in Aspen's Study Aid Timeline, which includes:

- Casenote *Legal Briefs*
- Emanuel *Law Outlines*
- *Examples & Explanations* Series
- *Introduction to Law* Series
- Emanuel *Law in a Flash* Flashcards
- Emanuel *CrunchTime* Series

Each of these series is designed to provide you with easy-to-understand explanations of complex points of law. Each volume offers guidance on the principles of legal analysis and, consulted regularly, will hone your ability to spot relevant issues. We have titles that will help you prepare for class, prepare for your exams, and enhance your general comprehension of the law along the way.

To find out more about Aspen Study Aid publications, visit us on-line at *http://lawschool.aspenpublishers.com* or e-mail us at *legaledu@aspenpubl.com*. We'll be happy to assist you.

Free access to Briefs on-line!

Download the cases you want using the full cut-and-paste feature accompanying Casenote Legal Briefs on-line. Fill out this form for full access to this useful feature provided by Loislaw. Learn more about Loislaw services on the inside front cover of this book or visit *www.loislawschool.com*.

Name	Phone
	( )

Address	Apt. No.

City	State	ZIP Code

Law School	Year (check one)
	☐ 1st ☐ 2nd ☐ 3rd

Cut out the UPC found on the lower left-hand corner of the back cover of this book. Staple the UPC inside this box. Only the original UPC from the book cover will be accepted. No photocopies or store stickers are allowed.

**Attach UPC
inside this box.**

E-mail (Print LEGIBLY or you may not get access!)

Title of this book (course subject)

Used with which casebook (provide author's name)

Mail the completed form to: Aspen Publishers, Inc.
Legal Education Division
Casenote On-line Access
130 Turner St., Building 3, 4th Floor
Waltham, MA 02453-8901

I understand that on-line access is granted solely to the purchaser of this book for the academic year in which it was purchased. Any other usage is not authorized and will result in immediate termination of access. Sharing of codes is strictly prohibited.

Signature _____

Upon receipt of this completed form, you will be e-mailed codes so that you may access the Briefs for this Casenote Legal Brief. On-line Briefs may not be available for all titles. For a full list of available titles, please check *http://lawschool.aspenpublishers.com*.

A. Decide on a Format and Stick to It

Structure is essential to a good brief. It enables you to arrange systematically the related parts that are scattered throughout most cases, thus making manageable and understandable what might otherwise seem to be an endless and unfathomable sea of information. There are, of course, an unlimited number of formats that can be utilized. However, it is best to find one that suits your needs and stick to it. Consistency breeds both efficiency and the security that when called upon you will know where to look in your brief for the information you are asked to give.

Any format, as long as it presents the essential elements of a case in an organized fashion, can be used. Experience, however, has led *Casenotes* to develop and utilize the following format because of its logical flow and universal applicability.

NATURE OF CASE: This is a brief statement of the legal character and procedural status of the case (e.g., "Appeal of a burglary conviction").

There are many different alternatives open to a litigant dissatisfied with a court ruling. The key to determining which one has been used is to discover *who is asking this court for what.*

This first entry in the brief should be kept *as short as possible.* Use the court's terminology if you understand it. But since jurisdictions vary as to the titles of pleadings, the best entry is the one that addresses who wants what in this proceeding, not the one that sounds most like the court's language.

RULE OF LAW: A statement of the general principle of law that the case illustrates (e.g., "An acceptance that varies any term of the offer is considered a rejection and counter-offer").

Determining the rule of law of a case is a procedure similar to determining the issue of the case. Avoid being fooled by red herrings; there may be a few rules of law mentioned in the case excerpt, but usually only one is *the* rule with which the casebook editor is concerned. The techniques used to locate the issue, described below, may also be utilized to find the rule of law. Generally, your best guide is simply the chapter heading. It is a clue to the point the casebook editor seeks to make and should be kept in mind when reading every case in the respective section.

FACTS: A synopsis of only the essential facts of the case, i.e., those bearing upon or leading up to the issue.

The facts entry should be a short statement of the events and transactions that led one party to initiate legal proceedings against another in the first place. While some cases conveniently state the salient facts at the beginning of the decision, in other instances they will have to be culled from hiding places throughout the text, even from concurring and dissenting opinions. Some of the "facts" will often be in dispute and should be so noted. Conflicting evidence may be briefly pointed up. "Hard" facts must be included. Both must be *relevant* in order to be listed in the facts entry. It is impossible to tell what is relevant until the entire case is read, as the ultimate determination of the rights and liabilities of the parties may turn on something buried deep in the opinion.

Generally, the facts entry should not be longer than three to five *short* sentences.

It is often helpful to identify the role played by a party in a given context. For example, in a construction contract case the identification of a party as the "contractor" or "builder" alleviates the need to tell that that party was the one who was supposed to have built the house.

It is always helpful, and a good general practice, to identify the "plaintiff" and the "defendant." This may seem elementary and uncomplicated, but, especially in view of the creative editing practiced by some casebook editors, it is sometimes a difficult or even impossible task. Bear in mind that the *party presently* seeking something from this court may not be the plaintiff, and that sometimes only the cross-claim of a defendant is treated in the excerpt. Confusing or misaligning the parties can ruin your analysis and understanding of the case.

ISSUE: A statement of the general legal question answered by or illustrated in the case. For clarity, the issue is best put in the form of a question capable of a "yes" or "no" answer. In reality, the issue is simply the Rule of Law put in the form of a question (e.g., "May an offer be accepted by performance?").

The major problem presented in discerning what is *the* issue in the case is that an opinion usually purports to raise and answer several questions. However, except for rare cases, only one such question is really the issue in the case. Collateral issues not necessary to the resolution of the matter in controversy are handled by the court by language known as *"obiter dictum"* or merely *"dictum."* While dicta may be included later in the brief, they have no place under the issue heading.

To find the issue, ask *who wants what* and then go on to ask *why did that party succeed or fail in getting it.* Once this is determined, the "why" should be turned into a question.

The complexity of the issues in the cases will vary, but in all cases a single-sentence question should sum up the issue.

In a few cases, there will be two, or even more rarely, three issues of equal importance to the resolution of the case. Each should be expressed in a single-sentence question.

Since many issues are resolved by a court in coming to a final disposition of a case, the casebook editor will reproduce the portion of the opinion containing the issue or issues most relevant to the area of law under scrutiny. A noted law professor gave this advice: "Close the book; look at the title on the cover." Chances are, if it is Property, you need not concern yourself with whether, for example, the federal government's treatment of the plaintiff's land really raises a federal question sufficient to support jurisdiction on this ground in federal court.

The same rule applies to chapter headings designating sub-areas within the subjects. They tip you off as to what the text is designed to teach. The cases are arranged in a casebook to show a progression or development of the law, so that the preceding cases may also help.

It is also most important to remember to *read the notes and questions* at the end of a case to determine what the editors wanted you to have gleaned from it.

HOLDING AND DECISION: This section should succinctly explain the rationale of the court in arriving at its decision. In capsulizing the "reasoning" of the court, it should always include an application of the general rule or rules of law to the specific facts of the case. Hidden justifications come to light in this entry; the reasons for the state of the law, the public policies, the biases and prejudices, those considerations that influence the justices' thinking and, ultimately, the outcome of the case. At the end, there should be a short indication of the disposition or procedural resolution of the case (e.g., "Decision of the trial court for Mr. Smith (P) reversed").

The foregoing format is designed to help you "digest" the reams of case material with which you will be faced in your law school career. Once mastered by practice, it will place at your fingertips the information the authors of your casebooks have sought to impart to you in case-by-case illustration and analysis.

B. Be as Economical as Possible in Briefing Cases

Once armed with a format that encourages succinctness, it is as important to be economical with regard to the time spent on the actual reading of the case as it is to be economical in the writing of the brief itself. This does not mean "skimming" a case. Rather, it means reading the case with an "eye" trained to recognize into which "section" of your brief a particular passage or line fits and having a system for quickly and precisely marking the case so that the passages fitting any one particular part of the brief can be easily identified and brought together in a concise and accurate manner when the brief is actually written.

It is of no use to simply repeat everything in the opinion of the court; record only enough information to trigger your recollection of what the court said. Nevertheless, an accurate statement of the "law of the case," i.e., the legal principle applied to the facts, is absolutely essential to class preparation and to learning the law under the case method.

To that end, it is important to develop a "shorthand" that you can use to make margin notations. These notations will tell you at a glance in which section of the brief you will be placing that particular passage or portion of the opinion.

Some students prefer to underline all the salient portions of the opinion (with a pencil or colored underliner marker), making marginal notations as they go along. Others prefer the color-coded method of underlining, utilizing different colors of markers to underline the salient portions of the case, each separate color being used to represent a different section of the brief. For example, blue underlining could be used for passages relating to the rule of law, yellow for those relating to the issue, and green for those relating to the holding and decision, etc. While it has its advocates, the color-coded method can be confusing and time-consuming (all that time spent on changing colored markers). Furthermore, it can interfere with the continuity and concentration many students deem essential to the reading of a case for maximum comprehension. In the end, however, it is a matter of personal preference and style. Just remember, whatever method you use, underlining must be used sparingly or its value is lost.

If you take the marginal notation route, an efficient and easy method is to go along underlining the key portions of the case and placing in the margin alongside them the following "markers" to indicate where a particular passage or line "belongs" in the brief you will write:

N   (NATURE OF CASE)
RL   (RULE OF LAW)
I   (ISSUE)
HL   (HOLDING AND DECISION, relates to the RULE OF LAW behind the decision)
HR   (HOLDING AND DECISION, gives the RATIONALE or reasoning behind the decision)
HA   (HOLDING AND DECISION, APPLIES the general principle(s) of law to the facts of the case to arrive at the decision)

Remember that a particular passage may well contain information necessary to more than one part of your brief, in which case you simply note that in the margin. If you are using the color-coded underlining method instead of margin notation, simply make asterisks or checks in the margin next to the passage in question in the colors that indicate the additional sections of the brief where it might be utilized.

The economy of utilizing "shorthand" in marking cases for briefing can be maintained in the actual brief writing process itself by utilizing "law student shorthand" within the brief. There are many commonly used words and phrases for which abbreviations can be substituted in your briefs (and in your class notes also). You can develop abbreviations that are personal to you and which will save you a lot of time. A reference list of briefing abbreviations can be found on page xii of this book.

C. Use Both the Briefing Process and the Brief as a Learning Tool

Now that you have a format and the tools for briefing cases efficiently, the most important thing is to make the time spent in briefing profitable to you and to make the most advantageous use of the briefs you create. Of course, the briefs are invaluable for classroom reference when you are called upon to explain or analyze a particular case. However, they are also useful in reviewing for exams. A quick glance at the fact summary should bring the case

to mind, and a rereading of the rule of law should enable you to go over the underlying legal concept in your mind, how it was applied in that particular case, and how it might apply in other factual settings.

As to the value to be derived from engaging in the briefing process itself, there is an immediate benefit that arises from being forced to sift through the essential facts and reasoning from the court's opinion and to succinctly express them in your own words in your brief. The process ensures that you understand the case and the point that it illustrates, and that means you will be ready to absorb further analysis and information brought forth in class. It also ensures you will have something to say when called upon in class. The briefing process helps develop a mental agility for getting to the *gist* of a case and for identifying, expounding on, and applying the legal concepts and issues found there. The briefing process is the mental process on which you must rely in taking law school examinations; it is also the mental process upon which a lawyer relies in serving his clients and in making his living.

acceptance	acp	offer	O
affirmed	aff	offeree	OE
answer	ans	offeror	OR
assumption of risk	a/r	ordinance	ord
attorney	atty	pain and suffering	p/s
beyond a reasonable doubt	b/r/d	parol evidence	p/e
bona fide purchaser	BFP	plaintiff	P
breach of contract	br/k	prima facie	p/f
cause of action	c/a	probable cause	p/c
common law	c/l	proximate cause	px/c
Constitution	Con	real property	r/p
constitutional	con	reasonable doubt	r/d
contract	K	reasonable man	r/m
contributory negligence	c/n	rebuttable presumption	rb/p
cross	x	remanded	rem
cross-complaint	x/c	res ipsa loquitur	RIL
cross-examination	x/ex	respondeat superior	r/s
cruel and unusual punishment	c/u/p	Restatement	RS
defendant	D	reversed	rev
dismissed	dis	Rule Against Perpetuities	RAP
double jeopardy	d/j	search and seizure	s/s
due process	d/p	search warrant	s/w
equal protection	e/p	self-defense	s/d
equity	eq	specific performance	s/p
evidence	ev	statute of limitations	S/L
exclude	exc	statute of frauds	S/F
exclusionary rule	exc/r	statute	S
felony	f/n	summary judgment	s/j
freedom of speech	f/s	tenancy in common	t/c
good faith	g/f	tenancy at will	t/w
habeas corpus	h/c	tenant	t
hearsay	hr	third party	TP
husband	H	third party beneficiary	TPB
in loco parentis	ILP	transferred intent	TI
injunction	inj	unconscionable	uncon
inter vivos	I/v	unconstitutional	unconst
joint tenancy	j/t	undue influence	u/e
judgment	judgt	Uniform Commercial Code	UCC
jurisdiction	jur	unilateral	uni
last clear chance	LCC	vendee	VE
long-arm statute	LAS	vendor	VR
majority view	maj	versus	v
meeting of minds	MOM	void for vagueness	VFV
minority view	min	weight of the evidence	w/e
Miranda warnings	Mir/w	weight of authority	w/a
Miranda rule	Mir/r	wife	W
negligence	neg	with	w/
notice	ntc	within	w/i
nuisance	nus	without prejudice	w/o/p
obligation	ob	without	w/o
obscene	obs	wrongful death	wr/d

Table of Cases

CHAPTER 1

Development of Liability Based upon Fault

Quick Reference Rules of Law

Anonymous

Parties not identified.

King's Bench, Y.B. 5 Edw. IV, folio 7, placitum 18 (1466).

NATURE OF CASE: [Nature of case not stated in casebook excerpt.]

FACT SUMMARY: [Facts not stated in casebook excerpt.]

RULE OF LAW
A person can be held liable for injuries resulting from lawful, unintentional conduct.

FACTS: [Facts not stated in casebook excerpt.]

ISSUE: Can a person be held liable for injuries resulting from lawful, unintentional conduct?

HOLDING AND DECISION: [Holding and decision not stated in casebook excerpt.]

▶ ANALYSIS

The answer to the implicit issue-question in *Anonymous* is "yes." A person can be held liable for injuries resulting from lawful, unintentional conduct. Today, considering the examples stated by counsel in *Anonymous*, the rule stated in this case might seem harsh and the extent of one's potential liability too broad. As the casebook observes, though [p. 2], one heightened purpose of early tort law was simply to keep the peace. If the range of potential liability stated in *Anonymous* accomplished nothing else, surely it encouraged a more cautious demeanor in the inhabitants of the realm. Note also the key distinction between this older rule, which permitted recovery for unintentional conduct, and today's law of negligence. The theory of negligence also permits recovery for unintentional conduct, of course, but today a negligence claim requires proof that the defendant behaved *un*lawfully by neglecting a duty of care.

Quicknotes

LIABILITY Any obligation or responsibility.

Weaver v. Ward

Injured soldier (P) v. Shooting soldier (D)

King's Bench, Hobart 134, 80 Eng. Rep. 284 (1616).

NATURE OF CASE: Action to recover damages for assault and battery.

FACT SUMMARY: During a military exercise, Ward's (D) musket accidentally discharged, injuring Weaver (P).

RULE OF LAW
An actor is liable for injury directly caused by his act unless he can prove himself utterly without fault.

FACTS: Ward (D) and Weaver (P) were participants in a military exercise. During the exercise, Ward's (D) musket accidentally discharged, injuring Weaver (P). Ward (D) contended that the accidental nature of his action should be a defense. The lower court held, as a matter of law, that a showing of accident alone is not a defense to an injury caused by Ward (D). The court gave judgment for Weaver (P) by sustaining his demurrer to the answer.

ISSUE: Is an actor excused from liability for the consequence of his act if he can prove that the injury occurred utterly without his fault?

HOLDING AND DECISION: Yes. The court held that an actor would be excused from liability if he could show the lack of any fault. However, the court considered the voluntary nature of the act of firing the musket as involving an aspect of fault and affirmed the judgment for Weaver (P). Apparently, the court would have found differently were the action of firing found to be involuntary.

ANALYSIS

This is one of the first cases clearly recognizing that some form of fault may be necessary for imposition of liability upon an actor. Modernly, the test for imposition of liability under a fault-based negligence theory is whether a reasonable man might have taken the defendant's action. If so, then there is no negligence, no fault, and, consequently, no liability.

■═■

Quicknotes

ACTION OF TRESPASS An action to recover damages resulting from the wrongful interference with a party's person, property or rights.

■═■

Brown v. Kendall

Injured dog owner (P) v. Stick-wielding dog owner (D)

Mass. Sup. Jud. Ct., 60 Mass. (6 Cush.) 292 (1850).

NATURE OF CASE: Trespass for assault and battery.

FACT SUMMARY: Kendall (D), while attempting to separate his dog from Brown's (P) dog, when the two dogs were fighting, accidentally struck Brown (P) with a stick.

🏛 RULE OF LAW
If in the prosecution of a lawful act, a casualty purely accidental arises, i.e., the injury was unavoidable, and the conduct of the defendant was free from blame, no action can be supported for an injury arising therefrom.

FACTS: Two dogs, owned by Brown (P) and Kendall (D) respectively, were fighting. Kendall (D) attempted to separate the dogs with a stick. When he raised the stick to strike the dogs, Kendall (D) stepped back to avoid the dogs as they approached him, and he accidentally struck Brown (P), who was behind him, in the eye, inflicting a serious injury. Brown (P) brought an action in trespass for assault and battery. The trial court instructed the jury that if it was not a necessary act, and Kendall (D) was not in duty bound to part the dogs, he was responsible for the consequences of the blow, unless it appeared he exercised extraordinary care, so the accident was inevitable. It further instructed that if Kendall (D) had no duty to separate the dogs, then the burden of proving extraordinary care was on him, as well as showing alternatively lack of ordinary care on the part of Brown (P). Following Kendall's (D) death, his executrix (D) excepted to the instructions.

ISSUE: If in the prosecution of a lawful act, a casualty purely accidental arises, can an action be supported for an injury arising therefrom?

HOLDING AND DECISION: (Shaw, C.J.) No. If in the prosecution of a lawful act, a casualty purely accidental arises, i.e., the injury was unavoidable, and the conduct of the defendant was free from blame, no action can be supposed for an injury arising therefrom. The instructions that should have been given are to the effect that Brown (P) could not recover: (1) if at the time of the accident both Kendall (D) and he were using ordinary care; (2) if Kendall (D) was using ordinary care and Brown (P) was not; or (3) if neither were using ordinary care. What constitutes ordinary care will vary with the circumstances, but, generally, it means that kind and degree of care which prudent and cautious people would use. Such is required under the circumstances and is necessary to guard against probable danger. An inevitable accident is one the defendant could not avoid by the use of the kind and degree of care necessary under the circumstances. Because the instructions to the jury placed the burden on Kendall (D) to show that he used extraordinary care or that Brown (P) failed to use ordinary care, rather than having placed the burden of proof on Brown (P) to prove his case, a new trial must be ordered.

▶ ANALYSIS

This case established that some form of fault, negligent or intentional, must form the basis of liability. Consequently, the loss from an unavoidable accident will stay where it falls. This case is also interesting because its discussion includes the concept of contributory negligence, which was fully accepted by the Massachusetts court, but which is losing favor to the concept of comparative negligence today.

■=■

Quicknotes

BILL OF EXCEPTIONS A writing setting forth the objections to a ruling, decision or instruction of the trial court for appeal.

COMPARATIVE NEGLIGENCE Doctrine whereby the court in assessing the appropriate measure of damages compares the relative fault of the parties and reduces the amount of damages to be collected by the plaintiff in proportion to his degree of fault.

CONTRIBUTORY NEGLIGENCE Behavior on the part of an injured plaintiff falling below the standard of ordinary care that contributes to the defendant's negligence, resulting in the plaintiff's injury.

DICTA Plural of dictum.

TRESPASS VI ET ARMIS Action to recover for damages resulting from the direct or immediate injury inflicted by one party against the person or property of another.

■=■

Cohen v. Petty

Injured passenger (P) v. Driver (D)

D.C. Ct. of App., 62 App. D.C. 187, 65 F.2d 820 (1933).

NATURE OF CASE: Action for injury negligently inflicted.

FACT SUMMARY: Petty (D) suffered a fainting spell while driving which caused an accident in which Cohen (P) was injured.

 RULE OF LAW
When injury results from an unforeseeable event there is no liability.

FACTS: Petty's (D) guest, Cohen (P), was injured when Petty (D) lost control of his car and it crashed. The evidence was that the loss of control was due to a fainting spell and that Petty (D) had never before experienced such fainting. The trial court directed a verdict in Petty's (D) favor and Cohen (P) appealed.

ISSUE: Is an actor liable for injury caused when an unforeseeable event causes him to lose control of his actions?

HOLDING AND DECISION: (Groner, J.) No. So long as the loss of control was not foreseeable, there is no negligence. Petty (D) had never fainted before and, consequently, the fainting was unforeseeable. Negligence is the failure to employ that degree of care that a reasonable man would use under the circumstances. If an event is unforeseeable, then a reasonable man would be unable to take any care to prevent it and would be under no duty to do so. There is no liability for the consequences of an unforeseeable event. Affirmed.

ANALYSIS

An unavoidable accident is one that could not have been prevented by the exercise of reasonable care. If an occurrence is unforeseeable it cannot be prevented. However, had Petty (D) known that he was subject to fainting spells, foreseeability would exist and driving would have become an unreasonable risk and injury therefrom would have resulted in liability. The case indicates that negligence is to be judged in terms of risk foreseeability.

Quicknotes

BINDING INSTRUCTIONS A jury instruction informing jurors how to resolve an action if specified circumstances are determined to exist.

FORESEEABILITY A reasonable expectation that an act or omission would result in injury.

Spano v. Perini Corp.

Garage and car owner (P) v. Blasting company (D)

N.Y. Ct. of App., 25 N.Y.2d 11, 250 N.E.2d 31 (1969).

NATURE OF CASE: Property damage based on strict liability.

FACT SUMMARY: Blasting by Perini Corp. (D), while building a tunnel, wrecked Spano's (P) garage on nearby property.

🏛 RULE OF LAW
One who sets off explosives is absolutely liable for damage caused without regard to trespass or fault.

FACTS: Spano (P) owned a garage, which was wrecked by shock waves from a dynamite blast set off by Perini Corp. (D) on nearby property. There was no physical trespass caused by the blast nor was there any proof of negligence on the part of the defendant. In addition to the foregoing, suit was also brought for damages to Davis's (P) automobile, which had been in the garage at the time of the blast. The two suits were consolidated and judgment was for Spano (P) and Davis (P). Perini Corp. (D) appealed, and the appellate court reversed. Davis (P) and Spano (P) appealed.

ISSUE:
(1) Is one who engages in blasting responsible for damage caused without any showing of fault?
(2) Is proof of trespass necessary to recovery in strict liability?

HOLDING AND DECISION: (Fuld, C.J.)
(1) Yes. This case recognizes that, under the doctrine of strict liability, an actor is liable for damage caused by abnormally dangerous activity without regard to fault. The rationale is that he who engages in an abnormally dangerous activity should bear the loss as opposed to the injured and innocent victim.
(2) No. The early common law would have distinguished between the physical invasion, which was a trespass, and the concussion, which would be a nuisance. For purposes of strict liability, the distinction has been abandoned.

▶ ANALYSIS

This case indicates the traditional approach to strict liability. If an activity cannot be made safe even by the exercise of utmost care, then strict liability applies. This is the majority view. In many jurisdictions, the protection of strict liability has been extended to food, drugs, and products. In those jurisdictions, if a defect exists in the product when it left the manufacturer, the manufacturer will be absolutely liable.

Quicknotes

STRICT LIABILITY Liability for all injuries proximately caused by a party's conducting of certain inherently dangerous activities without regard to negligence or fault.

■ ▬ ■

Intentional Interference with Person or Property

Quick Reference Rules of Law

Garratt v. Dailey

Arthritic woman (P) v. Five-year-old boy (D)

Wash. Sup. Ct., 46 Wash. 2d 197, 279 P.2d 1091 (1955).

NATURE OF CASE: Action to recover damages for battery.

FACT SUMMARY: Brian Dailey (D) pulled a chair out from under Ruth Garratt (P) as she began to sit down in it.

🏛 **RULE OF LAW**
The intent necessary for the commission of a battery is present when the person acts, knowing with substantial certainty that the harmful contact will occur.

FACTS: Ruth Garratt (P) alleged that Brian Dailey (D), who was 5 years old, pulled a chair out from under her as she was sitting down, thereby causing her to fall and break her hip. Brian Dailey (D) alleged that he picked up the chair and sat down in it, and then noticed that Ruth Garratt (P) was about to sit down where the chair had been. However, upon a second appeal, it was found that he knew, when he moved the chair, that Ruth Garratt (P) was about to sit down in it.

ISSUE: Is an intent to harm another necessary for the commission of a battery, when the defendant knows that his actions will result in an offensive contact?

HOLDING AND DECISION: (Hill, J.) No. While battery requires an intentional infliction of a harmful bodily contact, this does not mean that there must be an intent (or desire) to cause harm or even to cause the contact. A harmful bodily contact is inflicted intentionally when the person knows with substantial certainty that the contact will occur. In this case, the trial court ultimately found that Brian Dailey (D) moved the chair from under Ruth Garratt (P) while she was in the process of sitting down, and that he therefore knew with substantial certainty that she would attempt to sit down where the chair had been and that she would fall (come into contact with the ground). Brian's (D) intent to cause a harmful bodily contact is inferred from his knowledge that the contact would occur. Remanded.

▌ *ANALYSIS*

This decision's holding regarding the nature of the intent needed for a battery is representative of the nature of intent required for any intentional tort (such as assault, false imprisonment, trespass). Thus, the general view of intent is that where a reasonable person in the position of the defendant would believe that a certain result was substantially certain to follow his acts, the defendant will be considered to intend that result.

Quicknotes

BATTERY Unlawful contact with the body of another person.

Spivey v. Battaglia

Hugging victim (P) v. Hugger (D)

Fla. Sup. Ct., 258 So. 2d 815 (1972).

NATURE OF CASE: Appeal from summary denial of damages for personal injuries.

FACT SUMMARY: Spivey (P) appealed from a decision granting Battaglia's (D) motion for summary judgment contending his act of hugging Spivey (P), which caused her injury, was not assault and battery as a matter of law, but was negligence, and that as negligence, her action was not barred by the statute of limitations.

🏛 RULE OF LAW
In the context of ascertaining tortious intent, the knowledge and appreciation of a risk, short of substantial certainty, is not the equivalent of intent.

FACTS: Spivey (P) and Battaglia (D) were both employees at the same company. Battaglia (D) was aware of Spivey's (P) shyness. In an effort to tease her, Battaglia (D) intentionally put his arm around Spivey (P) and pulled her head towards him. She immediately experienced sharp pain and suffered partial facial paralysis. Some time later, Spivey (P) brought an action against Battaglia (D) for negligence and assault and battery. Battaglia (D) moved for summary judgment, contending that the "hug" was an assault and battery as a matter of law, and Spivey's (P) action was barred by the statute of limitations. The motion was granted and affirmed on appeal. From this decision, Spivey (P) appealed, contending that the action could be maintained on a negligence count, which was not barred by the statute of limitations.

ISSUE: Is knowledge and appreciation of a risk, short of substantial certainty, the equivalent of intent?

HOLDING AND DECISION: (Dekle, J.) No. In the context of ascertaining tortious intent, the knowledge and appreciation of a risk, short of substantial certainty, is not the equivalent of intent. The distinction between intent and negligence is a matter of degree. Where the known danger ceases to be only a foreseeable risk and becomes a substantial certainty, intent will be legally implied, and the actor's conduct becomes an assault and not unintentional negligence. In the present case, it cannot be said that the partial paralysis was "substantially certain" to occur as a result of Battaglia's (D) hug. As such, the negligence cause of action should have been submitted to the jury. Decision quashed; remanded with directions to reverse.

▶ **ANALYSIS**

The intent to bring about the consequences of one's actions, especially if the act is misdirected, is important in determining whether there has been an intentional tort. The determination is important, because a plaintiff may become entitled to punitive damages, or the availability of liability insurance may be affected.

■▬■

Quicknotes

ASSAULT AND BATTERY Illegal bodily contact.

NEGLIGENCE Conduct falling below the standard of care that a reasonable person would demonstrate under similar conditions.

■▬■

Ranson v. Kitner

Dog owner (P) v. Hunters (D)

Ill. Ct. App., 31 Ill. App. 241 (1889).

NATURE OF CASE: Appeal from award of damages for injury to personal property.

FACT SUMMARY: Appellants (D), while hunting wolves, killed appellee's (P) dog, believing it to have been a wolf.

🏛 RULE OF LAW
Mistake does not absolve an actor from liability for the harm caused by his intentional act.

FACTS: While hunting wolves, the appellants (D) spotted the appellee's (P) dog. Due to the dog's striking resemblance to a wolf, they mistakenly killed it. The appellee (P) sued the appellants (D) to recover the value of the dog, and the trial court awarded the appellee (P) $50 in damages. The appellants (D) appealed, arguing that they should not have been held liable for the harm caused by their conduct because they had acted in good faith.

ISSUE: Does mistake absolve an actor from liability for the harm caused by his intentional act?

HOLDING AND DECISION: (Conger, J.) No. Mistake does not absolve an actor from liability for the harm caused by his intentional act. The appellants (D) intended to kill the animal, and their good faith belief that it was a wolf does not relieve them from liability for the consequences of their act. Affirmed.

▶ ANALYSIS

The general rule is that mistake is no defense to an intentional tort. Because intent is held to be present when a result is substantially certain to occur, without regard to the actor's desire, the actor's belief as to the nature of the result of his conduct is normally irrelevant. Thus, in the case at hand, the tortfeasors were liable for killing the dog, despite the fact that they meant only to kill wolves, because they intended to kill the animal that was the victim of their hunt. All the same, it remained a loss for the dog's owner regardless of the tortfeasors' good faith mistake.

▬▬

Quicknotes

MISTAKE An act or failure to perform due to a lack of knowledge or a misconception as to a law or fact.

▬▬

McGuire v. Almy

Nurse (P) v. Violent ward (D)

Mass. Sup. Jud. Ct., 297 Mass. 323, 8 N.E.2d 760 (1937).

NATURE OF CASE: Action for damages for assault and battery.

FACT SUMMARY: Almy (D), an insane ward, injured her nurse, McGuire (P), during a rage.

RULE OF LAW
An insane person may be capable of entertaining the intent to commit a battery.

FACTS: McGuire (P), a registered nurse, had been hired to give 24-hour care to Almy (D), an insane person. Almy (D) had a violent attack during which she broke furniture and warned McGuire (P) not to enter her room or she would be killed. After entering, McGuire (P) approached Almy (D), who stood in striking position with a piece of furniture raised above her head. When McGuire (P) grabbed for the hand with the weapon, Almy (D) struck her. There was a jury verdict for McGuire (P). Almy (D) appealed the denial of her motion for a directed verdict.

ISSUE: May an insane person be liable for a battery?

HOLDING AND DECISION: (Qua, J.) Yes. An insane person is to be judged by the same standards as a normal person. Intent to do the act is the key to a battery, not the intent to harm. If an insane person can entertain that intent, then he can be liable for battery. The standard applies even though an insane person's acts may be uncontrollable. The loss is placed on the insane actor rather than on the innocent victim.

▶ ANALYSIS

This case represents a basic policy decision which is generally accepted. The policy reasons are: (1) the loss is better borne by the actor than the victim; (2) liability will encourage closer surveillance by custodians; and (3) insanity is easily feigned. The counter-argument is that one should not be liable for acts not within his control. This is not generally accepted.

━■━

Quicknotes

BATTERY Unlawful contact with the body of another person.

DIRECTED VERDICT A verdict ordered by the court in a jury trial.

━■━

Talmage v. Smith

Blinded boy (P) v. Property owner (D)

Mich. Sup. Ct., 101 Mich. 370, 59 N.W. 656 (1894).

NATURE OF CASE: Action for damages for trespass to person.

FACT SUMMARY: Smith (D) threw a stick at a boy, but instead hit Talmage (P).

RULE OF LAW
When one intends to harm another, it is no defense that an unintended person was instead harmed.

FACTS: Talmage (P) and several other boys were playing on the roofs of sheds on Smith's (D) property. Smith (D) ordered the boys to get down, but before they had succeeded in doing so, Smith (D) took a stick and threw it, hitting Talmage (P) in the eye with such force that the sight in that eye was lost. There was evidence that Smith (D) threw the stick intending to hit Byron Smith, another boy on the roof, and not Talmage (P).

ISSUE: When the defendant intends to harm one person but accidentally harms another person instead of the original victim, can the defendant be held liable for a battery to the second person?

HOLDING AND DECISION: (Montgomery, J.) Yes. When a defendant acts with the intention to inflict an unwarranted injury on someone, it does not matter that a person other than the one intended was harmed. Therefore, in this case, Smith (D) could not be relieved from liability because he hit Talmage (P) with the stick, instead of Byron Smith, the boy he intended to hit. Affirmed.

▎*ANALYSIS*

This decision provides an example of the prominent doctrine of "transferred intent." This doctrine holds that once there is an intent to commit an intentional tort, for example, battery, it does not matter that the person harmed was not the one intended. The intent is transferred from the person intended to the one actually harmed. The doctrine of "transferred intent" may perhaps represent the most peculiar aspect of "intent" in intentional interferences with persons or property, in that a defendant may be liable for harming another (or his property) even if he had no desire to harm, or even knowledge that such harm would occur to that person (or property). The reason for the doctrine may be because of the feeling that when the defendant does act intentionally with respect to one person, he is morally "at fault" and should not escape liability because of the fortuitous circumstance of injuring an unintended victim.

Quicknotes

TRESPASS UPON THE PERSON Cause of action to recover from any injuries to the plaintiff's person, resulting from the direct and immediate injury inflicted by another party.

■=■

Cole v. Turner

Parties not identified.

Nisi Prius, 6 Modern Rep. 149, 90 Eng. Rep. 958 (1704).

NATURE OF CASE: Action for assault and battery.

FACT SUMMARY: [No facts stated in casebook excerpt.]

🏛 RULE OF LAW
The least touching of another in anger is a battery. An unintentional touching without violence is not a battery. The use of violence in a rude manner is a battery. An attempt to pass through a narrow way resulting in a struggle sufficient to do injury is a battery.

FACTS: [No facts stated in casebook excerpt.]

ISSUE: [No issue stated in casebook excerpt.]

HOLDING AND DECISION: (Holt, C.J.) Yes. An unintentional touching without violence is not a battery. The use of violence in a rude manner is a battery. An attempt to pass through a narrow way resulting in a struggle sufficient to do injury is a battery.

▶ ANALYSIS

The interest protected by an action for battery is the interest in freedom from intentional and unpermitted contacts with the plaintiff's person. Consequently an unintentional or socially acceptable contact is not a battery. The gist of the action for battery is not the actor's wrongful intent but the absence of consent to the contact.

■■■

Quicknotes

BATTERY Unlawful contact with the body of another person.

NISI PRIUS A court having original jurisdiction over a matter.

■■■

Wallace v. Rosen

Student's mother (P) v. Teacher (D)

Ind. Ct. App., 765 N.E.2d 192 (2002).

NATURE OF CASE: Suit to recover damages for an alleged battery.

FACT SUMMARY: A high-school teacher touched a student's mother to encourage her to leave the school building during a fire drill. The student's mother fell down a stairway and alleged that the teacher's touching of her was a battery that caused the injuries she incurred in her fall.

🏛 RULE OF LAW
Intentionally touching another person cannot constitute battery if the touching does not occur in a rude, insolent, or angry manner.

FACTS: Mable Wallace (P) went to an Indianapolis high school to deliver homework to her daughter, who was a student at the school. Wallace (P) stopped to talk to her daughter near the top of a stairway in the school, and two of her daughter's friends joined them. Then the school initiated a fire drill. Students used the stairway to file out of the building. Wallace (P), though, moved to the landing at the top of the stairway, where she interfered with students as they tried to leave the building. One teacher, Harriet Rosen (D), noticed Wallace (P) and the three students with whom she was speaking at the top of the stairway. Wallace (P) did not hear Rosen (D) tell the group to "move it," so Rosen (D) touched Wallace (P) on the back to get Wallace's (P) attention. Wallace (P), who was recovering from foot surgery at the time, then fell down the stairs. At trial Rosen (D) admitted touching Wallace (P) on her back but denied pushing her. After the evidence closed, the trial judge refused to give the jury Wallace's (P) tendered instruction on battery, which in pertinent part defined battery as "the knowing or intentional touching of one person by another in a rude, insolent, or angry manner." The jury returned a verdict for Rosen (D) and the school district that employed her. Wallace (P) appealed, challenging, in part, the trial judge's refusal to instruct the jury on battery as Wallace (P) requested at trial.

ISSUE: Can intentionally touching another person constitute battery if the touching does not occur in a rude, insolent, or angry manner?

HOLDING AND DECISION: (Kirsch, J.) No. Intentionally touching another person cannot constitute battery if the touching does not occur in a rude, insolent, or angry manner. Battery requires intent—but it also requires more. In tort law, intent need not mean that a defendant behaves with hostility or wants to harm the plaintiff. What tortious intent does require is an intent to violate another person's interests in a legally prohibited way. When the alleged tort is battery, as in Rosen's (D) touching of Wallace (P) here, the alleged touching must have occurred both intentionally and in a rude, insolent, or angry manner. In today's crowded world, some touching is normal and necessary. The test for determining the tortious manner of an intentional touching, then, is whether it would offend an ordinary person who is not unduly sensitive about her personal dignity. Here, reviewing the evidence in the light most favorable to the judgment, Rosen (D) merely touched Wallace's (P) shoulder and turned toward the stairway during a fire drill. Such a touching cannot be the rude, insolent, or angry intentional touching that the law of battery requires. The evidence therefore supports the trial judge's discretionary rejection of Wallace's (P) tendered instruction. Affirmed.

▶ ANALYSIS

One of the concurring opinions in *Wallace*, Judge Sullivan's, would have affirmed the trial court's refusal of Wallace's (P) tendered instruction because the instruction's last portion would have instructed the jury that a reckless touching, and not necessarily an intentional touching, can constitute battery. As Judge Sullivan wrote, "[t]he alleged battery here was either an intentional touching in a rude, insolent, or angry manner, or it was no battery at all." 765 N.E.2d at 202. This distinction between mental states is a vestige of the ancient relationship between tort law and criminal law, with the contemporary law of battery requiring, as Judge Sullivan emphasized, a more culpable state of mind as a basis for liability. Compared to the mental states supporting liability in the examples cited in the 1466 case of *Anonymous* [p. 2], today's higher burden of culpability demonstrates the manner in which the law responds to the social forces that the law both organizes and serves.

■=■

Quicknotes

BATTERY Unlawful contact with the body of another person.

INTENT The state of mind that exists when one's purpose is to commit a criminal act.

■=■

Fisher v. Carrousel Motor Hotel, Inc.

Guest (P) v. Motor hotel (D)

Tex. Sup. Ct., 424 S.W.2d 627 (1967).

NATURE OF CASE: Action to recover damages for battery.

FACT SUMMARY: Fisher (P), while in line at a buffet luncheon, had his plate snatched from his hands by an employee of the Motor Hotel (D), who also insulted him.

🏛 RULE OF LAW
A battery may be committed even though there is no physical contact with the person's body, so long as there is contact with something that is attached to, or closely indentified with, the body.

FACTS: Fisher (P), a black man, was attending a meeting at the Carrousel Motor Hotel (D). While he was standing in a buffet lunch line, holding his plate, an employee of the hotel (D) came up to Fisher (P) and snatched his plate from his hands, shouting at the same time that the hotel (D) would not serve a black man. While Fisher (P) was not physically injured, the incident was highly offensive to him, and he sued the hotel (D) for damages for battery. A jury found for plaintiff, but the trial court handed down judgment for the defendants notwithstanding the verdict. The court of appeals affirmed and plaintiff appealed to the Supreme Court.

ISSUE: Is there a battery when there is no actual physical contact with the plaintiff's body, but only with something held in his hands?

HOLDING AND DECISION: (Greenhill, J.) Yes. Any offensive contact with a person's body or anything closely identified with the body is a battery. The reason for this is that battery involves an offense to the person's dignity, not just a physical injury. Therefore, an unpermitted invasion of the person's body is not necessary, because an unpermitted contact with something closely identified with the body, such as with something held in the hands, may be just as offensive as an unpermitted contact with the person. In this case, the snatching of the plate Fisher (P) held in his hands, in an offensive manner, was an unpermitted, offensive contact with something closely connected to Fisher's (P) body, and was therefore a battery.

▎▶ *ANALYSIS*

This decision is representative of the prevailing view that actual physical contact with the body is not necessary for battery. It should be noted that actual physical injury of the plaintiff is not a requirement of battery. The rationale for this is the same reason for not requiring actual physical contact with the person: battery protects not only a person's interest in not being physically harmed, but also protects his personal integrity. An unpermitted, offensive contact with the person or anything identified with the person, violates a person's integrity, even if he is not harmed. A battery, therefore, entitles the plaintiff to recover damages for mental disturbance—such as fright, or humiliation or embarrassment. Thus, in this decision, Fisher (P) recovered damages for the humiliation he suffered as a result of the battery.

■▬■

Quicknotes

BATTERY Unlawful contact with the body of another person.

HARMFUL OR OFFENSIVE CONTACT Contact that causes injury or annoyance to another individual.

■▬■

I de S et ux. v. W de S

Tavern owner and wife (P) v. Attacker (D)

At the Assizes, Y.B. Lib. Ass. Folio 99, Placitum 60 (1348).

NATURE OF CASE: Action to recover damages for trespass, because of an assault made upon the plaintiff.

FACT SUMMARY: W (D) struck at I's wife M (P) with a hatchet, but missed her.

> **RULE OF LAW**
> An act which causes another to be fearful of a harmful or offensive contact is known as an assault, and the plaintiff may recover damages, even though there is no actual physical contact or physical harm.

FACTS: W (D) was beating with a hatchet upon the door of I's (P) tavern, which was closed for the night. When I's (P) wife M (P) put her head out the window and ordered W (D) to stop, he struck at her with the hatchet. W (D) claimed there was no trespass for which the woman (P) could recover, since he did not actually harm her.

ISSUE: Is there a wrong and a trespass for which a plaintiff may recover damages, when the plaintiff is caused to fear for her safety, but not actually harmed?

HOLDING AND DECISION: (Thorpe, C.J.) Yes. An assault—making another fearful of a harmful contact—is a harm for which a plaintiff may recover. In this case, W (D) struck at I's (P) wife M (P) with a hatchet, thereby frightening her. The harm was in the assault itself, and she is entitled to recover damages from W (D).

▶ ANALYSIS

This case was one of the earliest decisions to recognize a mental, as opposed to physical, injury, and the need to compensate the plaintiff for such an injury. Thus, the law of assault developed to protect a person's interest in freedom from being fearful of a harmful or offensive contact upon his person, as opposed to battery, which protected a person from the injury itself.

■■■

Quicknotes

ASSAULT The intentional placing of another in fear of immediate bodily injury.

■■■

Western Union Telegraph Co. v. Hill

Husband and wife (P) v. Company employing agent (D)

Ala. Ct. of App., 25 Ala. App. 540, 150 So. 709 (1933).

NATURE OF CASE: Action to recover damages for assault.

FACT SUMMARY: Sapp allegedly made a grab for Hill's (P) wife over a counter, the dimensions of which made contact virtually impossible.

🏛 RULE OF LAW
There can be no assault unless there is an apparent ability to carry out a threatened contact.

FACTS: Sapp was an employee of Western Union (D). When Mrs. Hill (P) came to the office to have her clock repaired, Sapp, who had been drinking, suggested illicit sexual relations. Mrs. Hill (P) claimed that Sapp then made a grab for her shoulder over the counter, but she jumped back. The counter was 4'2" high, coming to Sapp's armpits, and so wide that by stretching over it Sapp's fingers barely reached the end of it. The photographs showed it was unlikely that Sapp could have reached Mrs. Hill (P). Judgment went for Hill (P) and Western Union (D) appealed, claiming there was no apparent ability to carry out the threat as a matter of law.

ISSUE: Can an assault be committed where the actor lacks the apparent ability to carry out his threat?

HOLDING AND DECISION: (Samford, J.) No. The apprehension raised by the alleged threat must be a reasonable one based on an apparent ability to carry out an immediate battery. The court found that there was a sufficient conflict in the evidence to raise a jury question on the existence of an apparent ability to carry out the battery. The case was reversed on other grounds relating to the liability of the corporation for the acts of its employees.

▶ ANALYSIS

This case illustrates the principle that the apprehension raised must be a reasonable one. Only an apparent ability to commit a battery could raise a reasonable fear and consequently only those may be redressed by the action for assault. The requirement of a reasonable fear is a policy limitation designed to guard against insubstantial or feigned fears as a ground for litigation. Alabama Code § 8264—Damages for injuries to person or reputation—all damages which the wife may be entitled to recover for injuries to her person or reputation, are her separate property. Section 8268—How wife sues; and must be sued—The wife must sue alone, at law or in equity, upon all contracts made by or with her, or for the recovery of her separate property, or for injuries to such property, or for its rents, income, or profits, or for all injuries to her person or reputation; and upon all contracts made by her, or engagements into which she enters, and for all torts committed by her, she must be sued as if she were sole. Prior to the enactment of the above statutes (1928) the wife could not sue alone for personal injuries but had to sue jointly with her husband and for his sole benefit.

◼━◼

Quicknotes

APPREHENSION Fear; anticipation of harm or injury.

ASSAULT The intentional placing of another in fear of immediate bodily injury.

BATTERY Unlawful contact with the body of another person.

EQUITY Fairness; justice; the determination of a matter consistent with principles of fairness and not in strict compliance with rules of law.

◼━◼

Big Town Nursing Home, Inc. v. Newman

Confined retiree (P) v. Nursing home (D)

Tex. Ct. Civ. App., 461 S.W.2d 195 (1970).

NATURE OF CASE: Appeal from award of damages for false imprisonment.

FACT SUMMARY: Big Town Nursing Home, Inc. (Big Town) (D) appealed from a judgment for Newman (P) for actual and exemplary damages in his false imprisonment action, arguing that the award of exemplary damages was improper in this case.

🏛 RULE OF LAW
One can be held liable for exemplary damages in a false imprisonment action if the false imprisonment is done intentionally in violation of the rights of the plaintiff.

FACTS: Newman (P) was taken to Big Town (D) by his nephew on September 19, 1968. The admission papers provided that he would not be kept in Big Town (D) for any length of time against his will. Three days later, Newman (P) decided he wanted to leave and attempted to call a taxi. He was prevented from leaving by Big Town's (D) employees. Newman (P) was advised that he could not leave or use the phone, and his grip and clothes were locked up. He attempted to leave on several occasions, but was caught and brought back against his will each time. He was locked up in Wing 3, a ward for senile patients, incorrigibles, alcoholics, etc. Payment of Newman's (P) social security checks was changed without his authorization. When he finally escaped on November 11, 1968, he had lost 30 pounds. He sued Big Town (D) for false imprisonment and received an award for actual and exemplary damages. From this decision, Big Town (D) appealed, arguing that the award of exemplary damages was improper in the case.

ISSUE: Can one be held liable for exemplary damages in a false imprisonment case if the false imprisonment is done intentionally in violation of the rights of the plaintiff?

HOLDING AND DECISION: (McDonald, C.J.) Yes. One can be held liable for exemplary damages in a false imprisonment action if the false imprisonment is done intentionally in violation of the rights of the plaintiff. False imprisonment is the direct restraint by one person of the physical liberty of another without adequate justification. The entire course of Big Town's (D) conduct was to prevent Newman (P) from leaving, in violation of his admission papers. There was no court order for Newman's (P) commitment, and the admissions papers clearly indicated to Big Town (D) Newman's (P) right to leave at will. Since Big Town (D) acted intentionally in violation of Newman's (P) rights, the award of exemplary damages was proper. [Newman (P) accepted a remittitur suggested by the Court.] Affirmed.

▶ ANALYSIS

Whether or not an action for false imprisonment will lie depends upon whether or not there is a reasonable means of escape available to the person confined. If an individual could remain imprisoned without risk of physical harm, there is authority for the proposition that one cannot recover for injuries suffered in making an unreasonably dangerous escape.

Quicknotes

EXEMPLARY DAMAGES Damages exceeding the actual injury suffered for the purposes of punishment, deterrence and comfort to plaintiff.

FALSE IMPRISONMENT Intentional tort whereby the victim is unlawfully restrained.

REMITTITUR The authority of the court to reduce the amount of damages awarded by the jury.

Parvi v. City of Kingston

Inebriated complainant (P) v. Municipality (D)

N.Y. Ct. App., 41 N.Y.2d 553, 362 N.E.2d 960 (1977).

NATURE OF CASE: Appeal from dismissal of false imprisonment action.

FACT SUMMARY: Parvi (P), who was picked up by police while intoxicated and driven by them to an abandoned golf course to "sleep it off," was unable to recall whether he was aware at that time of his confinement there.

▥ RULE OF LAW
A plaintiff's present recollection of a previous consciousness of confinement is not required to make out a prima facie case for false imprisonment.

FACTS: Parvi (P) was found by police in downtown Kingston (D), New York, in an intoxicated state. He told the officers he had nowhere to go, and they drove him to an abandoned golf course outside of town to "sleep it off." Parvi (P) brought an action for false imprisonment against the City (D) on the ground that the officers had confined him. The testimony as to whether Parvi (P) willingly went to the golf course conflicted. Parvi (P) testified that he could not presently recall whether he was conscious of being confined at the time he was taken out of town. The trial court dismissed the complaint and Parvi (P) appealed.

ISSUE: Is a plaintiff's present recollection of previous consciousness of confinement required to make out a prima facie case for false imprisonment?

HOLDING AND DECISION: (Fuchsberg, J.) No. While there is some division of authority in the United States as to the necessity of proof of consciousness of confinement in false imprisonment actions, the law of New York is settled on that point. False imprisonment, as a dignitary tort, is not suffered unless the victim knows the invasion or confinement. The trial court dismissed the case on the ground that Parvi (P) could not recall on the witness stand that he had been aware of his confinement when he was removed to the golf course. However, a plaintiff's present recollection of previous consciousness of confinement is not required to make out the prima facie case for false imprisonment. It may well be that the alcohol or Parvi's (P) injuries wiped out the memory of a consciousness that existed at the time the officers picked him up. This is not the same as saying he was unaware of the dignitary invasion when it occurred. Reversed.

DISSENT: (Breitel, C.J.) Parvi (P) has no memory of the entire incident and admitted that his only knowledge of it stemmed from subsequent conversations. He thus failed to make out even a prima facie case for false imprisonment.

▍ ANALYSIS

There remains some question among the various jurisdictions as to whether the action for false imprisonment will lie in the absence of knowledge of the confinement. A substantial number of states require such knowledge. The Restatement (Second) of Torts provides that the action will lie without such knowledge if the plaintiff suffers some actual injury or damage from the confinement.

━■━

Quicknotes

FALSE IMPRISONMENT Intentional tort whereby the victim is unlawfully restrained.

PRIMA FACIE CASE An action where the plaintiff introduces sufficient evidence to submit the issue to the judge or jury for determination.

SINA QUA NON Without which not; a necessary element or requirement.

━■━

Hardy v. LaBelle's Distributing Co.

Accused employee (P) v. Department store (D)

Mont. Sup. Ct., 661 P.2d 35 (1983).

NATURE OF CASE: Appeal from denial of damages for false imprisonment.

FACT SUMMARY: Hardy (P) contended she was falsely imprisoned by Labelle's (D) when interrogated about an alleged theft.

🏛 **RULE OF LAW**
False imprisonment exists upon the unlawful restraint of an individual against his will.

FACTS: Hardy (P), a temporary employee of Labelle's (D), was asked by another employee to tour the store. She was taken to the manager's office where she was detained and informed she had been accused of stealing a watch. Present in the office were other employees and at least one uniformed police officer. Hardy (P) denied the accusations and voluntarily underwent a polygraph examination. She passed and was given an apology. She brought suit for false imprisonment, contending she had been detained against her will. At trial, Hardy (P) testified she voluntarily stayed in the office to attempt to exonerate herself. The jury returned a verdict for Labelle (D), and Hardy (P) appealed.

ISSUE: Is false imprisonment the unlawful restraint of an individual against his will?

HOLDING AND DECISION: (Gulbrandson, J.) Yes. False imprisonment is the unlawful restraint of an individual against his will. In this case, Hardy (P) admitted she felt restrained from leaving the office, yet would have stayed anyway to exonerate herself. Thus, she was not restrained against her will and was not falsely imprisoned. Affirmed.

▌*ANALYSIS*

False imprisonment requires actual confinement, either through physical force or threats. The plaintiff also must know of the confinement. Thus, if an unconscious individual is confined, yet released before he awakens, no cause of action exists. Further, the existence of a safe, reasonable avenue of escape must be known by the plaintiff before such can be used by the defendant to preclude his liability.

■■■

Quicknotes

FALSE IMPRISONMENT Intentional tort whereby the victim is unlawfully restrained.

■■■

Enright v. Groves

Dog-at-large owner (P) v. Policeman and municipality (D)

Colo. Ct. App., 560 P.2d 851 (1977).

NATURE OF CASE: Appeal from award of damages for false imprisonment.

FACT SUMMARY: Officer Groves (D) appealed an award of damages to Mrs. Enright (P), whom he arrested for failure to produce her driver's license during his investigation of a "dog leash" ordinance violation.

🏛 RULE OF LAW
A claim for false arrest will not lie if an officer has a valid warrant or probable cause to believe that an offense has been committed and that the person who was arrested committed it.

FACTS: Groves (D), a uniformed police officer for the City of Ft. Collins (D), observed a dog running loose in violation of the Ft. Collins (D) "dog leash" ordinance. He saw the dog approach Mrs. Enright's (P) house, and he asked her 11-year-old son if the dog was his. The son replied that it was his dog, and that his mother was sitting in the car parked at the curb. Mrs. Enright (P) got out of the car and spoke with Groves (D). Groves (D) demanded her driver's license. Enright (P) gave her name and address but refused to produce her license. Groves (D) ordered her to produce her license or go to jail. She responded, "Isn't this ridiculous?" whereupon Groves (D) said, "Let's go," and arrested her. Enright (P), who was convicted of violating the "dog leash" ordinance, sought and was awarded $1,500 damages for false imprisonment. Groves (D) and Ft. Collins (D) appealed arguing that there was probable cause for the arrest, and that Enright (P) was convicted.

ISSUE: Will a claim for false arrest lie if an officer has a valid warrant or probable cause to believe that an offense has been committed and that the person who was arrested committed it?

HOLDING AND DECISION: (Smith, J.) No. A claim for false arrest will not lie if an officer has a valid warrant or probable cause to believe that an offense has been committed and that the person who was arrested committed it. Conviction of the crime for which one is specifically arrested is a complete defense to a subsequent claim for false arrest. In this case, Groves (D) did not arrest Enright (P) for violation of the "dog leash" ordinance. He arrested her for failure to produce her driver's license upon demand. No statute or case law requires a citizen to produce a driver's license upon demand unless that person is the driver of a vehicle and the demand is made in that connection. Enright (P) was not driving when the demand and arrest were made. Accordingly, Groves (D) was without authority to demand her license and to use force in arresting Enright (P). Affirmed.

▶ ANALYSIS

In *Whitman v. Atchison, T. & S. F. R. Co.*, 85 Kan. 150, 116 (1911), P. 234, a case of false imprisonment was made where the plaintiff, who fell and broke his leg while attempting to leave defendant's train, was detained by defendant's conductor. The conductor claimed that the law required him to have the injured plaintiff fill out a statement about the accident, but the plaintiff was unreasonably delayed for 20 minutes in getting medical help while in considerable pain. Note that a plaintiff can also hold a private citizen who aids a police officer in the making of a false arrest liable for damages. See Annot., 98 A. L. R. 3d 542 (1980).

▬▭▬

Quicknotes

FALSE ARREST The illegal arrest or restraint of a person's liberty.

PROBABLE CAUSE A reasonable basis for believing that a crime has been committed.

▬▭▬

Whittaker v. Sandford

Former cult member (P) v. Religious cult leader (D)

Me. Sup. Jud. Ct., 110 Me. 77, 85 A. 399 (1912).

NATURE OF CASE: Suit to recover damages for false imprisonment.

FACT SUMMARY: After crossing the Atlantic, the defendant failed to meet the terms of his agreement with plaintiff, thus making it impossible for plaintiff to reach shore, detaining her for over a month.

🏛 RULE OF LAW:
(1) To commit a false imprisonment it is not necessary that the tortfeasor actually apply physical force to the person of the plaintiff, but that plaintiff be physically constrained.
(2) A false imprisonment occurs when there is an intentional breach of an obligation to take active steps to release plaintiff.

FACTS: Plaintiff and defendant agreed that plaintiff would travel on defendant's yacht across the Atlantic, on the condition that defendant would not attempt to detain her on board for any purpose, particularly that of reconverting her to the religious movement with which he was affiliated. Upon arrival in port, defendant refused to furnish a boat so that plaintiff was detained on his yacht for over a month.

ISSUE:
(1) Is a false imprisonment committed when defendant exerts no physical force on plaintiff's person but obstructs plaintiff from leaving a confined area?
(2) Is a false imprisonment committed when there is a breach of a promise to take active steps to release plaintiff?

HOLDING AND DECISION: (Savage, J.)
(1) Yes. Even though defendant does not actually lay hands on plaintiff, there is still a false imprisonment because plaintiff's freedom of movement is limited.
(2) Yes. When defendant breaches his duty to take active measures to release plaintiff, he commits the tort of false imprisonment.

▶ ANALYSIS

Both holdings conform to well-established lines of precedents. Breach of duties such as a failure to let plaintiff out at the end of his sentence or to produce him in court constitutes a false imprisonment. However, whenever there is no duty to release plaintiff there is no tort.

Quicknotes

WRIT OF HABEAS CORPUS A proceeding in which a defendant brings a writ to compel a judicial determination of whether he is lawfully being held in custody.

State Rubbish Collectors Assoc. v. Siliznoff

Trash collectors' union (P) v. Holdout (D)

Cal. Sup. Ct., 38 Cal. 2d 330, 240 P.2d 282 (1952).

NATURE OF CASE: Appeal from damages awarded on cross-complaint alleging damages for mental suffering.

FACT SUMMARY: The State Rubbish Collectors Association (P) threatened to beat up Siliznoff (D), destroy his truck, or force him out of business unless he joined the Association (P) and paid dues to it.

🏛 RULE OF LAW
A complaint based on mental suffering caused by the outrageous conduct of defendant will be sustained if there was no privilege to act in such a manner.

FACTS: Siliznoff (D) had collected rubbish from a certain brewery while he was not a member of the State Rubbish Collectors Association (P). This action prompted the Association (P) to threaten to inflict bodily harm on Siliznoff (D), ruin his truck, or destroy his business unless he joined the ranks of their membership and paid them dues. The Association (D) sued to collect on notes it had forced Siliznoff (D) to sign, and he counterclaimed for damages for the emotional distress caused by the Association's (P) threats. The jury found for Siliznoff, and the Association (P) appealed.

ISSUE: Is a defendant who makes extremely anti-social threats on plaintiff, but who inflicts mental, not physical, injury, liable in a tort suit based on mental suffering?

HOLDING AND DECISION: (Traynor, J.) Yes. In the absence of a privilege, any conduct of defendant which exceeds the bounds of societal decency and causes extreme mental suffering, but no physical injury, constitutes the basis for a cause of action in mental suffering. The foundation of this opinion is that because mental suffering is an inherent element of the damages suffered in battery, assault, false imprisonment, and defamation, it is anomalous to deny recovery in cases in which the defendant's intentional misconduct fell short of producing some physical injury but produced intense mental distress. Affirmed.

▌ ANALYSIS

The case represents a breakthrough in the tort law; traditionally, recovery was only allowed for physical injury, and words of force which caused damage were not recognized as an invasion into an area protected by the tort law. One of the main reasons such claims were not recognized as valid was the absence of tangible physical injury and the existence of any injury was hard to prove.

Quicknotes

INTENTIONAL INFLICTION OF EMOTIONAL DISTRESS Intentional and extreme behavior on the part of the wrongdoer with the intent to cause the victim to suffer from severe emotional distress, or with reckless indifference, resulting in the victim's suffering from severe emotional distress.

Slocum v. Food Fair Stores of Florida

Insulted customer (P) v. Grocery store (D)

Fla. Sup. Ct., 100 So. 2d 396 (1958).

NATURE OF CASE: Suit to recover damages for mental suffering.

FACT SUMMARY: While shopping in Food Fair Stores of Florida (D), Slocum (P) was given an abusive reply to inquiries made to a grocery clerk. The rude remarks aggravated her heart condition and caused her emotional distress.

RULE OF LAW
No recovery is allowed for mental suffering when the abuse, insult, or profanity is not accompanied with serious threats to life or other affronts that amount to more than mere annoyances.

FACTS: While shopping in Food Fair Stores of Florida (D), Slocum (P) inquired into the price of an item and was met with a rude and malicious reply by an employee of said store. The remark upset Slocum (P) mentally and allegedly caused a heart attack.

ISSUE: Is abusive language that causes mental anguish enough to maintain a cause of action for emotional distress?

HOLDING AND DECISION: (Drew, J.) No. Defendants are not liable for mere insults, indignities, or even threats regardless of the consequences these words may have for plaintiff. In this case, Food Fair's (D) agent only refused to help Slocum (P) in a rude manner and made an adolescent comment about her bodily odor. This is enough to cause only little distress in the reasonable person. In order to recover, there must be severe emotional distress as an outgrowth of the conduct. The purpose of this is that if trivial insults were actionable at law then there could well be a curtailment of free speech, for those who fear legal repercussions for expressing disrespectful opinions might be deterred from speaking. Affirmed.

▶ ANALYSIS

Most jurisdictions accept the rule that there can be no recovery for mental suffering inflicted by petty insults. The judges expect that most individuals who interact in society are hardened and are thus prepared to deal with uncomplimentary affronts. Therefore, no tort remedy is necessary for the reasonable person. Further, courts see mental suffering as being much less quantitative and, hence, much less susceptible of proof than claims for physical injury so that there is a likelihood of many fictitious claims arising.

Quicknotes

ACTIONABLE Unlawful activity from which a cause of action may arise.

BUSINESS INVITEE A party invited onto another's property in order to conduct business to whom the owner owes a duty of care to protect against known dangers and those capable of discovery through reasonable care.

COMMON CARRIER An entity whose business is the transport of persons or property.

IN TOTO In whole.

RESPONDEAT SUPERIOR Rule that the principal is responsible for tortious acts committed by its agents in the scope of their agency or authority.

Harris v. Jones

Stutterer (P) v. Supervisor and employer (D)

Md. Ct. App., 281 Md. 560, 380 A.2d 611 (1977).

NATURE OF CASE: Appeal from denial of damages for intentional infliction of emotional distress.

FACT SUMMARY: Harris (P) sued his employer, GM (D), and a supervisor, Jones (D), for damages resulting from insulting and cruel behavior which allegedly worsened his stuttering condition.

RULE OF LAW
In order to recover damages resulting from the intentional infliction of emotional distress, a plaintiff must show that the distress suffered by him was "severe."

FACTS: Harris (P) worked at a General Motors (D) plant. He was a lifelong stutterer, was very self-conscious about the fact and, hence, also suffered from bad nerves. Harris (P) charged that Jones (D), a supervisor at the plant, "maliciously and cruelly" ridiculed him, causing him acute nervousness and resulting in an increase in his stuttering. Furthermore, Harris (P) charged that General Motors (D) had ratified Jones's (D) conduct. At trial for intentional infliction of emotional distress, a jury found for Harris (P) and awarded damages. The court then dismissed the verdict and entered judgment for Jones (D) and General Motors (D). Harris (P) appealed.

ISSUE: In order to recover damages resulting from the intentional infliction of emotional distress, must a plaintiff prove that the distress suffered was "severe"?

HOLDING AND DECISION: (Murphy, C.J.) Yes. Maryland is among the 37 jurisdictions recognizing that the intentional infliction of emotional distress, standing alone, may constitute a valid tort action. However, in order for such an action to lie, four separate elements must be shown: (1) the conduct must be intentional or reckless; (2) the conduct must be extreme and outrageous; (3) there must be a causal connection between the wrongful conduct and the emotional distress; and (4) the emotional distress must be severe. In the instant action, Harris (P) was not able to show the fourth element. He admitted that both his speech impediment and nervous conduct existed prior to his subjection to Jones's (D) insults. However, he contended, Jones's (D) conduct served to aggravate his problems. While this might be true, there is no evidence that such aggravation reached the level of severity required by the law governing the tort of intentional infliction of emotional distress. Absent such evidence, an action cannot lie. Thus, the judgment notwithstanding the verdict was properly granted. Affirmed.

ANALYSIS

Section 46 of the Restatement (Second) of Torts discusses the second element of intentional infliction of emotional distress, that of whether the defendant's conduct was extreme and outrageous, in comment D: "Liability has been found only where the conduct has been so outrageous in character, and so extreme in degree, as to go beyond all possible bounds of decency, and to be regarded as atrocious, and utterly intolerable in a civilized community." As such, mere insults, indignities, "or other trivialities" are not actionable.

Quicknotes

INTENTIONAL INFLICTION OF EMOTIONAL DISTRESS Intentional and extreme behavior on the part of the wrongdoer with the intent to cause the victim to suffer from severe emotional distress, or with reckless indifference, resulting in the victim's suffering from severe emotional distress.

JUDGMENT N.O.V. A judgment entered by the trial judge reversing a jury verdict if the jury's determination has no basis in law or fact.

Taylor v. Vallelunga

Victim's daughter (P) v. Assailant (D)

Cal. Ct. App., 171 Cal. App. 2d 107, 339 P.2d 910 (1959).

NATURE OF CASE: Suit to recover damages for battery and mental suffering caused by the battery.

FACT SUMMARY: Unknown to Vallelunga (D), Taylor (P) watched a physical attack upon her father by Vallelunga (D) and as a result suffered mental anguish.

RULE OF LAW
In order to recover damages for mental suffering that is the result of defendant's injury of a third person, the plaintiff must show that defendant reasonably anticipated mental stress would be inflicted on the plaintiff.

FACTS: Taylor (P) witnessed the beating of her father by Vallelunga (D), which caused her mental anguish. Taylor's (P) presence at the scene of the assault was unknown to Vallelunga (D) and he had no intent to inflict the severe emotional upset on Taylor (P).

ISSUE: Can damages for mental distress brought about by injury to a third person be recovered from one who had no cognizance of the presence of the emotionally upset plaintiff and no intent to cause that plaintiff mental injury?

HOLDING AND DECISION: (O'Donnell, J.) No. The defendant who does harm to a third party must be aware of plaintiff's presence and intend to cause the mental distress in plaintiff; otherwise, as in this case, plaintiff has no cause of action for the tort of mental suffering. Affirmed.

ANALYSIS

Most courts have analogous holdings to the present one, in disallowing recovery in situations where defendant has no knowledge of plaintiff's presence and no intent to injure the plaintiff mentally. These decisions have been rationalized by the doctrine of substantial certainty, i.e., given the injury to a third person there was a foreseeability of some mental effect on plaintiff. In cases where defendant has knowledge of plaintiff's presence and injures a third person, recovery for mental suffering is granted.

■■■

Quicknotes

GENERAL DEMURRER The assertion that the opposing party's pleadings are insufficient and that the demurring party should not be made to answer that does not specify the defendant's objections.

■■■

Dougherty v. Stepp

Landowner (P) v. Surveyor (D)

N.C. Sup. Ct., 18 N.C. 371 (1835).

NATURE OF CASE: Action to recover damages for trespass.

FACT SUMMARY: Stepp (D) entered the enclosed property of Dougherty (P) without permission.

RULE OF LAW
Every unprivileged entry onto the land of another is a trespass regardless of the amount of damages.

FACTS: Stepp (D) entered the enclosed property of Dougherty (P) without consent. While on the property, Stepp (D) surveyed the land. However, the surveying techniques involved no marking of trees or cutting of bushes. The jury found for Stepp (D), and Dougherty (P) appealed.

ISSUE: Is defendant liable for any entry onto the land of plaintiff although he creates no tangible damage?

HOLDING AND DECISION: (Ruffin, C.J.) Yes. An action for trespass can be maintained without proof of any actual damage. From every entry against the will of the landowner, the law implies some damage; "if nothing more, the treading down the grass or herbage." Reversed.

▶ ANALYSIS

The purpose of this decision is that at common law the trespass action was a safeguard against the repeated trespasser. Without the deterrent of legal liability for mere entry on the land without damage, the trespasser could after numerous entries onto the land claim an easement by prescription. The case also presents the old rule that a person is strictly liable for trespass, i.e., if he enters the land of another without permission, he is liable regardless of his intent or negligence in doing so. The present rule is that liability for trespass exists only if there is intentional or negligent intrusion.

Quicknotes

PRESCRIPTIVE EASEMENT A manner of acquiring an easement in another's property by continuous and uninterrupted use in satisfaction of the statutory requirements of adverse possession.

TRESPASS QUARE CLAUSUM FREIGIT Action for damages sustained as a result of the defendant's illegal entry onto plaintiff's property.

Bradley v. American Smelting and Refining Co.

Property owner (P) v. Copper smelter (D)

Wash. Sup. Ct., 104 Wash. 2d 677, 709 P.2d 782 (1985).

NATURE OF CASE: Action for trespass to land.

FACT SUMMARY: Bradley (P) brought an action for trespass to land against American Smelting and Refining Co. (American) (D), arguing that his land was damaged by particulate matter emitted from American's (D) plant.

> **RULE OF LAW**
> In order to sustain a cause of action for trespass to land, one must establish that he has suffered actual and substantial damages.

FACTS: American (D) operated its primary copper smelting plant some four miles form Bradley's (P) property. Various gasses and particulate matter, which cannot be detected by human senses, were emitted in the process. Bradley (P) brought an action against American (D) for trespass to land, arguing that his property was being damaged by the gasses and particulate matter being emitted.

ISSUE: In order to sustain a cause of action for trespass to land, must one establish that he has suffered actual and substantial damages?

HOLDING AND DECISION: (Callow, J.) Yes. In order to sustain a cause of action for trespass to land, one must establish that he has suffered actual and substantial damages. Trespass and private nuisance are separate fields of tort liability relating to actionable interference with the possession of land. They are not inconsistent and can be brought concurrently. Whether an invasion of property is a nuisance or a trespass depends upon the interest interfered with. When particulate emissions are involved, if the interference is transitory and quickly dissipated, the interference constitutes a nuisance. Where the particulates accumulate on the land, however, then a trespass has occurred. The particulate accumulation constitutes the actual and substantial damages necessary to sustain the action. If one brings a cause of action for trespass without the ability to show actual and substantial damages, his actions for trespass will be subject to dismissal upon motion for summary judgment.

▶ *ANALYSIS*

The distinction between the nuisance and the trespass theories is that trespass requires a physical incursion of the land by some tangible mass, whereas the nuisance theory only requires an interference with one's enjoyment or use of land. Another distinction is that in a trespass action, the socially beneficial or useful nature of the defendant's action is not relevant to whether a trespass has occurred.

■══■

Quicknotes

ACTUAL DAMAGES Measure of damages necessary to compensate victim for actual injuries suffered.

NUISANCE An unlawful use of property that interferes with the lawful use of another's property.

TRESPASS Unlawful interference with, or damage to, the real or personal property of another.

■══■

Herrin v. Sutherland

Property owner (P) v. Hunter (D)

Mont. Sup. Ct., 74 Mont. 587, 241 P. 328 (1925).

NATURE OF CASE: Suit to recover damages for trespass.

FACT SUMMARY: While hunting, the defendant fired shots over the property and possessions of the plaintiff.

RULE OF LAW
A trespass to the land occurs when bullets or other foreign particles violate the airspace above the land.

FACTS: While hunting, defendant repeatedly fired his shotgun at game birds in flight over plaintiff's property. These shots deprived plaintiff of the quiet, peaceful enjoyment of his home and property.

ISSUE: Does violation of the airspace immediately above the property by foreign objects constitute a trespass?

HOLDING AND DECISION: (Callaway, C.J.) Yes. If an alien object disturbs the airspace reasonably close to the surface of the land then a trespass is deemed to have been committed. The basis of the ruling is that the court envisions both the areas above and below the surface of the land as being legally protected from any unlawful intrusion; if these areas were not safeguarded by trespass laws, the property owner could not fully enjoy the premises. Further, the court fears that material crossing over the land in the airspace closely annexed to the property poses a potential source of danger to both persons and property. Affirmed.

▶ ANALYSIS

The case is one among many that stands for the proposition that a trespass occurs not only when there is a contact with or other entry onto the land, but also when there is intrusion in the space directly above the land. The case stands between the common-law notion that the owner's right to possession extends infinitely upward and the more modern view that only the airspace immediately above the land is protected by trespass laws.

■■■■

Quicknotes

AIR SPACE The area that exists directly above real estate.

DEFAULT Failure to carry out a legal obligation.

NOMINAL Small; trivial; with reference to name only.

TRESPASS Unlawful interference with, or damage to, the real or personal property of another.

■■■■

Rogers v. Board of Road Com'rs for Kent City

Decedent's wife (P) v. Snow fencer (D)

Mich. Sup. Ct., 319 Mich. 661, 30 N.W.2d 358 (1947).

NATURE OF CASE: Suit to recover damages for death based on negligence and trespass.

FACT SUMMARY: After the Board of Commissioners'(D) license to place a snow fence on Rogers' (P) property had expired, Rogers' (P) husband fatally injured himself due to the presence of the Board's (D) fencepost.

🏛 RULE OF LAW
Subsequent to the expiration of a license to enter land, any injury due to the continued presence of that object, regardless of the fact that negligence was not a cause of the injury, is a trespass.

FACTS: Two years prior to the date of the fatal injury of Rogers' (P) husband, the Board of Road Commissioners (D) obtained a license to place a winter snow fence on Rogers' (P) property on the condition that it be removed at the end of each winter season. In clear violation of the condition of the license, the fence was not taken down by the summer and thus as a result Rogers' (P) husband as he mowed the field hit the fence which caused him to fall and sustain a fatal injury.

ISSUE: Is an injury which is caused by the continued presence of an object after the privilege for that object's entry onto the land has terminated a trespass?

HOLDING AND DECISION: (Reid, J.) Yes. Although at one point there may have been a justification for the structure's presence on the land, after this justification is ended, any injury inflicted by the presence of that structure, whether negligent or not, is a trespass. Thus, even though the fence was licensed to be there during the winter, this license having terminated with the advent of the summer, any injury resulting from its unlawful presence entitled the landowner to damages for trespass. The court's decision reflects the concern of the law for the exclusiveness of possession. Reversed and remanded.

▶ ANALYSIS

The case belongs to a line of precedents that hold that once a trespass has been committed the intruder is liable for all the consequences of his trespass. His liability encompasses all tangible damage inflicted on the land itself, the person of the possessor and his family, and his chattels. The liability flows regardless of the foreseeability of the event. The reasoning that justifies such a rule is that the liability is based on the doctrine of transferred intent, not negligence, that is, the intent to enter the land unlawfully is transferred to establish a basis of liability for all other injuries caused. Hence, the fact that such harms could not be anticipated is irrelevant to building or attacking liability.

Quicknotes

CHATTEL An article of personal property, as distinguished from real property; a thing personal and moveable.

NEGLIGENCE Conduct falling below the standard of care that a reasonable person would demonstrate under similar conditions.

TRANSFERRED INTENT When a perpetrator acts with the intent to commit a crime against one person, and instead commits that crime against another person, the perpetrator's intent is transferred to the actual victim for the purposes of liability.

Glidden v. Szybiak

Wounded child (P) v. Dog owner (D)

N.H. Sup. Ct., 95 N.H. 318, 63 A.2d 233 (1949).

NATURE OF CASE: Suit to recover damages with a defense of trespass to chattel.

FACT SUMMARY: Elaine Glidden (P), a four-year-old child, played with and disturbed a dog belonging to Jane Szybiak (D), whereupon the dog bit Glidden (P).

RULE OF LAW
In order for a cause of action based upon trespass to chattels to be sustained, chattel owner must prove more than nominal damages to and intentional interference with the chattel.

FACTS: Four-year-old Elaine Glidden (P) encountered the dog, Toby, owned by Jane Szybiak (D), on the porch of a store. Glidden (P) played with and eventually provoked the dog, which snapped at her and inflicted wounds. Glidden (P) sued. Szybiak (D) argued that Glidden (P) was barred from recovery because she was trespassing at the time of her injury.

ISSUE: Can there be a defense of trespass to chattels when there are no more than nominal damages or intentional interference involving the chattel?

HOLDING AND DECISION: (Branch, C.J.) No. In order for a cause of action based upon trespass to chattels to be sustained, chattel owner must prove more than nominal damages to and intentional interference with the chattel. In this case, a trespass to chattels did not exist because there was no significant damage to the chattel. Since a trespass did not occur due to the fact that there was no willful intent to interfere with or do damage to the chattel, i.e., the dog, Szybiak (D) could not rely on an affirmative defense of trespass to chattel.

▶ ANALYSIS

This case represents a departure from the common-law view that no actual damage was necessary to sustain an action for trespass to chattels. Although a technical tort (a tort without actual damages) may be allowed to protect real property from trespass, the inviolability of personal property is not recognized by most contemporary courts.

■=■

Quicknotes

NOMINAL DAMAGES A small sum awarded to a plaintiff in order to recognize that he sustained an injury that is either slight or incapable of being established.

TRESPASS Unlawful interference with, or damage to, the real or personal property of another.

TRESPASS TO CHATTELS Action for damages sustained as a result of defendant's unlawful interference with plaintiff's personal property.

■=■

CompuServe Inc. v. Cyber Promotions, Inc.

Online service provider (P) v. Advertising company (D)

962 F. Supp. 1015 (S.D. Ohio 1997).

NATURE OF CASE: Application for preliminary injunction.

FACT SUMMARY: CompuServe (P) sought a preliminary injunction to restrain Cyber (D) from sending unsolicited e-mails to its subscribers.

🏛 RULE OF LAW
An action claiming trespass to chattels allows recovery for interference with the possession of chattels, not sufficient to rise to the level of conversion, and requires the defendant to pay the full value of the thing with which he has interfered.

FACTS: Cyber Promotions (D) is in the business of sending unsolicited e-mail advertisements on behalf of itself and its clients to Internet users. CompuServe (P), a national commercial online computer service, notified Cyber (D) that it was prohibited from sending its e-mails to CompuServe's (D) subscribers and requested that it cease doing so. Cyber (D) instead increased the number of e-mails it sent to CompuServe (P) subscribers. CompuServe (P) sought a preliminary injunction preventing Cyber (D) from sending the unsolicited e-mail advertisements to its subscribers, claiming Cyber's (D) transmission of electronic messages to its computer equipment is actionable under the common law theory of trespass to chattels.

ISSUE: Does an action claiming trespass to chattels allow recovery for interference with the possession of chattels?

HOLDING AND DECISION: (Graham, J.) Yes. An action claiming trespass to chattels allows recovery for interference with the possession of chattels, not sufficient to rise to the level of conversion, and requires the defendant to pay the full value of the thing with which he has interfered. The Restatement § 217(b) provides that a trespass to chattel is committed where the defendant intentionally uses or intermeddles with the chattel in possession of another. The comments define "intermeddling" as intentional physical contact. Electronic signals have been held to satisfy the definition of intermeddling. Here it is clear that CompuServe (P) has a possessory interest in its computer systems and that Cyber (D) has intentionally contacted such systems with its electronic signals. Cyber (D) argued that under the Restatement (Second) of Torts § 221, physical dispossession or substantial interference is required in order for the claim to be actionable. However, § 218 makes clear that an interference or intermeddling not meeting the § 221 definition is still actionable. Here Cyber's (D) mailings to CompuServe (P) subscribers demands disk space and drains CompuServe's processing powers, resulting in a diminution in value of its property. Motion for preliminary injunction granted.

▶ ANALYSIS

CompuServe (P) also argued that it suffered harm under § 218(d) to a legally protected interest, namely its goodwill and business reputation. Due to the large number of e-mail advertisements received, many of CompuServe's (P) customers closed their accounts. The court held that CompuServe's § 218(d) claim was actionable and rejected Cyber's (D) defense that CompuServe (P) was precluded from bringing suit in trespass since it connected itself with the Internet in the first place.

═■

Quicknotes

CHATTEL An article of personal property, as distinguished from real property; a thing personal and moveable.

PRELIMINARY INJUNCTION A judicial mandate issued to require or restrain a party from certain conduct; used to preserve a trial's subject matter or to prevent threatened injury.

TRESPASS Unlawful interference with, or damage to, the real or personal property of another.

═■

Pearson v. Dodd

U.S. Senator (P) v. Columnist (D)

410 F.2d 701 (D.C. Cir, 1969).

NATURE OF CASE: Appeal from partial summary judgment awarding damages for conversion.

FACT SUMMARY: Pearson (D) appealed from a grant of partial summary judgment for conversion, contending his actions in obtaining copies of certain information and publishing newspaper articles using this information did not amount to a conversion.

🏛 RULE OF LAW
The publication of information that does not amount to literary property, scientific invention, or secret plans formulated for the conduct of commerce, without an actual physical conversion of the documents containing the information, does not amount to conversion.

FACTS: Two former employees of Senator Dodd (P) secretly and without authority removed documents from Dodd's (P) files, copied and replaced them, and turned the copies over to Pearson (D). The information contained therein included contents of letters to Dodd (P) from supplicants and office records of an unknown nature. Pearson (D) published articles containing information obtained from the copies. Dodd (P) sued Pearson (D) on theories of conversion and invasion of privacy. The district court granted partial summary judgment in favor of Dodd (P) on the theory of conversion, and denied partial summary judgment in favor of Dodd (P) on the theory of invasion of privacy. From the court's grant of partial summary judgment on the theory of conversion, Pearson (D) appealed.

ISSUE: Does the publication of information that does not amount to literary property, scientific invention, or secret plans formulated for the conduct of commerce, absent an actual physical conversion of the documents containing the information, amount to conversion?

HOLDING AND DECISION: (Skelly Wright, J.) No. The publication of information that does not amount to literary property, scientific invention, or secret plans formulated for the conduct of commerce, without an actual physical conversion of the documents containing the information, does not amount to conversion. The measure of damages in a conversion action is the value of the goods converted. Because of the stringent measure of damages, not all interferences with property rights amount to conversions. It is clear from the facts that there has been no physical conversion of the actual original documents. Ideas or information are gen-

erally not protected by the law of conversion, but exceptions are made for literary work and scientific research, and information which has been gathered and can be sold as a commodity. The information contained herein does not appear to be this type of property. Since there was no actual conversion of the original documents, and the information utilized by Pearson (D) is not of the type normally protected by the law of conversion, the grant of partial summary judgment to Dodd (P) was improper. Reversed.

▶ ANALYSIS

Most actions brought for conversion involve settling title to disputed goods. Although there is authority for the proposition that a conversion may occur when one who is authorized to use a chattel exceeds the authorization, this view must be tempered in that the unauthorized use must involve a conversion adverse to the rights of the owner.

Quicknotes

CONVERSION The act of depriving an owner of his property without permission or justification.

INVASION OF PRIVACY The violation of an individual's right to be protected against unwarranted interference in his personal affairs, falling into one of four categories: (1) appropriating the individual's likeness or name for commercial benefit; (2) intrusion into the individual's seclusion; (3) public disclosure of private facts regarding the individual; and (4) disclosure of facts placing the individual in a false light.

PARTIAL SUMMARY JUDGMENT Judgment rendered by a court in response to a motion by one of the parties, claiming that the lack of a question of marital fact in respect to one of the issues warrants disposition of that issue without going to the jury.

TRESPASS TO CHATTELS Action for damages sustained as a result of defendant's unlawful interference with plaintiff's personal property.

TROVER An action for damages resulting from the unlawful conversion of, or to recover possession of, personal property.

Quick Reference Rules of Law

O'Brien v. Cunard S.S. Co.

Vaccinated passenger (P) v. Steamship company (D)

Mass. Sup. Jud. Ct., 154 Mass. 272, 28 N.E. 266 (1891).

NATURE OF CASE: Action to recover damages for assault and negligence.

FACT SUMMARY: O'Brien (P) held out her arm without objection to the doctor employed by Cunard S.S. Co. (D) to be vaccinated.

RULE OF LAW
Silence and inaction may imply consent to defendant's acts if the circumstances are such that a reasonable person would speak if he objected.

FACTS: In order to save its passengers the trouble of being vaccinated and quarantined when they reached the shores of the United States, the Cunard S.S. Co. (D) provided smallpox vaccinations on board ship. The Steamship Company (D) gave notice of this quarantine procedure and of its service in several languages. O'Brien (P) formed a part of the line of women who waited to have the doctor employed by the Steamship Company (D) inject her. Due to her presence in the line and her lack of objection to the vaccination, the doctor assumed that O'Brien (P) consented to receiving the smallpox vaccination. O'Brien (P) alleged that contamination of the vaccine or the site caused ulceration at the site and blistering on her body.

ISSUE: Is there consent to an assault when a person does nothing to resist the defendant's acts, if the situation is such that an average reasonable person would speak if he did not consent?

HOLDING AND DECISION: (Knowlton, J.) Yes. Consent will be implied from the plaintiff's conduct. In this case, the court looks to the facts that the plaintiff waited in the line designated for those who wished to be vaccinated and passively allowed the doctor to inject her. Affirmed.

▶ ANALYSIS

The case represents the great weight of authority that in determining whether there was consent the court must be guided by the overt words and acts of the plaintiff; subjective states of mind will not be considered.

▬▬▬

Quicknotes

CONSENT A voluntary and willful agreement by an individual possessing sufficient mental capacity to undertake an action suggested by another.

▬▬▬

Hackbart v. Cincinnati Bengals, Inc.

Football player (P) v. Opposing team (D)

601 F.2d 516 (10th Cir. 1979).

NATURE OF CASE: Appeal from denial of damages for battery.

FACT SUMMARY: Hackbart (P), a Denver Bronco's player, was intentionally injured by a member of the Cincinnati Bengals (D) during a professional football game.

RULE OF LAW
An injury inflicted by one player upon another during a professional football game may give rise to liability where the cause of the injury was an intentional blow.

FACTS: Hackbart (P), a member of the Denver Broncos football team, brought suit for injuries arising out of an intentionally administered blow during a regular season game. The blow was administered to the back of Hackbart's (P) head by "Booby" Clark, a member of the opposing team, the Cincinnati Bengals (D). The trial court, noting the violent nature of football and that incidents such as the one complained of by Hackbart (P) are not unusual, ruled that as a matter of law, liability could not issue in such a situation. Hackbart (P) appealed.

ISSUE: May an intentionally inflicted blow by an opposing player during a professional football game give rise to liability for injuries caused thereby?

HOLDING AND DECISION: (Doyle, J.) Yes. A review of the National Football League rules shows that an intentional blow to the head, such as the one complained of here, is clearly prohibited in a professional football game. As such, liability can result from the infliction of such a blow which gives rise to injuries in an opposing ballplayer. The trial court erroneously made its determination based on its observation regarding the violent nature of football as a sport rather than limiting its analysis to the evidence bearing on the liability of the Cincinnati Bengals (D) for the actions of its player. Reversed and remanded.

⏵ ANALYSIS

Not only cases involving injured players have arisen in the sporting context. In *Lang v. Amateur Softball Association of America*, 520 P.2d 659 (Okla. 1974), a fan injured by a softball thrown wildly over a fence by a pitcher warming up sued for damages. The court found that the defendant had utilized reasonable care to protect the fans, and that the spectators had impliedly assumed the risk of being hit when they entered the ballpark.

■=■

Quicknotes

ASSAULT The intentional placing of another in fear of immediate bodily injury.

ASSUMPTION OF RISK DOCTRINE An affirmative defense to a negligence suit by the defendant contending that the plaintiff knowingly and voluntarily subjected himself to the hazardous condition wholly absolving the defendant of liability for injuries incurred.

BATTERY Unlawful contact with the body of another person.

INTENT The state of mind that exists when one's purpose is to commit a criminal act.

NEGLIGENCE Conduct falling below the standard of care that a reasonable person would demonstrate under similar conditions.

RECKLESSNESS The conscious disregard of substantial and justifiable risk.

■=■

Mohr v. Williams

Patient (P) v. Ear specialist (D)

Minn. Sup. Ct., 95 Minn. 261, 104 N.W. 12 (1905).

NATURE OF CASE: Action to recover damages for battery.

FACT SUMMARY: Without Mohr's (P) permission in writing, or orally, Williams (D) operated on her ear.

> ## RULE OF LAW
> If the defendant's actions exceed the consent given, and he does a substantially different act than the one authorized, then he is liable.

FACTS: Mohr (P) was admitted to surgery so that her right ear might be operated upon by defendant. When Mohr (P) was unconscious, Williams (D) discovered the right ear was not that serious, but the left was infected. Thus, without awakening Mohr (P), Williams (D) operated on the left ear. He did this although he only had permission to operate on the right ear. The operation was successful but Mohr (P) nevertheless brought an action for battery. The jury awarded her $14,322, but the trial judge found the award excessive and granted a new trial. Both parties appealed.

ISSUE: If no emergency condition is found during the course of the operation to which plaintiff consented, is there valid consent to perform a different operation?

HOLDING AND DECISION: (Brown, J.) No. If the defendant's actions exceed the consent given, and he does a substantially different act than the one authorized, then he is liable. Unless the physician discovers a condition that endangers the life of his patient during the operation to which the plaintiff consented, there is no consent to a different operation. In this case, the diseased condition of Mohr's (P) left ear, was not discovered in the course of the authorized operation, but by independent examination after the operation was found to be unnecessary and, further, it was not an eminently dangerous condition. Affirmed.

▶ ANALYSIS

The case falls into the majority view. However, doctors have circumvented the problem of this decision by requiring the patient to give blanket consent to any remedy the physician thinks best.

■■■■

Quicknotes

BATTERY Unlawful contact with the body of another person.

CONSENT A voluntary and willful agreement by an individual possessing sufficient mental capacity to undertake an action suggested by another.

■■■■

De May v. Roberts

Woman in labor (P) v. Doctor (D) and friend (D)

Mich. Sup. Ct., 46 Mich. 160, 9 N.W. 146 (1881).

NATURE OF CASE: Action to recover damages for deceit, invasion of privacy, assault, and battery.

FACT SUMMARY: Dr. DeMay (D) arrived to deliver Roberts' (P) baby and introduced Scattergood (D) into the maternity room on the pretense that Scattergood (D) was Dr. DeMay's (D) assistant and, thus, Roberts (P) alleged that Scattergood (D) watched all that occurred, intruding on her privacy and indecently and wrongfully assaulting her.

RULE OF LAW:
(1) There exists no privilege of consent when the plaintiff has consented under a mistaken belief which has been instilled by defendant's deceit.
(2) An assault is perpetrated by the inducement of consent through misrepresentation.

FACTS: Dr. DeMay (D) entered Roberts' (P) bedroom where she was in labor, in order to perform delivery. With Dr. DeMay (D) was Scattergood (D), who appeared to be his assistant and whom Dr. DeMay (D) knew to be untrained professionally, as well as unmarried. The evidence disclosed that Scattergood (D) was present in Roberts' (P) room during labor and that he also took hold of Roberts' (P) hand and held her during a paroxysm of pain. Roberts (P), therefore, contended that Dr. DeMay's (D) deceit in passing off Scattergood (D) as a physician's aid caused an intrusion upon her privacy. Furthermore, Roberts (P) contended that Scattergood (D) assaulted her when he did indecently, wrongfully, and unlawfully lay hands upon her.

ISSUE:
(1) Is there consent when the defendant has misrepresented facts to a plaintiff and this misrepresentation has caused the plaintiff to consent?
(2) Has an assault been committed when the defendant induced plaintiff's consent by means of misrepresentation?

HOLDING AND DECISION: (Martson, C.J.)
(1) No. Consent which is gained through the defendant's misrepresentation is invalid. In this case, the defendant DeMay (D) introduced Scattergood (D) as a professional. Because she believed Scattergood (D) was examining her, Roberts (P) acquiesced to his presence at her bedside and to his laying his hands upon her. The reason for this rule seems to be that there can be no genuine consent where there is no understanding of the nature of the act to which one consents.
(2) Yes. An assault has been committed when misrepresentation induced plaintiff's consent, for the defense of consent does not exist in favor of one who has obtained that consent by misrepresentation. The policy behind this principle is that a variety of torts could be defended and justified by the commission of another tort, i.e., to gain consent to commit the first tort assault, a wrongdoer could induce consent by means of misrepresentation, another tort. Affirmed.

▶ *ANALYSIS*

Both holdings of this case seem to represent the mainstream of judicial authority. The case is also typical of early cases which did not recognize a remedy for the infliction of mental suffering unless it could be brought within the scope of some already existing tort remedy. Since it was possible without much pretense to grant recovery on a traditional assault theory, the court avoided granting relief on the then less acceptable doctrine of mental suffering. The case is an early forerunner of right to privacy as a basis of tort liability.

■■■■

Quicknotes

ASSAULT The intentional placing of another in fear of immediate bodily injury.

CONSENT A voluntary and willful agreement by an individual possessing sufficient mental capacity to undertake an action suggested by another.

MISREPRESENTATION A statement or conduct by one party to another that constitutes a false representation of fact.

PARTURITION The act of giving birth to a child.

■■■■

Katko v. Briney

Spring gun victim (P) v. Property owner (D)

Iowa Sup. Ct., 183 N.W.2d 657 (1971).

NATURE OF CASE: Action to recover compensatory and punitive damages due to physical injury caused by the firing of a spring gun set up by Briney (D).

FACT SUMMARY: In order to protect an uninhabited house, Briney (D) installed a mechanical spring gun whose fire was triggered by the opening of a door; Katko (P) opened the door and the gun fired, severely injuring him.

🏛 RULE OF LAW
No privilege exists to maintain a mechanical device that defends property by automatically inflicting serious bodily injury on those intruders who stimulate the firing mechanism.

FACTS: To guard an unoccupied, isolated house, which had been entered unlawfully on previous occasions, against future unlawful entries, Briney (D) took several precautions such as boarding up the house, posting no trespass signs, and setting up a shotgun trap. There was no warning of the spring gun device which was rigged so that it would fire when a door was opened. When Katko (P), a trespasser, opened the door, the gun blast seriously wounded him, blowing away a substantial portion of his leg. The wound left Katko (P) permanently disfigured with a shortened leg.

ISSUE: Does the landowner possess the privilege to install, for the purpose of protecting his property against unlawful intrusions, a mechanism whose sole function is the infliction of death or serious harm upon the intruders?

HOLDING AND DECISION: (Moore, C.J.) No. The fact that an intruder is acting unlawfully does not justify the maintenance of a mechanical device to protect property that can cause great physical injury. Such a man-killing mechanical device is only permissible if the intruder is committing a violent felony, endangering the lives of the occupants. Affirmed.

▌ ANALYSIS

The use of a mechanical device cannot expand the privilege to use physical violence in defense of property. There is a severe limitation on this privilege, for there is no right, whether by mechanical means or by the landowner's hand, to use force which may be lethal. This privilege to use physical force exists only after the landowner's mild methods of expulsion (verbal requests or constrained physical acts) have been met with resistance or when the violence directed at the land is redirected at its occupants. The amount of force which may be utilized can not exceed the apparent necessities of protecting the land in possession. The necessities are those which would be perceived by a reasonable individual in the property owner's position.

■━■

Quicknotes

SPRING GUN A gun that is set to fire when triggered by an external force.

■━■

Hodgeden v. Hubbard

Stove buyer (P) v. Stove sellers (D)

Vt. Sup. Ct., 18 Vt. 504, 46 Am. Dec. 167 (1846).

NATURE OF CASE: Action to recover damages for assault and battery and for taking and carrying away a stove; the defense is a privilege to recapture chattels.

FACT SUMMARY: Defendants (D) discovering immediately after the sale of goods that plaintiff (P) obtained goods from them fraudulently, pursued him and used force, once they caught him, to recapture goods.

🏛 RULE OF LAW
The law recognizes a privilege to recapture chattels when the owner has been defrauded of his rightful possession and he pursues the wrongful taker of his goods in fresh pursuit.

FACTS: Defendants (D) extended credit to plaintiff (P) on the sale of a stove. Immediately after this credit sale, defendants (D) discovered plaintiff (P) was in severe fiscal difficulties. Upon notice of plaintiff's (P) true financial status, defendants (D) rushed out in pursuit of plaintiff (P) and their stove. When they overtook plaintiff (P) a few miles away, they requested return of the stove. Plaintiff (P) resisted and drew his knife. While one defendant (D) held plaintiff (P), the other defendant (D) took possession of the stove.

ISSUE: Is there a privilege to recapture chattels by force, if the chattels have been obtained through misrepresentation and the true owner attempts to retake in fresh pursuit?

HOLDING AND DECISION: (Williams, C.J.) Yes. When possession is taken by one who obtained through fraud, the dispossessed owner may recapture by force, if he proceeds without unreasonable delay and as long as no unnecessary violence to person or breach of the peace occurs. No privilege exists in favor of the wrongdoer to resist, and if he does so, the owner may use any force necessary to defend his own person. The policy behind sanctioning the recapture privilege is that this self-help remedy enables the owner to recover his property promptly without wading through the cumbersome and lengthy legal procedures which ultimately may not even operate in time to recover the chattel or may be powerless to compel the return of the chattel. Reversed.

▶ ANALYSIS

The recapture privilege is founded on the concept that the original owner has a continuing right to possession. Thus, the privilege only exists when possession has been wrongfully taken. Courts have always acknowledged any forcible taking as a justification for the recapture privilege; the justification for the recapture privilege was extended to allow the privilege in cases such as this one where there was a wrongful taking by fraudulent methods. Any force designed to inflict serious bodily injury is excessive if exercised to effect the recapture of chattels. The amount of force which may be used is limited by the necessities of the situation as they would appear to a reasonable person in the recapturer's position. As a rule, a resort to force will not be privileged unless a demand first has been made for return of the chattels.

Quicknotes

CHATTEL An article of personal property, as distinguished from real property; a thing personal and moveable.

FRAUD A false representation of facts with the intent that another will rely on the misrepresentation to his detriment.

MISREPRESENTATION A statement or conduct by one party to another that constitutes a false representation of fact.

Bonkowski v. Arlan's Department Store

Shopper (P) v. Department store (D)

Mich. Ct. App., 12 Mich. App. 88, 162 N.W.2d 347 (1968).

NATURE OF CASE: Action to recover damages for false arrest and slander (defense to false arrest is the shopkeeper's privilege to detain a person he reasonably suspects of theft).

FACT SUMMARY: On the grounds of a reasonable suspicion, Arlan's Department Store's (D) detective detained Mrs. Bonkowski (P), and the detention resulted in Mrs. Bonkowski's (P) mental suffering.

🏛 RULE OF LAW
There is a shopkeeper's privilege to detain a customer for investigation if the shopkeeper has reason to suspect that customer has stolen goods.

FACTS: On the basis of a report that Mrs. Bonkowski (P) was shoplifting, Arlan's Department Store's (D) detective detained her outside the store and made her reveal the contents of her purse. Mrs. Bonkowski (P) produced sales slips for the items from the store, and this satisfied the detective that she had committed no theft. As a result of this detention, Mrs. Bonkowski (P) suffered psychological trauma.

ISSUE: Does a privilege exist by which a shopkeeper is able to detain a person for reasonable investigation whom he reasonably suspects has unlawfully taken merchandise?

HOLDING AND DECISION: (Fitzgerald, J.) Yes. If the merchant or his agent reasonably believes the individual has unlawfully taken goods held for sale in the merchant's store, then he enjoys the privilege to detain that individual for a reasonable investigation. The court's reasoning in allowing this privilege is that it guards the shopkeeper from the dilemma of either allowing the suspected person to walk away free, thus assuming the burden of loss for the stolen item himself, or the equally unpalatable choice of arresting the suspect, thus assuming the risk of paying damages in action for false arrest. Reversed and remanded.

▶ ANALYSIS

The case conforms to a line of cases which hold that a businessman who reasonably suspects a customer of theft may, in order to make reasonable inquiries, hold that person for a short time, if that customer has not left the store. The case at bar broadens this principle to allow detention of a customer who has already left the premises.

■ ≡ ■

Quicknotes

LARCENY The illegal taking of another's property with the intent to deprive the owner thereof.

JUDGMENT NOTWITHSTANDING THE VERDICT A judgment entered by the trial judge reversing a jury verdict if the jury's determination has no basis in law or fact.

REMITTITUR The authority of the court to reduce the amount of damages awarded by the jury.

SLANDER Defamatory statement communicated orally.

■ ≡ ■

Surocco v. Geary

Property owner (P) v. Mayor (D)

Cal. Sup. Ct., 3 Cal. 69, 58 Am. Dec. 385 (1853).

NATURE OF CASE: Action to recover damages for buildings and goods destroyed by a gunpowder blast; defense is necessity.

FACT SUMMARY: During a fire, Geary (D) blew up buildings owned by Surocco (P) in order to prevent the fire from spreading.

🏛 RULE OF LAW
The law recognizes a privilege to damage property to avert threatened disaster when necessary in exigent circumstances.

FACTS: To halt the spread of a conflagration that endangered a whole town, Geary (D) destroyed, by means of a gunpowder blast, Surocco's (P) store and house and the goods therein. This destruction was accomplished while Surocco (P) still had time to empty the buildings of goods.

ISSUE: Is an individual personally liable for the damage he creates when, in good faith and under apparent necessity, he destroys the property of another in order to save the surrounding area?

HOLDING AND DECISION: (Murray, C.J.) No. The right to destroy property is justified if it is done to prevent a fire or other disaster from proliferating and is done in the good-faith belief that it is a necessity. The purpose of sanctioning this privilege to destroy property in times of emergency is to insure the safety of the entire community, which could be jeopardized if the owner had a right to recover against the individual who saved the community. This right to recovery might deter the community's savior from acting. Reversed.

▌ANALYSIS

The case is one of a series which condones the individual who acts to avert peril which threatens the public. Such an individual is not liable to the owner whose property has been ruined as long as he acted believing reasonably that such a deed was necessary to prevent a public disaster. There is another body of case law dealing with necessity in which no public interest is at stake. The privilege to protect a private interest is narrowly circumscribed. One may trespass or damage property with immunity from tort liability only to save one's own life or the life of another.

Quicknotes

Vincent v. Lake Erie Transp. Co.

Dock owner (P) v. Steamship company (D)

Minn. Sup. Ct., 109 Minn. 456, 124 N.W. 221 (1910).

NATURE OF CASE: Action to recover damages for trespass, on appeal.

FACT SUMMARY: The crew of the Reynolds, a ship of the Lake Erie Transportation Co. (D), kept that ship tied to a dock belonging to Vincent (P) during a violent storm causing damage to the dock.

RULE OF LAW

Private necessity of avoiding destruction or damage to one's property gives rise to a privilege to invade the property of another, but this privilege is limited to entry and compensation must be made for any damage resulting from it.

FACTS: The steamship Reynolds, owned by Lake Erie Transportation Co. (D), was moored to Vincent's (P) dock for the purpose of discharging cargo. When a violent storm developed, instead of cutting the ship loose from the dock, the crew kept it tied up, with $500 damage resulting to the dock. Vincent (P) sued to recover for this damage. Upon judgment for Vincent (P), Lake Erie (D) appealed contending that the defense of necessity insulated them from liability.

ISSUE: Does the defense of private necessity relieve one of liability for damage done while protecting one's property?

HOLDING AND DECISION: (O'Brien, J.) No. Private necessity of avoiding destruction or damage to one's property gives rise to a privilege to invade the property of another, but this privilege is limited to entry, and compensation must be made for any damage resulting from it. It is true that normal property rights may be suspended where non-human conditions such as storms get out of control. In the landmark case of *Ploof v. Putnam*, 81 Vt. 471, 71 A. 188 (1908), however, the Vermont Supreme Court pointed out that where injury to property results from an emergency trespass, the damages must be compensated for, even though the trespass itself is privileged. Here, the deliberate act of the crew in not cutting the ship loose, though not a trespass, nevertheless resulted in trespassory harm to the dock of Vincent (P). This must be compensated for. The judgment must be affirmed.

▶ ANALYSIS

This case points up the general rule for the tort defense of private necessity. In addition to property, it, of course, also extends to situations in which nonhuman actions prevent a threat of death or serious bodily injury to the trespassing party. The privilege may be extended to the breaking into of buildings including dwellings, and supersedes the right of the owner to protect his property. (Therefore, any force used to expel someone acting out of necessity is wrongful and actionable.) Of course, the trespass involved must not be disproportionate to the danger avoided. Private necessity, of course, must be distinguished from public necessity. Unlike private necessity, public necessity carries with it a complete privilege (no liability for damages) whenever a trespass is necessary to avoid a public disaster (flood, etc.). Both public officers and private citizens may act in public necessity, and even deadly force may be justified in proper circumstances.

Quicknotes

ASSIGNMENT OF ERROR A complaint filed by an appellant setting forth the alleged errors of the trial court upon which he seeks a reversal.

PRIVATE NECESSITY A defense to liability for unlawful activity where the conduct is unavoidable and is justified by preventing the injury to life or health.

Sindle v. New York City Transit Authority

Injured student (P) v. Transit authority (D) and bus driver (D)

N.Y. Ct. App., 33 N.Y.2d 293, 307 N.E.2d 245 (1973).

NATURE OF CASE: Appeal from an award of damages for false imprisonment.

FACT SUMMARY: Sindle (P), a 14-year-old boy, was injured when he fell under the wheels of an Authority (D) school bus when he attempted to climb out after the bus driver (D) locked the doors to prevent vandals from escaping.

🏛 RULE OF LAW
A person falsely imprisoned is not relieved of the duty of reasonable care for his own safety in extricating himself from the unlawful detention.

FACTS: The students on an Authority (D) school bus were vandalizing the bus. The driver (D) inspected the damage after having warned the students and decided to take them to a police station. He locked the doors, bypassed regular bus stops, and proceeded to the police station. At one point, several students jumped out a bus window, apparently without injury. Sindle (P), a 14-year-old boy, decided to jump out, but as he was climbing out the window, the bus rounded a curve, and he fell out and was run over by the rear wheels. Sindle (P), joined with his father (P), sought damages for negligence and false imprisonment. At trial, Sindle (P) waived the negligence claim, and the court denied Authority's (D) motion to amend its answer to plead the defense of justification and excluded all evidence bearing on justification. Authority (D) appealed an award of damages to Sindle (P).

ISSUE: Is a person who is falsely imprisoned relieved of the duty of reasonable care for his own safety in extricating himself from the unlawful detention?

HOLDING AND DECISION: (Jasen, J.) No. A person who is falsely imprisoned is not relieved of the duty of reasonable care for his own safety in extricating himself from the unlawful detention. Accordingly, it was an abuse of the trial court's discretion to deny Authority's (D) motion. Authority (D) had the duty to plead justification, a defense which a plaintiff should expect in a false imprisonment, and, thus, Sindle (P) would not have been prejudiced by the court's granting Authority's (D) motion. Authority's driver (D) had a duty to care reasonably for the property entrusted him. The reasonableness of his actions bears on whether his conduct was justified. And, if Sindle (P) acted unreasonably in attempting to extricate himself, his damages for bodily injuries sustained as a result of the false imprisonment should be barred. Reversed and remanded for new trial.

▌ ANALYSIS

In cases where a person has attempted to alight from a moving vehicle absent some compelling reason, it has been held to be negligence per se. This would be a consideration upon retrial. Also, the actions of the bus driver might be compared to action allowed under the so-called "shopkeeper's privilege." Under that privilege, a shopkeeper may detain a suspected shoplifter. Here, the driver detained suspected vandals. This point goes to the issue of justification.

Quicknotes

FALSE IMPRISONMENT Intentional tort whereby the victim is unlawfully restrained.

JUSTIFICATION DEFENSE A reason recognized by law as an excuse for acting or failing to act.

NEGLIGENCE Conduct falling below the standard of care that a reasonable person would demonstrate under similar conditions.

Negligence

Quick Reference Rules of Law

Lubitz v. Wells

Injured nine-year-old (P) v. Golfer (D) and son (D)

Conn. Sup. Ct., 19 Conn. Supp. 322, 113 A.2d 147 (1955).

NATURE OF CASE: Action to recover damages for negligence.

FACT SUMMARY: Mr. Wells (D), father of defendant J. Wells, Jr. (D), left a golf club out in a place where children played, and his son (D) negligently failed to warn Lubitz (P) that he was intending to swing the club, thus injuring her.

> 🏛 **RULE OF LAW**
> Conduct which is reasonable and has low probability of resulting in harm to others is not negligence.

FACTS: The father (D) of J. Wells, Jr. (D) left a golf club out in his yard where both his son (D) and Lubitz (P) were playing. Wells, Jr. (D) swung the club without warning Lubitz (P) of his intention. As a result of his failure to warn her before swinging the golf club, Lubitz (P) was injured. Lubitz (P) sued the son (D) for his negligence in hitting her and sued the father (D) for his negligence in leaving the club in a position where it could inflict harm.

ISSUE: Is one who cannot anticipate that a child may use an instrument dangerously liable for negligence if he leaves that instrument within the child's reach?

HOLDING AND DECISION: (Troland, J.) No. A person is not negligent if there is little possibility that his conduct will injure another. In this case the chance that the child would inflict injury by means of the golf club was not foreseeable. A person cannot be shouldered with responsibility for acts which portend no harm. It would be unfair and unreasonable to hold someone to a standard of conduct beyond that which a prudent person could comply with.

▶ *ANALYSIS*

The case conforms to the weight of authority; courts generally do not expect people to guard against events which cannot reasonably be expected to cause harm. If minute risks were taken seriously, activity would decrease out of fear of injury to others.

■■■

Quicknotes

DEMURRER The assertion that the opposing party's pleadings are insufficient and that the demurring party should not be made to answer.

■■■

Blyth v. Birmingham Waterworks Co.

Flooded property owner (P) v. Fire plug installer (D)

Exchequer, 11 Exch. 781 (1856).

NATURE OF CASE: Action to recover damages for negligence on appeal.

FACT SUMMARY: An extraordinarily severe frost caused a fireplug owned by Waterworks (D) to flood the property of Blyth (P).

🏛 RULE OF LAW
Negligence involves the creation of an "unreasonable" risk, by act or omission, which a reasonable and prudent man would not create.

FACTS: Birmingham Waterworks Co. (D) installed water mains, including several fire plugs, in a street. The plugs worked well for 25 years. Then, during an extraordinarily cold frost one winter, one of the plugs got stopped up by ice, causing water from the pipes to flood and damage the property of Blyth (P). Blyth (P) sued for damages, alleging that Waterworks (D) was negligent for not taking adequate precautions to prepare for the contingency of this frost. Upon judgment for Blyth (P), Waterworks (D) appealed, contending that the frost was so extraordinary and unforeseeable that any damage resulted from mere accident.

ISSUE: May negligence liability be imposed where damage results from a mere accident, the contingency of which was wholly extraordinary?

HOLDING AND DECISION: (Alderson, B.) No. Negligence involves the creation of an "unreasonable" risk, by act or omission, which a reasonable and prudent man, guided upon those considerations which ordinarily regulate the conduct of human affairs, would not create. A reasonable person acts with reference to the average circumstances of ordinary times. He cannot be held, therefore, for extraordinary occurrences. Here, Waterworks (D) took all necessary precautions for ordinary frost. They cannot equitably be held responsible for a frost such as the one involved here, as such a frost is seldom seen south of the polar regions. The judgment must be reversed. The rationale here is that making Waterworks (D) responsible for all harm caused, even inadvertently, would be to make them insurers of all people they deal with. Reversed.

▶ ANALYSIS

This case points up the general rule for the negligence standard that all people owe: the objective "reasonable person under similar circumstances" test. If the conduct involved creates an "unreasonable risk" of harm, negligence can be found. Caution must be taken, however, to avoid confusing the foreseeability standard for standard of care (above) and the absence of this standard for proximate cause.

■▬■

Quicknotes

NEGLIGENCE Conduct falling below the standard of care that a reasonable person would demonstrate under similar conditions.

PROXIMATE CAUSE The natural sequence of events without which an injury would not have been sustained.

REASONABLE PERSON STANDARD The standard of care exercised by a hypothetical person who possesses the intelligence, education, knowledge, attention, and judgment required by society of its members when governing behavior; the standard applies to a person's judgment when determining breach of a duty under the theory of negligence.

UNFORESEEABLE A result that was not likely to occur from a particular act or failure to act.

■▬■

Gulf Refining Co. v. Williams

Burn victim (P) v. Gasoline distributor (D)

Miss. Sup. Ct., 183 Miss. 723, 185 So. 234 (1938).

NATURE OF CASE: Action to recover damages for negligence.

FACT SUMMARY: Gulf Refining Co. (D) sold gasoline in a nine-year-old drum with a bunghole of the same age which, when it came into contact with Williams (P), burst into flames, injuring him.

🏛 RULE OF LAW
An action for negligence exists when the defendant incurs a risk that makes the possibility of harm real enough so that a person of ordinary prudence would take some action to avert the threatened danger.

FACTS: Gulf Refining Co. (D) sold a nine-year-old gasoline drum with a worn bunghole of the same age. The threads of the bunghole were broken, bent, and jagged. This condition was known to one of Gulf's (D) employees but he failed to replace it. Hence, when Williams (P) began to unplug the bunghole, a fire began which caused injuries to Williams (P).

ISSUE: Is there a cause of action for negligence when there is only possibility of harm?

HOLDING AND DECISION: (Griffith, J.) Yes. There can be an action for negligence maintained if the possibility of harm is not entirely remote, but is a possibility which would induce a person of ordinary care to change his course of action to avoid that anticipated harm. It does not concern the court that the event is more likely than not to occur but that the chances of the harm occurring, weighted with the seriousness of the injury it would cause, induce a person acting according to the dictates of reasonable care to do something to preclude the event from happening. In this case, the defendant's employees could not have anticipated that it was more likely than not that the gasoline would explode, but there was a possibility of explosion due to the faulty bunghole and also if an injury did occur it would be of great magnitude. Affirmed.

▶ ANALYSIS
The case states a majority rule that there is the undertaking of an unreasonable risk and, thus, a breach of the duty of care, if the defendant performs an act that has a fairly low probability of occurring, but a fairly high probability of causing an accompanying injury. Thus, as the anticipated injury increases in magnitude, the apparent probability of its occurrence needs to be correspondingly less to constitute negligence.

Quicknotes

NEGLIGENCE Conduct falling below the standard of care that a reasonable person would demonstrate under similar conditions.

FORESEEABILITY OF HARM An inquiry into the relatedness of events that contributed to the plaintiff's injury; whether the harm was foreseeable determines whether the tortfeasor's conduct was the proximate cause of the injury.

Chicago B.&Q. R. Co. v. Krayenbuhl

Injured boy (P) v. Railway (D)

Neb. Sup. Ct., 65 Neb. 889, 91 N.W. 880 (1902).

NATURE OF CASE: Action to recover damages for personal injuries, caused by negligence, on appeal.

FACT SUMMARY: Krayenbuhl (P), age 4, had his foot severed while playing on a railroad turntable belonging to Chicago B.&Q. R. Co. (D), a railroad company.

🏛 RULE OF LAW
When the owner of dangerous premises knows, or has good reason to believe, that children trespassers, so young as to be ignorant of the danger, will be attracted to and will resort to such premises, he is under a duty of care to protect such children from the risks arising from such premises.

FACTS: Krayenbuhl (P), age 4, was known to have frequently trespassed upon the property of the railroad (D) to play on its turntable with other children. Though company policy was that the turntable was to be padlocked by the foreman when not in use, this policy was frequently ignored. On the day in question, Krayenbuhl (P), along with other children, entered the premises of the railroad (D), and either found the turntable unlocked or unlocked it themselves. It was unguarded. In the process of playing on it, Krayenbuhl's (P) foot was severed above the ankle. He sued to recover for personal injuries. Upon judgment in his favor, the Railroad (D) appealed, contending that the fact of the child's status as a trespasser took the case out of negligence liability.

ISSUE: Is the owner of dangerous premises justified in ignoring any duty of care to children trespassers, merely because they are trespassers?

HOLDING AND DECISION: (Albert, C.) No. When the owner of dangerous premises knows, or has good reason to believe, that children trespassers, so young as to be ignorant of the danger, will be attracted to and will resort to such premises, he is under a duty of care to protect such children from the risks arising from such premises. As such, the risks so created are unreasonable and unjustified. Though there is no general duty of care to trespassers, such a duty may often arise from peculiar circumstances (e.g., one cannot set up a spring gun to repel trespassers). The so-called "turntable doctrine" herein described recognized the peculiar circumstance of child trespassers as one such exception to the general rule. Here, the failure of the Railroad (D) to take precautions (locks, guards, etc.) to prevent children from playing on their dangerous premises (turntable) is an omission to act while under a duty of care. Such is negligence. [Reversed on other grounds.]

▶ ANALYSIS

This case points up the majority rule for children trespassers. It is more commonly called "the attractive nuisance doctrine" (rather than the "turntable" doctrine). Note that the duty of care here is higher than that normally imposed. The owner of land must not only maintain his premises such that no unreasonable risk is presented to those who have a right to be there, but he must also: (1) exercise due care to discover trespassing children, and (2) warn or, if necessary, protect them from the risks involved. Note also, however, that the doctrine is generally limited to cases involving artificial conditions on the land only (turntables, machinery, etc.). No special duty is owed where the condition or activity involved is natural (stream, etc.).

Quicknotes

ATTRACTIVE NUISANCE DOCTRINE The assignment of liability to an owner or occupier of land who permits a dangerous instrumentality to remain on the property, knowing that it is likely to attract children who have access to it, and who fails to take reasonable steps to prevent such injury.

DUTY OF CARE A principle of negligence requiring an individual to act in such a manner as to avoid injury to a person to whom he or she owes an obligatory duty.

NEGLIGENCE Conduct falling below the standard of care that a reasonable person would demonstrate under similar conditions.

TRESPASS Unlawful interference with, or damage to, the real or personal property of another.

TURNTABLE DOCTRINE Requires persons who maintain a condition on their premises which is likely to attract children to take precautions as would a reasonably prudent person to prevent injury.

Davison v. Snohomish County

Accident victim (P) v. County (D)

Wash. Sup. Ct., 149 Wash. 109, 270 P. 422 (1928).

NATURE OF CASE: Suit to recover damages for negligence.

FACT SUMMARY: Davison (P) was injured on the County's (D) bridge due to the fact that there was a weak guardrail, improper banking, and dirt on the approach to the bridge.

> ## 🏛 RULE OF LAW
> The burden in terms of monetary costs is too high for a public entity to protect against every anticipated accident.

FACTS: After Davison (P) crossed the County's (D) bridge, his car skidded and it struck the railing of the curve and broke through it. As a result of this accident, Davison (P) suffered severe injuries to his person and his automobile was also greatly damaged. Davison (P) alleged that the accident occurred because the guardrail was not sufficient in strength to hold the car, that there was dirt on the approach which contributed to the skidding, and that the approach to the bridge was improperly banked.

ISSUE: Does a county have the duty to prepare its roads so as to guard against all conceivable accidents?

HOLDING AND DECISION: (Beals, J.) No. There is no duty on the part of a public body to assume the burden of safeguarding against all conceivable accidents. In this case, the fact that the guardrail was not as sturdy as it should have been to protect against a car running off the road is inconsequential, for to insist on such a requirement would deter the county from opening roads to public access. In the era of the horse and buggy, if the county were to shield automobiles from leaving the road the costs of maintaining and establishing such protection would be too prohibitive for the county's expense account. Further, the fact that the incline was too steep was also irrelevant when the margin by which it was banked is compared to the height of the entire slope. The County (D) would not be expected to correct the whole slope to correct such a marginal error. Also, the court considered the fact that there was dirt on the road irrelevant as to the proof of negligence. The County (D) cannot be held for ordinary accumulation of dirt. Reversed.

▶ ANALYSIS

The case falls into a group of cases which consider the cost of the alternative courses of action which would prevent harm to the plaintiff. If the cost of prevention would halt the defendant from providing necessary services such as roads, then this cost should not be imposed. The converse is also considered, i.e., if the cost to post a warning or achieve some other safety measure is low, the defendant may be liable for not doing this inexpensive act.

■■■■

Quicknotes

NEGLIGENCE Conduct falling below the standard of care that a reasonable person would demonstrate under similar conditions.

■■■■

United States v. Carroll Towing Co.

State (D) v. Barge owner (P)

159 F.2d 169 (2d Cir. 1947).

NATURE OF CASE: Action to recover damages in admiralty for the sinking of a barge.

FACT SUMMARY: The attendant of the Conners Co. (P) barge left the vessel unwatched for 21 hours. During that period, the barge broke loose and was sunk.

RULE OF LAW

There is a duty of care to protect others from harm when the burden of taking adequate precautions is less than the product of the probability of the resulting harm and the magnitude of the harm.

FACTS: The attendant of the Conners Co. (P) barge left the vessel unwatched for 21 hours during the period when the harbor was full of vessels. During that 21-hour period, the barge broke loose from the pier through the negligence of Carroll Towing Co.'s (D) servant in shifting its mooring lines. The Conners Co. (P) barge was sunk. Conners Co. (P) sued Carroll Towing Co. (D) for negligence. The trial Court divided the damages.

ISSUE: Is the duty of care breached when defendant's conduct incurred a risk which could be avoided with very few precautions and which if it inflicts injury will cause a great amount of damage?

HOLDING AND DECISION: (Hand, J.) Yes. If the burden of preventing the injury is lower than the product of the probability of its occurring and the amount of harm that it will cause, then there is a breach of the duty of care and liability for negligence. In this case, the burden of preventing the accident was low; it only involved the watchman staying in the vicinity of the barge or recruiting someone else to stand by and watch it. The probability of the barge getting untied and striking another barge is undoubtedly a variable that changes with conditions, as is the amount of injury that will result. The existing conditions, the crowded harbor with barges constantly being moved about, made the probability of injury more than a negligible factor and made the magnitude of resulting injury an enormous figure. Thus, since the burden of preventing the collision was low and the product of the probability and the amount of injury projected is high, the fact that it occurred was a breach of duty. Affirmed.

ANALYSIS

This effort to formulate negligence, this "calculus of the risk," is an acceptable method of determining negligence. Behind this formula, however, is always the recognition that the measure of the reasonableness of the risk revolves around the specific circumstances of the situation. Conduct is relative to the particular occasion and need.

Quicknotes

DUTY OF CARE A principle of negligence requiring an individual to act in such a manner as to avoid injury to a person to whom he or she owes an obligatory duty.

NEGLIGENCE Conduct falling below the standard of care that a reasonable person would demonstrate under similar conditions.

Vaughan v. Menlove

Owner of burned cottages (P) v. Hay rick owner (D)

Common Pleas, 3 Bing. (N.C.) 468, 132 Eng. Rep. 490 (1837).

NATURE OF CASE: Action to recover damages for negligence.

FACT SUMMARY: Defendant erected a haystack near his neighbor's (P) property despite warnings that the haystack was a fire hazard. The defendant followed his own best judgment and allowed the haystack to remain. It burned, destroying the neighbor's (P) cottages.

🏛 RULE OF LAW
The standard of care is founded on the judgment of the person of ordinary prudence, not the subjective judgment of the defendant, even though this judgment was based on an honest attempt to act reasonably.

FACTS: Defendant built a hay rick close to the boundary of his property. Persons in the community told him that this rick was susceptible to the dangers of fire. He ignored their warnings on the grounds that his stock was insured and because he made an aperture through the rick as a precaution against fire. Nonetheless, the rick burned, and the fire caused injury to the neighbor's surrounding cottages.

ISSUE: Is there a cause of action for negligence if a person acts in conformity with his own best judgment, although this judgment causes him to behave in a less reasonable manner than a person who possesses ordinary prudence?

HOLDING: (Patterson, J.) The jury was instructed to consider whether Menlove's (D) gross negligence caused the fire. This consideration was necessary because Menlove (D) was obligated to exercise the reasonable caution that a prudent man in Menlove's (D) circumstances would have exercised. After a verdict for Vaughn (P), Menlove (D) was granted a new trial on the ground that the ordinary-prudence standard was too vague; Menlove (D) argued that he should be held only to a standard of whether he exercised his own judgment in good faith. If he complied with that subjective standard, he argued, he should not be held liable.

▶ ANALYSIS

This court follows the traditional concept that conduct in actions for negligence should be judged in terms of the mythical standard of the reasonable person instead of judging in terms of the defendant. The reasoning behind this seems apparent; if the behavior of tort litigants was judged on a personal standard, torts would be a subjective field. It would be necessary to probe and map every defendant rather than hold him to a minimum standard of care.

Quicknotes

BONA FIDE In good faith.

CASE PRMAE IMPRESSIONIS A new case that has no directly applicable precedent and must be decided entirely by reason as distinguished from authority.

HAY RICK A stack of hay.

NEGLIGENCE Conduct falling below the standard of care that a reasonable person would demonstrate under similar conditions.

REASONABLE PERSON STANDARD The standard of care exercised by a hypothetical person who possesses the intelligence, education, knowledge, attention, and judgment required by society of its members when governing behavior; the standard applies to a person's judgment when determining breach of a duty under the theory of negligence.

RULE NISI Motion by one party to make a final ruling against the opponent, unless the opponent can show cause as to why such ruling should not be ordered.

■▬■

Delair v. McAdoo

Car accident victim (P) v. Other driver (D)

Pa. Sup. Ct., 324 Pa. 392, 188 A. 181 (1936).

NATURE OF CASE: Action in trespass to recover damages for injury to person and property.

FACT SUMMARY: McAdoo (D), driving a car with dangerously worn tires, suffered a blow-out and crashed into Delair's (P) car.

RULE OF LAW

In exercising his duty of due care for the safety of others, every automobile driver and owner is charged with such knowledge of the safe condition of his car as can be ascertained through a reasonable inspection.

FACTS: McAdoo (D), unaware of the dangerous condition of his tires, attempted to pass Delair (P), when McAdoo's (D) left rear tire blew out, causing his car to crash into Delair's (P) car. At trial, witnesses testified that McAdoo's (D) tire was worn through to the inside lining. McAdoo (D) denied this. Delair (P) claimed that McAdoo (D) was negligent in driving with defective tires.

ISSUE: Is actual knowledge of the danger necessary to support a finding of negligence?

HOLDING AND DECISION: (Kephart C.J.) No. Every adult in the community is held to general knowledge of certain facts, such as the law of gravity, and the effect of pulling a trigger on a gun. Included here is the knowledge that worn tires are dangerous and should not be used. In addition, the owner or operator of a motor vehicle is charged with knowledge of whether or not his car is safe to drive, if such knowledge can be gained through reasonable inspection. Here, the evidence indicated that McAdoo's (D) tire was clearly and visibly worn. The law will not permit him, in defense of negligence, to assert his ignorance of the conditions of the tire, or the danger it represents. Affirmed.

ANALYSIS

This case incorporates a phenomenon of modern society, the automobile, into that class of objects and activities about which everyone is deemed to possess a minimum amount of knowledge. Everyone, for instance, should be aware of the danger of driving at night without headlights. Moreover, if someone is engaged in a particular activity, or stands in particular relationship to another, or is merely a stranger in the community, he may be under an affirmative duty to learn further facts. For example, as in the above case, a driver must inspect his tires; a landlord must investigate his premises before letting and advise his tenant of dangerous conditions; and a traveling motorist must advise himself of local traffic violations.

Quicknotes

NEGLIGENCE Conduct falling below the standard of care that a reasonable person would demonstrate under similar conditions.

Trimarco v. Klein

Injured tenant (P) v. Apartment owner (D)

N.Y. Ct. of App., 56 N.Y.2d 98, 436 N.E.2d 502 (1982).

NATURE OF CASE: Appeal from reversal of award of damages for negligence.

FACT SUMMARY: Klein's (D) tenant Trimarco (P) attempted to show that use of shatterproof glass for tub enclosures had become common over the years and that the regular glass enclosure on which he was injured, therefore, no longer met accepted safety standards.

RULE OF LAW
Evidence of custom and usage by others engaged in the same business is admissible as bearing on what is reasonable conduct under all the circumstances, which is the quintessential test of negligence.

FACTS: Trimarco (P), a tenant in Klein's (D) building, was injured when he fell through the glass door enclosing his tub. The glass looked like tempered glass but was just ordinary thin glass. In his negligence action, Trimarco (P) offered expert evidence that it had become common practice to use shatterproof glass in such enclosures so that by the date of his accident the glass door in his bathroom no longer conformed to accepted safety standards. The appellate division reversed a decision awarding Trimarco (P) damages, holding that even if the aforementioned evidence established a custom of using shatterproof glass in such enclosures, Klein (D) was nonetheless under no common-law duty to replace the glass unless he had prior notice of the danger (either from Trimarco (P) or from a similar accident in the building).

ISSUE: Does evidence of custom and usage have a bearing on what constitutes reasonable conduct under the circumstances of a particular case?

HOLDING AND DECISION: (Fuchsberg, J.) Yes. The quintessential test of negligence is whether a party's conduct was reasonable under all the circumstances of a particular case. Because evidence of custom and usage by others engaged in the same business bears on what is reasonable conduct, it is admissible, although it is not necessarily a conclusive or even compelling test of negligence. Customs and usages run the gamut, like everything else. As Holmes put it, "what usually is done may be evidence of what ought to be done, but what ought to be done is fixed by a standard of reasonable prudence, whether it usually is complied with or not." The trial court followed these principles in admitting the evidence of custom and usage, and it should not have been reversed. However, a new trial must be had here because the trial judge erroneously admitted certain other evidence.

ANALYSIS

There is only one area in which the courts have been willing to let prevailing custom serve to define the standard of care that must be met to avoid a charge of negligence, and that area is malpractice. Even where the standard of care is not set by prevailing custom in a particular field of endeavor, custom may still be important in deciding whether the actor behaved as would a reasonable person.

Quicknotes

CUSTOM AND USAGE A customary practice that is so widespread that it has become mandatory and has the force of law.

NEGLIGENCE Conduct falling below the standard of care that a reasonable person would demonstrate under similar conditions.

PRIMA FACIE CASE An action where the plaintiff introduces sufficient evidence to submit the issue to the judge or jury for determination.

REASONABLE MAN STANDARD A hypothetical person whose judgment represents the standard to which society requires its members to act in their private affairs and in their dealings with others.

Cordas v. Peerless Transportation Co.

Victim of runaway cab (P) v. Cab owner (D)

City Ct. of N.Y., 27 N.Y.S.2d 198 (1941).

NATURE OF CASE: Action to recover damages for negligence.

FACT SUMMARY: While being threatened by a passenger with a gun who was being pursued by a crowd, a taxi driver, employee of Peerless Transportation Co. (D), jumped out of the cab. The cab proceeded to hit Cordas (P).

RULE OF LAW
A person is not necessarily negligent if, in an emergency, he acts to avoid injury to himself and in doing so injures bystanders.

FACTS: A man jumped into a taxi cab owned by Peerless Transportation Co. (D). He pointed a gun at the driver and commanded him to go. The driver was frightened and complied. The driver was further frightened when he heard the man's pursuers following and yelling "Stop Thief." The driver quickly threw the car out of gear, slammed on his brakes, pulled the emergency brake, and, although he thought the motor was still running, jumped out of the car. The car proceeded to injure Cordas (P).

ISSUE: Is the duty of care required in an emergency or when one's life is in danger less strenuous than that required in ordinary circumstances?

HOLDING AND DECISION: (Carlin, J.) Yes. A person in an emergency demanding prompt action is not required to exercise the mature judgment or due care required in normal circumstances as long as the emergency is not of the person's own making. Here, the driver is not liable. The law does not require heroism of the average reasonable person.

ANALYSIS

The basis of the emergency doctrine is that the actor has no time for deliberation and cannot be held to the same standard as one who had opportunity to reflect before acting. The limitations on the doctrine are that the emergency must arise suddenly and unexpectedly and not be caused by the actor's own negligence. However, it is not really a lesser standard of care which is required of an actor in an emergency. The actor's conduct is compared to the average reasonable person's conduct in similar circumstances with the emergency being part of the circumstances. The actor will not be held negligent if he did what the average reasonable person would or might do in similar circumstances.

Quicknotes

DUTY OF CARE A principle of negligence requiring an individual to act in such a manner as to avoid injury to a person to whom he or she owes an obligatory duty.

REASONABLE PERSON STANDARD The standard of care exercised by a hypothetical person who possesses the intelligence, education, knowledge, attention, and judgment required by society of its members when governing behavior; the standard applies to a person's judgment when determining breach of a duty under the theory of negligence.

Roberts v. State of Louisiana

Bumped man (P) v. Blind man's employer (D)

La. Ct. App., 396 So. 2d 566 (1981).

NATURE OF CASE: Appeal from dismissal of action for negligence.

FACT SUMMARY: Roberts (P) appealed from the dismissal of his action against the State of Louisiana (D), contending that Burson, a blind concession stand operator, was negligent in traversing the area of the concession stand without the use of a cane.

🏛 RULE OF LAW
The standard of care applicable to handicapped persons is that they must take those precautions that ordinary, reasonable persons would if they were similarly handicapped.

FACTS: Roberts (P) fell and allegedly injured his hip as a result of being bumped by Burson, a blind concession stand operator, as Burson was traversing the concession stand area, located in a state building. Roberts (P) sued the State of Louisiana (D) through the Louisiana Health and Human Resources Administration (D), contending that it was liable in respondeat superior and negligent in failing to supervise and oversee the safe operation of the concession stand. Although Burson was not named, Roberts (P), relying on expert testimony alone, argued that Burson was negligent in traversing the concession area without the use of his cane. The expert had not examined Burson. Burson testified that he often made short trips in familiar areas without the use of a cane, relying on his facial sense. There was additional testimony to the extent that the use of the facial sense was not unreasonable in those circumstances. The trial court dismissed Roberts's (P) action, and from this decision, he appealed.

ISSUE: Is the standard of care applicable to handicapped persons that they must take those precautions that ordinary, reasonable persons would if they were similarly handicapped?

HOLDING AND DECISION: (Laborde, J.) Yes. The standard of care applicable to handicapped persons is that they must take those precautions that ordinary, reasonable persons would if they were similarly handicapped. Burson introduced a great deal of evidence that the manner in which he was traversing the concession area was not unreasonable. Roberts (P) relied solely on the testimony of his expert, who had not examined Burson. Further, Roberts (P) did not demonstrate that Burson had engaged in any other acts which could be characterized as negligent. Roberts (P) has failed to meet his burden of showing that Burson was negligent, and as a result, the action against the State of Louisiana (D) must fail. Affirmed.

▶ ANALYSIS

In essence, the standard applied to handicapped persons is not any different than the basic reasonable person standard, only the circumstance parameters within which the reasonable person acts have changed. This so-called handicapped standard applies both to physically handicapped individuals, and individuals handicapped by their particular circumstances.

■━■

Quicknotes

NEGLIGENCE Conduct falling below the standard of care that a reasonable person would demonstrate under similar conditions.

RESPONDEAT SUPERIOR Rule that the principal is responsible for tortious acts committed by its agents in the scope of their agency or authority.

STANDARD OF CARE A uniform degree of behavior against which a person's conduct can be measured when determining liability in negligence cases.

■━■

Robinson v. Lindsay

Accident victim (P) v. Snowmobiler (D)

Wash. Sup. Ct., 92 Wash. 2d 410, 598 P.2d 392 (1979).

NATURE OF CASE: Appeal from order of new trial in negligence action.

FACT SUMMARY: Robinson (P) was injured in a snowmobile accident caused by Anderson (D), a minor.

🏛 RULE OF LAW
A child will he held to an adult standard of care when he engages in an inherently dangerous activity, such as the operation of a powerful motor vehicle.

FACTS: An action seeking damages for personal injuries was brought on behalf of Kelly Robinson (P), who lost full use of her thumb as a result of a snowmobile accident. Robinson (P) was 11 years old at the time of the accident. The driver of the snowmobile, Anderson (D), was 13 years old. At trial, the jury was instructed to consider Anderson (D) to be bound by a duty to exercise the same care that a reasonably careful child of the same age would exercise under similar circumstances. Robinson (P) objected to the instruction contending that a child engaged in a dangerous activity such as driving a snowmobile must be held to an adult standard of care. The judge agreed and, after the jury found for Anderson (D), ordered a new trial. Anderson (D) appealed.

ISSUE: May a child be held to a lesser standard of care, even though he is engaged in an inherently dangerous activity?

HOLDING AND DECISION: (Utter, C.J.) No. It is true that, in general, a child is not held to adult standards of care in negligence actions. Instead, he is held only to the exercise of such degree of care and discretion as is reasonably to be expected from children of his age. However, an injustice would clearly result if a child who causes injuries while engaged in an inherently dangerous activity were permitted to defend himself by saying that he acted no more injudiciously than any other child his age would have acted. Accordingly, a general exception to the "children's standard of care" has been carved out. Thus, where a child engages in an inherently dangerous activity, he will be held to an adult standard of care. In the instant case, it is clear that Anderson (D) was engaged in an inherently dangerous activity. Snowmobiles may operate at very high speeds and they are the cause of hundreds of accidents each year. In operating such a machine, Anderson (D) must be held to the standard of care normally exercised by a reasonable adult. Accordingly, the new trial was properly ordered. Affirmed.

▶ ANALYSIS

Occasionally, a court has attempted to adopt a specific age limit as a guideline for children's negligence. For example, Pennsylvania borrowed from the criminal law rules relating to intent, and held that a child under the age of seven is incapable of negligence as a matter of law. A child between the ages of seven and 14 is presumed incapable of negligence, but evidence may be introduced proving otherwise (for children between the ages of 14 and 18, the rebuttable presumption is reversed). See *Kuhns v. Brugger*, 390 Pa. 331 (1957).

◼◼◼

Quicknotes

INHERENTLY DANGEROUS ACTIVITY An activity that is dangerous at all times so that precautions must be taken to avoid injury.

NEGLIGENCE Conduct falling below the standard of care that a reasonable person would demonstrate under similar conditions.

STANDARD OF CARE A uniform degree of behavior against which a person's conduct can be measured when determining liability in negligence cases.

◼◼◼

Breunig v. American Family Ins. Co.

Injured trucker (P) v. Insurer (D)

Wis. Sup. Ct., 45 Wis. 2d 536, 173 N.W.2d 619 (1970).

NATURE OF CASE: Action for damages for personal injury from negligence.

FACT SUMMARY: While overcome by a sudden state of insanity, Erma Veith, insured of American Family Ins. Co. (D), drove her automobile into Breunig's (P) truck.

🏛 RULE OF LAW
A person seized with a sudden mental disability for which he had no warning will be excused from the general rule of holding an insane person liable for his negligence.

FACTS: A psychiatrist testified that Ms. Veith, insured of American Family Ins. Co. (D), told him that while she was driving she believed God was directing her car. She saw a truck coming and stepped on the accelerator in order to become airborne, because she knew she could fly. Instead of flying, she collided with Breunig's (P) truck. At the time of the collision, Ms. Veith's automobile was on the left side of the road.

ISSUE: Is a sudden, unforeseen state of insanity a defense to liability for negligence?

HOLDING AND DECISION: (Hallows, C.J.) Yes. Sudden mental incapacity which strikes without warning is an exception to the general rule that an insane person will be held liable for negligence. Cases supporting the general rule generally involve preexisting or permanent insanity. The general rule is supported by the following policies: (1) where one of the two innocent persons must suffer a loss it should be borne by the one who occasioned it; (2) to induce those interested in the insane person's estate to restrain and control him/her; and (3) to deter persons from filing false claims of insanity to avoid liability. Sudden mental disability is equivalent to sudden physical disability such as heart attack, stroke, fainting, and epileptic seizure and should be treated alike and not under the general rule. Here, unless it is shown that Ms. Veith, insured of American Family Ins. Co. (D), had warning or knowledge that the mental disability would occur, she will not be held liable for acts she committed while suddenly mentally disabled. Affirmed.

▶ ANALYSIS

In nearly all cases, an insane person is held liable for negligence without reference to his insanity. However, this rule has been criticized, as in this case. A transitory sudden mental disability is commonly regarded as a circumstance depriving the actor of control over his conduct and relieving him of liability.

Quicknotes

INSANITY An affirmative defense to a criminal prosecution that the defendant suffered from a mental illness, thereby relieving him of liability for his conduct.

Heath v. Swift Wings, Inc.

Estate administrator (P) v. Pilot (D)

N.C. Ct. App., 40 N.C. App. 158, 252 S.E.2d 526 (1979).

NATURE OF CASE: Appeal from denial of damages for negligence.

FACT SUMMARY: Heath (P) claimed that the jury was erroneously instructed regarding the issue of standard of care of a pilot (D) whose plane crashed.

> ## 🏛 RULE OF LAW
> Even as to professionals, the standard of care is an objective one and may not be tailored to the individual characteristics of each defendant.

FACTS: Heath (P) a relative of two persons killed in a small plane crash, sued the pilot (D) and others, alleging that the crash occurred as a result of negligence. On that issue, the jury was instructed that negligence in a case of this sort is the "failure to exercise that degree of ordinary care and caution, which an ordinary prudent pilot having the same training and experience as [the pilot of the plane at issue], would have used in the same or similar circumstances." The jury returned a verdict finding the pilot (D) not negligent. Heath (P) appealed, alleging, in part, that the jury instructions were improper.

ISSUE: May the standard of care applying in a negligence action be expressed in subjective terms?

HOLDING AND DECISION: (Morris, C.J.) No. It is true that a professional will be held to the requisite degree of learning, skill, and ability called for in his particular occupation. However, the standard imposed, although higher than that imposed upon a lay person, is still an objective one, i.e., all professionals engaged in a particular occupation or specialty are held to the standard of care commonly exercised by the reasonable practitioner in the field. To instruct a jury otherwise, as did the trial court here, is to impose a different standard of care upon each defendant, according to the particular level of training and experience attained. Such a practice would be untenable. Accordingly, a new trial must be had. Reversed.

▶ ANALYSIS

A variation on the rule expressed in the Heath case occurs when a person engaging in a service represents that he possesses superior skill or training. In such a situation, the person is held to a higher standard, although it is still expressed in objective form. The same is true of specialists, who are held to exercise the reasonable care of the ordinary practitioner engaging in that particular specialty.

Quicknotes

PROFESSIONAL STANDARD OF CARE That degree of care as reasonable persons in the particular profession would exercise.

REASONABLY PRUDENT PERSON A hypothetical person whose judgment represents the standard to which society requires its members to act in their private affairs and in their dealings with others.

STANDARD OF CARE A uniform degree of behavior against which a person's conduct can be measured when determining liability in negligence cases.

Hodges v. Carter

Disappointed client (P) v. Attorneys (D)

N.C. Sup. Ct., 239 N.C. 517, 80 S.E.2d 144 (1954).

NATURE OF CASE: Appeal from dismissal of action for damages for negligence.

FACT SUMMARY: Hodges (P) engaged Topping (D) and Carter (D), attorneys, to bring suit against his insurers who did not pay a claim, but when the manner of service was invalidated by the state supreme court, Hodges (P) claimed his attorneys (D) were negligent.

RULE OF LAW

An attorney acting in good faith and with an honest belief that his actions are in the best interest of his client is not liable for mistaken advice in an area of unsettled law.

FACTS: Hodges' (P) drugstore and all property within was destroyed by fire. He filed claims with his four insurers who refused to pay on the claims. Hodges (P) engaged Topping (D) and Carter (D), attorneys, to bring suit against the insurers. Service was made in the usual manner by mail to the commissioner of insurance of the State of North Carolina who forwarded copies by registered mail to each foreign insurance company. Each of the four foreign insurance companies appeared specially to challenge jurisdiction. The North Carolina Supreme Court held the manner of service, the standard method for over 20 years, to be invalid. Hodges (P) sought damages from Topping (D) and Carter (D) for alleged negligence in the method of service used and for failure to sue out alias summons within 60 days (as the statute of limitations had by then run barring action against the insurers). A nonsuit was entered, and Hodges (P) appealed.

ISSUE: Is an attorney who acts in good faith and with an honest belief that his actions are in the best interest of his client liable for mistaken advice in an area of unsettled law?

HOLDING AND DECISION: (Barnhill, C.J.) No. An attorney acting in good faith and with an honest belief that his actions are in the best interest of his client is not liable for mistaken advice in an area of unsettled law. A lawyer will be held liable when a loss to a client is the proximate result of a want of a degree of knowledge and skill ordinarily possessed by others in the profession similarly situated, from an omission to use reasonable care and diligence; or from failure to exercise good faith in making a best judgment. Here, the manner of service used was a standard method for over two decades and had never been previously challenged. Topping (D) and Carter (D) had no reason to think otherwise. Affirmed.

► ANALYSIS

As for use of best judgment, lawyers have not been held liable for errors in interpretation of the Rule Against Perpetuities. Similarly, doctors are given wide discretion in making a diagnosis. The best example of a lawyer's failure to use due care is the failure to file a suit before the statute of limitations runs; no exercise of judgment is involved.

Quicknotes

DICTUM Statement by a judge in a legal opinion that is not necessary for the resolution of the action.

DUE DILIGENCE The standard of care as would be taken by a reasonable person in accordance with the attendant facts and circumstances.

GOOD FAITH An honest intention to abstain from any unconscientious advantage of another.

INVOLUNTARY NONSUIT The termination of a case without prejudice due to the plaintiff's failure to make out a case.

SCINTILLA Doctrine whereby if there is the least bit of evidence regarding a material question of fact then that issue should be left for determination by the jury.

STATUTE OF LIMITATIONS A law prescribing the period in which a legal action may be commenced.

Boyce v. Brown

Patient (P) v. Physician (D)

Ariz. Sup. Ct., 51 Ariz. 416, 77 P.2d 455 (1938).

NATURE OF CASE: Appeal from a directed verdict denying damages for medical malpractice.

FACT SUMMARY: Boyce's (P) fractured ankle was set by surgery with the use of a metal screw by Dr. Brown (D), but several years later the ankle began to swell and the pin had to be removed.

🏛 RULE OF LAW
Negligence on the part of a physician or surgeon, by reason of his departure from the proper standard of practice, must be established by expert medical testimony, unless the negligence is so grossly apparent that a layman would have no difficulty in recognizing it.

FACTS: In 1927, Boyce (P) saw Dr. Brown (D) to reduce a fracture in her ankle. An operation was performed by which the bone fragments were positioned and secured by use of a metal screw placed in the bone. Dr. Brown (D) continued to see Boyce (P) until recovery was apparent. No serious contention was made that Dr. Brown (D) did not follow approved medical standards of the day. In 1934, Boyce (P) returned to Dr. Brown (D) complaining of swelling in the ankle. He taped the ankle and filed the edge of her arch support which was worn sharp. After removing the tape, the pain and swelling worsened. In 1936, Boyce (P) saw Dr. Kent who found discoloration and swelling. An x-ray showed necrosis of the bone around the screw, which Dr. Kent removed. Recovery was complete. Boyce (P) alleged that Dr. Brown (D) was negligent in failing to take an x-ray. At trial, Dr. Kent testified as to what was proper to do in 1936 and was unable to express an opinion as to her condition in 1934. A directed verdict was given Dr. Brown (D), and Boyce (P) appealed on the basis of Dr. Brown's (D) failure to x-ray, which was argued to be negligence inferable by a layman.

ISSUE: Must negligence on the part of a physician or surgeon, by reason of his departure from the proper standard of practice, be established by expert medical testimony?

HOLDING AND DECISION: (Lockwood, J.) Yes. Negligence on the part of a physician or surgeon, by reason of his departure from the proper standard of practice, must be established by expert medical testimony, unless the negligence is so grossly apparent that a layman would have no difficulty recognizing it. Boyce's (P) treatment in 1934 consisted of taping the ankle, filing down the worn arch support, and untaping the ankle. She did not return to Dr. Brown (D) in 1934. She waited two years before seeing Dr. Kent. No evidence showed whether the screw should have been removed prior to 1936 or whether earlier removal would have been justifiable. Dr. Kent also said that he might have suspected arthritis had Boyce (P) come to him in 1934 and would have taken an x-ray, but no testimony showed the standard of medical care for 1934. The failure to take an x-ray is not negligence which is so obvious that it can be recognized by a layman. X-rays are not always an appropriate means of diagnosis. Affirmed.

▶ ANALYSIS

The court mentioned five other rather lengthy rules applicable to malpractice to which the student should refer. Professional standard of care rules refer to the locality in which the professional practices, particularly in regard to the profession of medicine.

Quicknotes

DIRECTED VERDICT A verdict ordered by the court in a jury trial.

EXPERT TESTIMONY Testimonial evidence about a complex area of subject matter relevant to trial, presented by a person competent to inform the trier of fact due to specialized knowledge or training.

NEGLIGENCE Conduct falling below the standard of care that a reasonable person would demonstrate under similar conditions.

PROFESSIONAL STANDARD OF CARE That degree of care as reasonable persons in the particular profession would exercise.

Morrison v. MacNamara

Patient (P) v. Nationally certified lab (D)

D.C. Ct. App., 407 A.2d 555 (1979).

NATURE OF CASE: Appeal from ruling disallowing expert testimony in medical malpractice action.

FACT SUMMARY: Morrison (P) appealed from a ruling refusing to allow the testimony of his expert witness as to the standard of care to be utilized in administering a urethral smear test, arguing that since the laboratory administering the test was nationally certified, it should be held to a national standard of care.

🏛 RULE OF LAW
The standard of care applicable to board certified physicians, hospitals, medical laboratories, and other health care providers is measured by the national standard of care.

FACTS: Morrison (P) reported to MacNamara (D), a nationally certified medical laboratory, for a urethral smear test for trichomonas. The test was administered while Morrison (P) was standing. Morrison (P) had an adverse reaction to the test and fainted, suffering serious injuries when he fell. Morrison (P) sued MacNamara (D), contending that there was negligence in administering the test to him while he was standing. He sought to introduce the testimony of an expert witness to testify that the standard of care nationally was to administer the test while the patient was either sitting or lying down. The court refused to allow the testimony, but allowed testimony presented by MacNamara (D) from local doctors that the test was always administered in the area with the patient standing. Morrison (P) appealed from the ruling, arguing that since MacNamara (D) was nationally certified, it should be held to a national standard of care.

ISSUE: Is the standard of care applicable to board certified physicians, hospitals, medical laboratories, and other health care providers measured by the national standard of care?

HOLDING AND DECISION: (Newman, C.J.) Yes. The standard of care applicable to board certified physicians, hospitals, medical laboratories, and other health care providers is measured by the national standards of care. The so-called locality rule was premised on notions of disparity and access to advances in medical science between urban and rural areas. The locality rule has no relevance to medical practice in this jurisdiction, and may serve to foster substandard medical care by judging conduct against other practitioners in the community. The doctrine is peculiar to the medical world, and the premises behind the rule are outmoded. Varying geographical standards of care are no longer valid in view of standards of uniform proficiency established by national board certification. Since clinical laboratories perform similar duties as to physicians and hospitals, they owe similar duties in their care and treatment of patients. MacNamara (D) admits that they are a nationally certified medical laboratory and hold themselves out to the public as such. The court should have allowed Morrison's (P) expert's testimony on the national standard of care, and should have allowed the jury to resolve the conflict of expert testimony. Reversed.

▶ ANALYSIS

As the factual basis for the so-called "locality rule" has been eroded, more and more jurisdictions are abandoning the doctrine, and the present case is indicative of this trend. An unfortunate by-product of the evolution of a national standard of care is the development of the professional expert witness in medical malpractice cases.

■■■

Quicknotes

EXPERT WITNESS A witness providing testimony at trial who is specially qualified regarding the particular subject matter involved.

NEGLIGENCE Conduct falling below the standard of care that a reasonable person would demonstrate under similar conditions.

STANDARD OF CARE A uniform degree of behavior against which a person's conduct can be measured when determining liability in negligence cases.

■■■

Scott v. Bradford

Patient (P) v. Surgeon (D)

Okla. Sup. Ct., 606 P.2d 554 (Okla. 1979).

NATURE OF CASE: Appeal from defendant's verdict in medical malpractice action.

FACT SUMMARY: Scott (P) sued in medical malpractice, alleging that she was not properly informed of the risks involved in a proposed operation.

RULE OF LAW
A doctor is under a legal obligation to disclose sufficient information to a patient to enable him to make an informed decision regarding a proposed medical treatment.

FACTS: Scott (P) developed complications following surgery performed by Bradford (D). She subsequently sued Bradford (D) in malpractice, contending that he failed to advise her as to the risks involved in her surgery or as to alternative methods of treatment. Furthermore, she asserted that had she been so advised, she would have refused the surgery and thus avoided the resultant complications. The case was submitted to the jury, which was advised in broad terms of the physician's duty to disclose. A verdict for Bradford (D) was returned, and Scott (P) appealed, claiming the jury instructions had been erroneously framed.

ISSUE: Must a doctor disclose sufficient information to a patient so as to enable him to make an informed decision regarding a proposed medical treatment?

HOLDING AND DECISION: (Doolin, J.) Yes. It is basic to our legal system that each person is considered to be his or her own master. Thus, a doctrine has evolved, known as the doctrine of informed consent, which prohibits a physician from substituting his judgment for that of the patient regarding treatment of the patient's medical problems. Instead, the doctor must adequately apprise the patient of all potential risks and consequences of a proposed procedure so that she may properly determine for herself whether she wishes to undergo the suggested treatment. Absent such appraisal, the doctor may be liable for any injuries caused by the unconsented-to treatment. In order to recover, a patient must prove: (1) the doctor failed to inform her adequately of a material risk before securing her consent to the proposed treatment; (2) had she been informed of the risks she would not have consented to the treatment; and (3) the non-disclosed risk of injury did in fact occur. In the instant case, factors (1) and (3) were shown by Scott (P). As to (2), she testified that she would not have undergone surgery had Bradford (D) advised her of the risks. The jury obviously disbelieved her since it rendered a verdict for Bradford (D). It appears that the jury was properly instructed as to the "informed consent" cause of action for medical malpractice. Affirmed.

CONCURRENCE: (Barnes, J.) The "reasonable patient" test regarding the second element of the informed consent test should be adopted.

ANALYSIS

The courts generally provide for three basic exceptions to the physician's duty to disclose. The first is where the risks are either already known by the patient or are so obvious that they ought to be known. The second is where full disclosure might be harmful to the patient, for example, where an emotionally upset patient would be unduly alarmed or shocked. Finally, an exception occurs where there is an emergency, and the patient is in no condition to determine for himself whether treatment is necessary.

Quicknotes

DOCTRINE OF INFORMED CONSENT Consent to a particular occurrence requiring full notification as to the consequence of that consent.

DUTY TO DISCLOSE The duty owed by a fiduciary to reveal those facts that have a material effect on the interests of the party that must be informed.

Moore v. The Regents of the University of California

Patient (P) v. Physician (D) and university regents (D)

Cal. Sup. Ct., 51 Cal. 3d 120, 793 P.2d 479 (1990).

NATURE OF CASE: Review of dismissal of action seeking damages for conversion, trespass, and personal injury.

FACT SUMMARY: Dr. Golde (D) developed and patented a genetic cell line using cells from patient Moore (P) without Moore's (P) consent.

🏛 RULE OF LAW
A physician has a duty to disclose to a patient intended research connected to the patient's treatment.

FACTS: Moore (P) was treated at UCLA Medical Center for a type of leukemia. Golde (D) was his treating physician. Tests revealed that Moore's (P) tissues had certain unique properties that made it valuable in genetic engineering research. Without informing Moore (P) of this area of inquiry, Golde (D) removed various tissues over a span of several years, including blood and his spleen. Golde (D), largely as a result of this research, obtained certain biomedical patents potentially worth large sums of money. Moore (P) later brought a suit claiming a proprietary interest in his tissues, as well as conversion, trespass, and breach of fiduciary duty. The trial court dismissed for failure to state a claim. The court of appeals affirmed, and the California Supreme Court granted review.

ISSUE: Does a physician have a duty to disclose to a patient intended research connected to the patient's treatment?

HOLDING AND DECISION: (Panelli, J.) Yes. A physician has a duty to disclose to a patient intended research connected to the patient's treatment. As an inherent ancillary to a patient's right to control his own body, a patient is entitled to make an informed choice in deciding whether to consent to treatment. When a physician has a pecuniary interest in the treatment, the patient has a right to be told this. This is because a pecuniary interest may influence a doctor's decisions regarding treatment, and the patient should be allowed to consider this possible conflict of interest in deciding whether to consent to treatment. A failure on the part of Golde (D) to disclose his research and financial interests in Moore's (P) cells constituted a breach of fiduciary duty, if proved. Reversed.

▶ ANALYSIS

This was a case closely watched by the medical community but not for the issue discussed here. Moore (P) had alleged conversion, claiming a proprietary interest in his tissues.

This held far-reaching implications for the medical research community if upheld. However, the Court rejected this claim, concluding that the common law doctrine of conversion did not apply to cells.

Quicknotes

DOCTRINE OF INFORMED CONSENT Consent to a particular occurrence requiring full notification as to the consequence of that consent.

BREACH OF FIDUCIARY DUTY The failure of a fiduciary to observe the standard of care exercised by professionals of similar education and experience.

INTER ALIA Among other things.

PROPRIETARY INTEREST An owner's interest and rights in property.

Pokora v. Wabash Ry. Co.

Injured driver (P) v. Railroad (D)

292 U.S. 98 (1934).

NATURE OF CASE: Action to recover damages for personal injury from negligence.

FACT SUMMARY: Pokora (P) drove a truck across a railroad crossing and was hit by a train.

🏛 RULE OF LAW
Unless reasonable minds could not differ on the point, the standard by which negligence is measured is for the jury to decide. Failure to get out of a vehicle and look before crossing a railroad track is not contributory negligence as a matter of law.

FACTS: Pokora (P) drove a truck up to a railroad crossing at which Wabash Ry. Co. (D) had four tracks. Because of boxcars on the first track, Pokora (P) could not see the tracks to the north. He stopped, looked, and listened, but heard nothing. He did not get out of his truck to walk forward and look down the tracks. As he drove slowly onto the main track, he was struck by a train coming from the north. The trial court took the case from the jury and granted a directed verdict for the Wabash Ry. (D) on the ground that Pokora's (P) conduct was contributory negligence as a matter of law. The case was affirmed by the Circuit Court of Appeals; the Supreme Court then granted certiorari.

ISSUE: Was Pokora's (P) failure to get out of the vehicle and walk forward to look down the track before driving forward contributory negligence as a matter of law?

HOLDING AND DECISION: (Cardozo, J.) No. It is for the jury to decide whether a plaintiff's conduct is contributory negligence unless the conduct is so obviously negligent that reasonable minds could not differ on the point. Whether one must stop, look, and listen or whether one must get out of the vehicle and reconnoiter depends on the situation. What is safe varies, and it is up to the jury to decide whether a particular conduct is safe for the particular situation. Reversed and remanded.

▌ *ANALYSIS*

This case reaffirms the proposition that, unless reasonable minds could not differ, it is up to the jury to decide whether a particular conduct is safe or negligent. Justice Cardozo, writing for the Supreme Court, warns about the danger of framing inflexible standards of behavior that amount to rules

of law applied by the judge. The Court then limits the stop, look, listen and/or get out rule enunciated by Justice Holmes in *B. & O. R. Co. v. Goodman* 275 U.S. 66 (1927).

Quicknotes

CONTRIBUTORY NEGLIGENCE Behavior on the part of an injured plaintiff falling below the standard of ordinary care that contributes to the defendant's negligence, resulting in the plaintiff's injury.

Osborne v. McMasters

Estate administrator (P) v. Clerk's employer (D)

Minn. Sup. Ct., 40 Minn. 103, 41 N.W. 543 (1889).

NATURE OF CASE: Action for damages for death of plaintiff's intestate.

FACT SUMMARY: McMasters' (D) clerk, in the course of his employment, sold poison without a label to Osborne's (P) intestate.

🏛 **RULE OF LAW**
When a statute imposes a legal duty, violation of the statute constitutes conclusive evidence of negligence, i.e., negligence per se.

FACTS: Osborne's (P) intestate bought a deadly poison from McMasters' (D) clerk, who was acting within the course of his employment at a drug store. The clerk sold the poison without labeling it "Poison," although a statute made it a crime to do so. The object of the statute was to protect the public. Osborne (P) claimed that a statute imposes a specific duty, and that one who neglects to perform the duty is liable to those for whose protection or benefit the duty was imposed. McMasters (D) claimed that, since no common-law duty to label poison existed, failure to label according to statute was not conclusive evidence of negligence in a civil action arising from a common-law right.

ISSUE: Does violation of a duty imposed by statute constitute negligence per se?

HOLDING AND DECISION: (Mitchell, J.) Yes. Where a statute or municipal ordinance imposes on any person a specific duty for the protection or benefit of others, if he neglects to perform that duty he is liable to those for whose protection or benefit it was imposed for any injuries which the statute was designed to prevent and which were proximately caused by such neglect. Negligence is the breach of a legal duty. It is immaterial whether the duty is imposed by the common law or by statute. The statute establishes a fixed standard by which the fact of negligence may be determined. Here, the master is civilly liable for the negligence of his servant committed in the course of his employment and resulting in injuries to third persons. Affirmed.

▶ *ANALYSIS*

This case establishes the proposition that violation of a criminal statute is conclusive evidence of negligence in a civil action where the statute was passed to protect a class of people (here, the public) of which the plaintiff is a mem-

ber. This is the majority view. Other courts, including California's, treat such violations as giving rise to a presumption of negligence, which becomes negligence as a matter of law unless rebutted. The presumption can only be rebutted by showing an excuse for the violation. A minority of about half a dozen states holds that the violation is only evidence of negligence, which the jury may accept or reject as it sees fit. A few states treat violations of statutes as negligence per se while violations of ordinances are only evidence of negligence. There is a similar conflict as to the effect of the regulations of administrative bodies, acting under statutory authority. Although such violations are sometimes treated as negligence per se there is more of a tendency here to treat them merely as evidence of negligence.

■=■

Quicknotes

NEGLIGENCE PER SE Conduct amounting to negligence as a matter of law because it is either so contrary to ordinary prudence or it is in violation of statute.

PLAINTIFF'S INTESTATE In this case, the term refers to the dead woman.

■=■

Stachniewicz v. Mar-Cam Corp.

Bar patron (P) v. Bar owner (D)

Or. Sup. Ct., 259 Or. 583, 488 P.2d 436 (1971).

NATURE OF CASE: Damages for negligence per se.

FACT SUMMARY: Stachniewicz (P), who was injured in a barroom brawl, sought damages on grounds that the bar's owner, Mar-Cam (D), violated a statute prohibiting the serving of liquor to obviously intoxicated persons.

🏛 **RULE OF LAW**
A violation of a statute or regulation constitutes negligence as a matter of law when violation results in injury to a member of the class of persons intended to be protected by the legislation and when the harm is of the kind which the statute or regulation was intended to prevent.

FACTS: A barroom fight erupted when American Indian patrons, sitting in a booth adjacent to the table where Stachniewicz (P) was seated with friends, were apparently offended by the refusal of one of the friends to permit his wife to dance with one of the Indians who was visibly intoxicated. Before the fight, the bartender, who had received complaints about insults from the Indians, warned Stachniewicz' (P) friends not to start any trouble with them. When police arrived, the Indians ran out a door with one of the friends in pursuit. The friend found Stachniewicz (P) lying just outside, his feet wedging the door open. He suffered retrograde amnesia and could not recall how he got there. At trial, Stachniewicz (P) contended that Mar-Cam (D) violated state regulations against serving liquor to visibly intoxicated persons and against boisterous or profane conduct or allowing visibly intoxicated persons on the premises. When the trial court did not find Mar-Cam's (D) action negligence per se, Stachniewicz (P) appealed.

ISSUE: Will a violation of a statute or regulation constitute negligence as a matter of law when violation results in injury to a member of the class of persons intended to be protected by the legislation and when the harm is of the kind which the statute or regulation was intended to prevent?

HOLDING AND DECISION: (Holman, J.) Yes. A violation of a statute or regulation constitutes negligence as a matter of law when violation results in injury to a member of the class of persons intended to be protected by the legislation and when the harm is of the kind which the statute or regulation was intended to prevent. Here, the regulation concerns matters having a direct relation to the start of fights which would create a likelihood of injury to customers. It can be assumed that the regulations were intended to insure the safety of bar patrons. It is an appropriate standard for awarding civil damages because Stachniewicz (P) was within the class of persons intended to be protected, bar patrons, and the harm suffered was the kind against which the statute was intended to protect. A jury could infer that his injuries were suffered as a result of the fight. Reversed and remanded.

▎ *ANALYSIS*

Many states have "Dram Shop Acts" which create tort actions against liquor sellers in specifically defined cases. Oftentimes, state legislative history is scanty, which gives a court wide latitude in determining the class to be protected and the harm against which the class is to be protected. The court in the case above simply assumed those factors in reaching its decision.

■=■

Quicknotes

DRAM SHOP ACT Law that imposes liability upon the seller of alcoholic beverages for injuries to a third party resulting from the intoxication of the buyer.

NEGLIGENCE PER SE Conduct amounting to negligence as a matter of law because it is either so contrary to ordinary prudence or it is in violation of statute.

■=■

Ney v. Yellow Cab Co.

Accident victim (P) v. Owner of stolen cab (D)

Ill. Sup. Ct., 2 Ill. 2d 74, 117 N.E.2d 74 (1954).

NATURE OF CASE: Appeal from award of damages for negligence.

FACT SUMMARY: Yellow Cab (D) was sued for injuries resulting from an accident involving one of its cabs, which was stolen when left unattended with the key in the ignition.

RULE OF LAW
The violation of a statute designed to protect the public safety constitutes prima facie evidence of negligence.

FACTS: A driver for Yellow Cab (D) left his taxi unattended with the key in the ignition. The cab was subsequently stolen and involved in an accident in which Ney (P) was injured. Ney (P) brought suit against Yellow Cab (D) for the negligence of its employee. He alleged that negligence was proven by the fact that the cabdriver's action in leaving his vehicle unattended with the key in the ignition was in violation of Article XIV, § 92 of the Illinois Uniform Traffic Act. The trial court found for Ney (P) upon jury verdict, and the court of appeals affirmed. Yellow Cab (D) appealed, arguing that the statute in question was intended as a traffic regulation only and, therefore, could not give rise to liability.

ISSUE: Does the violation of a statute designed to protect the public safety constitute prima facie evidence of negligence?

HOLDING AND DECISION: (Maxwell, J.) Yes. The key in this case is not whether the statute in question is labeled a traffic regulation or public safety measure, but rather what the intent of the legislature was in enacting the law. Judging from the statute in its entirety, it must be concluded that the legislature was interested in protecting the public safety. Furthermore, it is apparent that the legislature intended to guard against the dangers resulting from stolen vehicles, such as the ones existing in the instant case. Therefore, the violation of the statute by the Yellow Cab (D) driver constituted a prima facie act of negligence. However, Yellow Cab (D) will only be held liable if the negligent act was a proximate cause of the resulting injury to Ney (P). The question of proximate cause is made even more difficult by the fact that an intervening criminal act of a third party was involved. This question cannot be resolved as a matter of law, but instead was properly presented for determination to the jury. Their judgment that Yellow Cab (D) was liable will not be disturbed. Affirmed.

DISSENT: (Hershey, J.) The majority is clearly off-base in its determination that the statute at issue was intended to prevent injuries such as the one occurring here. Common experience proves that leaving the key in the ignition is only a minor cause of car theft. As such, the cabdriver's act cannot be considered a proximate cause of Ney's (P) injury.

ANALYSIS

The authors note that although both the majority and dissenting opinion rest heavily on proximate cause as an issue, the issue is virtually resolved by interpreting the purpose of the statute. Thus, the majority saw the statute as being intended to prevent car theft. Accordingly, its violation could clearly be deemed the proximate cause of a car theft. The dissent saw it otherwise. In either case, it is clear that statute interpretation is the key.

Quicknotes

A FORTIORI A method of reasoning whereby if one fact is true then a lesser fact, which is necessarily encompassed by the greater fact, must also be true.

NEGLIGENCE Conduct falling below the standard of care that a reasonable person would demonstrate under similar conditions.

PRIMA FACIE An action in which the plaintiff introduces sufficient evidence to submit an issue to the judge or jury for determination.

PROXIMATE CAUSE The natural sequence of events without which an injury would not have been sustained.

Perry v. S.N. and S.N.

Witnesses (D) v. Parents (P)

Tex. Sup. Ct., 973 S.W.2d 301 (1998).

NATURE OF CASE: Suit for damages resulting from injuries arising out of child abuse.

FACT SUMMARY: Parents (P) of a child who was abused at a day care center brought suit against alleged eyewitnesses to the abuse for failure to report the abuse pursuant to state statute.

🏛 RULE OF LAW
Violation of a mandatory child abuse reporting statute does not constitute negligence per se.

FACTS: B.N. and K.N. attended a day care center run by the Kellers (D). Their parents (P) brought suit against the Kellers (D) and three of their friends, Perry (D), White (D) and Quintero (D), alleging that during that period Daniel Keller (D) regularly abused their children physically and sexually. The parents (P) claimed that Perry (D), White (D) and Quintero (D) were negligent per se for violating a statute requiring any person that believes a child's physical or mental health or welfare has been or may adversely affected by abuse to file a report with the Department of Protective and Regulatory Services. They sought damages for pain, mental anguish, medical expenses and loss of income. Perry (D), White (D) and Quintero (D) moved for summary judgment for failure to state a cause of action. The trial court granted the motion and court of appeals affirmed as to the negligence claims, but reversed and remanded on the issues of negligence per se and gross negligence, holding that the violation of the statute was negligence per se.

ISSUE: Does the violation of a mandatory child abuse reporting statute constitute negligence per se?

HOLDING AND DECISION: (Phillips, C.J.) No. Violation of a mandatory child abuse reporting statute does not constitute negligence per se. The issue in negligence per se cases is whether the plaintiff belongs to the class the statute was intended to protect and whether the plaintiff's injury is of a type that the statute was designed to prevent. Here the legislature's intent was to protect children adversely affected by abuse or neglect. Here the children were clearly within the class of persons the statute was intended to protect and they suffered the type of injury the statute was designed to prevent. Next the court must determine whether the imposition of tort liability for violation of the statute is proper. Several factors may be considered in making this determination. First is whether there exists a relevant common law duty. Here, a negligence per se cause of action would derive the element of duty only from the Family Code. The court of appeals also mentioned several factors to be considered to deciding whether to apply negligence per se. These include whether the legislature has determined that compliance with criminal statutes is practicable and desirable and that the statutes give citizens notice of what conduct is required of them. With respect to notice, the court must consider whether the statute clearly defines the prohibited or required conduct. Here the statute imposes a duty to report when a person "has cause to believe" sexual abuse is occurring. This requirement does not clearly define what conduct is required in many situations. Next the court must consider whether applying negligence per se would create liability without fault. Here it would not because the statute only imposes liability for "knowing" failure to report. Third is whether negligence would impose liability disproportionate to the seriousness of the defendant's conduct. Here the penalty imposed for failure to report is far less than for abusers, weighing against the imposition of civil liability for nonreporters for damages resulting from the abuser's conduct. Last is whether the injury resulted directly or indirectly from violation of the statute. A majority of jurisdictions have held that failure to report child abuse is not negligence per se. Reversed.

▶ ANALYSIS

The decision in this case rests on the issue of whether the defendants had a duty under tort law requiring the imposition of liability for failure to exercise that duty. A court will not impose civil liability for violation of a criminal statute without the existence of a corresponding common law duty.

Quicknotes

CHILD ABUSE Conduct that is harmful to a child's physical or mental health.

NEGLIGENCE PER SE Conduct amounting to negligence as a matter of law because it is either so contrary to ordinary prudence or it is in violation of statute.

Martin v. Herzog

Unlit buggy rider (P) v. Car driver (D)

N.Y. Ct. App., 228 N.Y. 164, 126 N.E. 814 (1920).

NATURE OF CASE: Action for damages for death of plaintiff's intestate.

FACT SUMMARY: Martin's (P) decedent was killed in a collision between the buggy he was driving and Herzog's (D) automobile. Martin (P) was driving the buggy without lights, in violation of a criminal statute requiring lights.

RULE OF LAW
The unexcused omission to perform a statutory duty is negligence per se.

FACTS: Martin (P) was driving his buggy without lights when he was killed in a collision between the buggy and Herzog's (D) car. It was after dark and there was a criminal statute requiring lights. The trial judge refused Herzog's (D) request for an instruction that the absence of lights on Martin's (P) vehicle was prima facie evidence of contributory negligence, and instructed instead that the jury might consider the absence of lights as some evidence of negligence, but that it was not conclusive evidence. He granted Martin's (P) request for an instruction that the fact that Martin's intestate was driving without a light is not negligence in itself. The jury returned a verdict for Martin (P); the Appellate Division reversed; Martin (P) appealed to the court of appeals.

ISSUE: Is the unexcused omission of a statutory duty contributory negligence per se?

HOLDING AND DECISION: (Cardozo, J.) Yes. The unexcused omission of the statutory signals is more than just evidence of negligence; it is negligence in itself. Jurors have no power to relax the duty that one traveler on the highway owes under a statute to another traveler. It is error to instruct them that they have. The omission of lights, since it was unexcused, was negligence. However, a causal connection between the negligence and the injury must also be shown. Evidence of a collision occurring after dark between a car and an unlighted buggy is evidence from which a causal connection may be inferred between the collision and the lack of signals. If nothing is shown to break the connection, there is prima facie evidence of negligence contributing to the result. Affirmed.

▶ *ANALYSIS*

This case states the position, followed by a great majority of the courts, that violation of a statute is negligence per se when a statute applies to the facts and the violation is unexcused. Note, however, that the court emphasizes that one must not confuse the question of negligence with that of the causal connection between the negligence and the injury, and that conduct that is negligent is not always contributory negligence.

■≡■

Quicknotes

CONTRIBUTORY NEGLIGENCE Behavior on the part of an injured plaintiff falling below the standard of ordinary care that contributes to the defendant's negligence, resulting in the plaintiff's injury.

PRIMA FACIE An action in which the plaintiff introduces sufficient evidence to submit an issue to the judge or jury for determination.

STATUTORY DUTY An obligation owed by one individual to another pursuant to a particular statute.

■≡■

Zeni v. Anderson

Injured pedestrian (P) v. Car driver (D)

Mich. Sup. Ct., 397 Mich. 117, 243 N.W.2d 270 (1976).

NATURE OF CASE: Appeal from reversal of award of damages for negligence.

FACT SUMMARY: Zeni (P) was struck by a car and injured while walking on a well-worn snowpath with her back to oncoming traffic.

🏛 RULE OF LAW
Violation of a statute creates a presumption of negligence, which may be rebutted by a showing of inadequate excuse for the violation.

FACTS: On a snowy morning, Zeni (P) was walking to work. Instead of using the snow-covered sidewalk, she traveled along a well-used pedestrian snowpath, with her back to the oncoming traffic. A car driven by Anderson (D) struck Zeni (P), causing her severe injuries. There was evidence that Anderson (D) may have been traveling too close to the curb. At trial, the jury returned a verdict for Zeni (P), despite Anderson's (D) contentions that Zeni's (P) actions in walking in the street, rather than the sidewalk, constituted a violation of a state statute and as such was negligence per se, thus absolving Anderson (D) of liability. The court of appeals reversed. Zeni (P) appealed.

ISSUE: May the presumption of negligence arising from a statute violation be rebutted by evidence showing an adequate excuse for the violation?

HOLDING AND DECISION: (Williams, J.) Yes. It would be unreasonable to adhere to a rigid, automatic rule of negligence per se in all cases involving statutory violations. This is because in some circumstances, the violator may have reasonable justification for not acting in accordance with the statute. As such, she must be able to offer proof of such justification in order to allow the jury to determine whether she is a deserving plaintiff or an "innocent" defendant, despite the technical statute violation. Accordingly, the fairest approach is to hold that the violation of a statute creates a rebuttable presumption of negligence which may be overcome by a showing of an adequate justification for the violation. In the instant case, the issue of the violation, along with Zeni's (P) excuse, was properly presented to the jury. As such, the judgment for Zeni (P) should be reinstated. Reversed.

▶ *ANALYSIS*

Section 288A of the Restatement (Second) of Torts provides several valid excuses for the violation of a statute. These include: (1) where the actor's incapacity makes the violation reasonable; (2) where he is justifiably unaware of the need for compliance; (3) where he is unable due to the circumstances to comply with the statute; (4) where an emergency not caused by his own conduct makes it impossible to comply; and (5) where compliance would create a great risk to the actor or to others. The Restatement further notes that the list of excuses is meant to be illustrative and not exclusive.

■■■■

Quicknotes

IRREBUTTABLE PRESUMPTION A rule of law, inferred from the existence of a particular set of facts, that is not subject to dispute.

NEGLIGENCE PER SE Conduct amounting to negligence as a matter of law because it is either so contrary to ordinary prudence or it is in violation of statute.

■■■■

Goddard v. Boston & Maine R.R. Co.

Train passenger (P) v. Railroad company (D)

Mass. Sup. Jud. Ct., 60 N.E. 486 (1901).

NATURE OF CASE: Action for injuries sustained in a slip-and-fall.

FACT SUMMARY: A train passenger slipped on a banana skin and fell on a train-station platform shortly after he got off the train.

🏛 RULE OF LAW
A business owes no duty of reasonable care to ensure its patrons' safety unless the business has adequate notice that conditions on the premises are potentially dangerous.

FACTS: Goddard (P) got off a train at a station owned by the Boston & Maine Railroad Co. (D). Goddard (P) walked about the length of one train car on the platform. He then slipped and fell on a banana skin, sustaining injuries from his fall. The accident occurred shortly after Goddard's (P) train reached the station. Many passengers besides Goddard (P) were on the platform at the time. Goddard (P) sued the railroad company (D) for negligence. After the evidence at trial closed, the trial judge directed a verdict for the railroad company (D), and Goddard (P) appealed.

ISSUE: Does a business owe a duty of reasonable care to ensure its patrons' safety if the business does not have adequate notice that conditions on the premises are potentially dangerous?

HOLDING AND DECISION: (Holmes, C.J.) No. A business owes no duty of reasonable care to ensure its patrons' safety unless the business has adequate notice that conditions on the premises are potentially dangerous. Although a banana skin was on the platform, one of the other passengers who were present could have dropped it there within a minute of the accident. Affirmed.

▶ ANALYSIS

The lesson in the law of negligence in Chief Justice Holmes's succinct opinion in *Goddard* is clear: In Massachusetts at the turn of the twentieth century, courts did not impose a duty of reasonable care on a business for an alleged failure to correct a dangerous situation unless the business had a reasonable opportunity to discover the condition. The practice lesson in *Goddard* is just as clear and perhaps more durable: A trier of fact cannot base a verdict on mere speculation, which is all that the evidence on how long the banana skin

had been on the platform would permit a reasonable juror. As Chief Justice Holmes notes, the banana skin "may have been dropped within a minute" of Goddard's (P) fall, which is the same as saying that the skin also "may have been dropped" at a time sufficiently prior to the accident for the railroad company (D) to have owed Goddard (P) a particular duty of care. See, e.g., *Anderson v. Pre-Fab Transit Co.*, 409 N.E.2d 1157, 1160 (Ind. Ct. App. 1980) ("the 'might have' standard is not a correct statement of the burden of proof . . . [because it] invites the [trier of fact] to speculate"). Such inconclusive evidence cannot support a reasonable inference, and the trial judge therefore must direct a verdict for the defendant. When the burden of proof requires a preponderance of the evidence, a plaintiff must prove that an essential fact is more likely than not to have occurred as the law requires it to have occurred.

Quicknotes

BURDEN OF PROOF The duty of a party to introduce evidence to support a fact that is in dispute in an action.

DIRECTED VERDICT A verdict ordered by the court in a jury trial.

DUTY OF REASONABLE CARE Duty to exercise the degree of care as would a reasonably prudent person under like circumstances.

NEGLIGENCE Conduct falling below the standard of care that a reasonable person would demonstrate under similar conditions.

Anjou v. Boston Elevated Railway Co.

Slip-and-fall victim (P) v. Railroad (D)

Mass. Sup. Jud. Ct., 208 Mass. 273, 94 N.E. 386 (1911).

NATURE OF CASE: Action to recover damages for personal injuries due to negligence.

FACT SUMMARY: Anjou (P) was injured when she slipped on a dry, gritty, black banana peel lying on the platform at the Boston Elevated Railway Co.'s (D) station.

🏛 RULE OF LAW
Circumstantial evidence can sustain plaintiff's burden of proof of negligence only if a reasonable jury can draw from it the positive inference that defendant was negligent.

FACTS: Anjou (P) was a passenger who had just gotten off a train on the upper level of the Railway Company's (D) Dudley Street terminal. She waited until the arriving crowd had left the platform, then asked a uniformed employee of the Railway Co. (D) for directions to another car. She followed this employee along a narrow platform toward a stairway he indicated. She slipped on a banana peel, fell, and was injured. Witnesses described the peel as dry, gritty, black, trampled over; flattened down. The lower court directed a verdict for the Railway Co. (D).

ISSUE: May the issue of defendant's negligence go to the jury on circumstantial evidence where a reasonable jury can draw from it the positive inference that defendant was negligent?

HOLDING AND DECISION: (Rugg, J.) Yes. The issue of negligence must go to the jury as a question of fact once the court decides that a reasonable jury can draw from the evidence the positive inference that defendant was negligent. In this case, the Railway Co. (D) (through its employees) had a duty to use reasonable care to keep its station safe for passengers. This included a duty to observe and remove anything on the platform which might interfere with passengers' safety. From the appearance and condition of the banana peel, a reasonable jury might draw the inference that it had been lying on the platform for a long time. From this inference, the jury might conclude that to leave the banana peel lying there for so long was negligence on the part of the Railway Co. (D). The issue of negligence should have been submitted to the jury, and the lower court erred in directing a verdict for the Railway Co. (D). (In this case, rather than remand for a new trial, judgment is given for Anjou (P) "in accordance with the terms of the report.")

▶ ANALYSIS

The Goddard case is distinguished. The question of negligence was thought to hinge on how long the Railway Co. (D) had allowed the banana peel to lie on the platform. In Goddard, there was no evidence to show how long it had been there, whereas in this case there was evidence to indicate it had been there for a long time. Other instances in which the presence of litter has been held to be a breach of defendant's duty of due care toward users of the premises include a self-service cafeteria (garbage on the floor) and a department store (gum on the stairs). In those cases, it was not necessary to introduce evidence to show how long the specific piece of litter had been there, as it was for the offending banana peel here.

Quicknotes

CIRCUMSTANTIAL EVIDENCE Evidence that, though not directly observed, supports the inference of principal facts.

DUTY OF REASONABLE CARE Duty to exercise the degree of care as would a reasonably prudent person under like circumstances.

NEGLIGENCE Conduct falling below the standard of care that a reasonable person would demonstrate under similar conditions.

REMAND To send back for additional scrutiny or deliberation.

Joye v. Great Atlantic and Pacific Tea Co.

Slip-and-fall victim (P) v. Store owner (D)

405 F.2d 464 (4th Cir. 1968).

NATURE OF CASE: Appeal from an award of damages for negligence.

FACT SUMMARY: Joye (P) was injured when he slipped and fell on a banana at A&P's (D) supermarket.

🏛 RULE OF LAW
Without constructive notice of a dangerous condition, a defendant cannot be held liable for negligence.

FACTS: Joye (P) was injured when he slipped and fell on a banana in A&P's (D) supermarket. No direct evidence was offered as to how long the banana was on the floor before Joye (P) encountered it. The floor may not have been swept for as long as 35 minutes before the fall, and no one saw it until after Joye (P) fell. The banana was described as dark brown, having dirt and sand on it. The floor was dirty, and the banana was sticky about the edges. There was no evidence that A&P (D) put the banana on the floor or had actual notice of it. Joye (P) was awarded $10,000, and A&P (D) appealed arguing that it did not have constructive notice of the banana's being on the floor.

ISSUE: Can a defendant be held liable for negligence without constructive notice of the dangerous condition?

HOLDING AND DECISION: (Craven, J.) No. Without constructive notice of a dangerous condition, a defendant cannot be held liable for negligence. The case turns on the sufficiency of circumstantial evidence to establish constructive notice. From the evidence, a "jury could not tell whether the banana had been on A&P's (D) floor for 30 seconds or three days." Reversed.

▶ ANALYSIS

This case seems to be difficult to reconcile with *Anjou v. Boston Elevated Railway Co.*, 94 N.E. 386 (Mass. 1911). In both cases, brown, gritty bananas were involved. Liability may have ensued in Anjou on the basis of the higher duty to which common carriers are held. The court said that it was impossible to determine just how long the banana was on the floor, but the matter for determination would only seem to have been that the banana was on the floor for an unreasonably long time, which it would seem a jury could infer from the evidence.

Quicknotes

CIRCUMSTANTIAL EVIDENCE Evidence that, though not directly observed, supports the inference of principal facts.

CONSTRUCTIVE NOTICE Knowledge of a fact that is imputed to an individual who was under a duty to inquire and who could have learned of the fact through the exercise of reasonable prudence.

DANGEROUS CONDITION A condition of property that poses a reasonably foreseeable substantial risk of injury giving rise to liability for a public entity.

NEGLIGENCE Conduct falling below the standard of care that a reasonable person would demonstrate under similar conditions.

Ortega v. Kmart Corp.

Customer (P) v. Department store (D)

Cal. Sup. Ct., 36 P.3d 11 (2001).

NATURE OF CASE: Action for injuries sustained in a slip-and-fall.

FACT SUMMARY: A department-store customer sustained injuries when he slipped on a puddle of milk and fell. He could not prove how long the milk was on the floor before he slipped on it, but he did prove that the store probably had not checked the premises for at least 15-30 minutes before the accident.

🏛 RULE OF LAW
A store owner has a duty of reasonable care to inspect the store's premises within a reasonable period of time sufficient to permit discovery and correction of potentially dangerous conditions.

FACTS: While shopping in a Kmart (D) store, Ortega (P) slipped on a puddle of milk and fell, seriously injuring one of his knees. He sued Kmart (D) for his injuries, claiming that Kmart (D) was negligent for leaving the milk on the floor. Although Ortega (P) could not prove how long the milk was on the floor before he slipped on it, he could show that Kmart (D) had failed to inspect the premises within 15-30 minutes, and perhaps for as long as two hours, before the accident. Ortega (P) argued that such proof permitted jurors to infer that the milk had been on the floor long enough that Kmart's (D) employees should have discovered and removed the spill. Kmart (D), on the other hand, argued that Ortega (P) failed to show that the milk had been on the floor long enough to give the store constructive notice of the potentially dangerous condition. The jury awarded Ortega (P) $47,000. Kmart (D) appealed.

ISSUE: Does a store owner have a duty of reasonable care to inspect the store's premises within a reasonable period of time sufficient to permit discovery and correction of potentially dangerous conditions?

HOLDING AND DECISION: (Chin, J.) Yes. A store owner has a duty of reasonable care to inspect the store's premises within a reasonable period of time sufficient to permit discovery and correction of potentially dangerous conditions. Store owners owe their customers a duty to take reasonable measures to maintain reasonably safe premises. This duty is discharged by making reasonable inspections of those portions of the premises that are typically used by customers. If a plaintiff bases a negligence claim on a store's failure to correct a potentially dangerous condition, though, the evi-dence must show that the store had notice of the problem with enough time to remove the danger. Actual notice is not necessary. A store owner will be charged with constructive notice if the plaintiff shows that the potentially dangerous condition persisted long enough for a reasonably prudent store owner's employees to discover and correct the problem. The amount of time that suffices will vary from one case to another and is determined by the trier of fact. Plaintiffs can meet their burden on constructive notice by showing, as Ortega (P) did here, that the store's employees failed to inspect the premises within a reasonable period of time before an accident occurred. Affirmed.

▶ *ANALYSIS*

Although it's tempting to see *Goddard v. Boston & Maine R.R. Co.* as pro-business and *Ortega* as much less sympathetic toward business, it's also easy to reconcile the two decisions. In *Goddard*, the plaintiff showed only that the banana skin fell to the station platform only within some unspecified, wholly speculative timeframe. Here, the Court in *Ortega* merely establishes some relatively specific guidelines for what timeframe suffices to show that a store owner has exercised reasonably prudent care in maintaining safe premises for customers.

Quicknotes

DUTY OF REASONABLE CARE Duty to exercise the degree of care as would a reasonably prudent person under like circumstances.

Jasko v. F.W. Woolworth Co.

Slip-and-fall victim (P) v. Department store (D)

Colo. Sup. Ct., 177 Colo. 418, 494 P.2d 839 (1972).

NATURE OF CASE: Appeal from denial of damages for negligence.

FACT SUMMARY: Jasko (P) was injured when she slipped and fell on a piece of pizza that fell on the floor near the counter where pieces of pizza were sold in Woolworth's (D) store.

RULE OF LAW
When the operating methods of a proprietor are such that dangerous conditions are continuous or easily foreseeable, conventional notice requirements need not be met.

FACTS: Jasko (P) was injured when she fell on a piece of pizza that was on the terrazo (tile) floor near the "Pizza Hoagie Counter" in Woolworth's (D) store. Instead of showing actual or constructive notice to Woolworth (D) of the dangerous condition, Jasko (P) argued that Woolworth's method of selling pizza slices on waxed paper to customers who stand while eating created a reasonable probability that food would drop to the floor, and that steps taken to constantly clean the floor showed that Woolworth (D) recognized the danger. Judgment was for Woolworth (D), and Jasko (P) appealed.

ISSUE: When the operating methods of a proprietor are such that dangerous conditions are continuous or easily foreseeable, must conventional notice requirements be met?

HOLDING AND DECISION: (Groves, J.) No. When the operating methods of a proprietor are such that dangerous conditions are continuous or easily foreseeable, conventional notice requirements need not be met. Basic notice requirements arise from the view that dangerous conditions are not ordinary, and in such a situation a storekeeper is allowed a reasonable time to discover and correct the condition unless it is the direct result of his or her employee's acts. When the danger is continuous or easily foreseeable, the logical basis for the notice requirement does not exist. As actual or constructive notice was not required to be proved, the decision is reversed and remanded.

ANALYSIS

Note that in any case, a plaintiff has two burdens of proof to satisfy. In order to avoid a directed verdict against him, a plaintiff must satisfy the burden of coming forward with evidence to establish the element of his case, that it is more probable than not that he is correct. The second burden is to convince the jury by a preponderance of the evidence that he is correct. Above, by allowing a showing that the dangerous condition was continuous or reasonably foreseeable to be sufficient, the court presumed that the store had notice of the condition, which placed the burden on Woolworth (D) to show otherwise.

■=■

Quicknotes

DIRECTED VERDICT A verdict ordered by the court in a jury trial.

PREPONDERANCE OF THE EVIDENCE A standard of proof requiring the trier of fact to determine whether the fact sought to be established is more probable than not.

REASONABLE FORESEEABILITY A reasonable expectation that an act or omission would result in injury.

■=■

H.E. Butt Groc. Co. v. Resendez

Customer (P) v. Grocery store (D)

Tex. Sup. Ct., 988 S.W.2d 218 (1999).

NATURE OF CASE: Action for injuries sustained in a slip-and-fall.

FACT SUMMARY: A grocery-store customer slipped and fell near a grape display that permitted customer sampling. The customer sued the store for her injuries, claiming that merely displaying the produce for customer sampling created an unreasonable risk of harm.

🏛 RULE OF LAW
Merely displaying produce for customer sampling in a grocery store, without more, does not create an unreasonable risk of harm.

FACTS: The H.E. Butt Grocery Co. (HEB) (D) put up two grape displays in one of its stores. One of the displays had loose grapes in a bowl on a table for customer sampling; the bowl sat on ice about five inches below the top of the table. A three-inch rail surrounded the table's edge. The floor was a non-skid floor, floor mats had been placed around the tables, and warning cones also sat near the displays. Resendez (P) slipped near the displays and fell. At trial the jury returned a verdict for Resendez (P), and Texas's intermediate appellate court affirmed.

ISSUE: Does merely displaying produce for customer sampling in a grocery store, without more, create an unreasonable risk of harm?

HOLDING AND DECISION: (Per curiam) No. Merely displaying produce for customer sampling in a grocery store, without more, does not create an unreasonable risk of harm. Contrary to the Court of Appeals' reasoning, the law requires plaintiffs to show more than merely displaying produce for customer sampling to demonstrate an unreasonable risk of harm. Resendez's (P) burden required her to show (1) actual or constructive knowledge of the store's condition, (2) the existence of an unreasonable risk of harm in the condition, (3) HEB's (D) failure to exercise reasonable care to remove the risk, and (4) the failure to exercise care caused Resendez's (P) injuries. Unlike the plaintiff in *Corbin v. Safeway Stores*, 648 S.W.2d 292 (Tex. 1983), Resendez (P) failed to prove an unreasonable risk of harm. The plaintiff in *Corbin* proved more than the mere existence of a grape display; the determinative fact in *Corbin* was the slanted angle of the display in which the store offered its grapes without any floor mats around the display for further protection. Such additional evidence is not present in this case. Reversed.

▶ ANALYSIS

The store owners in *H.E. Butt* took several affirmative steps to ensure its customers' safety around a potentially dangerous produce display. Those facts further distinguish this case from the cited precedent, *Corbin*, where the defendant not only failed to take such steps but also admitted full prior awareness of the circumstances that caused the plaintiff's injuries in that case. *See* 648 S.W.2d at 296. Also worth noting is that *H.E. Butt* does not address the issue of actual or constructive notice at all. Is it possible that the store's affirmative exercises of caution had the effect of both admitting notice and turning that issue to the store's persuasive advantage by showing a diligent effort to discharge its duty of care?

■═■

Quicknotes

ACTUAL NOTICE The direct communication of information to a person.

CONSTRUCTIVE NOTICE Knowledge of a fact that is imputed to an individual who was under a duty to inquire and who could have learned of the fact through the exercise of reasonable prudence.

DUTY OF CARE A principle of negligence requiring an individual to act in such a manner as to avoid injury to a person to whom he or she owes a duty.

■═■

Byrne v. Boadle

Injured passerby (P) v. Shop owner (D)

Ct. of Exchequer, 2 H&C 722, 159 Eng. Rep. 299 (1863).

NATURE OF CASE: Action to recover damages for negligence.

FACT SUMMARY: While Byrne (P) was walking along the street, passing Boadle's (D) shop, a barrel fell from the shop window and struck Byrne (P), injuring him.

🏛 RULE OF LAW
When it is highly probable that an injury is due to the negligence of the defendant, and the defendant has better access to the evidence concerning the injury, the doctrine of res ipsa loquitur creates an inference that the defendant was negligent, and puts the burden on defendant to introduce contrary evidence.

FACTS: Byrne (P) was walking in a public street past Boadle's (D) flour shop, when a barrel of flour rolled out of the window above Byrne (P), striking and injuring him. The trial court nonsuited Byrne (P), ruling that there was no evidence of any negligence.

ISSUE: Can a presumption of negligence arise solely from the fact that an accident occurred?

HOLDING AND DECISION: (Pollock, C.B.) Yes. According to the ancient doctrine of res ipsa loquitur, "the thing speaks for itself." The mere fact that a barrel of flour fell on a passer-by outside of Boadle's (D) flour shop is prima facie evidence of the latter's negligence, and Byrne (P) cannot be expected to prove that it could not have happened without some negligence. If there are any facts inconsistent with a finding of negligence, it is for Boadle (D) to prove them.

▶ ANALYSIS

This is one of the earliest cases applying the doctrine of res ipsa loquitur. In a later English case, the rule was stated as follows: "There must be reasonable evidence of negligence; but where the thing is shown to be under the management of the defendant or his servants, and the accident is such as in the ordinary course of things does not happen if those who have the management use proper care, it affords reasonable evidence, in the absence of explanation by the defendants, that the accident arose from want of care." To invoke the doctrine, the plaintiff need not explain away all possibilities, as long as he shows that such accidents do not occur without negligence; the burden of proof is then shifted to the defendant.

Quicknotes

NEGLIGENCE Conduct falling below the standard of care that a reasonable person would demonstrate under similar conditions.

NONSUIT Judgment against a party who fails to make out a case.

RES IPSA LOQUITUR A rule of law giving rise to an inference of negligence where the instrument inflicting the injury is in the exclusive control of the defendant and where such harm could not ordinarily result in the absence of negligence.

RULE NISI Motion by one party to make a final ruling against the opponent, unless the opponent can show cause as to why such ruling should not be ordered.

McDougald v. Perry

Injured (P) v. Driver (D)

Fla. Sup. Ct., 716 So. 2d 783 (1998).

NATURE OF CASE: Personal injury action.

FACT SUMMARY: McDougald (P) sued Perry (D) for personal injuries sustained when a tire chained to the underside of Perry's (D) tractor-trailer struck McDougald's (P) windshield.

🏛 RULE OF LAW
The doctrine of res ipsa loquitur provides an injured plaintiff with an inference of negligence where direct proof is not available, if the plaintiff establishes that the instrumentality causing his injury was under the exclusive control of the defendant and the accident is one that would not, in the ordinary course of events, have occurred in the absence of negligence on the part of the one in control of the instrumentality.

FACTS: McDougald (P) sued Perry (D) for injuries sustained in an accident that occurred when McDougald (D) was driving behind a tractor-trailer driven by Perry (D). As Perry (D) drove over some railroad tracks, a 130-pound spare tire fell out of its cradle underneath the trailer and fell to the ground. The trailer's rear tires ran over the spare, which flew up into McDougald's windshield. Perry (D) testified that the tire had been held in place by the original chain that came with the trailer in 1969. He also stated that he conducted a pretrip inspection including an inspection of the chain; however, he stated that he did not check every link of the chain. After the accident the chain was dragging under the trailer. The judge instructed the jury on the doctrine of res ipsa loquitur and the jury returned a verdict for McDougald (P). The district court reversed on the basis that the trial court erred in instructing the jury on res ipsa loquitur. McDougald (P) appealed.

ISSUE: Does the doctrine of res ipsa loquitur provide an injured plaintiff with an inference of negligence where direct proof is not available?

HOLDING AND DECISION: (Wells, J.) Yes. The doctrine of res ipsa loquitur provides an injured plaintiff with an inference of negligence where direct proof is not available, if the plaintiff establishes the instrumentality causing his injury was under the exclusive control of the defendant and the accident is one that would not, in the ordinary course of events, have occurred in the absence of negligence on the part of the one in control of the instrumentality. Res ipsa loquitur means "the thing speaks for itself." The doctrine compels a finding of negligence under certain circumstances. The district court

concluded that McDougal (P) failed to show that this accident would not have occurred without negligence on the part of Perry (D). A plaintiff at trial must still present sufficient evidence, beyond the mere happening of the accident, allowing the jury to infer that the accident would not have occurred but for the defendant's breach of care. An injury alone does not indicate negligence unless it is accompanied by a sufficient showing of an immediate, precipitating cause. The doctrine only applies in rare instances. Here the accident is of the type that would not normally occur without the failure to exercise ordinary care by the person in control of the instrumentality. Reversed and remanded.

CONCURRENCE: (Anstead, J.) This is a classic situation in which an aged legal doctrine is still applicable today.

▶ ANALYSIS

The Restatement (Second) of Torts § 328D elaborates on the doctrine of res ipsa loquitur. The comments to that section set forth certain types of accidents that do not usually occur in the absence of someone's negligence. This conclusion is based on past experience and common sense.

━━▪

Quicknotes

DIRECT PROOF Proof derived from persons who actually observed the event or subject at issue.

ORDINARY CARE The degree of care exercised by a reasonable person when conducting everyday activities or under similar circumstances; synonymous with due care.

PERSONAL INJURY Harm to an individual's person or body.

RES IPSA LOQUITUR A rule of law giving rise to an inference of negligence where the instrument inflicting the injury is in the exclusive control of the defendant and where such harm could not ordinarily result in the absence of negligence.

━━▪

Larson v. St. Francis Hotel

Accident victim (P) v. Hotel (D)

Cal. App. Ct., 83 Cal. App. 2d 210, 188 P.2d 513 (1948).

NATURE OF CASE: Action to recover damages for personal injuries due to negligence.

FACT SUMMARY: Larson (P), walking on the sidewalk near the St. Francis Hotel (D), on V-J Day, was hit on the head by a falling overstuffed armchair.

🏛 RULE OF LAW
The doctrine of res ipsa loquitur applies only where the cause of the injury is shown to be under the exclusive control and management of the defendant.

FACTS: Amidst the celebrations of V-J Day, August 14, 1945, Larson (P) was walking on the sidewalk near the St. Francis Hotel (D) in San Francisco. Just after she stepped out from under the marquee, Larson (P) was hit on the head by a heavy, overstuffed armchair, knocked unconscious, and injured. No one saw where the chair came from. At the trial, Larson (P) relied on res ipsa loquitur and the judge granted a nonsuit against her. She appealed.

ISSUE: Does the doctrine of res ipsa loquitur apply to a case where an unexplained event might be due to the negligence of persons other than defendant?

HOLDING AND DECISION: (Bray, J.) No. The doctrine of res ipsa loquitur applies only where the cause of the injury is shown to be under the exclusive control and management of the defendant. It does not apply to a case where an unexplained event may have been attributable to one of several causes, for some of which the defendant is not responsible. In this case, the Hotel (D) did not have exclusive control of its furniture. The Hotel's (D) guests had partial control over the furniture. The injury to Larson (P) is as likely due to the fault of a guest or other person as to the Hotel (D). The most logical inference is that some such person threw the chair from a window. It thus appears that this occurrence is not such as ordinarily does not happen without the negligence of the party charged, but, rather, one in which the accident ordinarily might happen despite the fact that the defendants used reasonable care and were totally free from negligence. Affirmed.

▌*ANALYSIS*

Note the difference between this case and *Byrne v. Boadle* where a flour barrel fell on plaintiff. The nature of the hotel business is such that there are likely to be guests or visitors on the premises who may negligently throw furniture, whereas the nature of the flour warehousing business is such that no one except employees are likely to be on the premises who may negligently drop a flour barrel. The "exclusive control" rule is not always so literally or rigidly applied as this case might seem to indicate. Its purpose is basically to make sure that it is reasonable to pin the negligence on the defendant. Accordingly, where other causes for an event besides defendant's negligence (such as acts of third parties) are in the first instance equally probable, evidence which permits the jury to eliminate such causes will serve to make res ipsa loquitur applicable. It has been suggested that it would avoid confusion if this rule were not stated on terms of "control" at all, but rather were stated as a requirement that the apparent cause of the accident must be such that the defendant would be responsible for any negligence connected with it.

Quicknotes

EXCLUSIVE CONTROL RULE Necessary element of res ipsa loquitur doctrine that the defendant have total control of the instrument that inflicted the injury.

NEGLIGENCE Conduct falling below the standard of care that a reasonable person would demonstrate under similar conditions.

NONSUIT Judgment against a party who fails to make out a case.

RES IPSA LOQUITUR A rule of law giving rise to an inference of negligence where the instrument inflicting the injury is in the exclusive control of the defendant and where such harm could not ordinarily result in the absence of negligence.

Ybarra v. Spangard

Paralyzed patient (P) v. Physicians (D) and nurses (D)

Cal. Sup. Ct., 25 Cal. 2d 486, 154 P.2d 687 (1944).

NATURE OF CASE: Action to recover damages for personal injuries due to negligent malpractice.

FACT SUMMARY: Ybarra (P) suffered an injury to his right arm and shoulder while he was unconscious having his appendix removed under the care of six doctors and medical employees (D).

🏛 RULE OF LAW
Where an unexplained injury occurs during a medical procedure to a part of the body not under treatment, res ipsa loquitur applies against all of the doctors and medical employees who take part in caring for the patient.

FACTS: Ybarra (P) consulted Dr. Tilley (D), who diagnosed appendicitis. Dr. Tilley (D) arranged for an appendectomy to be performed by Dr. Spangard (D) at a hospital under the ownership and management of Dr. Swift (D). Ybarra (P) was wheeled into the operating room by nurse Gislor (D) and anesthetized by Dr. Reser (D). Dr. Reser (D) laid him back against two hard objects at the top of his shoulders. Ybarra (P) awoke the next morning in his hospital room attended by Thompson (D) and another nurse. When Ybarra (P) awakened he felt a sharp pain between his neck and his right shoulder. The pain spread down his arm, and after his release from the hospital he developed paralysis and atrophy of the muscles around the shoulder. Dr. Reser (D) and the nurses were employees of Dr. Swift (D); the other doctors (D) were independent contractors. The medical personnel (D) claimed that res ipsa loquitur should not apply against them because Ybarra (P) did not show an injury caused by an instrumentality under a defendant's control in that he did not show which of the several instrumentalities that he came in contact with in the hospital caused his injury, and did not show that any one particular defendant had exclusive control over any particular instrumentality. The court ruled for the defendants, and Ybarra (P) appealed.

ISSUE: Where an unexplained injury occurs during a medical procedure to a part of the body not under treatment, does res ipsa loquitur apply to permit negligence to be inferred against all of the doctors and medical employees who took part in caring for the injured patient?

HOLDING AND DECISION: (Gibson, C.J.) Yes. Where there has been an injury to a healthy part of the body not the subject of treatment, res ipsa loquitur applies to permit the inference of negligence against all doctors and medical employees who were entrusted with the patient's care. Every defendant in whose custody Ybarra (P) was placed for any period was under a duty to exercise ordinary care for his safety. The control at one time or another of one or more of the various agencies or instrumentalities which might have harmed Ybarra (P) was in the hands of every defendant or of his employees or temporary servants. Ybarra (P) was unconscious; it is unreasonable to require him to identify any one person as the one who did the negligent act in order to get his case before the jury. Reversed.

▶ ANALYSIS

This case is a prime example of the "smoking out the evidence" policy sometimes relied on by courts in invoking res ipsa loquitur. Obviously the medical personnel would keep silent to avoid implicating one of their number.

■■■

Quicknotes

ORDINARY CARE The degree of care exercised by a reasonable person when conducting everyday activities or under similar circumstances; synonymous with due care.

PROFESSIONAL STANDARD OF CARE That degree of care as reasonable persons in the particular profession would exercise.

RES IPSA LOQUITUR A rule of law giving rise to an inference of negligence where the instrument inflicting the injury is in the exclusive control of the defendant and where such harm could not ordinarily result in the absence of negligence.

■■■

Sullivan v. Crabtree

Parents of deceased passenger (P) v. Truck driver (D)

Tenn. Ct. App., 36 Tenn. App. 469, 258 S.W.2d 782 (1953).

NATURE OF CASE: Action for damages resulting from a car accident.

FACT SUMMARY: Sullivan was killed while a guest in a truck driven by Crabtree (D), who swerved into an embankment.

🏛 RULE OF LAW
The doctrine of res ipsa loquitur merely affords reasonable evidence, in the absence of an explanation, that injury was caused by negligence. Even if the facts are unexplained in a res ipsa loquitur situation, the jury may still refuse to make a finding of negligence.

FACTS: Sullivan was a guest in a motor truck driven by Crabtree (D). When Crabtree (D) was driving down a mountain, he suddenly swerved from his right side over to his left, ran off the left shoulder, overturned down a steep embankment, and crushed Sullivan to death. Sullivan's parents (P) sued Crabtree (D) and the owner (D) of the truck. The case went to trial against Crabtree (D) alone. Crabtree (D) testified that gravel on the road or the broken pavement might have caused him to lose control of the truck but he could not say definitely that the gravel or the pavement was the cause of the accident. The jury ruled for Crabtree (D), and the parents (P) appealed.

ISSUE: Does a finding of res ipsa loquitur prevent the jury from finding a defendant not negligent if the cause of the accident is unexplained?

HOLDING AND DECISION: (Felts, J.) No. The doctrine of res ipsa loquitur merely affords reasonable evidence, in the absence of an explanation, that the injury was caused by negligence. However, the jury still may choose the inference from the facts that it thinks is most probable. Here, the facts make up a case of res ipsa loquitur. This means that the facts of the accident show some evidence of negligence. Here, the jury refused to find that Crabtree (D) was negligent because it thought that it was more probable that Crabtree (D) was not negligent. The jury may find a defendant not to be negligent in a case of res ipsa loquitur, even if the defendant cannot explain what caused the accident, if it thinks that a finding of no negligence is more reasonable. Therefore, the court will uphold the jury's finding, in this case, that Crabtree (D) was not negligent, even though Crabtree (D) could not explain what caused the accident. Affirmed.

▶ ANALYSIS

The courts are in disagreement as to the precise effect that a finding of res ipsa loquitur has on the defendant's burden of proof. A finding of res ipsa loquitur in a case shifts the burden of proof to the defendant. Some courts have ruled that a finding of res ipsa loquitur warrants an inference that the defendant is negligent, which the jury may or may not agree with, as in this case. Other courts rule that it raises a presumption of negligence which requires the jury to find negligence if the defendant does not produce evidence sufficient to rebut the presumption. Other courts rule that it not only raises a presumption of negligence, but also shifts the ultimate burden of proof to the defendant and requires him to prove by a preponderance of all the evidence that the injury was not caused by his negligence. This case is in accord with the majority of the courts which hold that res ipsa loquitur still allows the jury to draw its own inference from the facts.

▬▬■

Quicknotes

INFERENCE A deduction from established facts.

NEGLIGENCE Conduct falling below the standard of care that a reasonable person would demonstrate under similar conditions.

PRESUMPTION A rule of law requiring the court to presume certain facts to be true based on the existence of other facts, thereby shifting the burden of proof to the party against whom the presumption is asserted to rebut.

RES IPSA LOQUITUR A rule of law giving rise to an inference of negligence where the instrument inflicting the injury is in the exclusive control of the defendant and where such harm could not ordinarily result in the absence of negligence.

▬▬■

CHAPTER 5

Causation in Fact

Quick Reference Rules of Law

Perkins v. Texas and New Orleans Ry. Co.

Deceased widow (P) v. Railroad (D)

La. Sup. Ct., 243 La. 829, 147 So. 2d 646 (1962).

NATURE OF CASE: Appeal of award of damages for wrongful death.

FACT SUMMARY: A locomotive traveling at an excessive speed was involved in an accident that would have occurred even if the train had not been speeding.

🏛 RULE OF LAW
Negligence will not give rise to liability if the injury would have happened even if the negligence had not occurred.

FACTS: Texas and New Orleans Railway (D) operated a line through Vinton, Louisiana. The legal train speed limit was 25 mph. At a blind intersection an accident occurred wherein the speed of the train was 37 mph and the speed of the automobile, which contained Perkins's (P) decedent, could not be determined. Evidence showed that even at 25 mph the train could not possibly have stopped before the crossing in the period after the auto became visible. A jury awarded Perkins (P) damages for wrongful death, and the court of appeals affirmed. The Railway (D) appealed.

ISSUE: Will negligence give rise to liability if the injury would have happened even if the negligence had not occurred?

HOLDING AND DECISION: (Sanders, J.) No. Negligence will not give rise to liability if the injury would have happened even if the negligence had not occurred. It is fundamental that negligence will lead to liability only if it is the sole or a substantial factor in bringing about the injury. Where the injury would have occurred even in the absence of negligence, the negligence cannot be said to be a substantial factor. Here, the engineer was negligent. However, even if he had been travelling 25 mph, a non-negligent speed, the train would have reached the crossing. Since no reliable evidence of the auto's speed exists, it is impossible to know whether the auto could have avoided the collision had the train been travelling slower. This being so, it has not been established that the engineer's negligence was a substantial factor in the injury. Reversed.

▶ ANALYSIS

The question of causation is often reduced to a "but for" test. The question is whether, but for the negligence, would no accident have occurred? If the answer is in the affirmative, then legal causation will exist.

Quicknotes

CAUSE IN FACT The event without which an injury would not have been incurred.

NEGLIGENCE Conduct falling below the standard of care that a reasonable person would demonstrate under similar conditions.

Reynolds v. Texas & Pac. Ry. Co.

Obese woman (P) v. Railroad (D)

La. Ct. App., 37 La. Ann. 694 (1885).

NATURE OF CASE: Action for damages caused by unlit stairs.

FACT SUMMARY: Mrs. Reynolds (P), who was heavy, fell down unlit stairs at a train depot owned by Texas & Pacific Ry. Co. (D).

🏛 RULE OF LAW
Although an injury might possibly have occurred even in the absence of another's negligence, if the negligence greatly multiplies the chances of accident to the injured person and is of a character naturally leading to the accident's occurrence—the mere possibility that the accident might have happened without the negligence is not sufficient to break the chain of cause and effect between the negligence and the injury.

FACTS: Mrs. Reynolds (P) weighed two hundred and fifty pounds. She emerged from the sitting room of a train depot, which was brightly lit, and went down unlit stairs. During her descent, she fell and was thrown beyond the narrow platform and the slope beyond, sustaining serious injuries. She was awarded $2,000 in damages, and Texas Ry. (D) appealed.

ISSUE: Is there sufficient proof that negligence caused a particular injury if the negligent party can show that there is a possibility that the injury would have occurred in the absence of the negligence?

HOLDING AND DECISION: (Fenner, J.) Yes. The fact that a defendant can show a possibility that an accident might have occurred without his negligence is insufficient proof that his negligence was not the "cause in fact" of the plaintiff's injuries, especially if his negligence greatly multiplied the plaintiff's chances of having an accident and is the type of negligence that usually causes the accident to occur. Here, there is a possibility that Mrs. Reynolds (P) might have fallen even if the stairs were well lit because she is heavy. But Texas Ry.'s (D) failure to light the stairs greatly increased the chances that she would fall. Unlit stairs often cause falls. Therefore, Texas Ry. (D) has not shown that its negligence did not cause her injuries. The court will look at what naturally happens, and not at remote speculations that there was a possibility that the accident was not connected with the negligence. Affirmed.

▶ ANALYSIS

This case illuminates the majority rule that a plaintiff is not required to prove his case beyond a reasonable doubt in order to recover. The plaintiff must prove that the defendant's negligence probably caused his injuries. The defendant cannot prove that his negligence was not a "cause in fact" merely by showing that there is a possibility that the plaintiff's injuries would have occurred without his negligence.

Quicknotes

POST HOC After this moment.

POST HOC ERGO PROPTER HOC The doctrine that because an occurrence followed a prior occurrence, it must have been the result of that prior occurrence.

NEGLIGENCE Conduct falling below the standard of care that a reasonable person would demonstrate under similar conditions.

Gentry v. Douglas Hereford Ranch, Inc.

Widower (P) v. Ranch company (D)

Mt. Sup. Ct., 290 Mont. 126, 962 P.2d 1205 (1998).

NATURE OF CASE: Wrongful death and survival suit.

FACT SUMMARY: Gentry (P) brought a wrongful death and survival suit against Bacon (D), the ranch company (D) and the cattle company (D), when his wife died as a result of Bacon's (D) rifle accidentally discharging when he allegedly stumbled on the deck steps.

🏛 RULE OF LAW
Cause in fact is established when a plaintiff can demonstrate that an event would not have occurred but for the defendant's conduct.

FACTS: Bacon (D) was preparing to hunt deer while his wife and their friend, Barbara Gentry, painted the inside of a house owned by Bacon's (D) wife's grandmother. He stumbled on the stairs and accidentally discharged the rifle, shooting Barbara in the head. She died several weeks later. Her husband (P) brought wrongful death and survival actions against Bacon (D), the ranch company (D) owned by the grandmother, and a cattle company (D) that owned part of the ranch, alleging Bacon (D) was negligent in handling the rifle and the ranch (D) and cattle companies (D) had been negligent in maintaining the stairs. Bacon (D) declared bankruptcy and was dismissed and the court entered summary judgment in favor of the ranch company.

ISSUE: Is cause in fact established when a plaintiff can demonstrate that an event would not have occurred but for the defendant's conduct?

HOLDING AND DECISION: (Trieweiler, J.) Yes. Cause in fact is established when a plaintiff can demonstrate that an event would not have occurred but for the defendant's conduct. In order to establish negligence, plaintiff must show that a duty existed, breach of that duty, causation and damages. If the plaintiff fails to establish any of these elements, then summary judgment for the defendant is proper. Proof of causation requires a showing of proof of both cause in fact and proximate cause. Cause in fact is established if the plaintiff can prove that the event would not have occurred but for the defendant's conduct. Here Gentry (P) claimed the ranch company (D) was negligent in failing to maintain the steps on which Bacon (D) tripped in a reasonably safe condition. He argued that the step was unstable and cluttered by debris. Bacon (D) testified, however, that his fall was not attributable to any of those circumstances. Rather, he could not remember what caused to him to stumble on the steps. A suspicion or speculation is not sufficient to raise a genuine issue of material fact so as to defeat a motion for summary judgment. Affirmed.

▶ ANALYSIS

In *Krone v. McCann*, 196 Mont. 260 (1982), plaintiff sought damages for an injury sustained when she tripped and fell over an object on defendant's property. The court affirmed summary judgment for the defendant on the basis that the plaintiff did not know what caused her to fall. The court stated that a plaintiff must show evidence leading the court to reasonably infer that the defendant's negligent conduct caused the injury.

Quicknotes

CAUSE IN FACT The event without which an injury would not have been incurred.

NEGLIGENCE Conduct falling below the standard of care that a reasonable person would demonstrate under similar conditions.

PROXIMATE CAUSE The natural sequence of events without which an injury would not have been sustained.

SUMMARY JUDGMENT Judgment rendered by a court in response to a motion by one of the parties, claiming that the lack of a question of material fact in respect to an issue warrants disposition of the issue without consideration by the jury.

WRONGFUL DEATH An action brought by the beneficiaries of a deceased person, claiming that the deceased's death was the result of wrongful conduct by the defendant.

Kramer Service Inc. v. Wilkins

Hotel guest (P) v. Hotel (D)

Miss. Sup. Ct., 184 Miss. 483, 186 So. 625 (1939).

NATURE OF CASE: Action for damages resulting from a defective door.

FACT SUMMARY: Wilkins (P) cut his forehead on a piece of glass which fell from a broken transom when he opened the door in Kramer's (D) hotel. Two years later, Wilkins (P) discovered that skin cancer had developed at the point of the glass injury.

> ## 🏛 RULE OF LAW
> One cannot recover for an injury if he shows just a possibility that the injury was caused by another's negligence.

FACTS: Wilkins (P) was a guest in Kramer's (D) hotel. Wilkins (P) was cut on his forehead when a piece of glass fell from a broken transom as he was opening a door. There was evidence that the hotel's disrepair had existed long enough so that Kramer (D) should have known about it. Wilkins's (P) wound did not heal and two years after the injury he went to a specialist in skin diseases, who found that at the point of the injury a skin cancer had developed.

ISSUE: Is the mere possibility that an injury was caused by another's negligence a sufficient basis for recovery?

HOLDING AND DECISION: (Griffith, J.) No. One cannot recover for an injury if he shows just a possibility that the injury was caused by another's negligence. Laymen have no experience with skin cancer, so the court must accept the undisputed testimony of specialists that there was, at most, a remote possibility that Wilkins's (P) cancer resulted from the original forehead cut. The jury should not be allowed to speculate when they have no experience with a disease and the medical experts are undisputed. This is an exception to the advisory. The mere possibility that Wilkins's (P) cancer might have been caused by his forehead cut is insufficient proof of causation and, therefore, will not sustain a verdict for Wilkins (P). While Wilkins (P) may recover for the forehead cut, he may not recover for the cancer. Affirmed as to liability; reversed and remanded as to damages.

▌ *ANALYSIS*

This case accords with the majority view that a mere possibility that negligence caused an injury is insufficient proof of "cause in fact." Accordingly, the court will direct a verdict for the defendant when the only proof of a causal connection is based on speculation.

■■■■

Quicknotes

POST HOC ERGO PROPTER HOC   The doctrine that because an occurrence followed a prior occurrence, it must have been the result of that prior occurrence.

Herskovits v. Group Health Cooperative of Puget Sound

Estate administrator (P) v. Hospital (D)

Wash. Sup. Ct., 99 Wash. 2d 609, 664 P. 2d 474 (1983).

NATURE OF CASE: Appeal of summary judgment dismissing action for damages for medical malpractice.

FACT SUMMARY: The negligence of Group Health (D) caused a reduction in the chances of survival in a patient whose chances of survival were already less than 50 percent.

🏛 RULE OF LAW
A plaintiff need not demonstrate that a decedent probably would have survived but for medical malpractice to state a cause of action for such malpractice.

FACTS: Group Health Cooperative (D) failed to diagnose lung cancer in Herskovits. He subsequently died. The trial court granted summary judgment when the estate (P), suing under a survivor statute, could not show that Herskovits would probably have survived but for the alleged malpractice. The estate (P) appealed. For purposes of the appeal, it was assumed that Group Health (D) was negligent and that Herskovits had a survival prospect of less than 50 percent when he was seen at Group Health.

ISSUE: Must a plaintiff demonstrate that a decedent probably would have survived but for medical malpractice to state a cause of action for such malpractice?

HOLDING AND DECISION: (Dore, J.) No. A plaintiff need not demonstrate that a decedent probably would have survived but for medical malpractice to state a cause of action for such malpractice. When the issue is breach of a duty to protect, the usual burden-of-proof situation changes. This is because a jury must look at not only what did happen, but also at what might have happened. This being so, it should be held that once a plaintiff has demonstrated that the defendant's acts or omissions have increased the risk of harm to another, a jury should decide what sort of harm was brought about by that increased risk. The jury should be permitted to so decide in this case. Reversed.

▶ ANALYSIS

At first glance, the rule here seems unfair, as it would seem to open the door for damages awarded on behalf of an individual who was not going to survive in any case. However, the court cautioned that only expenses and damages directly traceable to the malpractice may be recovered. Damages related to the inevitable death would not be recoverable.

■━■

Quicknotes

MEDICAL MALPRACTICE Conduct on the part of a doctor falling below that demonstrated by other doctors of ordinary skil and competency under the circumstances, resulting in damages.

NEGLIGENCE Conduct falling below the standard of care that a reasonable person would demonstrate under similar conditions.

SUMMARY JUDGMENT Judgment rendered by a court in response to a motion by one of the parties, claiming that the lack of a question of material fact in respect to an issue warrants disposition of the issue without consideration by the jury.

■━■

Daubert v. Merrell Dow Pharmaceuticals, Inc.

Injured (P) v. Pharmaceutical company (D)

43 F.3d 1311 (9th Cir. 1995).

NATURE OF CASE: Products liability suit.

FACT SUMMARY: Two minors (P) brought suit against Merrell Dow (D) claiming they suffered limb reduction birth defects because their mothers had taken Benedictin, a drug prescribed to treat morning sickness.

🏛 RULE OF LAW
Expert scientific testimony is admissible if it reflects "scientific knowledge," if the findings are "derived by the scientific method," if the work product amounts to "good science," and if it logically advances a material aspect of the proposing party's case.

FACTS: Two minors (P) brought suit against Merrell Dow (D) claiming they suffered limb reduction birth defects because their mothers had taken Benedictin, a drug prescribed to treat morning sickness. Expert testimony to establish that Benedictin had caused their injuries was admitted that was counter to the consensus within the scientific community. The district court granted summary judgment on this basis under the test set forth in *Frye*, which allows the admission of scientific evidence if based on a scientific technique generally accepted as reliable within the scientific community. This court affirmed. The Supreme Court reversed, holding that the Frye test was superceded by FRE 702, and remanded.

ISSUE: Is expert scientific testimony admissible if it reflects "scientific knowledge," if the findings are "derived by the scientific method," if the work product amounts to "good science," and if it logically advances a material aspect of the proposing party's case?

HOLDING AND DECISION: (Kozinski, J.) Yes. Expert scientific testimony is admissible if it reflects "scientific knowledge," if the findings are "derived by the scientific method," if the work product amounts to "good science," and if it logically advances a material aspect of the proposing party's case. Establishing that an expert's proffered testimony grows out of prelitigation research or that the expert's research has been subjected to peer review are the two ways the proponent of the proffered testimony can satisfy the first prong of FRE 702. Here none of the experts based his testimony on preexisting or independent research. None claims to have studied the effect of Benedictin on limb reduction defects. The proponent of the testimony may also satisfy its burden through the testimony of its experts, who must explain precisely how they came to their conclusions and point to an objective source to show they have followed a scientific method as followed by at least a recognized minority of scientists in their field. Plaintiffs here have made no such showing. The second prong of FRE 702 requires a valid scientific connection to the pertinent inquiry as a precondition to admissibility. Here the pertinent inquiry is causation. California tort law requires plaintiffs to show not merely that Benedictin increased the likelihood of injury, but that it more likely than not caused their injuries. The strongest inference to be drawn from the testimony is that Benedictin could have possibly caused the plaintiff's injuries. Affirmed.

▶ ANALYSIS

The relatively simple Frye test required the proponent of the expert testimony to show that it was based on the method generally accepted in the scientific community. The test set forth in *Daubert* focuses on the reliability of the expert's methodology; thus, it need not be the view espoused by the majority. However, the expert must explain his methodology and demonstrate its reliability in an objectively verifiable manner.

◼▬◼

Quicknotes

CAUSATION The aggregate effect of preceding events that bring about a tortious result; the causal connection between the actions of a tortfeasor and the injury that follows.

EXPERT TESTIMONY Testimonial evidence about a complex area of subject matter relevant to trial, presented by a person competent to inform the trier of fact due to specialized knowledge or training.

◼▬◼

Hill v. Edmonds

Injured passenger (P) v. Driver (D) and truck owner (D)

N.Y. Sup. Ct., 26 A.D.2d 554, 270 N.Y.S.2d 1020 (1966).

NATURE OF CASE: Appeal from dismissal of action for damages for negligence.

FACT SUMMARY: Although Edmonds (D), the driver of the car in which Hill (P) was a passenger, had acted negligently in running into a truck, the owner of the truck, Bragoli (D), also acted questionably in leaving it parked without lights in the middle of the road on a stormy night.

🏛 RULE OF LAW
When separate acts of negligence combine to produce directly a single injury, each tortfeasor is responsible for the entire result, even though his act alone might not have caused it.

FACTS: Bragoli (D) had left the truck he owned parked without lights in the middle of the road on a stormy night. Hill (P) suffered injuries when the car in which she was a passenger collided with the truck. She sued both parties for damages for personal injury. The testimony was that Edmonds (D), the driver of the car, had seen the truck when it was four lengths ahead of her and that she saw it in time to turn. However, Edmonds (D) also indicated that she did not know just what happened, that she swerved to avoid the truck, and the next thing she knew she was unconscious. The trial court concluded that Edmonds (D) was guilty of negligence and was solely responsible for the collision. It dismissed the complaint against Bragoli (D), and Hill (P) appealed.

ISSUE: Is each tortfeasor responsible for the entire result when separate acts of negligence combine to produce directly a single injury?

HOLDING AND DECISION: [Memorandum] Yes. Even though his act alone might not have caused it, each tortfeasor is responsible for the entire result when separate acts of negligence combine to produce directly a single injury. Assuming arguendo that Edmonds (D) was negligent, the fact remains that the accident could not have happened had not Bragoli (D) allowed his unlighted truck to stand in the middle of the roadway. Thus, the complaint against him must be reinstated and a new trial had.

▶ ANALYSIS

The rule of this case is known commonly as the "substantial factor" test. Ordinarily, the test arises in cases where it is uncertain which of two persons caused a third person's injury. In one well-known case, a man riding in a horsedrawn wagon was injured when two motorcycles passed simultaneously and frightened his horses. Both motorcyclists were held liable (*Corey v. Havender*, 65 N.E. 69 [Mass. 1902]).

Quicknotes

ARGUENDO Hypothetical argument.

NEGLIGENCE Conduct falling below the standard of care that a reasonable person would demonstrate under similar conditions.

SUBSTANTIAL FACTOR TEST In determining whether one of several joint acts was the proximate cause of an injury for purposes of tort liability, the inquiry is whether the act or omission was a substantial factor in causing the damage and whether the damage was the direct or probable result of the act or omission.

Anderson v. Minneapolis, St. P. & S. St. M. R.R. Co.

Burned-property owner (P) v. Railroad (D)

Minn. Sup. Ct., 146 Minn. 430, 179 N.W. 45 (1920).

NATURE OF CASE: Action for damages resulting from a fire which was negligently set.

FACT SUMMARY: A forest fire, caused by Minn. R.R.'s (D) negligence, merged with another fire of uncertain origin and both fires burned over Anderson's (P) property.

🏛 RULE OF LAW
If one negligently sets a fire which combines with another fire of no responsible origin, he is liable if his fire would have caused the damage independent of the other fire, or if his fire materially caused the damage. In other words, if one's negligence would have caused the damage complained of, he is liable and it is irrelevant whether, in fact, another force combined to cause the damage.

FACTS: Minn. R.R. (D) started a forest fire negligently. Before this fire reached Anderson's (P) property, it merged with another fire of independent and uncertain origins. The combined fires burned over Anderson's (P) property. Minn. R.R. (D) claimed that it should not be liable because the other fire alone could have caused the damage. It claimed that the jury instructions in the lower court were incorrect.

ISSUE: If a person's property is damaged by several fires combining and only one of these fires is of known origin, can he recover against the negligent party if the other fires alone could have produced the damage?

HOLDING AND DECISION: (Lees, C.) Yes. Even if the fire of unknown origins could have alone produced the damage, if the fire of known origins is a material element in causing the damage, the negligent originator of the known fire is liable. Here, Minn. R.R. (D) negligently set off a fire which combined with a fire of unknown origins and then did damage to Anderson's (P) property. Although the unknown fire alone could have destroyed the property, Minn. R.R. (D) is still liable because its fire was a material element in causing damage to Anderson's (P) property. This finding of liability is logical because if two known fires combine and cause damage, there is joint and several liability, even though either fire alone could have destroyed the property. Moreover, a statute compels the court to find liability under the facts at bar, although there would be liability even without this statute. Affirmed.

▶ ANALYSIS

This case illustrates the principle of concurrent liability. If a negligent party alone could cause injury, the fact that another party was concurrently causing the same injury does not exculpate the first party, unless he can show that his negligence was not a material element in causing the injury. If the rule were otherwise, it would be easy for a negligent party to escape liability by pointing to the other negligent party; the other party would in turn escape liability in the same manner.

━■━

Quicknotes

JOINT AND SEVERAL LIABILITY Liability amongst tortfeasors allowing the injured party to bring suit against any of the defendants, individually or collectively, and to recover from each up to the total amount of damages awarded.

JUDGMENT N.O.V. A judgment entered by the trial judge reversing a jury verdict if the jury's determination has no basis in law or fact.

━■━

Summers v. Tice

Shooting victim (P) v. Hunters (D)

Cal. Sup. Ct., 33 Cal. 2d 80, 199 P.2d 1 (1948).

NATURE OF CASE: Action for damages resulting from the negligent shooting of Summers (P).

FACT SUMMARY: Summers (P) was struck in the eye by a shot from one gun although the two defendants had both fired.

RULE OF LAW
When two defendants are both negligent, but only one of them could have caused the plaintiff's injury, the court will hold them both liable when it cannot determine which of the defendants caused the damage.

FACTS: Summers (P) and the two defendants were members of a hunting party. Both defendants, Tice (D) and Simonson (D), negligently fired, simultaneously, at a quail and in Summers' (P) direction. He was struck in the eye by a shot from one gun. There was no evidence from which to determine which gun had caused the injury.

ISSUE: When two defendants are both negligent, but only one of them could have caused the plaintiff's injury, will they be held jointly liable if there is no evidence proving which defendant caused the damage?

HOLDING AND DECISION: (Carter, J.) Yes. The judgment against both defendants may stand. Although the defendants were not acting in concert and there is insufficient evidence to determine which defendant was guilty of the negligence that caused the injuries, they are jointly liable because otherwise Summers (P) could not recover. It is logical that the defendants have the burden of proving that the other person was the sole cause of harm. It would be unfair to deny the injured person recovery simply because he cannot prove who did the damage when it is certain that between them they did all the damage. Therefore, the court shifts the burden of proof to the wrongdoers such that they must absolve themselves of the wrongdoing. Further, the defendants are in a better position to offer evidence to determine which one caused the injury. Affirmed.

▶ ANALYSIS

This case is in the majority. The doctrine of holding two negligent parties jointly liable when only one of the parties could have caused the damage is analogous to the doctrine of res ipsa loquitur, in the sense that it is the defendant who must come forward with evidence to absolve himself.

This case shifts the burden of proof to the defendants, just as the burden of proof is shifted in res ipsa loquitur cases. Were the rule otherwise, the plaintiff would hardly ever be able to prove who caused his injury.

Quicknotes

JOINT LIABILITY   Liability owed to an injured party by two or more parties where each party has the right to insist that the other tortfeasors be joined to the matter.

JOINT TORTFEASORS   Two or more parties that either act in concert, or whose individual acts combine to cause a single injury, rendering them jointly and severally liable for damages incurred.

RES IPSA LOQUITUR   A rule of law giving rise to an inference of negligence where the instrument inflicting the injury is in the exclusive control of the defendant and where such harm could not ordinarily result in the absence of negligence.

Sindell v. Abbott Laboratories

Child of drug user (P) v. Drug manufacturers (D)

Cal. Sup. Ct., 26 Cal. 3d 588, 607 P.2d 924 (1980).

NATURE OF CASE: Damages for products liability.

FACT SUMMARY: Abbott (D) and several other drug manufacturers sold DES, a drug designed to prevent miscarriages, but which caused later-life cancer in the female children born of the mothers using DES.

🏛 **RULE OF LAW**
Where several manufacturers produce and distribute a dangerously defective product, each should bear part of the damages due an injured plaintiff in proportion to the share of the total market it supplied.

FACTS: Sindell's (P) mother ingested the drug DES during pregnancy upon her physician's prescription. The drug was designed to prevent miscarriages. Many years after the pregnancy terminated with the birth of Sindell (P), it was discovered that the drug was inadequately tested by all of the manufacturers of it, and that it caused cancer of female human reproductive organs in the children of DES users. Sindell (P) became a victim of this cancer, and brought this action against five of the manufacturers of DES. Sindell (P) had no way of proving that Abbott (D) manufactured the drug taken by her mother, but the court held that because all of the defendants were negligent in manufacturing and distributing the drug, the burden of proof of causation shifted to the defendant companies, requiring them to show affirmatively that they did not manufacture the drug taken by Sindell's (P) mother. Abbott (D) appealed.

ISSUE: Where several manufacturers produce and distribute a dangerously defective product, should each bear part of the damages due an injured plaintiff in proportion to the share of the total market it supplied?

HOLDING AND DECISION: (Mosk, J.) Yes. The court below relied upon the ruling of this Court in *Summers v. Tice*, 33 Cal. 2d 80 (1948). There two negligent hunters discharged their weapons simultaneously, and the plaintiff was struck with a projectile. He was unable, however, to determine which of the hunters had shot him. The court shifted the burden of proof to the defendants to demonstrate that each was not the responsible party. This case requires some modification of that rule, however, because unlike Summers, all of the possibly responsible parties were not before the court here. The responsible manufacturer could escape liability in this case. Thus, we can reasonably measure the likelihood of each

of the defendants having supplied Sindell's (P) mother with DES by determining how much of the total market each supplied. Where several manufacturers produce and distribute a dangerously defective product, each should bear part of the damages due to an injured plaintiff in proportion to the share of the total market it supplied. Each of the defendants' liabilities for damages would be approximately equivalent to the injury caused by the DES it manufactured. Reversed.

▌ *ANALYSIS*

It is impossible to divorce this ruling from the fact that the case involved a dangerous drug causing personal injury. A similar result was reached in *Hardy v. Johns-Manville Sales Corp.*, 509 F. Supp. 1353 (1981), involving exposure to mineral asbestos and the personal injury caused thereby. However, where the injury caused is to property, the apparent public policy considerations at play in *Sindell* are not as strong, and it is less likely that the theory proportioning damages in the absence of proof of causation would be applied.

■=▪

Quicknotes

ENTERPRISE LIABILITY The apportionment of liability between each participant in an industry equal to the participant's market share.

FUNGIBLE GOODS Interchangeable or substitutable goods.

■=▪

CHAPTER 6

Proximate or Legal Cause

Quick Reference Rules of Law

Atlantic Coast Line R. Co. v. Daniels

Parties not identified.

Ga. Ct. App., 8 Ga. App. 775, 70 S.E. 203 (1911).

NATURE OF CASE: [Facts not stated in casebook excerpt.]

FACT SUMMARY: [Facts not stated in casebook excerpt.]

RULE OF LAW
The law will look to see whether the wrongful act was the proximate cause of the injury complained of in determining liability.

FACTS: [Facts not stated in casebook excerpt.]

ISSUE: Do courts use arbitrary limitations in establishing cause and effect?

HOLDING AND DECISION: (Powell, J.) Yes. Courts cannot deal with cause and effect in any absolute degree. It must be practically and arbitrarily limited. Words such as "proximate" and "natural" have been used to describe limits for the courts beyond which they will not attempt to find a connection between a cause and effect. The courts must determine whether the wrongful act which allegedly caused an injury was the proximate cause of that injury.

ANALYSIS

Once it is established that the defendant's act was one of the causes of the injury suffered by plaintiff, the question as to whether defendant should be held responsible for it legally arises. Prosser says it is sometimes "a question of whether the conduct has been so significant and important a cause that the defendant should be legally responsible." This can be restated as whether defendant had been under any duty to the plaintiff. Or it can be considered whether any duty defendant had included protecting the plaintiff against the consequences of the harmful act.

Quicknotes

PROXIMATE CAUSE The natural sequence of events without which an injury would not have been sustained.

REDUCTIO AS ABSURDUM The refuting of a legal argument by demonstrating its absurdity.

Ryan v. New York Central R.R. Co.

Owner of burned house (P) v. Railroad (D)

N.Y. Ct. App., 35 N.Y. 210, 91 Am. Dec. 49 (1866).

NATURE OF CASE: Action for damages for injury due to negligence.

FACT SUMMARY: Ryan's (P) house was destroyed by a fire which started when a spark from Central's (D) train engine ignited a wood shed. The fire spread through several houses before reaching Ryan's (P).

🏛 RULE OF LAW
Damages can be awarded only when the injury is immediate and not the remote result of defendant's negligence.

FACTS: Ryan's (P) home in Syracuse was destroyed by a fire which spread from Central's (D) woodshed which had been ignited by a spark from Central's (D) train engine either through careless management or insufficient condition. Ryan's (P) house was 130 feet from the shed. Several other houses were destroyed. The court found in favor of Central (D), and Ryan (P) appealed.

ISSUE: When a person's structure is set afire through his negligence or the negligence of his servant, is he liable for injury suffered to structures of all others to which the fire spreads?

HOLDING AND DECISION: (Hunt, J.) No. Liability would extend only to the owner of the first structure, that is, the structure upon which the spark lands. The result to be anticipated is that the structure upon which the spark lands will be damaged or destroyed. But the spread of the fire to other structures is not the necessary or usual result. The defendant has no control over that and cannot be responsible. The immediate result of the negligence was destruction of Central's (D) own woodshed. All other damage was remote. To hold defendant liable for all resulting damage would be to create a liability too great for any individual; all persons run some risk as to their neighbor's conduct. Affirmed.

▶ ANALYSIS

Supposedly, a defendant is liable for damage which is the natural and probable consequence of his act. In New York, there has been created an arbitrary rule that the wrongdoer is liable for fire only to the first, adjoining property, as illustrated above. Here, as the first structure to be struck by sparks belonged to Central (D), it was not liable to anyone. Thus, it would not make any difference whether the adjoining structure was one large building or thirty small stores. Only the owner of the first, adjoining property could recover. Even if the fire covered the entire block, burning a series of small stores, the ones after the first on the block to be ignited would not be covered. The court touched but did not rest its decision upon whether one should be liable for all damage from an intentionally set fire as opposed to a negligently set fire where liability may be limited to the first, adjoining property.

Quicknotes

NONSUIT Judgment against a party who fails to make out a case.

SUBROGATION The substitution of one party for another in assuming the first party's rights or obligations.

Bartolone v. Jeckovich

Car accident victim (P) v. Tortfeasors (D)

N.Y. Sup. Ct., 103 A.D.2d 632, 481 N.Y.S.2d 545 (1984).

NATURE OF CASE: Appeal of judgment n.o.v. in action seeking damages for personal injury.

FACT SUMMARY: Bartolone (P) suffered a total psychological breakdown following a seemingly minor accident.

🏛 RULE OF LAW
A tortfeasor bears responsibility for all damages proximately caused by tortious conduct, even if the damages appear disproportionate to the tortious conduct.

FACTS: Bartolone (P) was a bodybuilder involved in an accident caused by the negligence of Jeckovich (D). Bartolone's (P) physical injuries were minor, but he suffered an apparently total psychological breakdown, becoming psychotic. At trial, several mental health professionals opined that Bartolone (P), who had a traumatic childhood, had used bodybuilding as a coping mechanism, and when his routine was disturbed, he fell apart. A jury awarded $500,000. The trial court granted judgment n.o.v., holding that the evidence could not support the verdict. Bartolone (P) appealed.

ISSUE: Does a tortfeasor bear responsibility for all damages proximately caused by tortious conduct, even if the damages appear disproportionate to the tortious conduct?

HOLDING AND DECISION: (Denman, J.) Yes. A tortfeasor bears responsibility for all damages proximately caused by tortious conduct, even if the damages appear disproportionate to the tortious conduct. It is very well settled that a defendant takes a plaintiff as he finds him, and injuries seemingly excessive in comparison to the cause of harm will be compensable, if proven. Here, competent testimony that Bartolone (P) had a latent psychological weakness was believed by a jury, and it was well within its power to award damages as it did. Reversed.

▌ANALYSIS

This case is a textbook example of what is popularly called the "eggshell plaintiff" rule. A particularly sensitive plaintiff will be permitted to recover for seemingly disproportionate injuries. It is still required of a plaintiff that he convince a jury that the claimed damages are legitimate, however.

Quicknotes

EGGSHELL PLAINTIFF RULE Doctrine that the defendant is liable in tort for the aggravation of a plaintiff's existing injury or condition, regardless of whether the magnitude of the injury was foreseeable.

JUDGMENT NOTWITHSTANDING THE VERDICT (JUDGMENT N.O.V.) A judgment entered by the trial judge reversing a jury verdict if the jury's determination has no basis in law or fact.

TORTFEASOR Party that commits a tort or wrongful act.

In re Arbitration between Polemis and Furness, Withy & Co., Ltd.

Shipowner (Polemis) v. Ship charterer (Furness)

Ct. App., 3 K.B. 560 (1921).

NATURE OF CASE: Arbitration for damages for injury due to negligence.

FACT SUMMARY: The ship Polemis, while being unloaded, was destroyed by fire when Furness' servant negligently dropped a plank setting off a spark in the hold which exploded vapor seeping from the cargo of petrol and benzine.

🏛 RULE OF LAW
The fact that the kind of damage which an act might probably cause was not the damage anticipated is immaterial so long as the resulting damage is directly traceable to the negligent act, and not due to independent cause having no connection with the negligent act.

FACTS: Furness chartered the ship, Polemis, from its owners. It carried a cargo of petrol and benzine. While unloading in Casablanca, a heavy plank fell into the hold setting off a spark which ignited petrol vapor. The resulting explosion completely destroyed the Polemis. Arbitrators found that while a spark resulting from the dropping of the plank would not be reasonably foreseen, the dropping of the plank was due to negligence of Furness' servants. Also found was that some damage could be reasonably anticipated from the dropping of the plank. Damages were stated at £196 1s. 11d.

ISSUE: Were the damages too remote as to be recoverable?

HOLDING: (Bankes, L.J.) No. The arbitors are affirmed. It is immaterial that the spark could not be reasonably anticipated; the act of dropping the plank itself was negligent. If the act would or might probably cause damage, the fact that the damage it in fact causes is not the exact kind of damage one would expect is immaterial, so long as the damage is in fact directly traceable to the negligent act, and not due to the operation of independent causes having no connection with the negligent act, except that they could not avoid its results.

HOLDING: (Scrutton, J.) When damage is directly traceable to a negligent act, and no independent cause separates the damage from the negligent act, the unexpectedness of the specific kind of damage is irrelevant. In this case, the fact that some foreseeable damage would result from knocking down the planks makes the act negligent. That the resulting spark was unexpected is irrelevant because the negligent act directly caused the damage.

▶ ANALYSIS

This case follows the rule set out in *Christianson v. Chicago, St. P., M.G.O. Ry. Co.*, 69 N.W. 640 (1896), a minority rule in the United States. The rule is rather mechanical. Basically, if X can be foreseen to result in Y, but instead results in Z, the wrongdoer is still liable for Z even though it may be totally out of proportion to X. Z is proximate to X and, hence, there is liability. Prosser, among others, has called this decision "absurd." Basically, the criticism is that damages are usually just too high, with the rule being "artificial." This case remained a controversy for forty years until it was overruled in 1961.

Quicknotes

FORESEEABILITY A reasonable expectation that an act or omission would result in injury.

Overseas Tankship (U.K.) Ltd. v. Morts Dock & Engineering Co., Ltd. "Wagon Mound No. 1"

Wharf owner (P) v. Workmen's employer (D)

Privy Council 1961, A.C. 388 (1961).

NATURE OF CASE: Action for damages for injury due to negligence.

FACT SUMMARY: Morts' (P) wharf was seriously damaged when oil negligently discharged from Overseas' (D) ship, the Wagon Mound, spread across the water and later caught fire when molten metal dropped by Overseas' (D) workmen ignited cotton waste floating on the surface.

🏛 RULE OF LAW
Even though injury may result from a negligent act, liability for that injury is limited to the risk reasonably to be foreseen.

FACTS: Morts (P) operated a wharf in Port of Sydney, Australia. The ship, Wagon Mound, owned by Overseas (D) and moored about 600 feet away, carelessly discharged a large quantity of furnace oil which spread across the surface of the water and washed against Morts' (P) wharf. Damage was so minor that no claim was made. Cotton waste floating on the surface was ignited by molten metal dropped by Overseas' (D) workmen. This set the oil afire, seriously damaging Morts' (P) wharf. The trial court found that Overseas (D) did not know and could not reasonably know that the oil with a flashpoint of 170° could be set afire when spread on water. Morts (P) was awarded judgment and Overseas (D) appealed to the Privy Council (the Appeals Court for all Commonwealth Nations except England).

ISSUE: Should a defendant be liable for all damage directly resulting from his negligent act?

HOLDING AND DECISION: (Viscount Simonds) No. It is not "consonant with current ideas of justice and morality that for an act of negligence, however slight or venial, which results in some trivial foreseeable damage, the actor should be liable for all consequences, however unforeseeable and however grave, so long as they can be said to be 'direct.'" One should be responsible only for the probable consequences of his act, not the improbable. This keeps the rule from being too harsh while requiring all persons to observe a minimum standard of behavior. There should be some limitation on the consequences of a negligent act for which the wrongdoer will be held responsible and it seems unreasonable to substitute the reasonable foreseeability test with a direct causation test which leads to nothing but "insolvable problems of causation."

▶ ANALYSIS

This case overruled *In re Polemis,* Ct. of Appeals, 3 K.B. 560 (1921). One is responsible for the reasonably foreseeable or probable consequence of his negligent acts. The old rule of responsibility for all damage, foreseeable or not as long as some damage was reasonably foreseeable, was found unjust and harsh. This rule does not apply to the "eggshell skull" doctrine, as that deals with the inherent weakness of plaintiff while foreseeable consequences deals with extent of damage done.

Quicknotes

EGGSHELL SKULL DOCTRINE Doctrine that the defendant is liable in tort for the aggravation of a plaintiff's existing injury or condition, regardless of whether the magnitude of the injury was foreseeable.

FORESEEABILITY A reasonable expectation that an act or omission would result in injury.

NEGLIGENCE Conduct falling below the standard of care that a reasonable person would demonstrate under similar conditions.

Overseas Tankship (U.K.) Ltd. v. Miller Steamship Co.
"Wagon Mound No. 2"

Steamship owner (P) v. Ship owner (D)

Privy Council 1966, 1 A.C. 617 (1967).

NATURE OF CASE: Action for damages for injury due to negligence.

FACT SUMMARY: Miller's (P) two ships were damaged when oil negligently discharged from Overseas' (D) ship, the Wagon Mound, spread across the water and later caught fire when molten metal dropped by Overseas (D) workmen ignited cotton waste floating on the surface.

🏛 RULE OF LAW
One who is knowledgeable of a risk and can reasonably prevent it is liable for damages resulting from his failure to do so.

FACTS: Miller's (P) two ships were damaged when oil negligently discharged from Overseas' (D) ship, the Wagon Mound, spread across the water and later caught fire when molten metal dropped by Overseas' (D) workmen ignited cotton waste floating on the surface. The trial court made findings on foreseeability as follows: (1) reasonable people in the position of Wagon Mound officers would consider the furnace oil very difficult to ignite; (2) their personal experience would be that this probably occurred rarely; (3) risk of fire would have been regarded as a possibility but occurred only in exceptional circumstances; (4) the chances of fire would be considered remote; (5) damage to Miller's (P) ships would not be reasonably foreseeable, and, accordingly, damages could not be awarded.

ISSUE: Would a reasonable man having the knowledge and experience to be expected of the chief engineer of the Wagon Mound have known that there was a real risk of the oil on the water catching fire in some way?

HOLDING AND DECISION: (Lord Reid) Yes. Findings of the trial court show that the chief engineer should have known that it was possible to ignite the oil on the water. It does not follow that no matter what the circumstances may be that it is justifiable to neglect a risk of such small magnitude. The risk must be weighed against the difficulty of removing it. A reasonable man should not dismiss a small risk when it is so easy to remove it. There was no justification for discharging the oil into the water. In balancing the advantages and disadvantages it was the chief engineer's duty to stop the discharge immediately. Judgment was reversed.

▶ ANALYSIS

Here, the court is balancing what a reasonable man would foresee against the burden of obviating the risk. Overseas (D) should have known that despite the small chance of fire, a risk did exist, and as it was relatively easy to obviate that risk, it should have done so. This is not a throwback to *In re Polemis*, 3 K.B. 560 (1921) exactly, but more of an extension of Wagon Mound No. I which was distinguished on the facts. Here, the trial court made findings of fact that Overseas (D) should have known of the risk. Because the risk was known, the damage was foreseeable. Overseas (D) failed in its duty to remove the risk.

Quicknotes

NEGLIGENCE Conduct falling below the standard of care that a reasonable person would demonstrate under similar conditions.

REASONABLE PERSON STANDARD The standard of care exercised by a hypothetical person who possesses the intelligence, education, knowledge, attention, and judgment required by society of its members when governing behavior; the standard applies to a person's judgment when determining breach of a duty under the theory of negligence.

Palsgraf v. Long Island R.R. Co.

Injured bystander (P) v. Railroad company (D)

N.Y. Ct. App., 248 N.Y. 339, 162 N.E. 99 (1928).

NATURE OF CASE: Action for damages for personal injury due to negligence.

FACT SUMMARY: Mrs. Palsgraf (P) was injured on Long Island R.R. Co.'s (LIRR) (D) train platform when L.I.R.R.'s (D) servant helped a passenger aboard a moving train, jostling his package, causing it to fall to the tracks. The package, containing fireworks, exploded creating a shock which tipped a scale onto Mrs. Palsgraf (P).

🏛 **RULE OF LAW**
The risk reasonably to be perceived defines the duty to be obeyed.

FACTS: Mrs. Palsgraf (P) purchased a ticket to Rockaway Beach from LIRR (D) and was waiting on the train platform. While standing there, two men ran to catch a train which was pulling out from the platform. The first man jumped aboard, but the second man, who appeared as if he might fall, was helped aboard by the guard who had kept the door open so they could jump aboard. A guard on the platform also helped by pushing him onto the train. The man was carrying a package wrapped in newspaper. In the process, the man dropped his innocent-looking package, which fell to the tracks. The package contained fireworks and exploded. The shock explosion was apparently of great enough strength to tip over some scales at the other end of the platform which fell on Mrs. Palsgraf (P) and injured her. She was awarded damages and LIRR (D) appealed.

ISSUE: Did there exist a duty by LIRR (D) to Mrs. Palsgraf (P) by which LIRR (D) would be liable had it breached that duty by its negligence?

HOLDING AND DECISION: (Cardozo, C.J.) No. If there was no foreseeable hazard as the result of a seemingly innocent act with reference to the injured party, the act did not become a tort because it happened to be a wrong, though not to the injured party. Negligence is not enough upon which to base liability—there must be a duty to the injured party which could have been averted or avoided by observance of the duty. There can be no duty owed to an injured party when the wrong was committed towards someone else. The range of the duty is limited by the range of danger. The risk reasonably to be perceived defines the duty to be obeyed. There was nothing to suggest that the parcel from its appearance contained fireworks. Had the guard purposefully thrown down the package, he would have had no warning of a threat of

harm to Mrs. Palsgraf (P). Just because the act was inadvertent does not impose liability. In the abstract, negligence itself is not a tort. To be a tort, it must result in the commission of a wrong. A wrong imports the violation of a right. If the wrong was not willful, it must be shown by the plaintiff that the act as to him had such great possibilities of danger, so many and so apparent, as to entitle him to protection against it though the harm was unintentional. Had there been liability for the negligence towards Mrs. Palsgraf (P), she would recover for all injury "however novel or extraordinary." Accordingly, the judgment is reversed in favor of LIRR (D).

▶ **ANALYSIS**

Cardozo states that negligence is a matter of relationship between the parties. That relationship must be based upon the foreseeability of harm to the person who is, in fact, injured. Just because defendant's act was negligent, it is not necessarily wrong to the injured party. The act must be negligent and wrong to the injured party to enable him to sue in his own right. If there is no duty to the injured party, there can be no violation of a right, so even if an act was negligent it could not have violated a wrong to the injured party. The dissent on the other hand states that each person owes a duty of due care to society at large. Each person must refrain from any act which unreasonably threatens the safety of others. Accordingly, any party injured by a negligent act would suffer a wrong as the duty owed to each member of society at large would have been violated. A right of action must then arise despite the unforeseeability of the injury. The Restatement has accepted the view of this case that without any duty there can be no negligence, hence, never any liability to the unforeseeable injured party. Note that the determination of any question of duty is a question of law and never one for the jury. Cardozo, on the question of duty, went even further by suggesting that the defendant could owe a duty to one particular interest of the injured party but not to a different interest of the same party. That is to say that there could be a duty to the injured party's property interest but not to his person. So, if defendant negligently set a fire in plaintiff's unoccupied building, and the plaintiff is injured extinguishing the blaze, damages only to the building are recoverable, or vice versa depending upon the original duty. This theory advanced in the dictum of Palsgraf was approved by the Restatements § 281, but it has been

Continued on next page.

widely opposed by most other courts. In fact, there is much authority against it and even Prosser has called this aspect of Cardozo's view "artificial." There are, of course, interests which, as a matter of public policy, should not be protected against certain types of wrongful conduct, but it does not follow from this that protection should always be limited to the interest which is threatened in advance.

■═■

Quicknotes

FORESEEABILITY The reasonable anticipation that damage is a likely result from certain acts or omissions.

NEGLIGENCE Failure to exercise that degree of care which a person of ordinary prudence would exercise under similar circumstances.

PROXIMATE CAUSE Something which in natural and continuous sequence, unbroken by any new intervening cause, produces an event and without that the injury would not have occurred.

UNFORESEEABLE A result that was not likely to occur from a particular act or failure to act.

■═■

Yun v. Ford Motor Co.

Estate representative v. Automobile manufacturer (D)

N.J. Super. Ct. App. Div., 276 N.J. Super. 142, 647 A.2d 841 (1994).

NATURE OF CASE: Products liability suit.

FACT SUMMARY: Yun (P) brought suit on behalf of her deceased father's estate against Ford (D) and other defendants for injuries sustained by the father when he ran across the freeway in an attempt to retrieve an allegedly defective tire assembly that fell off the back of her van.

🏛 RULE OF LAW
A claim of strict liability may be defeated if the defendant can show that an intervening superceding event or another sole proximate cause resulted in the plaintiff's injury.

FACTS: Chang was a passenger in a 1987 Ford (D) van owned and driven by his daughter Yun (P). Yun (P) heard a rattling noise coming from the rear of the van. The spare tire and plastic cover screwed to the rear of the van landed directly behind the van and rolled across both lanes of traffic resting against the wooden guard rail. Yun (P) drove the van to the right side of the highway and stopped. Chang ran across the freeway to get the spare tire and was struck by a vehicle driven by Linderman (D). Yun (P) sued Ford (D), Miller (D), Universal (D), Castle (D), the Lindermans (D) and Kim's Automobile Center (D). Summary judgment was granted to defendant and Yun (P) appealed.

ISSUE: May a claim of strict liability be defeated if the defendant can show that an intervening superceding event or another sole proximate cause resulted in the plaintiff's injury?

HOLDING AND DECISION: (Villanueva, J.) Yes. A claim of strict liability may be defeated if the defendant can show that an intervening superceding event or another sole proximate cause resulted in the plaintiff's injury. This action falls within the Products Liability Act. Yun (P) must show the alleged defect in the spare tire bracket proximately caused Chang's injuries. Proximate cause is defined as any cause in the natural sequence of events, unbroken by a sufficient intervening cause, that results in the injury and without which the injury would not have occurred. This refers to conduct setting off a foreseeable sequence of events that is a substantial factor in bringing about the injury and that is not superceded by another event. Here the question is whether Chang's conduct was reasonably foreseeable or highly extraordinary. Here the circumstances were highly extraordinary. Chang's attempt to retrieve the tire by running across the freeway was extraordinarily dangerous and does not conform to the standard of conduct of normal persons. Furthermore, the alleged defect

in the tire was not the cause of Chang's injury. A tortfeasor is responsible for negligent conduct if it constitutes a substantial factor in bringing about the plaintiff's injuries. If concurrent events are involved, the manufacturer of a product may defeat a claim of strict liability by showing an intervening, superceding cause or another sole proximate cause that resulted in the injury. Even if the defective tire was a proximate cause of Chang's injuries, his conduct in running across the freeway constituted an intervening, superceding cause. In addition, Yun (P) and Chang's joint decision not to fix the allegedly defective assembly 30 days earlier constituted an intervening superceding cause as well. Affirmed.

CONCURRENCE AND DISSENT: (Baime, J.) The judgments in favor of Ford (D) and Kim's (D) should be affirmed since the record fails to demonstrate facts sufficient for a finding of negligence. However, Yun's (P) evidence with respect proximate cause on the part of the remaining defendants was sufficient to present an issue of material fact for the jury.

▶ ANALYSIS

Typically the issue of proximate cause is a question for the jury. However, where the issue of proximate cause is a policy question then the court will resolve the issue. This occurs when the consequences of the conduct are highly extraordinary so that the imposition of liability would not be equitable.

Quicknotes

INTERVENING ACT An event whose occurrence breaks the causal chain between the tortfeasor's acts and the resulting injury.

NEGLIGENCE Conduct falling below the standard of care that a reasonable person would demonstrate under similar conditions.

PROXIMATE CAUSE The natural sequence of events without which an injury would not have been sustained.

STRICT LIABILITY Liability for all injuries proximately caused by a party's conducting of certain inherently dangerous activities without regard to negligence or fault.

SUMMARY JUDGMENT Judgment rendered by a court in response to a motion by one of the parties, claiming that the lack of a question of material fact in respect to an issue warrants disposition of the issue without consideration by the jury.

Derdiarian v. Felix Contracting Corp.

Injured workman (P) v. Contractor (D)

N.Y. Ct. App., 51 N.Y.2d 308, 414 N.E.2d 666 (1980).

NATURE OF CASE: Action for damages for negligence.

FACT SUMMARY: Derdiarian (P) was severely injured while working at an excavation site constructed by Felix (D), when an automobile driven by Dickens (D), an epileptic, careened onto the site.

🏛 RULE OF LAW
An intervening act will not serve as a superseding cause, relieving the defendant of liability, where the risk of the intervening act occurring is the very same risk which rendered the defendant negligent.

FACTS: Derdiarian (P), an employee of a subcontractor, was working at an excavation site constructed by Felix (D), a general contractor, when a car came careening onto the site. Derdiarian (P) was struck by the car and seriously injured. The driver of the car, Dickens (D), had neglected to take his regular medicine and had suffered an epileptic seizure immediately prior to the accident. Derdiarian (P) alleged that Felix's (D) negligence stemmed from its failure to provide adequate protection around the excavation site. Felix (D) contended that even if it had been negligent, the intervening act of Dickens's (D) negligence severed any proximate causation connecting Felix's (D) conduct and the injuries suffered by Derdiarian (P). A verdict against Felix (D) was returned. It appealed.

ISSUE: May a foreseeable intervening act by a third party serve as a superseding cause, thereby relieving the negligent defendant of liability?

HOLDING AND DECISION: (Cooke, C.J.) No. Occasionally the difficult question of proximate causation can be decided as a matter of law where an intervening act by a third party is involved. Thus, it has been held that where the intervening act was unforeseeable and where the resulting injuries were different in kind than those normally associated with the defendant's negligence, the defendant, as a matter of law, will not be held to be a proximate cause of the plaintiff's injuries. However, the situation presented here is different. In the instant case, the very reason that Felix's (D) conduct was negligent was that it created a risk of injury due to automobile accidents. Thus, the fact that the risk materialized in a somewhat different fashion than anticipated or that the intervening actor was also negligent, cannot serve to absolve Felix (D) of liability as the proximate cause of Derdiarian's (P) injuries. Affirmed.

▶ ANALYSIS

For another case decided on similar grounds, see *Weirum v. RKO General, Inc.*, 15 Cal. 3d 40 (1975). In that case, a radio station conducted a contest whereby its generally young listeners were instructed to locate a personality through clues broadcast periodically. In the course of the contest, a car driven by a teenager at high speed collided with another car and killed the driver. The radio station was held liable, despite the intervening negligence of the teen-age driver, since the risk created by its actions was precisely the risk that resulted—an accident resulting from dangerous driving.

Quicknotes

FORESEEABILITY A reasonable expectation that an act or omission would result in injury.

INTERVENING ACT An event whose occurrence breaks the causal chain between the tortfeasor's acts and the resulting injury.

NEGLIGENCE Conduct falling below the standard of care that a reasonable person would demonstrate under similar conditions.

PROXIMATE CAUSE The natural sequence of events without which an injury would not have been sustained.

Watson v. Kentucky & Indiana Bridge & R.R. Co.

Burn victim (P) v. Railroad (D)

Ky. Ct. App., 137 Ky. 619, 126 S.W. 146 (1910).

NATURE OF CASE: Action for damages for injury due to negligence.

FACT SUMMARY: Through R.R.'s (D) negligence, a tank car full of gasoline derailed and began leaking. Duerr then struck a match, causing the vapor to explode and injure Watson (P).

⚖ RULE OF LAW
The mere fact that an intervening act was unforeseen will not relieve the defendant guilty of primary negligence from liability unless the intervening act is something so unexpected or extraordinary as that it could not or ought not to be anticipated.

FACTS: Through R.R.'s (D) negligence, a tank car full of gasoline derailed and its valve broke, allowing gasoline to run into the street. Duerr then struck a match, igniting the vapor and causing an explosion which injured Watson (P). There was conflicting evidence as to whether Duerr lit the match deliberately to cause a fire or innocently to light his cigar. The trial court directed a verdict for R.R. (D).

ISSUE: Was Duerr's intervening act so unexpected and extraordinary as that it could not or ought not to be anticipated?

HOLDING AND DECISION: (Settle, J.) As it is not clear whether Duerr's act was deliberate, the issue cannot be decided; judgment must be reversed, and a new trial ordered. As the lighting of the match resulted in the explosion, the question arose as to whether the act was merely a contributing cause or the proximate cause of injury. There was conflicting evidence on the point but the trial court erroneously directed a verdict and did not permit the jury to determine the fact. It was probable that a match would be lit after the accident and in such case not be the proximate cause of the explosion as the explosion could not have occurred at all without the original negligence of R.R. (D). However, if the lighting of the match was deliberate or malicious, it could not or ought not to have been foreseen that such a thing would be done for such evil purpose. If so, the R.R. (D) could not have reasonably anticipated or guarded against a malicious act and would not be liable. That issue remains to be decided in a new trial. Reversed.

▶ ANALYSIS

For an intervening cause to be one that will not relieve the original negligent party from liability, it must be one which in ordinary human experience can be reasonably anticipated under the circumstances. Generally, malicious and wanton acts and criminal acts are not foreseeable and will relieve the original negligent party of liability. The procedural error by the court took the issue away from the jury when the jury was supposed to determine all questions of fact, one of which was the deliberateness of Duerr's act.

Quicknotes

CONTRIBUTORY CAUSE Any factor that contributes to the happening of an event.

DIRECTED VERDICT A verdict ordered by the court in a jury trial.

INTERVENING ACT An event whose occurrence breaks the causal chain between the tortfeasor's acts and the resulting injury.

NEGLIGENCE Conduct falling below the standard of care that a reasonable person would demonstrate under similar conditions.

PROXIMATE CAUSE The natural sequence of events without which an injury would not have been sustained.

Fuller v. Preis

Executor of deceased estate (P) v. Car driver (D)

N.Y. Ct. App., 35 N.Y.2d 425, 322 N.E.2d 263, 363 N.Y.S.2d 568 (1974).

NATURE OF CASE: Wrongful death.

FACT SUMMARY: Fuller's (P) decedent committed suicide, allegedly the irresistible impulse of head injuries suffered in a car accident.

> 🏛 **RULE OF LAW**
> As a matter of law, an act of suicide is not a superseding cause in negligence law precluding liability.

FACTS: Dr. Lewis, Fuller's (P) decedent, was injured in an auto accident seven months before he committed suicide. He suffered head injuries, which damaged the part of the brain controlling emotion and motor control. Epileptic seizures occurred 38 times, including three times on the day of the suicide. Dr. Lewis was physically and emotionally healthy prior to the accident. The seizures could not be controlled by drugs and became progressively more severe. He became depressed, unsteady on his feet, irritable, and experienced headaches. A neurologist testified that on the day of death, Dr. Lewis was in postconvulsive psychosis, which placed his conduct beyond his control. Suicide notes were left in which Dr. Lewis stated he was sane. Fuller (P) sought damages for wrongful death against Preis (D), who allegedly caused the accident which Fuller (P) argued was the proximate cause of the suicide. A jury verdict for $200,000 was reversed on appeal and the complaint dismissed as contrary to the weight of credible evidence.

ISSUE: As a matter of law, is an act of suicide a superseding cause in negligence law precluding liability?

HOLDING AND DECISION: (Breitel, C.J.) No. As a matter of law, an act of suicide is not a superseding cause in negligence law precluding liability. A tortfeasor may be liable for the wrongful acts of a third party if foreseeable, e.g., a doctor's malpractice. The same applies when death results from an "involuntary" suicidal act of the victim as a direct consequence of the wrongful conduct. There is neither public policy nor precedent barring recovery for suicide of a tortiously injured person driven "insane" by the consequence of the tortious act. The issue at trial was whether the suicide was the result of an "irresistible impulse" caused by traumatic organic brain damage. Medical testimony showed that such result was more likely than not. Even though the decedent believed he was sane, sanity is never established by self-serving certification. Insane persons often are unable to accept or recognize their mental state. In tort law, it is recognized that one may retain the power to intend, to know, and yet act

from involuntary and irresistible impulse. The jury only had to find that Preis's (D) negligence substantially contributed to the suicide. Reversed.

▶ *ANALYSIS*

The early view did not allow recovery when the suicide retained even the slightest awareness of what he was doing. The suicide was thus a superseding cause, a view strongly influenced by ecclesiastical law which held that one who knowingly committed suicide was a culpable wrongdoer. This case gives a broad interpretation to the irresistible impulse test. Many courts will find an irresistible impulse only when the decedent takes his own life in a sudden frenzy.

■▬■

Quicknotes

IRRESISTIBLE IMPULSE RULE A defense to a criminal prosecution that the defendant, due to some mental disease or defect, was unable to resist the impulse to commit the crime due to his inability to control his actions.

NEGLIGENCE Conduct falling below the standard of care that a reasonable person would demonstrate under similar conditions.

■▬■

McCoy v. American Suzuki Motor Corp.

Injured rescuer (P) v. Automobile manufacturer (D)

Wash. Sup. Ct., 961 P.2d 952, 136 Wash. 2d 350 (1998).

NATURE OF CASE: Products liability action.

FACT SUMMARY: McCoy (P) sued Suzuki (D) claiming that the injuries he sustained while rescuing two individuals from a Suzuki Samurai were proximately caused by a defective condition in the automobile.

🏛 **RULE OF LAW**
The rescue doctrine may be invoked in products liability cases, requiring the rescuer-plaintiff to prove that the defendant's conduct was the proximate cause of his injuries.

FACTS: McCoy (P) was driving on the interstate when the car in front of him, a Suzuki, swerved off the road and rolled. He stopped to render assistance and found the driver of the car badly injured. A state trooper stopped and asked McCoy (P) to place flares along the road. After the accident was cleared, McCoy (P) was walking along the roadway back to his car when he was struck by a hit-and-run driver. He and his wife (P) brought suit against the driver and passenger of the Suzuki for negligence, the State for the trooper's negligence, and American Suzuki (D) for its allegedly defective car. Suzuki (D) moved for summary judgment on the basis that the rescue doctrine does not apply to products liability actions and even if it does, McCoy (P) cannot prove Suzuki (D) proximately caused his injuries. Summary judgment was granted for Suzuki (D) and McCoy (P) appealed. The court of appeals reversed, holding that the rescue doctrine applies to products liability cases but that the injured rescuer need not prove that the defendant proximate caused the rescuer's injuries, only that defendant proximately caused the danger and that the rescuer was injured while rescuing.

ISSUE: May the rescue doctrine be invoked in products liability cases?

HOLDING AND DECISION: (Sanders, J.) Yes. The rescue doctrine may be invoked in products liability cases, requiring the rescuer-plaintiff to prove that the defendant's conduct was the proximate cause of his injuries. The rescue doctrine allows an injured rescuer to sue a party causing the danger that required the rescue. The rescue doctrine imposes a duty on the tortfeasor towards the rescuer on the basis that it is foreseeable that a person will come to the rescue of a person placed in danger by the tortfeasor's conduct. The doctrine also negates the presumption that the rescuer assumed the risk of injury by undertaking the rescue as long as he did not act

rashly or recklessly. McCoy (P) argued that the rescue doctrine relieved him of demonstrating that Suzuki's (D) wrongdoing proximately caused his injuries. He argued that a rescuer may prevail if he shows the defendant proximately caused the dangerous condition and that plaintiff was injured while rescuing. The court of appeals erred. The rescuer must still demonstrate the defendant proximately caused his injuries. Thus the issue is whether McCoy (P) has shown that Suzuki (D) proximately caused his injuries. Suzuki (D) argued that it was totally unforeseeable that a rescuer would be injured by a third car under the circumstances of this case and that the court should rule in its favor as a matter of law. The court concludes the issue of forseeability of the intervening close should be determined by the jury, not the court. The court may dismiss an action without trial for lack of legal cause where the defendant's actions are too remote so as to be a cause of the plaintiff's injuries. Here Suzuki's (D) alleged fault is not so remote to conclude as a matter of law that its actions were too remote to be the cause of McCoy's (P) injuries. Remanded.

▎ *ANALYSIS*

In order to demonstrate rescuer status, a rescuer must show: (1) the defendant was negligent to the rescued person and such negligence gave rise to the danger; (2) the danger was imminent; (3) a reasonably prudent person would have concluded the danger existed; and (4) the rescuer acted with reasonable care. Here McCoy (P) introduced sufficient evidence to obtain rescuer status.

■▬■

Quicknotes

PRODUCT LIABILITY The legal liability of manufacturers and sellers for damages and injuries suffered by buyers, users, and even bystanders because of defects in goods purchased.

PROXIMATE CAUSE The natural sequence of events without which an injury would not have been sustained.

REASONABLY PRUDENT PERSON A hypothetical person whose judgment represents the standard to which society requires its members to act in their private affairs and in their dealings with others.

RESCUE DOCTRINE One whose conduct places a person in danger is liable to a third party for any injuries incurred in effecting a reasonable rescue attempt.

■▬■

Kelly v. Gwinnell

Injured party (P) v. Driver (D) and host (D)

N.J. Sup. Ct., 96 N.J. 538, 476 A.2d 1219 (1984).

NATURE OF CASE: Appeal of summary judgment dismissing action for damages for personal injury.

FACT SUMMARY: Kelly (P), involved in an accident with Gwinnell (D), who was intoxicated, sued Zak (D), Gwinnell's (D) host.

🏛 RULE OF LAW
A social host may be liable for furnishing alcohol to an intoxicated guest.

FACTS: Gwinnell (D) was a guest at Zak's (D) home. Zak (D) furnished alcohol to Gwinnell (D) beyond the point of intoxication. Gwinnell (D) later was in an accident with Kelly (P), who sued both Gwinnell (D) and Zak (D). The trial court granted summary judgment dismissing Zak (D), and the appellate court affirmed. Kelly (P) appealed.

ISSUE: May a social host be liable for furnishing alcohol to an intoxicated guest?

HOLDING AND DECISION: (Wilentz, C.J.) Yes. A social host may be liable for furnishing alcohol to an intoxicated guest. In terms of duty, the law already imposes a duty not to serve an intoxicated minor, and for a business not to serve an intoxicated patron. This, along with a strong social policy against drunk driving, makes the next step of holding hosts serving alcohol to intoxicated guests a logical one. In terms of causation, it is quite foreseeable that serving alcohol to an intoxicated guest may cause an accident. Here, the allegation was that Zak (D) served alcohol to an intoxicated Gwinnell (D), and this court believes liability should be possible in this situation. Reversed.

DISSENT: (Garibaldi, J.) Before imposing such a high duty on social hosts, many factors and interests need to be weighed. The legislature is in a better position to do this. This decision is improper judicial legislation, and the result is therefore also improper.

▌ANALYSIS

Social host liability is the minority rule. Historically, some states have had "dram shop acts" which imposed liability on establishments, but such liability on social hosts has been uncommon. California, one of the first states to judicially impose host liability, changed this by statute in 1978.

■▬■

Quicknotes

CAUSATION The aggregate effect of preceding events that bring about a tortious result; the causal connection between the actions of a tortfeasor and the injury that follows.

FORESEEABILITY A reasonable expectation that an act or omission would result in injury.

SOCIAL HOST LIABILITY Responsibility imposed upon a person who offers alcoholic beverages to a third party for injuries resulting from the intoxication of the individual.

SUMMARY JUDGMENT Judgment rendered by a court in response to a motion by one of the parties, claiming that the lack of a question of material fact in respect to an issue warrants disposition of the issue without consideration by the jury.

■▬■

Enright v. Eli Lilly & Co.

Granddaughter of DES user (P) v. DES manufacturer (D)

N.Y. Ct. App., 77 N.Y.2d 377, 570 N.E.2d 198 (1991).

NATURE OF CASE: Review of dismissal of personal injury action.

FACT SUMMARY: Enright (P) sought damages for injuries allegedly resulting from her grandmother's ingestion of the drug DES.

> ## 🏛 RULE OF LAW
> An injury to a mother which results in injuries to a later-conceived child does not establish a cause of action in favor of the child against the original tortfeasor.

FACTS: Enright's (P) grandmother ingested the drug DES while pregnant with Enright's (P) mother, Patricia, in 1960. Allegedly, this ingestion led to latent damage to Patricia's reproductive system while being formed in utero. Patricia's injuries, in turn, resulted in congenital defects suffered by Enright (P), who was born prematurely. Enright (P) brought a personal injury action against Eli Lilly (D), the drug's manufacturer. The trial court dismissed, refusing to recognize a cause of action in favor of a child for injuries suffered as a result of a preconception tort committed against the mother. The appellate division affirmed, and the court of appeals (New York's highest court) granted review.

ISSUE: Does an injury to a mother which results in injuries to a later-conceived child establish a cause of action in favor of the child?

HOLDING AND DECISION: (Wachtler, C.J.) No. An injury to a mother which results in injuries to a later-conceived child does not establish a cause of action in favor of the child. To recognize such a cause of action would pose vexing questions with staggering implications in terms of unlimited liability for drug manufacturers. While products liability (as well as negligence liability, for that matter) exists in part to deter unsafe conduct, limiting liability to those who either ingested the drug, like Enright's (P) grandmother, or who were exposed to it in utero, like Patricia, still serves this purpose. On the other hand, to extend liability to those who were never exposed to a dangerous product would lead to such uncertainty in the pharmaceutical industry that the negative impacts on the development of new and much needed drugs would be significant. Consequently, the policy decision must be that the occasional tragedy of individual injury is outweighed by society's need to avoid overdeterrence in the drug industry. Here, Enright (P) was injured as a consequence of injuries to her mother's reproductive system; she was not

herself exposed to DES. Therefore, she has no cause of action against Eli Lilly (D). Affirmed.

▶ *ANALYSIS*

This case provides an excellent example of the difference between cause in fact and proximate (or legal) cause. Cause in fact is just that—a certain act or omission resulting in a certain consequence. Proximate cause is a policy decision, a recognition that at some point cause in fact becomes so attenuated that liability should not be recognized, either because of unforeseeability, the intervention of other acts, or the conduct of a third party.

■■■

Quicknotes

LOSS OF CONSORTIUM An action brought based on willful interference with the marital relationship.

MARKET SHARE LIABILITY The apportionment of liability between each participant in an industry equal to the participant's market share.

STRICT LIABILITY Liability for all injuries proximately caused by a party's conducting of certain inherently dangerous activities without regard to negligence or fault.

■■■

CHAPTER 7

Joint Tortfeasors

Quick Reference Rules of Law

Bierczynski v. Rogers

Accident victims (P) v. Drag racers (D)

Del. Sup. Ct., 239 A.2d 218 (1968).

NATURE OF CASE: Action to recover damages for negligence.

FACT SUMMARY: Race (D) and Bierczynski (D) were drag racing on a public highway and during the fact hit a car in which C. and S. Rogers (P) were riding.

🏛 RULE OF LAW
Individuals who are party to a motor vehicle race on a highway are tortfeasors acting in concert and each participant is liable for harm to a third person arising from tortious conduct because he has engaged in and induced the wrong.

FACTS: Race (D) and Bierczynski (D) were participants in a drag race on a highway. As the two cars involved in the race were coming over a hill, the Rogers' (P) car came into sight. Race (D) attempted to swing his car back into the proper lane but he lost control of the car and it hit the Rogers' (P) car at about 70 miles per hour. The trial court awarded substantial damages in favor of the Rogers (P), holding both Race (D) and Bierczynski (D) jointly liable. Bierczynski's (D) car never actually hit the Rogers' (P) vehicle; thus, he appealed claiming he was not liable for any of the damage.

ISSUE: Is a defendant who participates in a motor race on a public highway wherein the car of the other participant strikes the car of the plaintiff, liable for the damages inflicted upon that third party?

HOLDING AND DECISION: (Herrmann, J.) Yes. A defendant who engages in a motor vehicle race on a public street is liable for the injury caused by the other participant to the plaintiff. In this instance even though Bierczynski (D) never came in contact with the Rogers' (P) car, he was engaged in the race and thus acted in concert to cause the injury to the Rogers (P). The reason for the rule is that it would be unfair to hold only one party liable if both caused the accident, for presumably the defendant who actually contacted the plaintiff might be insolvent. Further, it seems unfair to the defendant who actually collided to make him bear the entire brunt of the damages when the other individual was also responsible for the injuries. Affirmed.

▶ ANALYSIS

The case conforms to the mainstream of opinion that there need not be actual harm done by the party if that party is engaged in the activity which causes the harm. All that is necessary to be a joint tortfeasor is to have encouraged or aided in the harm-producing activity. Further, a tacit understanding, as in this case where two automobiles are in a speed competition, is enough to establish liability. However, the defendant must take some active part in the activity which causes the harm. Mere presence or knowledge of the conduct of another person which may cause harm is not enough to establish liability, for there is no duty for observers to take affirmative action to prevent a tort.

■≡■

Quicknotes

JOINT LIABILITY Liability owed to an injured party by two or more parties where each party has the right to insist that the other tortfeasors be joined to the matter.

JOINT TORTFEASORS Two or more parties that either act in concert, or whose individual acts combine to cause a single injury, rendering them jointly and severally liable for damages incurred.

NEGLIGENCE Conduct falling below the standard of care that a reasonable person would demonstrate under similar conditions.

■≡■

Coney v. J.L.G. Industries, Inc.

Decedent's administrator (P) v. Manufacturing company (D)

III. Sup. Ct., 97 III. 2d 104, 454 N.E. 2d 197 (1983).

NATURE OF CASE: Hearing on issue of law certified to the state supreme court in wrongful death action.

FACT SUMMARY: J.L.G. Industries (D) contended that joint and several liability no longer was applicable in a comparative negligence situation.

🏛 RULE OF LAW
The adoption of comparative negligence does not require the abolition of joint and several liability.

FACTS: Jasper was killed while using a product made by J.L.G. Industries (D). J.L.G. (D) contended that Jasper's employer was partially negligent, and that since Illinois had adopted comparative negligence, the doctrine of joint and several liability had also been abolished, and any judgment against it should be reduced by the percentage of fault attributable to the employer. This issue was certified for decision by the state supreme court.

ISSUE: Does the adoption of comparative negligence require the abolition of joint and several liability?

HOLDING AND DECISION: (Moran, J.) No. The adoption of comparative negligence does not require the abolition of joint and several liability. The effect of comparative negligence is to reduce a plaintiff's verdict by the amount of fault attributable to him. It has nothing to do with the relative faults of two or more defendants. The policy behind joint and several was, and still is, that a plaintiff should not bear the consequences of a judgment-proof defendant. Rather, it is the tortfeasor who should. To abolish joint and several liability would have the effect of reducing a plaintiff's recovery beyond the amount of fault attributable to him, and the adoption of comparative negligence did not contemplate this. Affirmed.

▌ ANALYSIS

The typical situation these days is for a plaintiff to sue all potential defendants and for the defendants to cross or third-party complain against each other. If for some reason a plaintiff elects not to proceed against all defendants, the potential defendants will probably be brought in by the existing defendants. As the case states, contributory or comparative negligence as a doctrine has little to do with this.

■■■

Quicknotes

COMPARATIVE NEGLIGENCE Doctrine whereby the court in assessing the appropriate measure of damages compares the relative fault of the parties and reduces the amount of damages to be collected by the plaintiff in proportion to his degree of fault.

JOINT AND SEVERAL LIABILITY Liability amongst tortfeasors allowing the injured party to bring suit against any of the defendants, individually or collectively, and to recover from each up to the total amount of damages awarded.

■■■

Bartlett v. New Mexico Welding Supply, Inc.

Accident victim (P) v. Other car's owner (D)

N.M. Ct. App., 98 N.M. 152, 646 P.2d 579 (1982).

NATURE OF CASE: Appeal of new trial order in action for damages for personal injury.

FACT SUMMARY: Bartlett (P) argued that joint and several liability should be applied in a pure comparative negligence jurisdiction.

🏛 RULE OF LAW
Joint and several liability will not be applied when pure comparative negligence is adopted.

FACTS: Bartlett (P) was injured in an accident with a vehicle under the control of New Mexico Welding (D). A third, unidentified vehicle was also involved. Bartlett (P) sued New Mexico Welding (D). The jury found Bartlett (P) nonnegligent and New Mexico Welding (D) 30 percent responsible. New Mexico was a pure comparative negligence state. Bartlett (P) argued that under joint and several liability, New Mexico Welding (D) should pay all damages. The trial court refused to enter judgment, but ordered a new trial. New Mexico Welding (D) sought an interlocutory appeal.

ISSUE: Will joint and several liability be applied when pure comparative negligence is adopted?

HOLDING AND DECISION: (Wood, J.) No. Joint and several liability will not be applied when pure comparative negligence is adopted. Pure comparative negligence is based on the notion that blame should be apportioned as it is found to exist. Joint and several liability is that the plaintiff should not bear the burden of an insolvent defendant. However, where there is only one defendant, the plaintiff bears this burden, and the court does not see why an additional defendant should change this. Here, the unidentified tortfeasor was 70 percent responsible, so New Mexico Welding should bear 30 percent of the damages. Reversed and remanded.

▶ ANALYSIS

Joint and several liability has been, in recent years, in the forefront of tort reform debate. Many have argued that it has constituted a strain on municipalities and the insurance industry. Proposals to abolish or modify the rule have been hotly debated in the public arena. Probably the best known attempt at reform was California's 1986 Proposition 51, a compromise which abolished joint and several liability for general damages only.

Quicknotes

INTERLOCUTORY APPEAL The appeal of an issue that does not resolve the disposition of the case, but is essential to a determination of the parties' legal rights.

Bundt v. Embro

Car passengers (P) v. Car owner/drivers (D)

N.Y. Sup. Ct., Queens Co., 48 Misc. 2d 802, 265 N.Y.S.2d 872 (1965).

NATURE OF CASE: Motion for leave to file amended answers in action for damages for personal injuries.

FACT SUMMARY: Bundt (P) and other plaintiffs had recovered against the State of New York for injuries resulting from an auto accident before suing Embro (D) and other defendants.

RULE OF LAW
When individuals are joint tortfeasors with the state, satisfaction from the state discharges the individuals.

FACTS: Two autos were involved in an accident. Various passengers sued the various owners and operators. Some of the defendants moved to amend their answers to include the defense of discharge when they learned that the plaintiffs had sued and recovered on the same accident against the state in the state court of claims.

ISSUE: When individuals are joint tortfeasors with the state, does satisfaction from the state discharge the individuals?

HOLDING AND DECISION: (Groat, J.) Yes. When individuals are joint tortfeasors with the state, satisfaction from the state discharges the individuals. While there can be many perpetrators of a wrongful act, there remains but one act, and there can be but one recovery therefor. Once a plaintiff has been fully compensated for the wrong, all other possible tortfeasors are discharged. The fact that it is the state that compensated for the wrong is of no consequence; in this situation, the state will be treated as would any tortfeasor. Motion granted.

ANALYSIS

The general rule discussed here, almost universally followed, is not an all-or-nothing proposition. It will sometimes happen that one of two or more joint tortfeasors will be able to pay only part of a judgment. When this occurs, the other joint tortfeasor will only be obligated to pay what the other did not. Also, where one party settles out of court before judgment, the settlement monies are credited against the judgment.

Quicknotes

JOINT TORTFEASORS Two or more parties that either act in concert, or whose individual acts combine to cause a single injury, rendering them jointly and severally liable for damages incurred.

PERSONAL INJURY Harm to an individual's person or body.

Cox v. Pearl Investment Co.

Injured party (P) v. Site's owner (D)

Colo. Sup. Ct., 168 Colo. 67, 450 P.2d 60 (1969).

NATURE OF CASE: Action to recover damages for negligence.

FACT SUMMARY: Cox (P) sought recovery against Pearl Investment Co. (D) which owned the property upon which she was injured. Pearl Investment (D) sought to be released from liability on the basis of the fact that Cox (P) had released from liability Goodwill Industries, the tenant of the property.

🏛 RULE OF LAW
Plaintiff does not relinquish his cause of action against a tortfeasor by releasing a joint tortfeasor, if the plaintiff expressly reserves the right to sue others who may be liable.

FACTS: Cox (P) was injured on property owned by Pearl Investment Co. (D) and leased by Goodwill Industries. Cox (P) had covenanted with Goodwill Industries to release it from liability beyond $2,500. In the covenant, Cox (P) expressly reserved the right to sue any other persons who might be liable for the damage. Indeed, Cox (P) sued Pearl Investment Co. (D). At trial, Pearl (D) moved for summary judgment on the basis of the common-law rule that a release of one tortfeasor releases all others who may have liability. The motion was granted by the trial court.

ISSUE: Does a plaintiff, who releases one of several joint tortfeasors from liability but has, in her release, expressly retained the right to recover from the other tortfeasors, relinquish the right to sue the tortfeasors who were not released?

HOLDING AND DECISION: (Hodges, J.) No. A plaintiff who expressly reserves the right to recover against the remaining tortfeasors does not relinquish the right to pursue an action against the nonreleased parties. In this case, the covenant between Goodwill and Cox (P) contained a clause expressing Cox's (P) desire to maintain her right to hold Pearl (D), the other tortfeasor, liable for the injuries. The reasons the court does not allow the covenant made with Goodwill to foreclose Cox's (P) cause of action against Pearl Investment (D) are these: (1) the principle of contract law is that the intentions manifested by the parties shall govern the situation; here the intention of Cox (P) was not to release her cause of action against Pearl Investment (D); (2) there is no danger of double compensation for the court can credit the judgment debtor, Pearl Investment (D), with the amount Cox (P) received from the party released; and (3) the non-settling tort-

feasor is not prejudiced by this rule, but rather benefitted, since he is entitled to have the judgment against him reduced by the amount paid by his co-tortfeasor. Reversed.

▶ ANALYSIS

The case is within the majority faction; until recently, most jurisdictions followed the common-law rule that if one tortfeasor, were released all stood released from liability. This rule was justly condemned and changed by all U.S. jurisdictions except two. The reason for this shift as discussed by Prosser is that the common-law rule placed the plaintiff in the untenable position of either forfeiting the partial compensation he could derive through settlement without suit or foregoing his entire claim against the other without full compensation. Although the release of one tortfeasor had no relation to the breach of the other's duty, the law nevertheless released him from liability.

■■■

Quicknotes

COVENANT A written promise to do, or to refrain from doing, a particular activity.

NEGLIGENCE Conduct falling below the standard of care that a reasonable person would demonstrate under similar conditions.

RELEASE The relinquishment of a claim against another party.

SUMMARY JUDGMENT Judgment rendered by a court in response to a motion by one of the parties, claiming that the lack of a question of material fact in respect to an issue warrants disposition of the issue without consideration by the jury.

TORTFEASOR Party that commits a tort or wrongful act.

■■■

Elbaor v. Smith

Malpractice victim (P) v. Physician (D)

Tex. Sup. Ct., 845 S.W.2d 240 (1992).

NATURE OF CASE: Appeal from verdict awarding damages for personal injury.

FACT SUMMARY: Smith (P) obtained a large judgment against Elbaor (D) after the other defendants had entered into a "Mary Carter" agreement with Smith (P).

🏛 RULE OF LAW
"Mary Carter" settlement agreements, whereby the settling defendant agrees to testify against any remaining defendants in exchange for an offset, are void as against public policy.

FACTS: Smith (P) sued doctors Elbaor (D), Syrquin (D), and Stephens (D) for medical malpractice. Syrquin (D) and Stephens (D) entered into a particular type of settlement agreement with Smith (P) known as the "Mary Carter" arrangement. In the agreement, Syrquin (D) and Stephens (D) guaranteed Smith (P) at least $425,010 if she did not recover that amount from Elbaor (D). Smith (P) agreed to pay them back the $425,010 out of any excess judgment recovered at trial from Elbaor (D). The case proceeded to trial, and Stephens (D) and Syrquin (D) "ganged up" on Elbaor (D). The jury found Elbaor (D) 88 percent responsible and returned a verdict against him of $1,872,848. Elbaor (D) appealed.

ISSUE: Are "Mary Carter" settlement agreements valid?

HOLDING AND DECISION: (Gonzalez, J.) No. "Mary Carter" settlement agreements are void. It is the policy of the law to promote settlements, because doing so promotes judicial economy. However, the "Mary Carter" agreement does just the opposite; it virtually guarantees a trial. Beyond this, it is antithetical to the quest for truth embodied by a trial because it fosters collusion between ostensibly opposing parties. Consequently, these sort of arrangements shall be deemed void as contrary to public policy. Reversed.

DISSENT: (Doggett, J.) The trial court correctly disclosed the existence of the "Mary Carter" agreements to the jury and otherwise took great care to safeguard the adversarial nature and fairness of the proceedings. So long as at least two parties with antagonistic interests remain—here, Smith (P) and Elbaor (D)—the search for truth is not diminished.

▍ANALYSIS

The "Mary Carter" agreement is often used when a "deep pocket," such as a governmental entity or large corporation, is a defendant. It depends, for its utility, on joint and several liability. Some states, like California, have either modified or done away with joint and several liability, which has resulted in less frequent use of "Mary Carters."

Quicknotes

COLLUSION An agreement between two or more parties to engage in unlawful conduct or in other activities with an unlawful goal, typically involving fraud.

JOINT AND SEVERAL LIABILITY Liability amongst tortfeasors allowing the injured party to bring suit against any of the defendants, individually or collectively, and to recover from each up to the total amount of damages awarded.

MARY CARTER AGREEMENT Agreement between plaintiff and defendants in multiparty litigation to pay a specified amount regardless of the jury's determination.

MEDICAL MALPRACTICE Conduct on the part of a doctor falling below that demonstrated by other doctors of ordinary skill and competency under the circumstances, resulting in damages.

Knell v. Feltman

Cab driver (P) v. Other car's driver (D)

174 F.2d 662 (D.C. Cir. 1949).

NATURE OF CASE: Action to recover damages for negligence and for contribution.

FACT SUMMARY: A guest passenger in Knell's (D) car was injured because of the negligence of Knell (D) and Feltman (P); Feltman (P) attempted to convince the court to make Knell (D) contribute to the payment of damages caused by his and Knell's (D) negligence.

🏛 RULE OF LAW
When a tort is committed by the concurrent negligence of two or more individuals who did not intentionally inflict injury, contribution should be required of the co-tortfeasor even though no joint judgment was obtained by the plaintiff himself.

FACTS: While riding as a passenger in Knell's (D) car, Langland was injured when it collided with Feltman's (P) taxi. Langland was a personal friend of Knell (D), and so she did not sue him; however, she did sue Feltman (P), who filed a third-party complaint against Knell (D) (making him a defendant and himself a plaintiff for purposes of this case) in an action to determine if Knell's (D) negligence was a sole or contributing factor in the causation of Langland's injuries.

ISSUE: If a tort is committed by two persons concurrently through negligence rather than intentionally, should contribution be awarded even though the plaintiff did not obtain a joint judgment?

HOLDING AND DECISION: (Miller, J.) Yes. When a tort is committed due to the concurrent negligence of two persons, contribution should be demanded of the co-tortfeasor, even though the plaintiff has not obtained a joint judgment to compensate for his injuries. In the present case, the injured party, Langland, did not file a complaint against Knell (D) because she was a personal acquaintance; thus, Langland did not obtain a joint judgment against both Knell (D) and Feltman (P). However, Feltman (P) brought Knell (D) into the action through means of a third-party complaint so that the jury was able to determine that his negligence was one source of Langland's injuries. Hence, it is clear that Knell (D) is liable for the injuries. To allow the injured party (Langland) to select who should foot the bill would be unfair to the defendant who is burdened with the total payment. To allow this situation the law would be a party to collusion between the plaintiff and a tortfeasor. Affirmed.

▶ ANALYSIS

There is a split among state jurisdictions on this question of whether to allow contribution among joint tortfeasors. The common-law rule does not allow contribution. Twenty-two states currently adhere to the common-law rule. Seven states allow contribution only between those defendants against whom a joint judgment has been obtained. Sixteen permit contribution from a joint tortfeasor whether joined as a defendant or not and apportion the damages equally. Five permit contribution from a joint tortfeasor whether joined or not and divide damages according to relative degrees of fault.

Quicknotes

CONCURRENT NEGLIGENCE Where the negligence of two independent actors result in a single injury.

CONTRIBUTION The right of a person or party who has compensated a victim for his injury to seek reimbursement from others who are equally responsible for the injury in proportional amounts.

JOINT TORTFEASORS Two or more parties that either act in concert, or whose individual acts combine to cause a single injury, rendering them jointly and severally liable for damages incurred.

Yellow Cab Co. of D.C., Inc. v. Dreslin

Cab company (D) v. Other car driver and passengers (P)

181 F.2d 626 (D.C. Cir. 1950).

NATURE OF CASE: Action to recover damages for negligence and for contribution.

FACT SUMMARY: Mrs. Dreslin (P) was injured in a crash of two motor vehicles caused by the negligence of her husband (D) and Yellow Cab Co. (D).

🏛 RULE OF LAW
Since neither husband nor wife is liable for the torts perpetrated against the other, the spouse cannot he held on contribution theory to pay damages for injury to the other spouse because, in order for a right of contribution to exist, there must be coexistent liability.

FACTS: Mrs. Dreslin (P) was injured as a result of the negligence of both her husband (D) and the Yellow Cab Co. (D in relation to Mrs. Dreslin and P in relation to Mr. Dreslin). Mrs. Dreslin (P) sued Yellow Cab Co. (D), and Yellow Cab (as P) cross-claimed against Mr. Dreslin (D) for contribution for any sums recovered by the plaintiffs against it.

ISSUE: Assuming the jurisdiction is one in which there is interspousal tort immunity, can one spouse be required to contribute to the co-tortfeasor for the damages recovered against that tortfeasor by the spouse?

HOLDING AND DECISION: (Proctor, J.) No. Due to the application of the doctrine of interspousal tort immunity, there is no liability on the part of the spouse-tortfeasor; hence, because there is no liability, there can be no right of contribution. The purpose of the immunity doctrine is to preserve the domestic peace; if the co-tortfeasor could extract damages indirectly through the contribution doctrine, the purpose of shielding spouses from liability for torts committed against the other spouse would be destroyed. Affirmed.

▌ANALYSIS

The case falls within the prevailing view that the contribution defendant must be liable for the plaintiff who sustained injuries. If there was never any liability, as in a case of interfamilial immunity, assumption of the risk, contributory negligence, guest statute, or some other doctrine which nullifies the contribution defendant's liability to the plaintiff, then he is not liable for contribution. The statutes dealing with contribution also follow this principle. The case conforms to the modern view of contribution which many states have codified in statutes. The statutes generally al-

low contribution in cases of negligence but not in cases of intentional injury. Generally, liability is divided among tortfeasors on a pro rata share; however, some jurisdictions apportion liability on the basis of comparative fault. In the situation where a plaintiff gives a release or covenant not to sue to one defendant, that defendant is usually required to contribute his pro rata share later.

Quicknotes

ASSUMPTION OF RISK DOCTRINE An affirmative defense to a negligence suit contending that the plaintiff knowingly and voluntarily subjected himself to a hazardous condition absolving the defendant of liability for injuries incurred.

CONTRIBUTION The right of a person or party who has compensated a victim for his injury to seek reimbursement from others who are equally responsible for the injury in proportional amounts.

CONTRIBUTORY NEGLIGENCE Behavior on the part of an injured plaintiff that combines with the defendant's negligence, resulting in injury to the plaintiff.

GUEST STATUTE A state statute requiring a specified level of culpability, usually more than mere negligence, on the part of the driver of an automobile in order for the owner/driver to be liable for injuries resulting to a gratuitous passenger.

INTERSPOUSAL IMMUNITY A common law doctrine precluding spouses from commencing actions against one another. Some states have abolished the doctrine.

NEGLIGENCE Conduct falling below the standard of care that a reasonable person would demonstrate under similar conditions.

PRO RATA In proportion.

TORTFEASOR Party that commits a tort or wrongful act.

Slocum v. Donahue

Parents (P) v. Driver (D)

Mass. Ct. of App., 44 Mass. App. Ct. 937, 693 N.E.2d 179 (1998).

NATURE OF CASE: Vehicular homicide proceeding.

FACT SUMMARY: Donahue (D) sought indemnity and contribution from Ford, claiming Ford was negligent and in breach of the warranties of merchantability and fitness for a particular purpose, causing his automobile to accelerate and resulting in the death of the Slocum's (P) eighteen-month-old son.

🏛 RULE OF LAW
When a release is given in good faith to one of two or more persons liable in tort for the same injury, it discharges the tortfeasor to whom it is granted from all liability for contribution to the other tortfeasor.

FACTS: Donahue (D) pled guilty to a motor vehicle homicide in which he killed the Slocum's (P) eighteen-month-old son. The Slocums (P) filed suit against Donahue (D) alleging negligence and gross negligence. Donahue (D) filed a third-party complaint against Ford denying negligence and seeking contribution and indemnity, alleging Ford was negligent and in breach of its warranties of merchantability and fitness for a particular use. Donahue (D) claimed that when he started to back the car out of the driveway, the engine raced and the car continued to accelerate even though he stepped on the brakes. The car's rear wheels hit the curb across the street, causing the car to become airborne, hitting a fence. When Donahue (D) got out of the car he found Todd Slocum lying on the lawn. Donahue's (D) expert testified the floor mat of the car was defective, causing it to interfere with the operation of the brakes. Prior to trial the Slocums (P) and Ford entered a settlement agreement providing Ford would pay them $150,000 in exchange for release of any claim. Ford moved for summary judgment as to Donahue's (D) claims stating that there was no basis for Donahue's (D) indemnity claims. Donahue (D) appealed from a final judgment dismissing his claims against Ford.

ISSUE: When a release is given in good faith to one of two or more persons liable in tort for the same injury, does it discharge the tortfeasor to whom it is granted from all liability for contribution to the other tortfeasor?

HOLDING AND DECISION: (No judge listed.) Yes. When a release is given in good faith to one of two or more persons liable in tort for the same injury, it discharges the tortfeasor to whom it is granted from all liability for contribution to the other tortfeasor. The Donahues (D) argued that

the settlement was not made in good faith and was collusive because the settlement amount was far less than the value of the case and Ford offered the Slocums (P) the use of their experts. Facts were introduced showing the settlement was fair and reasonable. Here there was a high likelihood that a jury would find Donahue (D) liable due to his admission of liability and in light of the fact that he was drinking from a bottle of vodka in a brown paper bag under the driver's seat. Here there was no indication of bad faith or collusion in the settlement negotiations. Nor is there evidence that the Slocums (P) use of experts originally retained by Ford was collusive. Nor did the trial court err on the issue of indemnification. Indemnity allows a party without fault to recover from the tortfeasor the amount of his loss, with reasonable attorney's fees. Indemnity is allowed only when the party seeking indemnity is not responsible for the negligent conduct and where the indemnitee is held vicariously liable for the acts of the tortfeasor. Here indemnity would not have been appropriate since the jury found Donahue solely negligent and his liability was not vicarious. The motion for summary judgment was properly allowed. Affirmed.

▶ ANALYSIS

In addition to its substantive rulings on contribution and indemnity, *Slocum* illustrates a cardinal principle for all practicing attorneys and their clients: Settlement gives parties an opportunity to control their own destinies in litigation without incurring the extraordinary risk of allowing other persons to impose outcomes upon the parties. Here, the court politely understates the obvious by finding it "reasonably predictable" that the criminally liable Donahue (D) would be found civilly liable if the case proceeded to trial. The trial, of course, bore out that predictability, with the jury returning a verdict against Donahue (D). Based on the casebook excerpt, Donahue (D) proceeded to trial because he saw no way to make a $25,000 payment for his share of a proposed settlement. After trial, with third-party defendant Ford now out of the case after making a $150,000 payment to the Slocums (P), Donahue (D) himself presumably would have been liable for a verdict for much more than the $25,000 portion he originally thought he could not pay; even if the jury awarded the Slocums (P) only the amount of their original settlement offer ($400,000), Donahue (D) himself would have had to pay $275,000 to the Slocums (P) after applying his insurance provider's maximum benefit of $125,000. Much of the time, as here, stubbornness actually does not advance a client's best interests.

Bruckman v. Pena

Auto accident victim (P) v. Truck driver (D) and owner (D)

Colo. Ct. App., 29 Colo. App. 357, 487 P.2d 566 (1971).

NATURE OF CASE: Action for personal injuries.

FACT SUMMARY: Pena (P) was first injured in an auto accident with Bruckman (D) and then later had his injuries aggravated in another accident with another party.

🏛 RULE OF LAW
It is error for a court to instruct that a plaintiff may recover damages for injuries received subsequent to any act of negligence by the defendant and from causes for which the defendant is in no way responsible.

FACTS: Pena (P) was injured on July 21, 1964, in an auto accident as a result of Bruckman's (D) negligence. Armored (D) owned the truck driven by Bruckman (D). On June 11, 1965, his injuries were aggravated in another accident in which Bruckman (D) was in no way involved. Pena (P) filed this action against Bruckman (D) and Armored (D). At the close of evidence, the court instructed the jury that it was their duty to apportion the damages caused to Pena (P) between Bruckman (D), Armored (D), and the subsequent tortfeasor. In addition, the court further instructed the jury "if you find the evidence does not permit such an apportionment, then the defendants are liable for the entire disability." The jury returned judgment for Pena (P) in the amount of $50,000. Bruckman (D) and Armored (D) challenged the quoted instruction on appeal.

ISSUE: Is it error to instruct a jury that they may hold one defendant liable for all injuries caused to a tort plaintiff if they (the jury) are unable to apportion such injuries between that defendant and a subsequent tortfeasor who aggravated the plaintiff's injuries?

HOLDING AND DECISION: (Dwyer, J.) Yes. As a general rule, the burden of proof is on the plaintiff in a personal injury case to establish that the damages he seeks were proximately caused by the negligence of the defendant; and, as such, it is error for a court to instruct that a plaintiff may recover any damages for injuries received subsequent to the act of negligence by the defendant and from causes for which the defendant is in no way responsible—regardless of the difficulty of apportioning the plaintiff's total damages between the defendant's acts and the acts of any subsequent tortfeasor who may have aggravated plaintiff's original injuries. It is true that where subsequent trauma aggravates a preexisting diseased condition, the tortfeasor causing the trauma will be liable for the total injuries caused. The reverse is not true,

however, as Pena (P) would have us believe here, since no causation link between prior negligence and subsequent injuries can be established. Reversed.

▶ ANALYSIS

This case points up the connection between the rules of causation and the apportionment of tort damages. Only damages proximately caused by a tortfeasor may be assigned to him. Note that it has been held that a jury apportionment will be upheld as long as there is "some evidence to sustain the apportionment made, even though, due to circumstances of the particular case, the proofs do not attain the degree of precision which would make possible an exact dividing line between the injuries." *McAllister v. Pennsylvania*, 324 Pa. 65 (1936).

Quicknotes

APPORTIONMENT OF DAMAGES The allocation of damages between two parties typically in ratio to their respective fault or risk.

CAUSATION The aggregate effect of preceding events that bring about a tortious result; the causal connection between the actions of a tortfeasor and the injury that follows.

NEGLIGENCE Conduct falling below the standard of care that a reasonable person would demonstrate under similar conditions.

PERSONAL INJURY Harm to an individual's person or body.

Michie v. Great Lakes Steel Division, Nat'l Steel Corp.

Canadian residents (P) v. American polluters (D)

495 F.2d 213 (6th Cir. 1974).

NATURE OF CASE: Action for nuisance damages.

FACT SUMMARY: Michie (P) and others (P) filed a nuisance action against three corporate defendants alleging damages from air pollution.

🏛 RULE OF LAW
Individual tortfeasors may be held jointly and severally liable even though their tortious acts were wholly independent of one another.

FACTS: Michie (P) and 36 other Canadian residents (P) filed this federal diversity nuisance action against three American corporations operating plants across the Detroit River in Michigan, of which Great Lakes Steel (D) was only one. Each of the Canadians (P) claimed between $11,000 and $35,000 in individual damages as a result of the pollution which the three American corporations had discharged into the air. Because the harm separately caused by the three corporations is admittedly indivisible, Great Lakes (D) moved to have the complaint dismissed on the ground that it failed to allege the $10,000 federal diversity minimum damages against any one of the three corporations. This appeal followed on the question of whether the parties could be jointly and severally liable (permitting an aggregation of the claims against them).

ISSUE: May individual tortfeasors be jointly and severally liable even though their tortious acts were wholly independent of one another?

HOLDING AND DECISION: (Edwards, J.) Yes. Individual tortfeasors may be held jointly and severally liable even though their tortious acts were wholly independent of one another. Where harm caused by multiple tortfeasors is individual, there is a manifest unfairness in putting the impossible burden of proving the specific shares of harm done by each upon the shoulders of the injured party. It is true that this theory has not heretofore been applied to nuisance cases, at least not in Michigan (the controlling law state). Yet, recent Michigan cases clearly indicate a policy toward shifting the burden of assigning relative harm to all multiple tortfeasors. As such, Michie (P) et al. have met the $10,000 requirement by their aggregate claim against all three corporations. Affirmed.

▶ ANALYSIS

This case points up the clear trend of modern authority toward apportioning relative liability for indivisible injuries caused by independent multiple tortfeasors. Indeed, it is the majority rule today. Prosser explains the rule as a function of simple expediency, when apportionment cannot be rationally made. Note that it is also consistent with the basic rationale of all tort law, i.e., the equitable distribution of losses from civil wrongs, since permitting the wrongdoers to escape liability would be clearly inequitable. This court is correct, however, in characterizing the application of this rule to nuisance liability as unusual. Most courts will hold polluters liable only for injuries particularly shown to have been individually caused.

Quicknotes

DIVERSITY The authority of a federal court to hear and determine cases involving $10,000 or more and in which the parties are citizens of different states, or in which one party is an alien.

EQUITABLE DISTRIBUTION The means by which a court distributes all assets acquired during a marriage by the spouses equitably upon dissolution.

JOINT AND SEVERAL LIABILITY Liability amongst tortfeasors allowing the injured party to bring suit against any of the defendants, individually or collectively, and to recover from each up to the total amount of damages awarded.

Dillon v. Twin State Gas & Electric Co.

Estate administrator (P) v. Gas company (D)

N.H. Sup. Ct., 85 N.H. 449, 163 A. 111 (1932).

NATURE OF CASE: Suit to recover damages for a wrongful death action.

FACT SUMMARY: Decedent, a fourteen-year-old boy, was sitting on the beam of a public bridge and lost his balance; to save himself from falling to certain death or severe injury, the decedent grabbed one of the wires belonging to the Electric Co. (D), thus electrocuting himself before he could fall to his death.

🏛 RULE OF LAW
Damage may be apportioned in a seemingly indivisible injury if a potential danger from one source has diminished the value of the loss actually inflicted.

FACTS: The Electric Co. (D) maintained aerial wires over the bridge upon which the decedent stood. As he leaned over while he was sitting on one of the girders of the bridge, he lost his balance. In order to save himself from falling downward to an almost certain death, the boy reached out and got hold of one of the wires owned by the Electric Co. (D). Thus, he was electrocuted prior to his fall.

ISSUE: Should the court consider, in determining damages, the value of the object or person harmed in relation to potential harms which may reduce its or his value?

HOLDING AND DECISION: (Allen, J.) Yes. The court holds that the damages for wrongful death, generally considered an indivisible harm, should be apportioned because of the potential harm which clearly diminished the value of the young man's life. The court considers heavily the fact that the boy's life was in effect almost valueless because, but for the wires, he would have been killed or crippled for life. Thus, the Electric Co. (D) should only be liable for the loss of earning capacity of the boy in an injured condition if it were determined that severe injury crippling the young man would have resulted; or if death was determined to be the result of the fall then the Electric Co. (D) should be relieved of paying damages for lost earning capacity and be only responsible for damages sustained as a result of conscious shock, which the boy felt.

▶ *ANALYSIS*
The analysis utilized by the judge in this opinion is unusual. The closest analogy to this reasoning wherein the plaintiff's injuries are assigned a value according to the possibility of other harms is when damages are awarded on the basis of prior events in a wrongful death action which may limit the plaintiff's life expectancy and correspondingly restrict the value of the plaintiff's life.

Quicknotes

APPORTIONMENT OF DAMAGES The allocation of damages between two parties typically in ratio to their respective fault or risk.

WRONGFUL DEATH An action brought by the beneficiaries of a deceased person, claiming that the deceased's death was the result of wrongful conduct by the defendant.

Quick Reference Rules of Law

Winterbottom v. Wright

Mail coach driver (P) v. Breaching coach repairer (D)

Exchequer of Pleas, 10 M. & W. 109, 152 Eng. Rep. 402 (1842).

NATURE OF CASE: Action for damages based on negligence.

FACT SUMMARY: Winterbottom (P) was injured while driving a defective mail coach which the government had bought from Wright (D) pursuant to a supply-maintenance contract.

🏛 RULE OF LAW
A contracting party, unless he has undertaken a public duty, has no liability to third parties who are injured as a result of a breach of the contract.

FACTS: Wright (D) agreed to supply and maintain mail coaches for the use of the Postmaster General. Atkinson also had a contract with the Postmaster General to supply horses and coachmen to operate the mail coaches. Winterbottom (P), one of Atkinson's coachmen, was injured when one of the coaches supplied by Wright (D) broke down. Winterbottom (P) brought suit against Wright (D), contending that his injuries were the result of Wright's (D) negligent performance of the contract with the Postmaster General.

ISSUE: Is a contracting party who has not undertaken a public duty liable to third persons who are injured as a result of a breach of the contract?

HOLDING AND DECISION: (Lord Abinger, J.) No. Parties to a contract are liable only to each other for breaches of the contract, unless the duty undertaken was to the public. Third parties have no privity with respect to the contract and, therefore, may not sue either party to the contract. If such an action were permitted, contracting parties would be exposed to a potentially unlimited number of suits by strangers to the contract, even in the situation where the breach has been excused or waived. Winterbottom (P) was not privy to the contract between the Postmaster General and Wright (D), and, therefore, may not maintain an action against him.

CONCURRENCE: (Alderson, J.) If we were to hold that the plaintiff could sue in this case, there is no point at which such actions would stop. The only safe rule is to confine the right to recover to those who enter into the contract.

CONCURRENCE: (Rolfe, J.) "This is one of those unfortunate cases in which there has been damnum [wrong], but it is damnum absque [without] injuria [injury]; it is, no doubt, a hardship upon the plaintiff to be without a remedy, but by that consideration we ought not to be influenced."

▶ ANALYSIS

The harsh Winterbottom decision was followed by the majority of courts in the United States during the second half of the 19th century, but a number of exceptions developed. The New York court in *Thomas v. Winchester*, 6 N.Y. 397, allowed a negligence action, by a woman who was poisoned, against a chemist who had sold the falsely labeled poison to her druggist. The court's rationale was that the poison was an "imminently dangerous" article, while the defective mail coach in Winterbottom was not. Other applications of the "imminently dangerous" exception proved difficult, however, and the New York court in *MacPherson v. Buick Motor Co.*, 217 N.Y. 382 (1916), finally formulated a general rule of liability of remote manufacturers which eliminated privity as a requirement.

■━■

Quicknotes

BREACH OF CONTRACT Unlawful failure by a party to perform its obligations pursuant to contract.

DAMNUM ABSQUI INJURIA When an injury is sustained but the law affords no means of recovery.

NEGLIGENCE Conduct falling below the standard of care that a reasonable person would demonstrate under similar conditions.

PRIVITY OF CONTRACT A relationship between the parties to a contract that is required in order to bring an action for breach.

■━■

MacPherson v. Buick Motor Co. (I)

Injured automobile owner (P) v. Car manufacturer (D)

N.Y. Ct. of App., 217 N.Y. 382, 111 N.E. 1050 (1916).

NATURE OF CASE: Negligence action.

FACT SUMMARY: MacPherson (P) sued Buick (D) for injuries sustained when a defective wheel in the automobile he purchased collapsed.

🏛 RULE OF LAW
A manufacturer breaches a duty of care to a foreseeable user of its product if the product was likely to cause an injury if negligently made and it places the product on the market without conducting a reasonable inspection.

FACTS: Buick (D), an automobile manufacturer, sold a car to a retail dealer who in turn sold it to MacPherson (P). While MacPherson (P) was in the car it suddenly collapsed due to the wheel being made out of defective wood. While the wheel was not manufactured by Buick (D), there was evidence that a reasonable inspection would have revealed the defects. The supreme court held in favor of MacPherson and the appellate division affirmed. Buick (D) appealed.

ISSUE: Does a manufacturer breach a duty of care to a foreseeable user of its product if the product was likely to cause an injury if negligently made and it places the product on the market without conducting a reasonable inspection?

HOLDING AND DECISION: (Cardozo, J.) Yes. A manufacturer breaches a duty of care to a foreseeable user of its product if the product was likely to cause an injury if negligently made and it places the product on the market without conducting a reasonable inspection. A product is dangerous if it is reasonably certain to place life and limb in peril when negligently made. If the manufacturer knows the item will be used by person other than the purchaser, he is under a duty to manufacture the item carefully. There must be knowledge of a probable danger and that the danger will be borne by others in addition to the buyer in the normal course of events. The proximity or remoteness of the transaction is also to be considered. If the manufacturer of a finished product places it on the market without inspection, then mobility will attach. Buick (D) was not relieved from its duty to inspect because it bought the wheels from a reputable manufacturer. Buick (D) had a duty to inspect the component parts of its automobiles before placing them on the market. Affirmed.

▶ ANALYSIS

There was a traditional distinction between cases involving nonfeasance and misfeasance. Nonfeasance was actionable under contract law and resulted where there was a promise and a subsequent breach of that promise. Misfeasance was actionable in tort and existed when the defendant attempted to perform a contract and did so in error.

Quicknotes

DUTY OF CARE A principle of negligence requiring an individual to act in such a manner as to avoid injury to a person to whom he or she owes an obligatory duty.

MISFEASANCE The commission of a lawful act in a wrongful manner.

NEGLIGENCE Conduct falling below the standard of care that a reasonable person would demonstrate under similar conditions.

NONFEASANCE The omission, or failure to perform, an obligation.

H. R. Moch Co. v. Rensselaer Water Co.

Warehouse owner (P) v. Waterworks company (D)

N.Y. Ct. App., 247 N.Y. 160, 159 N.E. 896 (1928).

NATURE OF CASE: Action to recover damages for negligence.

FACT SUMMARY: Rensselaer Water Co. (D) made a contract with a city to supply water. Moch's (P) building caught fire. Water was not supplied, and the building burned.

RULE OF LAW
A water company that contracts with a city to supply water is not liable to a citizen whose house burns when water service fails.

FACTS: Rensselaer Water Co. (D) made a contract with a city to supply water. Water service to fire hydrants and private citizens was included in the contract. During the term of this contract a fire from a nearby building spread to Moch's (P) warehouse, destroying it and its contents. Moch (P) alleged that Rensselaer Water Co. (D) was promptly notified of the fire, but failed to supply water and as a result of this failure, Moch's (P) building was destroyed.

ISSUE: Does a private citizen have an action against a water company that has contracted with the citizen's city to supply the city with water and did not do so, thus causing the citizen harm?

HOLDING AND DECISION: (Cardozo, C.J.) No. The water company's (D) performance on the contract did not bring it into such relation with each citizen that its failure to continue performance without reasonable notice was a tort. The court defined nonfeasance as inaction at the stage of a contract when the inaction is merely the withholding of a benefit. Misfeasance can be inaction also, but the conduct must have gone so far that inaction would result in injury. If inaction is found to be misfeasance, there exists a relation out of which arises a duty to go forward. The court decided here that Rensselaer Water Co.'s (D) failure to supply the water was nonfeasance. Hence, there was no relation, no duty, and no liability. To support its decision the court cites a parade of horribles which would occur if liability were allowed. Coal dealers and manufacturers would be liable if their supply ran low, and anyone making a contract would be held to have a duty to an indefinite number of potential beneficiaries once performance had begun. Affirmed.

▶ ANALYSIS

This case represents the prevailing rule which has been criticized but is followed in all but a few states. The rationale for the rule is that to hold the water company (D) liable would place an undue burden on the company. Prosser states that the following three arguments demolish the decisions. First, the water company has commenced performance and supplied water, so its failure to continue to supply is misfeasance, not nonfeasance. Second, its performance gives it the status of a public utility and a relation with individual members of the public. This relation imposes a duty. Third, by commencing performance it has induced the city and its citizens to rely upon it and to forego other protection.

Quicknotes

MISFEASANCE The commission of a lawful act in a wrongful manner.

NEGLIGENCE Conduct falling below the standard of care that a reasonable person would demonstrate under similar conditions.

NONFEASANCE The omission, or failure to perform, an obligation.

PUBLIC UTILITY A private business that provides a service to the public which is of need.

RELIANCE Dependence on a fact that causes a party to act or refrain from acting.

Clagett v. Dacy

High bidder (P) v. Attorney (D)

Md. Ct. Spec. App., 47 Md. App. 23, 420 A.2d 1285 (1980).

NATURE OF CASE: Appeal from grant of demurrer in malpractice action.

FACT SUMMARY: Dacy (D), an attorney conducting a foreclosure sale, was sued for malpractice by the high bidder at the sale.

RULE OF LAW
In the absence of an underlying contractual attorney-client relationship, an attorney owes no duty of care to a third party.

FACTS: Dacy (D), an attorney, was employed by a mortgagee of land to conduct a foreclosure sale. Because he failed to follow the proper procedures, the sale was set aside on two separate occasions. The resulting delay permitted the mortgage debtor to discharge the loan and thus redeem the property. Clagett (P), the high bidder at the invalidated sales, sued Dacy (D) for malpractice, alleging that his incompetence deprived Clagett (P) of the opportunity to purchase the land and realize a profit on resale. Dacy (D) demurred on the ground that he owed no duty of care toward Clagett (P) and thus could not be negligent. The trial court granted the demurrer. Clagett (P) appealed.

ISSUE: May an attorney owe a duty to a third party where there is no underlying contractual attorney-client relationship?

HOLDING AND DECISION: (Wilner, J.) No. Recently the rule requiring strict privity between the parties in an attorney malpractice action has been relaxed to a modest degree. It is now possible for a third party, not privy to the contract between the attorney and client, to sue for malpractice, where that party is a third party beneficiary to the employment contract. Thus, the beneficiary of a will may sue an attorney, employed by the testator, who negligently drafted the instrument. However, some underlying contractual attorney-client relationship is still required before a duty of care will be imposed as regards a third party. In the instant case, Clagett (P), as a bidder on the foreclosed property, can hardly be deemed a third-party beneficiary to the contract between Dacy (D) and the mortgagee. Dacy (D) was not charged with looking after Clagett's (P) interests. In fact, the opposite was true. As an attorney for the mortgagee, Dacy (D) was seeking the highest price possible for the land. Clagett (D) was interested in obtaining the lowest possible price. Obviously, their interests were antagonistic, rather than mutually dependent. Affirmed.

ANALYSIS

The case of *Donald v. Garry*, 19 Cal. App. 3d 769 (1971), cited by the *Clagett* court, held that "an attorney may be liable for damages caused by his negligence to a person intended to be benefitted by his performance irrespective of any lack of privity of contract between the attorney and the party to be benefitted." The *Clagett* court declined to interpret the case as advocating a broad right to sue for attorney malpractice and instead read it as merely requiring the elements of a third party beneficiary to be shown.

Quicknotes

DEMURRER The assertion that the opposing party's pleadings are insufficient and that the demurring party should not be made to answer.

DUTY OF CARE A principle of negligence requiring an individual to act in such a manner as to avoid injury to a person to whom he or she owes an obligatory duty.

FORECLOSURE An action to recover the amount due on a mortgage of real property where the owner has failed to pay their debt, terminating the owner's interest in the property which must then be sold to satisfy the debt.

PRIVITY OF CONTRACT A relationship between the parties to a contract that is required in order to bring an action for breach.

Hegel v. Langsam

Student's parents (P) v. University

Ohio Ct. of Common Pleas, 273 N.E.2d 351 (1971).

NATURE OF CASE: Action for negligence damages.

FACT SUMMARY: Hegel's (P) daughter became a drug user and associated with criminals while a student at the University of Chicago.

> 🏛 **RULE OF LAW**
> Colleges and universities are under no affirmative duty to regulate the private lives of their students.

FACTS: Hegel's (P) seventeen-year-old daughter was enrolled as a freshman at the University of Chicago and assigned to a dormitory. During her freshman year, the University exercised no control over her comings and goings at the dormitory. She began staying away from it, soon became associated with Chicago's criminal element, was seduced, and became a drug user. Her parents demanded that the University return her to them but school officials could not. This action was soon thereafter filed against the University (D) by the Hegels (P) alleging that the school's negligent failure to perform supervisory duties had resulted in the damage to the Hegel's (P) daughter. The University (D) thereupon made a motion for judgment (in their favor) on the pleadings.

ISSUE: Are colleges and universities under any affirmative duty to control the activities of their students so as to protect them from getting into trouble?

HOLDING AND DECISION: (Bettman, J.) No. Colleges and universities are under no affirmative duty to regulate the private lives of their students. A university is an institution of learning—nothing more. It is neither a nursery school, boarding school, nor prison. No one is required to attend and the school is under no duty to require attendance. It is presumed that anyone enrolled in such an institution will have the necessary maturity to take care of himself or herself without the school being forced to supervise them. As such, no duty to do so is imposed upon the school. Since there can be no negligence recovery without some duty, the motion for judgment against Hegel (P) on the pleadings is affirmed.

▶ ANALYSIS

This case points up recognition of the demise of the "in loco parentis" principle for the administration of institutions of higher education. Indeed, the current trend of authority is to wholly absolve such schools of any actionable duty to its students as students (e.g., no duty to supervise private affairs, provide courses of true educational value, etc.). Note

that the court in *Hegel* wholly disregards the question of whether the school's (D) state status (as a governmental unit) should have any bearing upon its relative legal responsibilities to its students. As such, it appears that the court has adopted a virtual "hands-off" policy on university responsibility questions.

■■■

Quicknotes

AFFIRMATIVE DUTY An obligation to undertake an affirmative action for the benefit of another.

IN LOCO PARENTIS A situation in which a person has assumed the responsibilities and obligations of a lawful parent without undergoing the legal adoption process.

JUDGMENT ON THE PLEADINGS Motion for judgment after the pleadings are closed.

NEGLIGENCE Conduct falling below the standard of care that a reasonable person would demonstrate under similar conditions.

■■■

L.S. Ayres & Co. v. Hicks

Escalator victim (P) v. Store (D)

Ind. Sup. Ct., 40 N.E.2d 334 (1942).

NATURE OF CASE: Motion for new trial in action for damages.

FACT SUMMARY: Hicks (P) fell and got his fingers caught in an escalator; Ayres (D) store unreasonably delayed in stopping the escalator.

> ## RULE OF LAW
> One who is an invitor or has control of an instrumentality that causes injury has a legal obligation to take affirmative steps to rescue a person who is helpless or in a situation of peril. The invitor or one who has control of an instrumentality has the legal obligation to aid a helpless person, even if he did not cause the original situation that the helpless person finds himself in.

FACTS: Hicks (P), a six-year-old boy, went with his mother to go shopping at Ayres (D) department store. Hicks (P) fell on the escalator in Ayres (D) store and as a result, he got his fingers caught in the escalator. Ayres (D) did not immediately stop the escalator but kept it running and as a result Hicks (P) was hurt severely. After an unreasonable time, Ayres (D) did stop the escalator. It was found liable and moved for a new trial.

ISSUE: Does one who has control of an instrumentality that causes harm to another have a legal duty to rescue him from the instrumentality?

HOLDING AND DECISION: (Shake, C.J.) Yes. An invitor or one who has control of an instrumentality that causes harm to another has a legal duty to rescue that other person, even if he is not negligent. The mere occurrence of this type of accident creates a relation that gives rise to a legal duty to aid the injured person. Thus, it is irrelevant whether the injured person was contributorily negligent or whether his potential rescuer was negligent or legally responsible for the original injury. Here Ayres (D) was an invitor and had control of the instrumentality causing harm, it had a duty to affirmatively act and to exercise reasonable care to avoid aggravation of the injury. However, Hicks (P) is entitled to recover only for the injuries that resulted when Ayres (D) had the duty to act but failed to do so for an unreasonable time. Reversed. Motion for new trial granted.

▶ ANALYSIS

This case is an exception to the general rule that one has no duty to rescue another unless he caused the predicament. Other exceptions to the rule, accepted in some jurisdictions, include the following situations: where a seaman falls overboard; where an employer can save a helpless employee; carrier and passenger; innkeeper and guest; jailer and prisoner; where one assumes the care of another, e.g., schoolteacher and pupil; and landowner and business visitor, on premises open to the public as in this case.

Quicknotes

CONTRIBUTORY NEGLIGENCE Behavior on the part of an injured plaintiff falling below the standard of ordinary care that contributes to the defendant's negligence, resulting in the plaintiff's injury.

DUTY TO RESCUE The duty to take some action to assist another in danger; such a duty is only imposed under certain circumstances.

INVITOR An individual that induces another to enter upon his property.

REASONABLE CARE The degree of care observed by a reasonably prudent person under similar circumstances; synonymous with due care or ordinary care.

J.S. and M.S. v. R.T.H.

Parents (P) v. Abuser (D)

N.J. Sup. Ct., 155 N.J. 330, 714 A.2d 924 (1998).

NATURE OF CASE: Suit for damages resulting from child abuse.

FACT SUMMARY: The parents of two girls brought suit against their neighbor and his wife, seeking damages based on his sexual abuse of their daughters.

> 🏛 **RULE OF LAW**
> When a spouse has actual knowledge or special reason to know of the likelihood that his or her spouse is engaging in sexually abusive behavior against a particular person, the spouse has a duty of care to take reasonable steps to prevent or warn of the harm and a breach of that duty constitutes a proximate cause of the resultant sexual abuse of the victim.

FACTS: Two young girls spent substantial period of time with their neighbor at his horse barn. The man, R.T.H. (D), sexually abused the girls. The girls' parents (P) brought suit against the man and his wife (D) for damages, arguing that the wife's (D) negligence rendered her liable for their injuries as well. In an amended answer, the wife (D) argued that she owed no duty of care to the plaintiffs, that any alleged negligence on her part was not the proximate cause of the injuries and that any damages were the result of a third party whose actions were beyond her control. The trial court entered summary judgment for the wife (D) and the appellate division reversed and remanded. The wife (D) appealed.

ISSUE: When a spouse has actual knowledge or special reason to know of the likelihood that his or her spouse is engaging in sexually abusive behavior against a particular person, does the spouse have a duty of care to take reasonable steps to prevent or warn of the harm and does a breach of that duty constitute a proximate cause of the resultant sexual abuse of the victim?

HOLDING AND DECISION: (Handler, J.) Yes. When a spouse has actual knowledge or special reason to know of the likelihood that his or her spouse is engaging in sexually abusive behavior against a particular person, the spouse has a duty of care to take reasonable steps to prevent or warn of the harm and a breach of that duty constitutes a proximate cause of the resultant sexual abuse of the victim. In determining whether to impose a duty, the court must weigh several factors including the nature of the underlying risk of harm, its foreseeabilty and severity, the opportunity and ability to exercise care to prevent the harm, the comparative interests or relationships between the parties, and the societal interests in the proposed solution based on public policy and fairness. The fundamental element in determining whether a duty of care is owed is foreseeability. This is based on the defendant's knowledge of the risk of injury as determined from an objective standard. Such knowledge may be actual or constructive. Where the type of harm is difficult to ascertain, the court may require the defendant have special reason to know that a particular plaintiff or class of plaintiffs would suffer from the particular type of injury. Moreover, where the risk of harm is that posed by third persons, the plaintiff may be required to show that the defendant knew or had reason to know from past experience that such conduct was likely. Whether a legal duty may be imposed requires a balancing of the conflicting interests of the parties. This requires an assessment of the defendant's responsibility for conditions creating a risk of harm and an analysis of whether the defendant had sufficient control, opportunity and ability to avoid the harm. The question of whether to impose a duty also depends upon public policy and fairness. The court must also consider the scope or boundaries of the duty under the totality of the circumstances and such scope must be reasonable. This includes a consideration of the risk of harm involved and the practicality of preventing it as determined by an objective standard on the particular facts of the case. It is highly foreseeable that a wife's failure to prevent or warn of her husbands sexual abuse or propensity for sexual abuse would result in the occurrence or continuation of such abuse. The wife's (D) negligence was the proximate cause of their injuries. Affirmed.

▶ ANALYSIS

The court engages in a balancing of the competing interests of the parties. On the one hand is the strong public interest in protecting society from the threat of potential sexual abuse. On the other is the defendant's interests in marital privacy. The court concluded that the protection against potential abuse outweighs the interests in marital privacy.

■=■

Quicknotes

ACTUAL KNOWLEDGE Knowledge that presently and objectively exists.

CHILD ABUSE Conduct that is harmful to a child's physical or mental health.

CONSTRUCTIVE KNOWLEDGE Knowledge that is imputed to an individual as a result of its being either in the public record or discoverable through the exercise of reasonable care.

■=■

Tarasoff v. Regents of University of California

Murder victim's parents (P) v. Psychiatrists (D) and their employer (D)

Cal. Sup. Ct., 17 Cal. 3d 425, 551 P.2d 334 (1976).

NATURE OF CASE: Action for wrongful death.

FACT SUMMARY: Doctors from the University of California (D) were aware that one of their outpatients intended to kill Tatiana Tarasoff but neglected to warn her of it.

🏛 RULE OF LAW
A doctor bears a duty to exercise reasonable care and warn potential victims about known violent tendencies or intentions of a patient.

FACTS: While a mental outpatient at a University of California (D) Hospital, Poddar disclosed his intention to kill Tatiana Tarasoff because she had spurned his romantic advances. The psychologist who learned of this intention, Dr. Moore, notified both the campus police and three staff psychiatrists; but, after a cursory investigation, it was decided that no action to confine Poddar was necessary. Tatiana was not warned of Poddar's intentions. Two months later, Poddar shot and killed Tatiana. At his trial, it was learned that Poddar had discontinued his treatment at the U.C. (D) hospital after the incident two months earlier. Tatiana's parents (P) thereupon filed this action against U.C. (D) alleging that the hospital's negligent failure to warn Tatiana of Poddar's intention had caused her wrongful death. This appeal followed.

ISSUE: Are doctors under any duty to warn potential victims about known violent tendencies and intentions of their patients?

HOLDING AND DECISION: (Tobriner, J.) Yes. A doctor bears a duty to exercise reasonable care and warn potential victims about known violent tendencies or intentions of a patient. There is no reason why the rule requiring doctors to take such action to prevent harm from physical illness should not be extended to mental illness situations as well. U.C. (D) contends that the burden of deciding which of the many threats which doctors hear should be taken seriously is too great; but, there is nothing improper in the law requiring a professional to exercise his professional judgment. U.C. further (D) contends that requiring disclosure of such threats will destroy the confidentiality necessary to effective psychotherapy; but the interest of society in protecting itself from physical violence must take precedence. The action may proceed.

▶ ANALYSIS

This case marks a diversion from the traditional attitude of the courts regarding the duty of a doctor to warn about threats made by a patient in confidence. As Justice Clark in his unreported (in the casebook) dissent pointed out here, there is nothing unusual in holding a psychotherapist liable for harm which results from the "negligent discontinuance" of psychotherapy. Pre-*Tarasoff*, however, there was no precedent for predicating liability on a mere failure to disclose dangerous intentions. Note that this new rule is consistent with the psychotherapist-patient privilege since such privilege is expressly inapplicable in situations in which the safety or welfare of any individual is threatened.

Quicknotes

AMICUS BRIEF A brief submitted by a third party, not a party to the action, that contains information for the court's consideration in conformity with its position.

State of Louisiana ex rel. Guste v. M.V. Testbank

State on behalf of oil spill victims (P) v. Negligent shipper (D)

752 F.2d 1019 (5th Cir. 1985).

NATURE OF CASE: Appeal from denial of damages for economic loss.

FACT SUMMARY: Guste (P) contended he could recover his economic loss caused by Testbank's (D) shipping accident even though he suffered no physical property damage.

> ### 🏛 RULE OF LAW
> Claims for economic loss unaccompanied by physical damage to a proprietary interest are not recoverable in maritime tort.

FACTS: In 1980, Testbank's (D) ship collided with another vessel causing toxic fumes to escape and endanger sea life. Guste (P) suffered economic loss due to the closing of the waterway; however, he suffered no physical damage to any property. Testbank (D) successfully moved for summary judgment on the basis no damages are recoverable in maritime tort without physical damage. Guste (P) appealed.

ISSUE: Are claims for economic loss unaccompanied by physical damage to a proprietary interest recoverable in maritime tort?

HOLDING AND DECISION: (Higginbotham, J.) No. Claims for economic loss unaccompanied by physical damage to a proprietary interest are not recoverable in maritime tort. This is a rule of long standing and is necessary to keep some limit on recovery. Without this bright line, liability for maritime torts would be unlimited. Because a bright line rule is used, some cases, approaching the borderline, will be resolved inequitably. However, no good cause exists to alter the long-standing rule. Use of such a rule also adds an element of predictability, which allows people to govern and plan their behavior accordingly. Thus, no recovery is available. Affirmed.

CONCURRENCE: (Gee, J.) Expanding the scope of liability usually leads to opening the door to ridiculous extremes allowing recovery in cases not contemplated in the original holding.

DISSENT: (Wisdom, J.) This long-standing rule is outdated and no longer serves a legitimate purpose. Conventional tort theories of proximate causation and foreseeability are in conflict with this rule. There is no reason to abandon traditional tort concepts for maritime law. Those directly affected by the tort should recover their lost profits.

DISSENT: (Rubin, J.) *Robins* has no application to cases, such as this one, in which persons sustain real economic injury from negligent acts, through no fault of their own, but they cannot be made whole. If Congress will not address this problem, this court should.

▌ *ANALYSIS*

The court rejected Guste's (P) alternative argument that he could recover on a nuisance theory. The court stated that it would be too difficult to determine whether individuals suffered harm distinct from the public at large to allow for recovery on a private nuisance theory. The dissent would allow recovery on this theory if particular damages could be shown.

■▬■

Quicknotes

EX REL. Actions brought in the name of the state on behalf of a private party.

PURE ECONOMIC LOSS Pecuniary loss unaccompanied by any physical damage to person or property.

■▬■

Daley v. LaCroix

Mother (P) and son (P) v. Driver of car (D)

Mich. Sup. Ct., 384 Mich. 4, N.W.2d 390 (1970).

NATURE OF CASE: Action for negligent infliction of emotional distress.

FACT SUMMARY: The Daleys (P) suffered emotional distress after LaCroix's (D) car crashed into their house.

🏛 **RULE OF LAW**
Whenever a definite and objective physical injury is produced as a result of emotional distress proximately caused by a tortfeasor's negligent conduct, the injured party may recover damages for such physical consequences to himself notwithstanding the absence of any physical impact upon him at the time of the emotional shock.

FACTS: In July 1963, a car driven negligently by LaCroix (D) careened off the road and sheared off a utility pole, causing an electrical explosion that damaged the Daleys' (P) house. Though there was no physical impact on either Estelle Daley (P) or her son Timothy (P), both suffered extensive emotional distress which manifested itself in severe nervousness. As a result, Estelle (P) and Timothy (P) filed this action against LaCroix (D) for negligent infliction of emotional distress. Because such an action is not traditionally permissible absent proof of some "physical impact" (absent here) on the injured party, the trial court directed a verdict for LaCroix (D). This appeal followed.

ISSUE: May a tort victim recover damages for negligent infliction of emotional distress absent proof of some "physical impact" upon him which created such distress?

HOLDING AND DECISION: (Kavanagh, J.) Yes. Whenever definite and objective physical injury is produced as a result of emotional distress proximately caused by a tortfeasor's negligent conduct, the injured party may recover damages for such physical consequences to himself, notwithstanding the absence of any physical impact upon him at the time of the emotional shock. It is true that damage awards for physical reactions (e.g., nervousness) to emotional distress have traditionally only been recoverable when the emotional distress was accompanied by some immediate "physical impact" on the victim (e.g., blow to the head), from and as a part of the tortfeasor's act. This court's examination of this rule, in light of the increasing sophistication of both the scientific and legal communities regarding it, indicates that it is time to change it. As such, since testimony below was sufficient to raise a jury question of fact as to whether the nervous condition of the Daleys (P) was caused by LaCroix (D), the directed verdict must be reversed.

DISSENT: (Brennen, J.) Traumatic neuroses, nervous upsets, etc., must be subjected to a "physical impact" requirement if spurious claims are to be avoided.

▌ *ANALYSIS*

This case points up the clear trend of modern authority toward rejecting the "physical impact" requirement for negligent infliction of emotional distress. Traditionally, only such outrageous conduct as the negligent mishandling of corpses had been insulated from the "physical impact" requirement for recovery of mental disturbance damages. Several objections have traditionally been made to such recovery. It has been said that mental disturbance is too difficult to measure in terms of money. It has been contended that such "injuries" are too "remote."

■▬■

Quicknotes

DIRECTED VERDICT A verdict ordered by the court in a jury trial.

NEGLIGENT INFLICTION OF EMOTIONAL DISTRESS Violation of the duty of care owed to another that occurs when an individual creates a foreseeable risk of injury to the other person, which causes emotional distress resulting in some physical harm to that person.

PROXIMATE CAUSE The natural sequence of events without which an injury would not have been sustained.

SUI GENERIS Peculiar to its own type or class.

THE "IMPACT RULE" Doctrine that in order to recover damages for negligent infliction of emotional distress an external impact is required.

■▬■

Thing v. La Chusa

Injured son's mother (P) v. Driver (D)

Cal. Sup. Ct., 48 Cal. 3d 644, 771 P.2d 814 (1989).

NATURE OF CASE: Review of order reversing dismissal of action seeking damages for emotional distress.

FACT SUMMARY: Thing (P) sought emotional distress damages for injuries to her son which she did not contemporaneously observe.

> 🏛 **RULE OF LAW**
> One may recover emotional distress damages for injury to a relative only if he observes the injury-producing event.

FACTS: Thing's (P) son was injured when an automobile driven by La Chusa (D) struck him. Informed of the accident by her daughter, Thing (P) ran to the scene and saw her son lying bloody and unconscious in the road. Thing (P) sued La Chusa (D) for emotional distress. The trial court granted La Chusa's (D) motion for summary judgment, dismissing the action because Thing (P) had not actually observed the accident. The court of appeals reversed, and the California Supreme Court granted review.

ISSUE: May one recover emotional distress damages for injury to a relative only if he observes the injury-producing event?

HOLDING AND DECISION: (Eagleson, J.) Yes. One may recover emotional distress damages for injury to a relative only if he observes the injury-producing event. Emotional distress is part of the human condition and can be inflicted by an unlimited number of traumatic events. On a societal level, it is unacceptable to impose tort liability on a defendant whenever he causes another such distress partly because of the deleterious effects of unlimited liability and because injury is often out of proportion to the level of negligence. A bright-line outer limit of liability for emotional distress caused by trauma to another must be drawn. The most logical point to draw this line is to limit recovery to (1) close relatives, by blood or marriage, who (2) contemporaneously observe the event that causes the injury and the injury itself, and who (3) suffer a serious emotional reaction. Here, Thing (P) did not actually observe her son's accident, so she may not recover. The judgment of the court of appeal is reversed.

CONCURRENCE: (Kaufman, J.) Liability for emotional distress caused by injuries to third parties should be confined to those in the zone of danger put in fear of their own safety.

▶ ANALYSIS

The common law originally recognized the "impact rule," which requires physical injury for emotional trauma damages. The California Supreme Court jettisoned this requirement in *Dillon v. Legg*, 68 Cal. 2d 728 (1968), which allowed recovery for observing injury to another. In the years between 1968 and 1988, liability in this area had been gradually expanding. The present case closed the door on such growth.

Quicknotes

EMOTIONAL DISTRESS Extreme personal suffering which results from another's conduct and for which damages may be sought.

IMPACT RULE Doctrine that in order to recover damages for negligent infliction of emotional distress an external impact is required.

SUMMARY JUDGMENT Judgment rendered by a court in response to a motion made by one of the parties, claiming that the lack of a question of material fact in respect to an issue warrants disposition of the issue without consideration by the jury.

Endresz v. Friedberg

Stillborn twins' parents (P) v. Driver (D)

N.Y. Ct. App., 24 N.Y.2d 478, 248 N.E.2d 901 (1969).

NATURE OF CASE: Action for wrongful death.

FACT SUMMARY: Endresz' (P) seven-months-pregnant wife (P) delivered stillborn twins after being injured in an auto accident with Friedberg (D).

🏛 **RULE OF LAW**
The parents of an unborn fetus whose birth was prevented by negligent conduct may not bring a wrongful death action to redress the wrong that was done.

FACTS: Janice Endresz (P) was seven months pregnant when she was involved in an auto accident negligently caused by Friedberg (D). As a result of the accident, her twins were stillborn two days later. The Endreszes (P) thereupon filed wrongful death actions on behalf of the twins alleging $100,000 in damages for "loss of anticipated care, comfort, and support" and a personal injury action on behalf of Janice (P). The trial court, however, dismissed the wrongful death actions on the ground that such were not maintainable on behalf of an unborn fetus. The Endreszes (P) appealed, contending that since the court had recently recognized the right of a child to sue for prenatal injuries, it must logically extend such rights to the child's survivors in a wrongful death action.

ISSUE: May a wrongful death action be maintained by the parents of an unborn fetus whose birth was prevented by negligent conduct?

HOLDING AND DECISION: (Fuld, C.J.) No. The parents of an unborn fetus whose birth was prevented by negligent conduct may not bring a wrongful death action to the redress the wrong that was done. The rationale for allowing a child, in his own right, to recover damages for prenatal injuries is that it is unfair to force the child to go through life "bearing the seal of another's fault." Where the child dies, however, no such injustice arises. Since the parents may recover for their suffering, loss of consortium, etc., in a simple personal injury action, the basic underlying policy of the law to compensate for loss is fully served without permitting wrongful death recovery. Affirmed.

DISSENT: (Burke, J.) It is elementary that every wrong must have a remedy. The decision today leaves the wrong done to the unborn twins here without redress.

▶ *ANALYSIS*

This case reaffirms the traditional rule regarding the rights of parents to recover for the wrongful death of their unborn children. In essence, of course, the logical import of this decision is that society owes no duty of care to the unborn child. Note, of course, that this rule changes when the fetus may be classified as "viable"—i.e., capable of surviving outside of the mother. The definition of "viability," of course, varies greatly from jurisdiction to jurisdiction. Some permit recovery only if the child is capable of independent respiration prior to its death. Others permit recovery if respiration is maintainable only by a respirator.

Quicknotes

DUTY OF CARE A principle of negligence requiring an individual to act in such a manner as to avoid injury to a person to whom he or she owes a duty.

PAIN AND SUFFERING Refers to a type of recovery in tort for both physical and mental injuries.

PERSONAL INJURY Harm to an individual's person or body.

WRONGFUL DEATH An action brought by the beneficiaries of a deceased person, claiming that the deceased's death was the result of wrongful conduct by the defendant.

Procanik by Procanik v. Cillo

Birth-defective child (P) v. Doctors (D)

N.J. Sup. Ct., 97 N.J. 339, 478 A.2d 755 (1984).

NATURE OF CASE: Appeal of summary adjudication dismissing causes of action seeking special and general damages for "wrongful life."

FACT SUMMARY: An allegedly negligent diagnosis by Cillo (D) prevented Procanik's (P) mother from knowing he would be born with serious handicaps, which had she known might have caused her to terminate the pregnancy.

🏛 RULE OF LAW
An infant plaintiff may recover special damages for "wrongful life" but may not recover general damages therefor.

FACTS: Procanik's (P) mother contracted rubella during the first trimester of her pregnancy. Such an infection causes a great risk of serious birth defects, a danger that proved true in Procanik's (P) case. He was born with serious handicaps. Cillo (D) and other medical personnel had failed to diagnose rubella in the mother. Procanik (P) brought an action seeking, among other things, special damages for extra expenses he would incur throughout his life as a result of the alleged malpractice, on the theory that his mother might have terminated the pregnancy had she been diagnosed and informed of such diagnosis. He also sought general damages for an impaired life. No allegation was made that any defendant had brought about Procanik's (P) handicaps. The trial court dismissed the "wrongful life" causes of action. The appellate court affirmed. Procanik (P) appealed.

ISSUE: May an infant plaintiff recover special and general damages for "wrongful life?"

HOLDING AND DECISION: (Pollock, J.) No. An infant plaintiff may recover special damages for "wrongful life," but may not recover general damages therefor. Earlier decisions held that neither parents nor children could recover special damages for negligent diagnosis that prevented a mother from making an informed choice regarding termination. This was largely due to a judicial reluctance to recognize the legitimacy of abortion. However, in the intervening years, the U.S. Supreme Court has legitimized abortion, and this court has permitted parents to recover special damages from negligent doctors when the negligence prevented them from properly considering termination. There is no logical reason to deny the same rights to the infant itself, as the expenses will prove just as real through the lifetime of the child. General damages for diminished value of life, however, present an entirely different issue. Beyond the weighty philosophical issue of whether no life can be preferable to impaired life, the damages in such a situation cannot be measured in any rational way. Since such damages would be pure speculation, they cannot be permitted. Here, Procanik (P) may proceed on special damages, but not general ones. Affirmed in part; reversed in part.

▶ ANALYSIS

Needless to say, the issues raised here go to the outer edge of judicial competence, being more fit for religious or moral debate than judicial decision. Not surprisingly, the jurisdictions that have spoken on this matter have come down in different directions. Some deny specials and generals; others allow both.

Quicknotes

GUARDIAN AD LITEM Person designated by the court to represent an infant or ward in a particular legal proceeding.

WRONGFUL BIRTH A cause of action brought by the parents of a child born with severe birth defects against a doctor for negligent treatment or advice.

WRONGFUL LIFE A medical malpractice action brought by the parents of a child born with severe birth defects against a doctor, claiming that but for the doctor's negligent treatment or advice they would not have given birth to the child.

CHAPTER 9

Owners and Occupiers of Land

Quick Reference Rules of Law

Taylor v. Olsen

Injured driver (P) v. Tree owner (D)

Or. Sup. Ct., 282 Or. 343, 578 P.2d 779 (1978).

NATURE OF CASE: Appeal from denial of damages for negligence.

FACT SUMMARY: Taylor (P) injured herself when she crashed into a tree, which had fallen onto a highway from Olsen's (D) property.

🏛 RULE OF LAW
It is generally a question of fact as to whether a landowner has taken reasonable care in protecting people outside his land from dangerous conditions existing upon the land.

FACTS: Taylor (P) suffered injuries when her car, on a dark and windy January evening, struck a tree, which had fallen across the highway from Olsen's (D) adjacent property. The trial court, noting that there was no evidence suggesting Olsen (D) could have reasonably known about the tree's hazardous condition before it fell, directed verdict for Olsen (D). Taylor (P) appealed.

ISSUE: Is the question of whether a landowner has taken reasonable care in protecting people outside his land from dangerous conditions existing upon the land generally one of fact?

HOLDING AND DECISION: (Linde, J.) Yes. Usually such a question would be presented to the jury. However, in cases where no evidence has been introduced from which a reasonable jury could impute liability, a directed verdict is proper. The instant action is such a case. Although Taylor (P) testified that an examination of the tree after the accident revealed that the center had decayed, there was no evidence that Olsen (D) could have, through reasonable inspection, determined that fact beforehand. Furthermore, no evidence was adduced suggesting that drilling to the center of a tree to look for decay is a common method of examining trees, absent any external indications that the tree was not structurally sound. As such, Olsen (D) could not be held liable for Taylor's (P) injuries. Affirmed.

▶ ANALYSIS

The general American rule is that a landowner has no duty to protect persons outside his property from natural conditions existing on the property. However, liability has been assessed where the landowner knew of the structural defects of a tree and failed to take reasonable precautions against resulting damage. *Turner v. Ridley,* 144 A.2d 269 (D.C. 1958). There is also a line of cases which distinguish between the care which must be exercised by a rural landowner, and one residing in an urban area. However, this distinction is rejected in Taylor.

━■

Quicknotes

DIRECTED VERDICT A verdict ordered by the court in a jury trial.

━■

Salevan v. Wilmington Park, Inc.

Foul ball victim (P) v. Ball park owner (D)

Del. Sup. Ct., 72 A.2d 239 (1950).

NATURE OF CASE: Action for personal injuries.

FACT SUMMARY: Salevan (P) was injured by a foul ball while walking on a public street adjacent to Wilmington's (D) ball park.

🏛 RULE OF LAW
Landowners whose property is adjacent to public sidewalks or highways owe a duty of care to take reasonable precautions for the protection of the traveling public.

FACTS: Wilmington Park (D) was engaged in the operation of a baseball park located adjacent to East Thirtieth Street in the City of Wilmington. One day, while walking on East Thirtieth Street, Salevan (P) was struck with a foul ball emanating from this park. Salevan (P) thereupon filed this action for personal injuries. At trial, it was adduced that in the course of the average game, some two to three foul balls normally got out of the park, landing on East Thirtieth Street. Though Wilmington Park (D) was aware of this, it took few precautions to protect pedestrians there during any of 68 games played during the season.

ISSUE: Do landowners owe any duty of care to pedestrians on public highways abutting their land?

HOLDING AND DECISION: (Wolcott, J.) Yes. Landowners whose property is adjacent to public sidewalks or highways owe a duty of care to take reasonable precautions for the protection of the traveling public. Breach of the duty to not interfere with such rights is clearly actionable. The inherent nature of the game of baseball is such as to require a landowner to take reasonable effective precautions to protect the traveling public nearby. While Wilmington Park (D) evidently undertook some cursory precautions here, the fact that two or three balls normally endanger pedestrians on East Thirtieth Street every game anyway should have put them, as landowners, on notice that the precautions they took were inadequate. Judgment for Salevan (P); $2,500 awarded.

▌ *ANALYSIS*

This case points out the general duty (due care) assignable to landowners regarding people outside of their land when some dangerous activity is going on on the land. Note that, as a general rule, landowners owe no duty to people outside their land for natural conditions on the land. Furthermore, a duty of due care arises even for artificial conditions (e.g., ditch) on a landowner's land only if the artificial condition abuts adjacent public land (e.g., excavation next to a road). These general duties, of course, arise out of the common law. Note that some jurisdictions (e.g., California) have done away with them.

■=■

Quicknotes

DUTY OF CARE A principle of negligence requiring an individual to act in such a manner as to avoid injury to a person to whom he or she owes an obligatory duty.

DANGEROUS CONDITION A condition of property that poses a reasonably foreseeable substantial risk of injury giving rise to liability for a public entity.

FORESEEABILITY A reasonable expectation that an act or omission would result in injury.

■=■

Sheehan v. St. Paul & Duluth Ry. Co.

Rail walker (P) v. Railroad (D)

76 F. 201 (7th Cir. 1896).

NATURE OF CASE: Action to recover damages for personal injury.

FACT SUMMARY: While Sheehan (P) was walking on St. Paul & Duluth's (D) railroad track, his foot got caught and was run over by St. Paul & Duluth's (D) train.

🏛 RULE OF LAW
A landowner owes a duty of care to a trespasser only after he or she has discovered the presence of the trespasser.

FACTS: While Sheehan (P) was walking on St. Paul & Duluth's (D) railroad track, his foot slipped and became stuck in the rail. He was unable to get it out before the train ran over his foot. The train crew did not see Sheehan (P) until the train was almost upon him and it was too late to stop. Sheehan (P) filed suit, but the court directed a verdict for St. Paul & Duluth (D). Sheehan (P) appealed.

ISSUE: Does a landowner have a duty of care to a trespasser before s/he is aware of the trespasser's presence and peril?

HOLDING AND DECISION: (Seaman, J.) No. The landowner has no duty of care to the unknown trespasser. Only after the landowner discovers the trespasser is a duty of reasonable care owed. In this case, the railroad did not have a duty to foresee that a reasonable person would trespass on the track at a place not open to travel. Hence, the St. Paul & Duluth (D) railroad owed no duty of care to trespasser Sheehan (P), since it had no notice of his presence. "The trespasser who ventures to enter upon a track for any purpose of (her or) his own assumes all risks of the conditions which may be found there, including the operation of engines and cars." At public crossings, the railroad does owe a duty of care to the public. The determinative factor is not that the public's passage at these crossings is lawful, but that the crossings by their existence give notice to the railroad. Such notice gives rise to a duty of care. Since there was no notice of Sheehan's (P) presence in this case, St. Paul & Duluth's (D) duty of care did not arise until the train crew discovered his predicament. The only question of liability would be whether after discovering Sheehan's (P) peril, St. Paul & Duluth's (D) train crew was negligent in averting injury to him. Affirmed.

▶ ANALYSIS

This case follows the general rule that the landowner owes no duty of care to the unknown trespasser. Reasons given to support the rule are: that the trespasser is contributorily negligent or a wrongdoer, or that the trespasser's presence is unanticipated and so a reasonable person would not take steps to protect him/her. The latter rationale was used in this case. Prosser feels that the true explanation is that in a society based on private ownership, it is not socially desirable to interfere with a landowner's use of his/her land by imposing the burden of watching for and protecting trespassers. The landowner's immunity has been criticized, and the courts have created exceptions to it. The exceptions are as follows: once the landowner knows of the trespasser's presence, reasonable care is required (as mentioned in this case); where it is known to the landowner that a substantial number of persons frequently trespass in a limited area, a duty is owed; and where the landowner anticipates the presence of trespassers and carries on activity that might be highly dangerous to them, liability may be found. Each of the exceptions is based on the landowner's notice or anticipation of trespassers' presence.

Quicknotes

DUTY OF CARE A principle of negligence requiring an individual to act in such a manner as to avoid injury to a person to whom he or she owes an obligatory duty.

IMMUNITY Exemption from a legal obligation.

PERSONAL INJURY Harm to an individual's person or body.

TRESPASSERS Persons present on the land of another without the knowledge or express permission of the owner, and to whom only a minimum duty of care is owed for injuries incurred while on the premises.

Barmore v. Elmore

Assaulted guest (P) v. Assailant's father (D)

Ill. App. Ct., Second Dist., 83 Ill. App. 3d 1056, 403 N.E.2d 1355 (1980).

NATURE OF CASE: Appeal from denial of damages for negligence.

FACT SUMMARY: Barmore (P) sued Elmore (D) for injuries received from an attack by Elmore's (D) disturbed adult son during a business visit to Elmore's (D) home.

🏛 RULE OF LAW
As to a licensee, the owner of premises is only required to warn his guest of any hidden dangers of which the owner has knowledge.

FACTS: Barmore (P) and Elmore (D) were officers and members of a Masonic Lodge. In August 1977, Barmore (P) visited Elmore (D) at his house for the purpose of discussing Lodge business. While he was there, Barmore (P) was attacked by Elmore's (D) disturbed adult son and injured. He brought suit against the elder Elmore (D) alleging that as a landowner, he was negligent in failing to protect Barmore (P) from a dangerous condition upon the premises, namely his son, who had a history of mental illness. The trial court, holding that Barmore (P) was a licensee, rather than an invitee, held that Elmore (D) had not breached any duty toward his guest. Accordingly, he directed a verdict for Elmore (D). Barmore (P) appealed.

ISSUE: Is the duty of a landowner toward a licensee limited to a warning regarding any hidden dangers of which the owner has knowledge?

HOLDING AND DECISION: (Lindberg, J.) Yes. Initially, Barmore's (P) contention that he was an invitee must be dismissed. The primary benefit of Barmore's (P) visit ran not to Elmore (D) but to the lodge of which both parties were members. As such, Barmore (P) must be classified as a licensee. Accordingly, Elmore's (D) duty to Barmore (P) extended only to warning him of any hidden dangers on the premises of which Elmore (D) was aware. It cannot be said that he breached this duty. Although his son had a history of mental illness, there is no evidence suggesting that Elmore (D) knew or could have known that Barmore's (P) visit that night would result in an attack. Therefore, a directed verdict in his favor was properly granted. Affirmed.

▌ANALYSIS

Some courts have abolished the distinction between a landowner's duty toward a business invitee and that owed to a guest or licensee. In such jurisdictions, a general duty of reasonable care is invoked. See *Rowland v. Christian*, 69 Cal. 2d 108 (1968). The destruction of the business invitee/licensee distinction was accomplished statutorily in at least one jurisdiction. See Conn. Gen. Stat. § 5255.7(a). However, the rule applied in Barmore, i.e., that a greater duty is owed to business invitees than to licensees, is still the rule in the majority of American jurisdictions.

Quicknotes

INVITEE A person who enters upon another's property by an express or implied invitation and to whom the owner of the property owes a duty of care to guard against injury from those hazards that are discoverable through the exercise of reasonable care.

LICENSEE A person who enters upon the land of another by the land owner's express or implied consent to whom the land owner owes a duty of reasonable care to protect against reasonably discoverable hazards; the recipient of a license.

Campbell v. Weathers

Customer (P) v. Lessee (D)

Kan. Sup. Ct., 153 Kan. 316, 111 P.2d 72 (1941).

NATURE OF CASE: Action to recover damages for negligence.

FACT SUMMARY: On his way to the toilet in Weather's (D) place of business, Campbell (P) stepped into a trap door and was injured.

RULE OF LAW
A regular customer of a business establishment who enters the establishment but does not buy anything is considered to be an invitee.

FACTS: Weathers (D) operated a cigar stand and lunch counter at which Campbell (P) was a regular customer. Campbell (P) entered the cigar stand, loitered there for about fifteen minutes without making a purchase and then went to use the toilet. On his way to the toilet he stepped into an open trap door and was injured. The toilet was open to the public. Weathers' (D) demurrer was sustained, and Campbell (P) appealed.

ISSUE: Is a regular customer of a business establishment who on a particular occasion enters the establishment and uses the toilet but does not make a purchase an invitee?

HOLDING AND DECISION: (Wedell, J.) Yes. A regular or prospective customer of a place of business does not have to make a purchase on a particular occasion to be considered an invitee. Here, since Campbell (P) was a regular customer, the fact that he did not make a purchase on the day of his injury does not affect his status as an invitee. However, if it appears that a person had no intention of presently or in the future becoming a customer he could not be held to be an invitee. Reversed.

ANALYSIS

This case follows the mutual benefit rationale for distinguishing between invitees and licensees. The landowner has no financial interest in the entry of a licensee. Therefore, the licensee is entitled to nothing more than an honest disclosure of the dangers which are known to the landowner. But the visit of an invitee (or business visitor) may be financially beneficial to the landowner or possessor. Such visitor is entitled to expect that the possessor will take reasonable care to discover dangerous conditions and either make them safe or warn invitees. The theory is that the duty of affirmative care to make the premises safe is the price the occupier must pay for the present or prospective benefit to be derived from the visitor. The alternative theory, which is accepted by the majority of courts, is that the basis of liability is the representation implied when a possessor encourages others to enter: that reasonable care has been taken to make the place safe. It is not just the invitation but also an implied assurance accompanying the invitation that the place will be safe (which is not found to be present in the case of social guests).

Quicknotes

DANGEROUS CONDITION A condition of property that poses a reasonably foreseeable substantial risk of injury giving rise to liability for a public entity.

DUTY OF CARE A principle of negligence requiring an individual to act in such a manner as to avoid injury to a person to whom he or she owes an obligatory duty.

Whelan v. Van Natta

Customer (P) v. Shopkeeper (D)

Ky. Ct. App., 382 S.W.2d 205 (1964).

NATURE OF CASE: Action to recover damages for personal injury.

FACT SUMMARY: Whelan (P) was injured in a back room of Van Natta's (D) grocery store while looking for a box he'd (P) requested.

> 🏛 **RULE OF LAW**
> An invitee retains the status of an invitee only as long as he remains on that part of the premises to which the land occupier's invitation extends.

FACTS: Whelan (P) entered Van Natta's (D) grocery store and made a purchase. He then asked about a box and was told to go to the back room. While looking for the box in the back room, which was dark, Whelan (P) fell through an unseen stairwell and was injured. Following a court judgment for Van Natta (D), Whelan (P) appealed.

ISSUE: Can a person who is on the premises as an invitee lose the status of an invitee by going to another area of the premises?

HOLDING AND DECISION: (Montgomery, J.) Yes. The land occupier is subject to liability to another as an invitee only for harm sustained while he is on the land within the scope of the land occupier's invitation. The invitation extends to the part of the land upon which the land possessor gives the visitor reason to believe that his presence is desired for the purpose for which he has come. If the invitee goes outside the area of the invitation, he becomes a trespasser or a licensee depending upon whether he goes there with or without the possessor's consent. In this case, Whelan (P) requested a box for his own purpose. He was not invited into the back room as part of his business in the grocery store. He went there to get the box he requested. In going to the back room he left the area of invitation, that is, the area in which Van Natta (D) gave him reason to believe that his presence was desired for the purpose of doing business in the grocery store. Hence, Whelan (P) lost his status as an invitee and became a licensee (since he did have permission to go to the back room). Affirmed.

▶ ANALYSIS

An invitee will also cease to be an invitee if he stays on the land after the expiration of a reasonable time within which to accomplish the purpose for which he is invited. These cases are decided upon and uphold the "invitation" test rather than the "mutual" or "economic" benefit test. The benefit to the land occupier is the same, whether the invitee stays within the area of invitation or not. As in this case, the benefit to Van Natta (D) did not diminish when Whelan (P) went into the back room.

■══■

Quicknotes

BUSINESS INVITEE A party invited onto another's property in order to conduct business to whom the owner owes a duty of care to protect against known dangers and those capable of discovery through reasonable care.

INVITEE A person who enters upon another's property by an express or implied invitation and to whom the owner of the property owes a duty of care to guard against injury from those hazards that are discoverable through the exercise of reasonable care.

■══■

Rowland v. Christian

Injured guest (P) v. Apartment renter (D)

Cal. Sup. Ct., 69 Cal. 2d 108, 443 P.2d 561 (1968).

NATURE OF CASE: Appeal from summary judgment for the defense in action to recover damages for personal injury.

FACT SUMMARY: While a guest in Christian's (D) house, Rowland (P) was injured by a defective faucet in the bathroom.

RULE OF LAW
An injured person's status as a trespasser, licensee, or invitee will not be determinate as to liability, although the status may have some bearing on the question of liability.

FACTS: Rowland (P) was a social guest in Christian's (D) home. He asked to use the bathroom, and, while there, was injured when a cracked faucet handle broke. Christian (D) had known that the handle was cracked and had complained to the building manager, but did not warn Rowland (P) of its condition. Rowland (P) filed a personal injury action, but the trial court, concluding that Rowland (P), as a social guest, must take the premises as he found them, entered summary judgment for Christian (D). Rowland (P) appealed.

ISSUE: Does an injured person's status as a trespasser, licensee, or invitee determine the possessor's liability?

HOLDING AND DECISION: (Peters, J.) No. The proper test to determine the possessor's liability is whether in the management of his property, he has acted as a reasonable person in view of the probability of injury to others. Liability is determined by balancing the following factors: foreseeability of harm to the plaintiff, the closeness of the connection between the possessor's conduct and the injury, the moral blame attached to the possessor's conduct, the policy of preventing future harm, the extent of the burden to the possessor, the consequences to the community of imposing a duty of care, and the availability and prevalence of insurance. A plaintiff's status may have a bearing in some cases on some of these factors. In this case Christian (D) was aware of the dangerous condition, that the defect was not obvious, and that Rowland (P) was about to come into contact with it. She neither remedied the condition, nor warned Rowland (P). A guest should reasonably be entitled to a warning of a dangerous concealed condition. Her failure to warn constituted negligence. The court feels that the distinctions and immunities attached to trespasser, licensee, and invitee are not justified in light of modern society and the attempt to use the categories in a just manner has given rise to a confused and complex system. "The common law rules obscure rather than illuminate the proper considerations which should govern determination of the question of duty." Reversed.

DISSENT: (Burke, J.) The distinctions among trespassers, licensees and invitees have been developed and applied by the courts over a period of many years. Tort law should be modified by the legislature, not by the courts.

ANALYSIS

In rejecting the categories the court follows a position adopted by an English statute in 1957. The statute declares that the possessor owes the same duty of care to invitees and licensees, with the matter of entry bearing only on the issue of reasonable care. The U.S. Supreme Court has refused to apply the categories to a guest on a ship. The position followed here, that the plaintiff's status is irrelevant as to the duty of reasonable care owed, but may be relevant to the question whether the possessor acted reasonably, is a minority position, followed so far only in California and Hawaii.

Quicknotes

DUTY OF REASONABLE CARE Duty to exercise the degree of care as would a reasonably prudent person under like circumstances.

INVITEE A person who enters upon another's property by an express or implied invitation and to whom the owner of the property owes a duty of care to guard against injury from those hazards that are discoverable through the exercise of reasonable care.

LICENSEES Persons known to an owner or occupier of land, who come onto the premises voluntarily and for a specific purpose although not necessarily with the consent of the owner.

PERSONAL INJURY Harm to an individual's person or body.

SUMMARY JUDGMENT Judgment rendered by a court in response to a motion by one of the parties, claiming that the lack of a question of material fact in respect to an issue warrants disposition of the issue without consideration by the jury.

TRESPASSERS Persons present on the land of another without the knowledge or express permission of the owner, and to whom only a minimum duty of care is owed for injuries incurred while on the premises.

Borders v. Roseberry

Injured guest (P) v. Landlord (D)

Kan. Sup. Ct., 216 Kan. 486, 532 P.2d 1366 (1975).

NATURE OF CASE: Action for personal injuries.

FACT SUMMARY: Borders (P) slipped and fell on the icy steps of the house in which Roseberry (D) was landlord, while visiting as a social guest.

🏛 RULE OF LAW
Landlords are liable for defective conditions existing at the time of leasing to a tenant only in regard to: (1) undisclosed dangerous conditions known to lessor and unknown to lessee; (2) conditions dangerous to persons outside of the premises; (3) premises leased for admission of the public; (4) parts of land retained in lessor's control which lessee is entitled to use; (5) situations in which lessor contracts to repair; and/or (6) negligence by lessor in making repairs.

FACTS: Borders (P) went to premises, over which Roseberry (D) was a landlord, as a social guest of the tenants. While there, he slipped and fell on the front steps of the premises, injuring himself. Water had dripped from the roof on to these steps and frozen, creating the slippery condition which occasioned the fall. Though Roseberry (D) had promised to repair the roof and install guttering, no such work had been done at the time of the fall. Borders (P) filed this personal injury action against Roseberry (D), but the trial court concluded, as a matter of law, that Roseberry (D) was under no duty to anyone to make the proposed repairs or maintain the premises in a safe condition. Borders (P) appealed.

ISSUE: Is a landlord under a general duty of care to social guests of his tenants to remedy defective conditions on his land?

HOLDING AND DECISION: (Prager, J.) No. Landlords are liable for defective conditions existing at the time of leasing to a tenant in regard to: (1) undisclosed dangerous conditions known to lessor and unknown to lessee; (2) conditions dangerous to persons outside of the premises; (3) premises leased for admission of the public; (4) parts of land retained in lessor's control which lessee is entitled to use; (5) situations in which lessor contracts to repair; and/or (6) negligence by lessor in making repairs. There is no general duty, only the above-mentioned six exceptions. Exceptions 1 through 4 are clearly inapplicable. Exception 5 is also inapplicable since Roseberry's (D) mere promise to repair hardly constitutes a contract to do so. Finally, exception 6 is also inapplicable since the lessee here obviously knew of the dangerous condition of the steps—thereby neutralizing the risk for Roseberry (D). Affirmed.

▶ ANALYSIS

This case points up the generally recognized rule and exceptions governing the duties of landlords (i.e., lessors) to their lessees and their lessees' guests. At common law, a lease was considered a sale of property for a term. For such term, the lessee assumed all risks of liability normally associated with ownership except where unusual circumstances (i.e., the six exceptions above) gave rise to a special duty for the landlord. Note, of course, that this rule is subject to challenge and revision in many jurisdictions in which statutory duties to repair and court-implied warranties of habitability have been imposed upon landlords.

■◼■

Quicknotes

DUTY OF CARE A principle of negligence requiring an individual to act in such a manner as to avoid injury to a person to whom he or she owes an obligatory duty.

PERSONAL INJURY Harm to an individual's person or body.

■◼■

Pagelsdorf v. Safeco Ins. Co. of America

Injured guest (P) v. Landlord (D) and his insurer (D)

Wis. Sup. Ct., 91 Wis. 2d 734, 284 N.W.2d 55 (1979).

NATURE OF CASE: Appeal from denial of damages for negligence.

FACT SUMMARY: Pagelsdorf (P), an invitee of a tenant of Mahnke's (D) building, was injured due to a structural defect in the building, the failure of a balcony railing.

RULE OF LAW
A landlord must exercise ordinary care toward his tenants and toward others on the premises with the tenants' permission.

FACTS: Pagelsdorf (P) was assisting Blattner, a tenant of Mahnke's (D) building, in moving some furniture. He was injured when a balcony railing upon which he was leaning collapsed. The railing had dry rot and should have been replaced. At trial, Pagelsdorf (P) was termed a licensee of Mahnke (D). Accordingly, the jury returned a verdict for Mahnke (D), finding that he had no knowledge that the railing was defective. Pagelsdorf (P) appealed, contending that Mahnke (D) should have been held to a higher standard of care.

ISSUE: Must a landlord exercise ordinary care toward both his tenants and their invitees?

HOLDING AND DECISION: (Callow, J.) Yes. Traditionally a landlord, with certain exceptions, has been held not liable for injuries to his tenants and their visitors resulting from defects in the premises. However, this rule is grounded in outdated concepts of a lease as a property conveyance. The modern lease is recognized as a contract for land and services. Thus, an implied warranty of habitability in residential leases has been found in many modern jurisdictions, including Wisconsin. Using the same logic, the ancient cloak of immunity enjoyed by landlords toward their tenants and visitors must be abolished. A landlord must now exercise reasonable ordinary care toward both his tenants and their guests, or be liable for the consequences. Reversed and remanded.

ANALYSIS

As mentioned in the principal case, the traditional landlord's "cloak of immunity" was riddled with exceptions. One such exception is described in § 379 of the Restatement (Second) of Torts: "A lessor of land who transfers its possession in a condition which he realizes or should realize will involve unreasonable risk of physical harm to others outside of the land, is subject to the same liability for physical harm subsequently caused to them by the condition as though he had remained in possession." A similar provision, contained in § 358, made the landlord liable for injuries to tenants in certain situations.

Quicknotes

IMPLIED WARRANTY OF HABITABILITY A warranty implied by a landlord that the premises are suitable, and will remain suitable, for habitation.

LEASE An agreement or contract which creates a relationship between a landlord and tenant (real property) or lessor and lessee (real or personal property).

NEGLIGENCE Conduct falling below the standard of care that a reasonable person would demonstrate under similar conditions.

ORDINARY CARE the degree of care exercised by a reasonable person when conducting everyday activities or under similar circumstances; synonymous with due care.

Kline v. 1500 Massachusetts Ave., Apartment Corp.

Assault victim (P) v. Lessor (D)

439 F.2d 477 (D.C. Cir. 1970).

NATURE OF CASE: Action for personal injuries.

FACT SUMMARY: Kline (P) was assaulted in a common area of her apartment building, owned by Apt. Corp. (D).

🏛 RULE OF LAW
A landlord is under a duty to take precautions to protect tenants from foreseeable criminal acts committed by third parties.

FACTS: Sarah Kline (P) was a tenant of Apt. Corp. (D) residing in a 585-unit combination office-apartment building at 1500 Massachusetts Ave. in Washington, D.C. At approximately 10:15 p.m. one evening, she was criminally assaulted and robbed in the common hallway of the complex. Though the building had been the scene of several such crimes in the past, Apt. Corp. (D) had discontinued the posting of a doorman and had not installed any electronic security devices in the building. Alleging that this failure breached a duty to her, Kline (P) filed this personal injury action against Apt. Corp. (D). The district court dismissed her complaint and this appeal followed on the question of whether any such duty is owing from an urban landlord to his tenant.

ISSUE: Is a landlord under any duty to take precautions to protect tenants from foreseeable criminal acts committed by third parties?

HOLDING AND DECISION: (Wilkey, J.) Yes. A landlord is under a duty to take precautions to protect tenants from foreseeable criminal acts committed by third parties. A landlord must take reasonable care to minimize the predictable risk of crime to his tenants where: (1) he has notice of repeated crimes in the past; (2) he has notice that these crimes occurred in "common areas" retained in his control; (3) he has every reason to expect reoccurrence of such crimes; and, (4) he has the exclusive power to take preventive action. Though he is not an insurer of his tenants, a landlord is the only one who is in a position to make the building, as a whole, safe. Though he is not a policeman, he is the only one who can take protective measures in hallways, garages, etc., that policemen cannot be expected to patrol. Finally, though the exact measures necessary will vary from building to building, it is fair to say here that Apt. Corp. (D) should be held to a duty to provide roughly the same protection today as it promised Kline (D), by contract, in 1959 when she moved in. Reversed.

▶ ANALYSIS

Though this case points up the decidedly minority rule, it does reflect an increasing judicial sensitivity to the rights of crime victims. Note that the duty imposed by the courts is analogous to that which an innkeeper is held to owe to his patrons (as well as third parties in dram-shop act jurisdictions), as a result of the innkeeper's control of his premises. Similar duties are imposed upon common carriers, hospitals, landowners regarding invitees and other businessmen regarding the (invitee) patrons. Note, of course, that the question of what precautions are necessary is a difficult question of fact, to be resolved in each case by the trier of fact.

Quicknotes

COMMON CARRIER An entity whose business is the transport of persons or property.

DUTY TO PROTECT/AID A moral duty and not one imposed by law; no liability attaches to those persons who fail to undertake a rescue or otherwise aid a person in need absent a special relationship between them.

FORESEEABILITY A reasonable expectation that an act or omission would result in injury.

PERSONAL INJURY Harm to an individual's person or body.

Damages

Quick Reference Rules of Law

Anderson v. Sears, Roebuck & Co.

Burn victim's guardian (P) v. Heater manufacturer (D)

377 F. Supp. 136 (E.D. La. 1974).

NATURE OF CASE: Motion for remittitur in action for personal injuries.

FACT SUMMARY: A small child was severely burned in a fire caused by a heater which had been defectively manufactured by Sears (D).

RULE OF LAW
In determining whether a damage award is excessive in a personal injury case, the court must individually examine each of the five cardinal elements of damages: (1) past physical and mental pain; (2) future physical and mental pain; (3) future medical expenses; (4) loss of earning capacity; and (5) permanent disability and disfigurement.

FACTS: Anderson (P) filed this action on behalf of Helen Britain, a young child, who was severely burned in a fire which destroyed her home. The blaze was started by a defective heater which had been defectively manufactured by Sears (D). At trial it was proved, inter alia, that she had been burned over 40 percent of her body, causing extreme scarring, the adhesion of her fingers, and a permanent bend in her elbow, that she had and would for the rest of her life require several operations of enormous cost, that her future earning capacity would be severely limited and that she would be permanently disfigured. The jury returned a $2,000,000 judgment. Sears (D) thereupon moved for remittitur (lowering of the award as legally excessive).

ISSUE: Should a motion for remittitur (i.e., lowering of a damage award as legally excessive) be granted on the mere ground that the aggregate award is enormous?

HOLDING AND DECISION: (Cassibry, J.) No. In determining whether a damage award is excessive in a personal injury case, the court must individually examine each of the five cardinal elements of damages: (1) past physical and mental pain (here arising from the grotesque and deforming pain, fever, vomiting, infection, etc., associated with such injuries); (2) future physical and mental pain (here, arising from the future operations which will be necessary to restore any semblance of normalcy to Helen's life); (3) future medical expenses (here, arising from 27 projected operations, psychiatric counseling, etc.); (4) loss of earning capacity (here, arising from the probability that Helen will never be self-supporting); and (5) permanent disability and disfigurement (including loss of speech, hair, skin, and use of legs and fingers). Viewed in such a context, the award was not legally excessive. Motion denied.

ANALYSIS

This case catalogues the major personal injury damage elements. While some elements are easily computed, most require complex economic calculations involving inflation, discounting future losses, etc. Note that large awards are regularly reported in various legal journals so as to permit comparisons by attorneys in similar cases. Indeed, services are available which inform attorneys of the going rate for arms, legs, etc., within a jurisdiction. Note also that "remittitur" is the motion by which a defendant may have a jury award reduced. Though it is permitted in many jurisdictions, "additur" (adding to insufficient award) is considered unconstitutional unless defendant consents.

Quicknotes

INTER ALIA Among other things.

REMITTITUR The authority of the court to reduce the amount of damages awarded by the jury.

Richardson v. Chapman

Injured (P) v. Driver (D)

Ill. Sup. Ct., 175 Ill. 2d 98, 676 N.E.2d 621 (1997).

NATURE OF CASE: Suit for damages in a personal injury suit.

FACT SUMMARY: Chapman (D) challenged the award of damages for injuries sustained by Richardson (P) when he drove a semi-trailer into her car while it was stopped at a traffic light.

🏛 RULE OF LAW
An award of damages may be deemed excessive if it exceeds the range of fair and reasonable compensation, is the result of passion or prejudice, or is so large that it shocks the conscience.

FACTS: Richardson (P) was driving a car with McGregor as a passenger when they were hit from behind by a semi-trailer driven by Chapman (D). The trial judge directed a verdict in favor of Richardson (P) and against Chapman (D) and his employer on the issue of liability. The jury returned verdicts in favor of Richardson (P) and McGregor (P) in the respective amounts of $22,358,814 and $102,215. The defendants challenged these verdicts on the basis that Richardson's (P) expert witness testified as to an incorrect calculation concerning the present value of her future economic losses and on the basis that the award of damages was excessive.

ISSUE: Will an award of damages be deemed excessive if it exceeds the range of fair and reasonable compensation, is the result of passion or prejudice, or is so large that it shocks the conscience?

HOLDING AND DECISION: (Miller, J.) Yes. An award of damages may be deemed excessive if it exceeds the range of fair and reasonable compensation, is the result of passion or prejudice, or is so large that it shocks the conscience. Richardson (P) argued that the larger damages award was attributable to the jury's decision to award her expenses that were likely to include in the future but were not specifically included in the expert's calculations. While the trier of fact enjoys some leeway in awarding medical costs that are likely to arise in the future but are not specifically itemized in the testimony, here the award was $1.5 million more than the higher of the two figures presented at trial. Such a difference cannot be attributable simple to miscellaneous costs. Thus it is proper for the court by remittitur to reduce by $1 million that differential. The remainder of the damages award is not excessive as claimed by Chapman (D). The issue of damages is a question for the trier of fact. Such an award of damages is excessive if it falls outside the range of fair and reasonable compensation or results from passion or prejudice, or is so large

that it shocks the conscience. When reviewing the amount of compensatory damages award for a nonfatal injury, the court may consider the permanency of the plaintiff's condition, the possibility of future deterioration, the extent of the medical expenses, and the restrictions imposed on the plaintiff by the injuries. Richardson (P) suffered devastating injuries a result of the accident and thus it cannot be found that the damages award shocks the conscience or lacks evidentiary support. Likewise McGregor's award is not excessive. Affirmed in part, reversed in part and vacated in part.

CONCURRENCE AND DISSENT: (McMorrow, J.) The majority erred by reducing the plaintiffs' jury awards. The evidence showed that Richardson's (P) award of $1.5 million for present cash value of future medical expenses was based on a minimum estimate of her expected medical-care needs. Reducing that portion of her award by two-thirds of the amount that the jury found reasonable is an improper, arbitrary invasion of the jury's function. Furthermore, the reduction of the other plaintiff's award for pain and suffering, from $100,000 to $50,000, suffers the same fundamental flaw. On this second award, too, the majority has merely substituted its own subjective assessment of the evidence for that of the jury.

▶ ANALYSIS

In personal injury cases such as this, a plaintiff may be compensated for both present and future medical expenses. Present medical expenses are easily ascertainable by introducing into evidence bills reflecting services rendered or testimony. Future medical expenses, however, must be demonstrated through expert testimony of the predicted costs. Where the injury results in the plaintiff's being permanently removed from the workplace, he may also recover for loss or impairment of future earning capacity. This requires expert testimony in order to establish what the plaintiff would have earned in his lifetime had he not sustained the injuries.

Quicknotes

COMPENSATORY DAMAGES Measure of damages necessary to compensate victim for actual injuries suffered.

DIRECTED VERDICT A verdict ordered by the court in a jury trial.

PERSONAL INJURY Harm to an individual's person or body.

REMITTITUR The authority of the court to reduce the amount of damages awarded by the jury.

Montgomery Ward & Co., Inc. v. Anderson

Retail store (D) v. Customer (P)

Ark. Sup. Ct., 334 Ark. 561, 976 S.W.2d 382 (1998).

NATURE OF CASE: Personal injury suit seeking damages for medical expenses.

FACT SUMMARY: Montgomery Ward (D) sought to exclude evidence of the total medical expenses incurred by Anderson (P) as a result of falling in its Little Rock store, and to instead admit evidence of actual expenses incurred by Anderson (P) after a negotiated discount.

RULE OF LAW
Gratuitous or discounted medical services are a collateral source and are not to be considered in assessing the damages owed by a tortfeasor to a plaintiff in a personal injury suit.

FACTS: Anderson (P) was injured when she fell in Montgomery Ward's (D) Little Rock store. Montgomery Ward (D) sent her to the hospital to be treated. Anderson (P) underwent surgical and other medical procedures incurring expenses of approximately $25,000. Montgomery Ward (D) moved in limine to prohibit Anderson (P) from introducing the total amount billed by the hospital as proof of her medical expenses and asked that her evidence be limited to actual expenses for which she was responsible to pay. Anderson's (P) attorney had agreed with the hospital that her expenses would be discounted 50 percent. Anderson (P) argued that the collateral source rule prohibited Montgomery Ward (D) from introducing evidence of the discount. The trial court denied the motion in limine, ruled that the discount was a collateral source and allowed evidence to be introduced of the total amount of expenses. Montgomery Ward (D) appealed from the ruling and the denial of its motion for a new trial.

ISSUE: Are gratuitous or discounted medical services a collateral source, not to be considered in assessing the damages owed by a tortfeasor to a plaintiff in a personal injury suit?

HOLDING AND DECISION: (Newbern, J.) Yes. Gratuitous or discounted medical services are a collateral source and are not to be considered in assessing the damages owed by a tortfeasor to a plaintiff in a personal injury suit. The collateral source rule applies unless evidence of the benefits from the collateral source is relevant for a purpose other than mitigation of damages. Here the issue is whether the forgiveness of a debt for medical services is a collateral source to be protected by the rule. The collateral source rule requires the trial court to exclude evidence of payments received by an injured party from sources collateral to the tortfeasor. Such recoveries are not to inure to the benefit of the wrongdoer, even if they result in multiple recoveries. There are four circumstances under which the rule does not apply: (1) to rebut testimony of the plaintiff that he returned to work prematurely or did not receive additional medical care from financial need; (2) the plaintiff's condition was attributable to some other cause; (3) for impeachment purposes of plaintiff's testimony that he paid the medical expenses himself; or (4) to show plaintiff continued to work if he claimed to be out of work. None of the exceptions apply here. Both the Restatement (Second) of Torts § 920A and case law have also held that gratuitous medical services fall under the collateral source rule. Affirmed.

ANALYSIS

The Restatement (Second) of Torts § 920A provides that payments or benefits received by an injured party from a collateral source are not credited against the tortfeasor's liability, although they cover all or a part of the harm for which the tortfeasor is liable. The comments also provide that plaintiff is allowed to keep any benefits received. Moreover, if the plaintiff receives gratuities of cash or services those sources are not to be deducted from the tortfeasor's liability, since he must compensate the injured party for the total harm sustained, not just his net loss.

Quicknotes

COLLATERAL SOURCE RULE The doctrine that compensation given to an injured party from a third party should not be considered in assessing the damages to be paid by the party who inflicted the injury.

MOTION IN LIMINE Motion by one party brought prior to trial to exclude the potential introduction of highly prejudicial evidence.

PERSONAL INJURY Harm to an individual's person or body.

Zimmerman v. Ausland

Accident victim (P) v. Other driver (D)

Or. Sup. Ct., 266 Or. 427, 513 P.2d 1167 (1973).

NATURE OF CASE: Action for personal injuries.

FACT SUMMARY: Part of the damages recovered by Zimmerman (P) included loss of the ability to engage in strenuous activity—even though such could be remedied by an operation.

🏛 RULE OF LAW
A tort victim may not recover damages for a permanent injury if an operation could correct the injury and a reasonable person under similar circumstances would submit to treatment.

FACTS: Zimmerman (P) suffered a torn cartilage in an auto accident caused by Ausland's (D) negligence. She filed this action for personal injury damages, alleging, inter alia, that the torn cartilage in her knee was a permanent injury which would prevent her from engaging in the strenuous physical education activity which was required by her job as a substitute teacher. At trial, Ausland (D) introduced evidence that Zimmerman (P) could recover completely if she would submit to surgery on it. The jury returned a $7,500 judgment for Zimmerman (P). Though Ausland (D) had not requested an instruction to the jury on whether the failure to have the operation constituted a failure to mitigate, he appealed contending that the trial court should not have allowed a question of "permanent" injury damages to get to the jury because of such failure.

ISSUE: May a tort victim recover damages for a permanent injury if an operation could correct the injury and a reasonable person under similar circumstances would submit to treatment?

HOLDING AND DECISION: (Tongue, J.) No. A tort victim may not recover damages for a permanent injury if an operation could correct the injury and a reasonable person under similar circumstances would submit to treatment. Whether or not a reasonable person would have such a surgery is a question of fact for the trier of fact to determine. As such, it is for the jury to decide whether Zimmerman (P) failed to mitigate the permanency of her damages by not submitting to an operation. The court has no right to preclude this determination. Since the jury here, after hearing the testimony about the proposed operation, decided nevertheless that Zimmerman's (P) injuries were "permanent" there is no reason to disturb the judgment. Affirmed.

▶ ANALYSIS

The question of whether failure to have an operation constitutes a failure to mitigate damages is precisely the kind of delicate fact weighing process normally assigned to the jury. Basically, it requires the balancing of three factors: risk, cost, and probability of success. It is elementary, of course, that tort victims are under a duty of care to mitigate whatever damages they receive. This duty is often called the "avoidable consequences rule" and operates essentially as a limitation on recoverable tort damages. Note, finally, of course, that refusal to undertake a reasonable operation will not cut off immediate pain and suffering, etc., damages.

Quicknotes

AVOIDABLE CONSEQUENCES RULE Doctrine requiring the nonbreaching party to a contract to exercise ordinary care in attempting to minimize the damages incurred as a result of the breach.

PERSONAL INJURY Harm to an individual's person or body.

REASONABLE PERSON STANDARD The standard of care exercised by a hypothetical person who possesses the intelligence, education, knowledge, attention, and judgment required by society of its members when governing behavior; the standard applies to a person's judgment when determining breach of a duty under the theory of negligence.

Cheatham v. Pohle

Ex-wife (P) v. Ex-husband (D)

Ind. Sup. Ct., 789 N.E.2d 467 (2003).

NATURE OF CASE: Appeal from a punitive-damages award in a suit for invasion of privacy and intentional infliction of emotional distress.

FACT SUMMARY: After the parties divorced, the ex-husband publicly displayed copies of nude photos of his former wife, as well as photos of the couple performing a consensual sexual act. A jury awarded the ex-wife punitive damages, but Indiana's punitive-damages statute required 75 percent of her punitive-damages award to be deposited into a state fund for public benefit.

🏛 RULE OF LAW
The Takings Clauses of the federal and Indiana Constitutions do not prohibit the Indiana state legislature from requiring 75 percent of punitive-damages awards to be deposited into state-operated funds for public benefit.

FACTS: Doris Cheatham (P) and Michael Pohle (D) divorced. Four years later, Pohle (D) distributed at least sixty copies of nude photos of Cheatham (P), as well as photos of Cheatham (P) and Pohle (D) performing a consensual sexual act. The recipients of the copies of the photos were all in the small Indiana community where both Cheatham (P) and Pohle (D) still lived and worked. Cheatham (P) sued Pohle (D) for invasion of privacy and intentional infliction of emotional distress. The jury agreed with Cheatham (P), awarding her $100,000 in compensatory damages and $100,000 in punitive damages. Cheatham (P) based an appeal on her punitive-damages award, arguing that Indiana's punitive-damages statutory scheme reduced the punitive-damages award she actually collected by violating the Takings Clauses of the federal and Indiana Constitutions. Indiana's punitive-damages statutes provided that a recipient of a punitive-damages award shall actually collect only 25 percent of such an award; under the statute, the remaining 75 percent of the award went to Indiana's Violent Crimes Victims Compensation Fund.

ISSUE: Do the Takings Clauses of the federal and Indiana Constitutions prohibit the Indiana state legislature from requiring 75 percent of punitive-damages awards to be deposited into state-operated funds for public benefit?

HOLDING AND DECISION: (Boehm, J.) No. The Takings Clauses of the federal and Indiana Constitutions do not prohibit the Indiana state legislature from requiring 75 percent of punitive-damages awards to be deposited into state-operated funds for public benefit. Punitive damages are quasi-criminal awards and have no basis in traditional compensatory notions of making the plaintiff whole or otherwise valuing the plaintiff's injuries. There is therefore no right to punitive damages because such awards do nothing to compensate an injured party. Based in the common law as they are, punitive damages are completely subject to the legislative will; under the federal constitution, no rights vest in anyone in any common-law rule. Legislatures thus may abolish punitive damages altogether or, as in Indiana, they may impose an intermediate approach to punitive damages, punishing the defendant with a punitive-damages award but limiting a plaintiff's recovery under the award. Because any interest a plaintiff holds in a punitive-damages award derives entirely from state law, it also follows that the plaintiff has no property interest in a punitive-damages award, which in turn means that no property of Cheatham's (P) is taken and deposited into Indiana's Violent Crimes Victims Compensation Fund. It is of no consequence that a punitive-damages award must be supported by a compensatory award: requiring a basis in an award to which plaintiffs do have a right does not change the nature of any subsequent award of punitive damages. Affirmed.

▶ ANALYSIS

Cheatham was a 3-2 decision, a fact that puts the confidence of Justice Boehm's discussion in the majority opinion in perspective. The casebook excerpt does not address the disturbing, more general question of whether requiring deposit of part of a money judgment does constitute a taking of "property." Justice Dickson, writing in dissent, argued that such a requirement is a taking of property because, regardless of the quasi-criminal nature of punitive damages, "[a] judgment for money is property," 789 N.E.2d at 477 (quoting *Wilson v. Berkshire*, 126 Ind. 497, 506, 25 N.E. 131, 134 (1890)), and because "[i]t is not within the power of a legislature to take away rights [that] [*sic*] have been once vested by a judgment." *Id.* at 478 (quoting *McCullough v. Virginia*, 172 U.S. 102, 123-124 (1898)). Defendants still would be punished under Justice Dickson's analysis. The only difference would be that plaintiffs would get to keep all of the punitive damages that they are awarded as, Justice Dickson argued, the federal and Indiana Constitutions require.

━■━

Quicknotes

COMPENSATORY DAMAGES Measure of damages necessary to compensate victim for actual injuries suffered.

━■━

State Farm Mutual Automobile Ins. Co. v. Campbell

Insurer (D) v. Insured (P)

538 U.S. 408 (2003).

NATURE OF CASE: Certiorari review of damages awarded in a bad faith, fraud, and intentional infliction of emotional distress action.

FACT SUMMARY: Campbell (P) sued State Farm Mutual Automobile Insurance Co. (State Farm) (D), his automobile insurer, for bad faith, fraud, and intentional infliction of emotional distress action when State Farm (D) refused to settle a claim brought against Campbell (P) by Ospital's estate and by Slusher.

> 🏛 **RULE OF LAW**
> In determining the validity of a punitive damages award, consideration is given to the degree of reprehensibility of the defendant's misconduct, the disparity between the actual or potential harm suffered by the plaintiff and the punitive damages award, and the difference between the punitive damages award by the jury and the civil penalties authorized or imposed in comparable cases.

FACTS: Campbell (P) caused a collision which killed Ospital and left Slusher permanently disabled. Ospital's estate and Slusher sued Campbell (P) for wrongful death and in tort. Campbell's (P) insurance company, State Farm (D) refused to settle with Ospital and Slusher even though Ospital and Slusher agreed to settle for the policy limit of $25,000 each. State Farm (D) assured Campbell (P) that State Farm (D) would represent Campbell's (P) interests, that Campbell's (P) assets were safe and that Campbell (P) did not need to procure separate counsel. A jury found Campbell (P) to be at fault and awarded $185,849 to Ospital and Slusher. Initially, State Farm (D) refused to cover the $135,849 in excess liability and refused to post a bond so Campbell (P) could appeal. State Farm (D) told Campbell (P) that he may as well put a For Sale sign on his house. Campbell (P) obtained his own attorney, filed his appeal and, in the meantime, agreed to let Slusher and Ospital's attorney represent him (P) in a case against State Farm (D) for bad faith, fraud, and intentional infliction of emotional distress. In exchange, Slusher and Ospital agreed not to seek satisfaction from Campbell (P), but would play a central role in the bad faith action, including receiving 90 percent of any verdict against State Farm (D). The appeals court denied Campbell's (P) appeal in the wrongful death and tort actions and State Farm (D) paid the entire judgment, including the amounts in excess of the policy limits. Despite State Farm's (D) payment, Campbell (P) filed suit against State Farm (D)

alleging bad faith, fraud, and intentional infliction of emotional distress. The trial court found in favor of Campbell (P) and awarded him $2.6 million in compensatory damages and $145 million in punitive damages. The award was subsequently reduced to $1 million and $25 million, respectively. The appeals court affirmed the $1 million and reinstated the $145 million in punitive damages. The U.S. Supreme Court granted certiorari.

ISSUE: Is an award of $145 million in punitive damages, where full compensatory damages are $1 million, excessive and in violation of the Due Process Clause?

HOLDING AND DECISION: (Kennedy, J.) Yes. An award of $145 million in punitive damages, where full compensatory damages are $1 million, is excessive and in violation of the Due Process Clause because the reprehensibility of State Farm's (D) misconduct could have been punished in a more modest way and still have satisfied State objectives. The disparity between the actual or potential harm suffered by Campbell (P) and the punitive damages awarded was significant, and the difference between the punitive damages award by the jury and the civil penalties authorized or imposed in comparable cases was great. Although States have discretion over the amount of punitive damages allowed, there are constitutional limitations on these awards. The imposition of grossly excessive or arbitrary punishments on a tortfeasor are prohibited because of fundamental notions of fairness. Moreover, because defendants subjected to punitive damages in civil cases do not have the same protections applicable in criminal proceedings, such awards pose an acute danger of arbitrary deprivation of property. In the present case, it was erroneous for the $145 million to be reinstated. Although State Farm's (D) handling of the claims against Campbell (P) was reprehensible, in that they would probably get a judgment over the policy limits, but still went to trial and then told Campbell (D) to sell his house, a more modest punishment for these actions could have satisfied the State's legitimate objectives. Instead, this case was used to expose State Farm's (D) perceived nationwide deficiencies, and a State does not have a legitimate concern in imposing punitive damages to punish a defendant for unlawful acts committed outside the State's jurisdiction. A State cannot punish a defendant for conduct that may have been lawful where it occurred. Lawful out-of-state conduct may be probative when

Continued on next page.

it demonstrates the deliberateness and culpability of the defendant's action in the State where it is tortuous, but that conduct must have a nexus to the specific harm suffered by the plaintiff. Moreover, the courts erred in awarding punitive damages to punish and deter conduct that bore no relation to Campbell's (P) harm. Due process does not permit courts to adjudicate the merits of other parties' hypothetical claims against a defendant. Furthermore, the disparity between the actual or potential harm suffered by Campbell (P) and the punitive damages award is much too large to be valid. Few awards exceeding a single-digit ratio between punitive and compensatory damages will satisfy due process. Usually an award of no more than four times the amount of compensatory damages is the maximum. The ratio in the present case is 145 to 1. The measure of punishment in this case was neither reasonable nor proportionate to the amount of harm to Campbell (P) and to the general damages recovered. The harm Campbell (P) suffered was minor economic damage and not physical, and the excess verdict was paid before the complaint was filed. Lastly, the disparity between the punitive damages award and the civil penalties authorized or imposed in comparable cases is great. The civil sanction is a $10,000 fine for an act of fraud. Reversed and remanded.

▐ *ANALYSIS*

There is much analysis in legal literature concerning the theoretical basis and practical operation of punitive damages in tort cases.

■≡■

Quicknotes

BAD FAITH Conduct that is intentionally misleading or deceptive.

DUE PROCESS CLAUSE Clauses found in the Fifth and Fourteenth Amendments to the United States Constitution providing that no person shall be deprived of "life, liberty, or property, without due process of law."

FRAUD A false representation of facts with the intent that another will rely on the misrepresentation to his detriment.

INTENTIONAL INFLICTION OF EMOTIONAL DISTRESS Intentional and extreme behavior on the part of the wrongdoer with the intent to cause the victim to suffer from severe emotional distress, or behavior performed with reckless indifference, resulting in the victim's suffering from severe emotional distress.

PUNITIVE DAMAGES Damages exceeding the actual injury suffered for the purposes of punishment, deterrence and comfort to plaintiff.

■≡■

CHAPTER 11

Wrongful Death and Survival

Quick Reference Rules of Law

Moragne v. States Marine Lines, Inc.

Longshoreman's widow (P) v. Vessel's owner (D)

398 U.S. 375 (1970).

NATURE OF CASE: Appeal from denial of a wrongful death action.

FACT SUMMARY: After Edward Moragne, a longshoreman, was killed aboard a vessel in navigable waters, his widow (P) brought an action against States Marine Lines (D), owner of the vessel, to recover damages for wrongful death.

🏛 RULE OF LAW
Although Congress has not enacted a specific remedy for wrongful death in admiralty, an action for wrongful death does lie under maritime common law for death caused by violation of maritime duties.

FACTS: Edward Moragne, a longshoreman, was killed in navigable waters while working aboard the vessel Palmetto State. Thereafter, Moragne's widow (P) brought an action against the States Marine Lines, Inc. (D), owner of the Palmetto State. However, the state court held that maritime law (applicable because Edward's death occurred in navigable waters) did not afford a cause of action for wrongful death. Thereupon, Moragne's widow (P) appealed.

ISSUE: Is there a cause of action for wrongful death under general maritime law?

HOLDING AND DECISION: (Harlan, J.) Yes. Although Congress has not enacted a specific remedy for wrongful death in admiralty, an action for wrongful death does lie under maritime common law for death caused by violation of maritime duties. Although *The Harrisburg*, 119 U.S. 199 (1886), held that there is no cause of action for wrongful death under U.S. maritime law, today *The Harrisburg* must be overruled. The fact that every state in the United States has enacted a wrongful death statute makes it clear that there is a general policy today in favor of allowing wrongful death actions. This policy is based upon the reasoning that "where existing law imposes a primary duty, violations of which are compensable if they cause injury, nothing in ordinary notions of justice suggests that a violation would be nonactionable simply because it was serious enough to cause death." Of course, this reasoning is equally applicable to maritime law. As such, whenever a violation of maritime duties causes a death, the appropriate persons, a category to be defined through future litigation, should be allowed to bring an action for wrongful death. Reversed.

▶ ANALYSIS

This case illustrates the general rejection of the "felony-murder doctrine." Under this English doctrine (generally adopted by American courts before this century), there was no civil recovery for an act that resulted in death—that is, for an act that constituted both a tort and a felony. This doctrine was founded upon the fact that the punishment for a felony was death of the felon and forfeiture of his property to the Crown. As such, nothing remained of the felon or his property on which to base a civil action. As noted in this case, however, every state in the United States now has a wrongful death act which allows for civil recovery.

Quicknotes

ADMIRALTY That area of law pertaining to navigable waters.

MARITIME LAW That area of law pertaining to navigable waters.

WRONGFUL DEATH An action brought by the beneficiaries of a deceased person, claiming that the deceased's death was the result of wrongful conduct by the defendant.

Selders v. Armentrout

Accident victim's parents (P) v. Other driver (D)

Neb. Sup. Ct., 190 Neb. 275, 207 N.W.2d 686 (1973).

NATURE OF CASE: Appeal from damages award for a wrongful death.

FACT SUMMARY: When the Selders (P) brought an action to recover damages for the wrongful deaths of three of their minor children, a jury only awarded them medical and funeral expenses as damages.

🏛 RULE OF LAW
The measure of damages recoverable by a parent for the wrongful death of a minor child includes the loss of society, comfort and companionship of the child, as well as any pecuniary loss.

FACTS: The Selders (P) were involved in an automobile accident with the Armentrouts (D). As a result of this accident, three of the Selders' (P) minor children were killed. Thereafter, the Selders (P) brought an action against the Armentrouts (D) to recover damages for the wrongful deaths of their minor children. Before the jury deliberated on a verdict, the court instructed it that, "except for medical and funeral expenses, the damages should be the monetary value of the contributions and services which the parents could reasonably have expected to receive from the children less the reasonable cost to the parents of supporting the children." Thereafter, the jury found the Armentrouts (D) negligent and returned a verdict for the Selders (P) in the amount of the medical and funeral expenses of the three children. Thereupon, the Selders (P) brought this appeal to recover further damages.

ISSUE: In an action for the wrongful death of a minor child is the parent entitled to compensation for the loss of society, comfort and companionship of the child?

HOLDING AND DECISION: (McCown, J.) Yes. The measure of damages recoverable by a parent for the wrongful death of a minor child includes the "loss of society, comfort and companionship" of the child, as well as any pecuniary loss. Of course, to limit damages to any pecuniary loss (i.e., to the monetary value of the services which the parent could reasonably have expected to receive from the child less the reasonable cost of supporting the child) would be to "stamp almost all modern children as worthless in the eyes of the law." Since this would be grossly unfair, the Selders (P) are entitled to recover for loss of "society, comfort and companionship" of their children. Affirmed as to liability; reversed as to damages.

DISSENT: (White, C.J.) A jury should not be allowed to translate emotional, conjectural, and speculative sentimental values incapable of having any objective standards applied to them, into an award of money.

▶ ANALYSIS

This case illustrates a very recent trend which specifically allows compensation for the "loss of companionship" of a child wrongfully killed. The general rule, however, is still that damages are limited to any pecuniary loss. Note, though, that even those states that limit damages to "pecuniary" loss usually allow substantial damages for the loss of a child, on the theory that the child would have "eventually" made a substantial monetary contribution to his parents.

Quicknotes

LOSS OF COMPANIONSHIP An action brought based on willful interference with the marital relationship.

WRONGFUL DEATH An action brought by the beneficiaries of a deceased person, claiming that the deceased's death was the result of wrongful conduct by the defendant.

Murphy v. Martin Oil Co.

Burn victim's widow (P) v. Property owner (D)

Ill. Sup. Ct., 56 Ill. 2d 423, 308 N.E.2d 583 (1974).

NATURE OF CASE: Action under both a wrongful death statute and a survival statute.

FACT SUMMARY: After Mr. Murphy died from a fire on the Martin Oil Co.'s (D) land, his wife (P) brought an action against the Oil Co. (D) to recover for his wrongful death and for his damages suffered during the interval between his injury and death.

🏛️ **RULE OF LAW**
When an injury caused by tortious conduct results in death, survivors of the decedent can recover from the tortfeasor both under the Illinois Wrongful Death Statute for the decedent's death and under the State Survival Statute for any damages suffered by the decedent during the interval between his injury and death.

FACTS: Mr. Murphy died several days after he suffered injuries in a fire on the Martin Oil Co.'s (D) premises. Thereafter, his wife (P) brought a negligence action against the Oil Co. (D) in two counts. First, she claimed damages to herself (as a result of her husband's death) under the Illinois Wrongful Death Statute. Second, she claimed damages under the State Survival Statute for Mr. Murphy's mental and physical suffering before his death, for his loss of wages following the injury and for his loss of clothing worn at the time of the injury. The state court, though, dismissed the wife's (P) claim under the Survival Statute on the ground that Illinois law makes wrongful death recovery the exclusive remedy in such situations. This appeal followed.

ISSUE: Is recovery for wrongful death the exclusive remedy when death results from injuries caused by tortious conduct?

HOLDING AND DECISION: (Ward, J.) No. When an injury caused by tortious conduct results in death, survivors of the decedent can recover from the tortfeasor both under the Illinois Wrongful Death Statute for the decedent's death and under the State Survival Statute for damages suffered by the decedent during the interval between his injury and death. Of course, under the older view, an action for personal injury did not survive death under the Survival Statute if death resulted from the tortious conduct which caused the injury (i.e., wrongful death recovery was the exclusive remedy in such cases). However, such limitation was unfair since it denied full liability for wrongs and full recovery for victims. As such, Murphy's wife (P) is entitled to recovery under the

Wrongful Death and Survival Statutes. Affirmed in part and reversed in part.

▶ **ANALYSIS**

This case illustrates the general rule (in states which have both of the discussed statutes) that recovery may be had under both Wrongful Death and Survival Statutes concurrently. Note that most jurisdictions today have Survival Statutes covering actions for injury to tangible property and for personal injury actions. Very few states, however, provide for the survival of intangible interests in personality (e.g., defamation actions).

Quicknotes

SURVIVAL STATUTE Law providing a cause of action to a deceased person's estate for certain unlawful acts committed upon the deceased person up until the time of his death.

WRONGFUL DEATH An action brought by the beneficiaries of a deceased person, claiming that the deceased's death was the result of wrongful conduct by the defendant.

Quick Reference Rules of Law

Butterfield v. Forrester

Injured horseback rider (P) v. Road blocker (D)

King's Bench, 11 East 59 (1809).

NATURE OF CASE: Action to recover damages for personal injury.

FACT SUMMARY: While riding very fast, Butterfield (P) ran into an obstruction Forrester (D) had put in the road and was injured.

🏛 RULE OF LAW
A plaintiff will not be able to recover where his lack of due care contributed to the occurrence of the accident.

FACTS: Forrester (D) was making some repairs on his house and put up a pole across a road. However, passage was still possible. Butterfield (P) was riding very fast on the road, did not see the pole, and ran into it. He fell with his horse and was injured. There was no evidence of his being intoxicated. There was evidence that it was possible to see 100 yards away at the time of the accident and that, had Butterfield (P) not been riding so fast, he might have seen and avoided the pole.

ISSUE: Can a plaintiff who has not used reasonable care to avoid an accident recover for injury caused by the accident?

HOLDING: (Bayley, J. [who also tried the case]) By riding his horse as fast as possible, Butterfield (P) failed to exercise ordinary care. He therefore was entirely responsible for the accident.

HOLDING: (Ellenborough, C.J.) One person's fault does not relieve another from the duty to exercise ordinary care himself. Butterfield (P) thus could have prevailed here only by showing that Forrester (D) wrongly obstructed the road, and that Butterfield (P) himself exercised ordinary care to avoid the obstruction.

DECISION: (Per curiam) Rule refused.

▶ ANALYSIS

This case states the defense of contributory negligence. The following theories have been used to support the theory: Plaintiff is denied recovery to punish him for his own misconduct; plaintiff must come into court with "clean hands"; the defense is a deterrent to plaintiffs' negligence; plaintiff's negligence is a superseding cause which makes the defendant's negligence no longer the proximate cause. The same standard is used as to determine negligence: the average reasonable person.

Quicknotes

NEGLIGENCE Conduct falling below the standard of care that a reasonable person would demonstrate under similar conditions.

REASONABLE PERSON STANDARD The standard of care exercised by a hypothetical person who possesses the intelligence, education, knowledge, attention, and judgment required by society of its members when governing behavior; the standard applies to a person's judgment when determining breach of a duty under the theory of negligence.

Davies v. Mann

Donkey's owner (P) v. Wagon driver (D)

Exchequer, 10 M.&W. 546, 152 Eng. Rep. 588 (1842).

NATURE OF CASE: Action to recover damages for negligence.

FACT SUMMARY: Davies (P) left his donkey on a public highway, and Mann (D) drove into it, killing it.

🏛 **RULE OF LAW**
The last clear chance doctrine is that where plaintiff's negligence has put him in a dangerous position, and defendant discovers plaintiff's danger and fails to use due care to avoid injuring plaintiff, plaintiff's negligence will not bar his recovery.

FACTS: Davies (P) fettered the forefeet of his ass and turned it onto a public highway. It was grazing off the side of the road when Mann's (D) wagon, which was coming at a fast pace, knocked it down and killed it.

ISSUE: If defendant fails to use due care to avoid injuring a plaintiff who has negligently put himself in a dangerous position, does plaintiff's negligence bar his recovery?

HOLDING: (Lord Abinger, C.B.) No. A plaintiff's negligently placing himself in a dangerous condition does not excuse defendant's failure to use due care to avoid injury to plaintiff. In this case, whether Davies' (P) ass was lawfully or wrongfully on the road makes no difference, since Mann (D) might, by using proper care, have avoided hitting the ass and did not. He is liable for the consequences of his negligence, even though the ass might have been there improperly.

HOLDING: (Parke, J.) Even if Davies (P) wrongfully placed the ass in the highway, Mann (D) still had a duty to drive his wagon at a pace enabling him to avoid the accident.

▶ *ANALYSIS*

The following reasons have been given for the last clear chance doctrine: (1) If the defendant has the last clear opportunity to avoid the harm, the plaintiff's negligence is no longer a proximate cause of the resulting injury; and (2) the later negligence of the defendant involves a higher degree of fault. The assumption is that he is the more culpable because his opportunity to avoid the injury was later. Prosser feels that the real explanation for the doctrine is the dislike for the defense of contributory negligence. Prosser further states that "as an ultimate, just solution, it is obviously inadequate" since usually it merely transfers from the plaintiff to the defendant an entire loss due to the fault of both.

Quicknotes

CONTRIBUTORY NEGLIGENCE Behavior on the part of an injured plaintiff falling below the standard of ordinary care that contributes to the defendant's negligence, resulting in the plaintiff's injury.

PERSONAL INJURY Harm to an individual's person or body.

REASONABLE CARE The degree of care observed by a reasonably prudent person under similar circumstances; synonymous with due care or ordinary care.

McIntyre v. Balentine

Pickup truck driver (P) v. Tractor driver (D)

Tenn. Sup. Ct., 833 S.W.2d 52 (1992).

NATURE OF CASE: Appeal from jury verdict rejecting claim for personal injury.

FACT SUMMARY: After he and another driver were both found to have been at fault in a car accident, McIntyre's (P) claim for personal injury was rejected based on the defense of contributory negligence.

> ## 🏛 RULE OF LAW
> Contributory negligence is abolished as a defense.

FACTS: McIntyre (P) was involved in an auto accident with Balentine (D). Both were intoxicated. McIntyre (P) sued for personal injury. The jury found both parties equally negligent. Based on a contributory negligence instruction, the jury returned a defense verdict. McIntyre (P) appealed.

ISSUE: Is contributory negligence abolished as a defense?

HOLDING AND DECISION: (Drowota, J.) Yes. Contributory negligence is abolished as a defense. The doctrine was originally based on the notion that a person should not benefit from his own wrongdoing. It may have arisen out of the all-or-nothing nature of issue pleading in commonlaw England. To vitiate its more egregious characteristics, rather artificial doctrines such as last clear chance and superseding cause have been grafted onto the contributory negligence doctrine. However, it appears that the best approach at this time would simply be to adopt a system of comparative fault. Some states have adopted "pure" comparative fault, where a plaintiff can recover even if he is 90 percent or more at fault. However, a modified comparative fault system, wherein a plaintiff can recover only if he is less than 50 percent at fault, is more consistent with a fault-based compensation system. In this case, the jury would probably not have found McIntyre (P) and Balantine (D) equally at fault if it had considered an instruction based on the rule announced here, so a new trial is necessary. Reversed in part, affirmed in part, and remanded.

▶ ANALYSIS

Almost all states (forty-six, in fact) have jettisoned contributory negligence in favor of comparative fault. As the opinion intimates, two main forms of comparative fault exist: the form adopted here and "pure" comparative negligence. For an example of an opinion that opted for pure comparative fault, see *Li v. Yellow Cab Co.*, 13 Cal. 3d 804, 532 P.2d 1226 (1975).

Quicknotes

COMPARATIVE FAULT Doctrine whereby a plaintiff's damages are reduced by a percentage equal to that of his own causal fault so long as the plaintiff's fault is not the sole proximate cause of the injury.

CONTRIBUTORY NEGLIGENCE Behavior on the part of an injured plaintiff falling below the standard of ordinary care that contributes to the defendant's negligence, resulting in the plaintiff's injury.

MODIFIED COMPARATIVE FAULT Under modified comparative fault, the plaintiff will be barred from all recovery if her fault is as great as (or, in some jurisdictions, greater than) that of the defendant.

PERSONAL INJURY Harm to an individual's person or body.

PURE COMPARATIVE FAULT Under pure comparative fault, the plaintiff can recover as long as her fault is not the sole proximate cause of her injury.

Seigneur v. National Fitness Institute, Inc.

Customer (P) v. Fitness club (D)

Md. Ct. Sp. App., 752 A.2d 631 (2000).

NATURE OF CASE: Negligence action against a fitness club.

FACT SUMMARY: A fitness-club customer injured her right shoulder during her initial evaluation on the club's weight machines. She and her husband sued the club for negligence. The club moved to dismiss, arguing that she had assumed all risk for any injuries sustained at the club by signing an agreement that contained an express exculpatory clause.

🏛 **RULE OF LAW**
An express exculpatory clause in an agreement can excuse a defendant's negligence.

FACTS: Gerilynne Seigneur (P) signed a written agreement when she started her membership with her fitness club, National Fitness Institute, Inc. ("NFI") (D). The agreement contained an express provision in which Seigneur (P) agreed to assume all risk for any injuries she might incur at NFI's (D) facilities. The provision also stated an express waiver of all claims for negligence against NFI (D). Seigneur (P) then injured her right shoulder at her initial evaluation on NFI's (D) weight machines. She and her husband sued NFI (D) for negligence—vicariously for the allegedly negligent conduct of the NFI (D) employee who conducted the evaluation, and directly for allegedly negligently hiring and training the employee. NFI (D) responded with a motion to dismiss, arguing that Seigneur (P) had assumed all risk by entering her agreement with the club, and that the club therefore was entitled to judgment against her. On NFI's motion to dismiss, which the trial court treated as a motion for summary judgment, Seigneur (P) contended that the agreement was an adhesion contract, the agreement's assumption-of-risk provision violated public policy, and the agreement was ambiguous. The trial judge entered summary judgment in favor of NFI (D). Seigneur (P) appealed.

ISSUE: Can an express exculpatory clause in an agreement excuse a defendant's negligence?

HOLDING AND DECISION: (Salmon, J.) Yes. An express exculpatory clause in an agreement can excuse a defendant's negligence. Maryland law requires an exculpatory agreement to be clear and specific in releasing a defendant from liability for his negligence; the agreement here meets that standard, and the agreement did not result from any improper purpose on the part of NFI (D), either. Further, no public policy typically prohibits an exculpatory clause that is clear and

freely entered by the parties. There are, however, three exceptions: (1) when the protected party engages in intentionally, recklessly, wantonly harmful conduct, or in grossly negligent harmful conduct, (2) when the bargaining power between the parties is grossly unequal, and (3) when the public has an interest in the transaction. Here, Seigneur (P) bases her appeal on the second and third exceptions; neither ground, however, is persuasive in this case. The agreement was indeed an adhesion contract, but that fact alone does not mean that the parties were grossly unequal in bargaining power. Seigneur (P) was free to go elsewhere for the non-essential services provided by a fitness club. Nor does the transaction implicate the larger public interest. To determine public interest in this context, courts consider the totality of the circumstances, focusing on such concerns as whether the business is publicly regulated, whether the protected party provides a service of great public importance, whether the protected party actively performs the service for any person meeting set requirements or for any member of the public, whether the protected party has a distinctly greater bargaining power against his clients and confronts his public with a standard adhesion contract, and whether the purchaser's person or property becomes subject to the seller's (i.e., the protected party's) control. Under these factors, NFI's (D) exculpatory clause does not patently offend Maryland sensibilities because the club does not perform an essential public service. Affirmed.

▶ **ANALYSIS**

In this intersection of tort law and contract law, the sanctity of contract prevails. As the court notes [p. 603], parties generally are free to govern their own destinies by their agreements. That principle applies even when, as in *Seigneur*, the agreement permits one party to avoid potential liability in tort.

◼▬◼

Quicknotes

ADHESION CONTRACT A contract, usually in standardized form, that is prepared by one party and offered to another, whose terms are so disproportionately in favor of the drafting party that courts tend to question the equality of bargaining power in reaching the agreement.

Continued on next page.

ASSUMPTION OF RISK DOCTRINE An affirmative defense to a negligence suit contending that the plaintiff knowingly and voluntarily subjected himself to a hazardous condition absolving the defendant of liability for injuries incurred.

EXCULPATORY CLAUSE A clause in a contract relieving one party from liability for certain unlawful conduct.

NEGLIGENCE Conduct falling below the standard of care that a reasonable person would demonstrate under similar conditions.

SUMMARY JUDGMENT Judgment rendered by a court in response to a motion made by one of the parties, claiming that the lack of a question of material fact in respect to an issue warrants disposition of the issue without consideration by the jury.

WILLFUL AND WANTON MISCONDUCT Unlawful intentional or reckless conduct without regard to the consequences.

Rush v. Commercial Realty Co.

Injured tenant (P) v. Landlord (D)

N.J. Sup. Ct., 7 N.J. Misc. 337, 145 A. 476 (1929).

NATURE OF CASE: Action to recover damages for personal injury.

FACT SUMMARY: While a tenant of Commercial Realty Co. (D), Rush (P) fell through the outhouse floor and was injured.

🏛 RULE OF LAW
The defense of assumption of risk requires that plaintiff has voluntarily encountered the risk, and the risk is not assumed where defendant has left plaintiff no reasonable alternatives.

FACTS: Rush (P) was a tenant of Commercial Realty Co. (D). Commercial Realty Co. (D) provided an outhouse for the use of its tenants. Rush (P) went to use the outhouse and fell through a trap door in the floor, thereby sustaining injuries. Rush (P) testified that the floor was in bad condition. Commercial Realty Co. (D) appealed the denial of its motion for nonsuit and its motion for a directed verdict.

ISSUE: Where defendant's negligence creates a risk and defendant provides no reasonable alternatives, is a plaintiff who encounters the risk and is injured barred recovery by the defense of assumption of risk?

HOLDING AND DECISION: (Per curiam) No. The defense requires that plaintiff's choice to assume the risk was free and voluntary. If defendant has left plaintiff no reasonable alternatives, it will not be assumed that plaintiff's choice to assume the risk was a voluntary one. Here, Rush (P) had no choice but to use the facilities provided by Commercial Realty Co. (D). Her use was not assumption of risk. She was not required to leave her home and go elsewhere. The jury might find that her stepping on the floor which she knew was in bad repair was contributory negligence, but her use was not assumption of risk. The denial of Commercial Realty Co.'s (D) motion is affirmed.

▌ANALYSIS

This case represents the general rule that voluntariness cannot be assumed where no reasonable alternative exists. Likewise, those who dash in to save their property or lives or the property of others, from a peril caused by defendant's negligence, do not assume the risk. Of course, the value of plaintiff's interest may not be sufficient to warrant the risk in some situations. Then plaintiff might be charged with contributory negligence, not assumption of risk.

Quicknotes

ASSUMPTION OF RISK DOCTRINE An affirmative defense to a negligence suit by the defendant contending that the plaintiff knowingly and voluntarily subjected himself to the hazardous condition wholly absolving the defendant of liability for injuries incurred.

DIRECTED VERDICT A verdict ordered by the court in a jury trial.

PERSONAL INJURY Harm to an individual's person or body.

Blackburn v. Dorta

Parties not identified.

Fla. Sup. Ct., 348 So. 2d 287 (1977).

NATURE OF CASE: Consolidated appeals in negligence actions.

FACT SUMMARY: The court was called upon to rule on the continued invalidity of the assumption of risk defense after comparative negligence had been adopted.

🏛 RULE OF LAW
The defense of assumption of risk is interchangeable with the concept of contributory negligence and, as such, is merged into the principles of comparative negligence.

FACTS: On appeal, several cases were consolidated, all involving the defense of assumption of risk. The principal question concerned the validity of the defense after the case of *Hoffman v. Jones*, 280 So. 2d 431 (Fla. 1973), which adopted the principles of comparative negligence in Florida. The court was asked to rule that assumption of risk, as an affirmative defense, was no longer viable after the Hoffman decision.

ISSUE: Can the defense of assumption of risk be asserted subsequent to the adoption of the rules of comparative negligence?

HOLDING AND DECISION: (Sundberg, J.) No. To begin with, it must be noted that assumption of risk has always been a confused and disfavored doctrine. There are various categories of assumption of risk: express and implied; primary and secondary; strict and qualified. For various reasons, only one of these categories has ever had any significance in tort law—that of implied-secondary-qualified assumption of risk. However, upon examination of this doctrine, it becomes clear that it is indistinguishable from the discarded law of contributory negligence. As such, it must be held that for purposes of Florida tort law, the assumption of risk defense has been merged into the principles of comparative negligence, as described in the *Hoffman* decision.

▶ ANALYSIS

As the principal case notes, the defense of assumption of risk has always been looked upon with some degree of disfavor by the courts. This is principally because it could often operate to bar an otherwise deserving claim. In at least some jurisdictions, it has been held that the public interest in public safety mandates that the defense not be permitted in cases involving the violation of safety statutes. See, e.g., *Casey v. Atwater*, 22 Conn. Supp. 225 (1960).

Quicknotes

ASSUMPTION OF RISK DOCTRINE An affirmative defense to a negligence suit by the defendant contending that the plaintiff knowingly and voluntarily subjected himself to the hazardous condition wholly absolving the defendant of liability for injuries incurred.

COMPARATIVE NEGLIGENCE Doctrine whereby the court in assessing the appropriate measure of damages compares the relative fault of the parties and reduces the amount of damages to be collected by the plaintiff in proportion to his degree of fault.

CONSOLIDATION The combining of two or more separate companies into a single new corporation.

Teeters v. Currey

Unsterilized woman (P) v. Doctor (D)

Tenn. Sup. Ct., 518 S.W.2d 512 (1974).

NATURE OF CASE: Malpractice action.

FACT SUMMARY: Over three years after Currey (D), a physician, performed an operation to sterilize Mrs. Teeters (P), she discovered that the operation was a failure.

🏛 RULE OF LAW
The statute of limitations for a medical malpractice action for negligently performed surgery runs not from the date of the injury, but from the time that the patient discovers, or should have reasonably been expected to discover, the injury.

FACTS: On June 5, 1970, Mrs. Teeters (P) gave birth to a normal child with Dr. Currey (D) as the attending physician. At that time, because of complications, Dr. Currey (D) performed a bilateral tubal ligation to prevent future pregnancies. However, on December 6, 1972, Mrs. Teeters (P) discovered she was again pregnant. Thereafter, on March 9, 1973, she delivered a premature child and there were severe complications. On November 15, 1973, Mrs. Teeters (P) instituted a suit against Dr. Currey (D) on the basis that the earlier tubal ligation was negligently and inadequately performed. In response, Dr. Currey (D) alleged that the one-year statute of limitations barred any action against him. After a lower court held for Currey (D), Mrs. Teeters (P) appealed.

ISSUE: Does the statute of limitations for a medical malpractice action for negligently performed surgery begin to run from the date of the injury?

HOLDING AND DECISION: (Henry, J.) No. The statute of limitations for a medical malpractice action for negligently performed surgery runs not from the date of the injury, but from the time that the patient discovers, or should have reasonably been expected to discover, the injury. This rule is based upon the rationale that an injured patient should not be denied recovery (and a doctor allowed to escape liability) merely because the injury is not evident for a long period of time. Here, Mrs. Teeters (P) did not discover Dr. Currey's (D) negligence and her own injury until three years after the operation. However, after discovering her injury, Mrs. Teeters (P) brought an action within the time allowed by the statute of limitations. As such, her action is not barred. Reversed.

▶ ANALYSIS

This case illustrates the majority rule for medical malpractice actions. However, some courts still use the time-of-damage approach. Others have held that the statute of limitations begins to run when the doctor-patient relationship ends, even if the patient has not discovered the injury. Still others have limited the time-of-discovery rule to negligent surgical practices and applied the time-of-damage rule to cases of negligent diagnosis.

■——■

Quicknotes

STATUTE OF LIMITATIONS A law prescribing the period in which a legal action may be commenced.

STATUTE OF REPOSE A law prescribing the period of time in which an action can be commenced that begins to run upon the delivery of goods or the completion of performance.

■——■

Freehe v. Freehe

Husband (P) v. Wife (D)

Wash. Sup. Ct., 81 Wash. 2d 183, 500 P.2d 771 (1972).

NATURE OF CASE: Action for negligence damages.

FACT SUMMARY: Clifford Freehe (P) brought an action against his wife, Hazel Freehe (D), to recover for personal injuries caused by negligence.

🏛 **RULE OF LAW**
Interspousal tort immunity in personal injury cases is hereafter abandoned.

FACTS: Clifford Freehe (P) was injured by a tractor owned by Hazel Freehe (D), his wife, as her separate property. This tractor was also located on Hazel Freehe's (D) separate property farm. After his injury, Clifford Freehe (P) brought an action against Hazel Freehe (D) to recover compensation for his injuries. This action was based on Hazel Freehe's (D) negligent maintenance of the tractor and her failure to warn Clifford Freehe (P) of its unsafe condition. In response, Hazel Freehe (D) brought a motion for summary judgment on the basis of interspousal tort immunity. After the trial court granted Hazel's (D) motion, Clifford (P) brought this appeal.

ISSUE: Must the doctrine of interspousal tort immunity be followed today in personal injury cases?

HOLDING AND DECISION: (Neill, J.) No. Interspousal tort immunity in personal injury cases is hereafter abandoned, since those reasons previously advanced in support of it are no longer valid. First, husband and wife are no longer considered to be "one person" (i.e., the identity of the wife is not merged with that of the husband). Second, there is no validity to the argument that allowance of tort actions between spouses will destroy marital "peace and tranquility." "If a state of peace and tranquility exists between spouses, then the situation is such that either no action will be commenced or that the spouses . . . will allow the action to continue only so long as their personal harmony is not jeopardized." Finally, criminal and divorce laws do not provide adequate alternatives to tort actions (i.e., neither compensates for damages done or provides any remedy for nonintentional torts). Here, therefore, Clifford (P) is entitled to maintain an action for negligence against his wife (D). Reversed.

▶ **ANALYSIS**

This case illustrates the rule followed in approximately half of the states—i.e., complete abandonment of interspousal tort immunity. Furthermore, many other states have partially abandoned such immunity by creating various exceptions. For example, most states exempt from immunity any intentional tort actions. Note that a majority of the states do still retain intrafamily tort immunity in order to prevent suits between parent and child.

■■■

Quicknotes

IMMUNITY Exemption from a legal obligation.

INTERSPOUSAL IMMUNITY A common law doctrine precluding spouses from commencing actions against one another for their torts.

SUMMARY JUDGMENT Judgment rendered by a court in response to a motion by one of the parties, claiming that the lack of a question of material fact in respect to an issue warrants disposition of the issue without consideration by the jury.

■■■

Renko v. McLean

Injured daughter (P) v. Mother (D)

Md. Ct. of App., 346 Md. 464, 697 A.2d 468 (1997).

NATURE OF CASE: Negligence action.

FACT SUMMARY: Renko (P) brought suit against her mother (D) for injuries sustained when she drove their car into the rear of another vehicle.

🏛 RULE OF LAW
In Maryland there is no exception to the parent-child immunity doctrine in motor tort cases based on the existence of compulsory automobile liability insurance coverage.

FACTS: Renko (P) suffered serious injuries when her mother negligently drove their car into the rear of another vehicle. After her eighteenth birthday Renko (P) filed suit against her mother (D) for negligence. Her mother (D) filed a motion to dismiss passed on the parent-child immunity doctrine. Renko (P) asked the court to recognize an exception to the doctrine to allow emancipated children to file actions against their parents for injuries sustained in motor vehicle accidents occurring when the minor is between 15 and 18 years old. The trial court entered judgment for the mother (D) and Renko (P) appealed.

ISSUE: Is there an exception in Maryland to the parent-child immunity doctrine in motor tort cases based on the existence of compulsory automobile liability insurance coverage?

HOLDING AND DECISION: (Karwacki, J.) No. In Maryland there is no exception to the parent-child immunity doctrine in motor tort cases based on the existence of compulsory automobile liability insurance coverage. Renko (P) argued that the court should abrogate the parent-child immunity doctrine for the following reasons: (1) adult children should be allowed to maintain actions against their parents for injuries occurring during their minority; (2) no justification exists to apply the doctrine here in light of the compulsory motor vehicle liability insurance law; and (3) application of the doctrine violates the Maryland and federal constitutions. With respect to the first argument Renko (P) contends that since this court has allowed children to maintain actions against their parents for acts occurring after attaining majority, the court should also allow children who have attained majority to bring suit for acts occurring during their minority. This reading would result in a total abrogation of the doctrine and is rejected. With respect to the second argument, while the court recognizes that most jurisdictions have abrogated the doctrine as applied to motor torts, this court believes the rule is in the best interests of both children and parents and that abrogating such immunity would result in familial discord and interfere in the raising and discipline of the children. The assertion that the doctrine violates state and federal law is meritless as well. Affirmed.

▶ ANALYSIS

The parent-child immunity doctrine was a common law bar to tort actions between parents and children. The rationale supporting the doctrine was that it would promote family harmony and the integrity of the familial unit.

━━■

Quicknotes

NEGLIGENCE Conduct falling below the standard of care that a reasonable person would demonstrate under similar conditions.

PARENTAL IMMUNITY The immunity of a parent from liability in actions brought by his or her child claiming negligence.

━━■

Abernathy v. Sisters of St. Mary's

Patient (P) v. Hospital (D)

Mo. Sup. Ct., 446 S.W.2d 599 (1969).

NATURE OF CASE: Personal injury negligence action.

FACT SUMMARY: Abernathy (P) brought an action against the Sisters of St Mary's Hospital (D), a charitable institution, for damages for personal injuries allegedly suffered as a result of the Hospital's (D) negligence.

🏛 RULE OF LAW
The doctrine of immunity of charitable institutions from liability for torts is hereafter abolished.

FACTS: Abernathy (P) was injured in the Sisters of St. Mary's Hospital (D) when an employee of the Hospital (D) negligently failed to assist him as he moved from his bed to the bathroom. Thereafter, Abernathy (P) brought an action against the Hospital (D) to recover damages for his personal injuries. In response, the Hospital (D) moved for summary judgment on the basis it was immune from liability for torts as a charitable institution. After the lower court held for the Hospital (D), Abernathy (P) brought this appeal.

ISSUE: Is a charitable institution liable for its torts today?

HOLDING AND DECISION: (Henley, C.J.) Yes. The doctrine of immunity of charitable institutions from liability for torts is hereafter abolished. As such, a charitable institution "is liable for its own negligence and for the negligence of its agents and employees acting within the scope of their employment." Such liability is necessary since immunity only "fosters neglect and breeds irresponsibility, while liability promotes care and caution." Furthermore, today charity is "big business" which can afford to pay for its torts. Here, therefore, the Hospital (D) is not immune from liability for its torts. Reversed and remanded for further proceedings.

▌ *ANALYSIS*

This case does not illustrate the majority view. That is, most jurisdictions have not "completely abolished" charitable immunity. However, most have "partially abolished" it by creating various exceptions (e.g., many have limited immunity to "recipients of the benefits of the charity"). Note that there are two principal arguments which have been used to support charitable immunity. First, there is the theory of "implied waiver." Under this theory, "he who accepts the benefit of charity impliedly agrees he will not assert against the institution any right of recourse for wrong done him."

Second, there is the "trust fund" theory. Under this theory, a charitable institution's funds are held in trust for charitable purposes and cannot be used to "pay" judgments resulting from tort claims.

■■■

Quicknotes

CHARITABLE IMMUNITY A rule absolving charities from liability for tortious activity.

■■■

Ayala v. Philadelphia Board of Public Education

Parents of injured student (P) v. School board (D)

Pa. Sup. Ct., 453 Pa. 584, 305 A.2d 877 (1973).

NATURE OF CASE: Personal injury negligence action.

FACT SUMMARY: After William Ayala, Jr. (P) was injured at school in his upholstery class, he and his father (P) brought an action against the Philadelphia Board of Public Education (D).

🏛 RULE OF LAW
The doctrine of state and local governmental immunity from liability for torts is hereafter abolished.

FACTS: While William Ayala, Jr. (P) was in the upholstery class at the Carrol School in Philadelphia, he caught his arm in a shredding machine. As a result of the injuries caused by this machine, William's (P) arm had to be amputated. Thereafter, William (P) and his father (P) brought an action against the Philadelphia Board of Public Education (D) to recover damages. This action was brought on the ground that the Board's (D) employees were negligent in failing to supervise the upholstery class. In response, the Board (D) asserted the defense of governmental immunity from liability for torts. After the lower court and superior court held for the Board (D), the Ayalas (P) appealed.

ISSUE: Should the doctrine of governmental immunity from liability for torts be followed today?

HOLDING AND DECISION: (Roberts, J.) No. The doctrine of state and local governmental immunity from liability for torts is hereafter abolished for two central reasons. First, "it is better that the losses due to tortious conduct should fall upon the municipality rather than the injured individual." As such, the torts of public employees should be regarded as a "cost of the administration of government, which should be distributed by taxes to the public." Second, "exposure of the government to liability for its torts will have the effect of increasing governmental care and concern for the welfare of those who might be injured by its actions." Here, therefore, a negligence action may be brought against the Philadelphia Board of Public Education (D). Reversed.

▶ ANALYSIS

This case illustrates the rule followed by a number, although minority, of jurisdictions. Note that many of those jurisdictions which allow state and local governmental immunity have developed exceptions to such immunity. An exception followed by many of such jurisdictions is based upon a distinction between "proprietary" and "governmental" functions. Under this exception, there is no immunity for a city when it engages in activity that is normally carried out by the private sector of the economy (i.e., when it engages in "proprietary" functions). However, immunity remains for other activities (i.e., for "governmental" functions).

■═■

Quicknotes

GOVERNMENTAL IMMUNITY Implied immunity of state and federal governments from taxation by the other.

■═■

Riss v. New York

Assault victim (P) v. Municipality (D)

N.Y. Ct. App., 22 N.Y.2d 529, 240 N.E.2d 860 (1968).

NATURE OF CASE: Action for personal injuries.

FACT SUMMARY: Despite repeated pleas to the police for protection, Riss (P) was blinded and maimed by a criminal who had openly threatened her for years.

RULE OF LAW
Absent a specific legislative mandate to the contrary, the government is not liable for the negligent failure of police authorities to protect citizens from crime.

FACTS: For over six months in 1959, Linda Riss (P) was terrorized and threatened by a rejected suitor named Burton Pugach, described by the court as a "miscreant masquerading as a respectable attorney." Specifically, he threatened, "If I can't have you, no one else will have you, and when I get through with you, no one else will want you." Though she repeatedly reported such threats to the police, pleading for help, none was given in any significant way. Finally, on June 14, 1959, at an engagement party for Riss (P), who was to marry another man, a "thug" hired by Pugach threw acid in Riss's (P) face, blinding her in one eye and scarring her for life. Riss (P) filed this action against the City of New York (D) alleging that the negligent failure of NYPD to protect her was the cause of her injuries. From a dismissal of the complaint, she appealed contending that New York (D) was under a duty to protect her.

ISSUE: Are municipalities immune from liability arising out of the negligent failure of police authorities to protect citizens from crime?

HOLDING AND DECISION: (Breitel, J.) Yes. Absent a specific legislative mandate to the contrary, the government is not liable for the negligent failure of police authorities to protect citizens from crime. Such immunity applies even where specific threats have been made known to the authorities by particularly endangered persons. Though such immunity superficially appears harsh, any other holding could only result in interference with the allocation of police manpower by the courts. Such a decision is for the legislature, not the court, to make. The dismissal is affirmed.

DISSENT: (Keating, J.) The court today readopts one of the law's most enduring nonsequiturs: "Because we owe a duty to everybody, we owe it to nobody." Examination of the traditional justifications for this rule recommends its demise. First, it is suggested that permitting recovery in cases such as this would subject the city to "limitless liability"—but this ra-

tionale has long been discredited by the results of rejection of the general doctrine of sovereign immunity. Second, it is suggested that permitting recovery would invite a suit every time a crime is committed—but this rationale ignores the fact that such litigants would still be forced to prove causation, etc., before they could recover—a clear deterrent to spurious actions. Third, it is suggested that permitting recovery would interfere with police manpower allocation—but what is in fact threatened is merely tort liability for negligent allocation. More fundamentally, liability is necessary here to effect the most important function of tort law: redistribution of the burden of loss arising from crime to society as a whole.

ANALYSIS

Though the court here states the clear majority rule today, Justice Keating's eloquent dissent points up what may develop into a trend of authority. More and more states have adopted statutes providing for the compensation for crime victims (e.g., California) under some circumstances. Furthermore, anti-crime liability insurance is encouraged and available to personal and business customers. Most writers agree, however, that it is highly unlikely that general tort immunity in this area will ever be supplanted.

Quicknotes

MUNICIPAL IMMUNITY Immunity from liability for local government entities.

PERSONAL INJURY Harm to an individual's person or body.

DeLong v. Erie County

Decedent's widower (P) v. County (D) and city (D)

N.Y. Sup. Ct., 89 A.D.2d 376, 455 N.Y.S.2d 887 (1982).

NATURE OF CASE: Appeal of award of damages against a municipality for negligent withholding of police protection.

FACT SUMMARY: After DeLong dialed 911 to report a burglar, the official handling the call mistakenly recorded the address she gave and the police did not follow standard verification procedures.

🏛 RULE OF LAW
Liability may arise when standard procedures are not followed in an emergency summons for police help.

FACTS: DeLong, discovering a burglar attempting to force entry, dialed 911. The official receiving the call mistakenly recorded the address she gave. When the police found a non-existent address, they dismissed the call as a prank. Standard procedure was to have the tape of the call reviewed to see if the address was correct. This was not done. DeLong was killed by the burglar, and her survivors (P) sued for wrongful death. A jury awarded damages against the village of Kenmore (D), which had responded to the call. The village appealed.

ISSUE: May liability arise when standard procedures are not followed in an emergency summons for police help?

HOLDING AND DECISION: (Hancock, J.) Yes. Liability may arise when standard procedures are not followed in an emergency summons for police help. The standard rule is that a general failure to provide police protection is not compensable because allocation of police resources is a decision best left to the legislative and executive branches of government. When, however, a special relationship is formed between police and an individual, negligent execution of duties may lead to liability. Common examples of individuals with special relationships include undercover informants and protected witnesses. One placing an emergency call and told help is on the way is in a special relationship, as that individual is now relying on assurances that the police will arrive and may, therefore, not take defensive measures he otherwise might. This appears to have been the case here, as DeLong did not flee the house. Affirmed.

▶ ANALYSIS

Tort immunity regarding municipal and county government may be characterized as a dichotomy. The two elements are discretionary and ministerial functions. Historically, liability may not arise in a situation where an official exercises discretion in some matter, but liability may arise when a ministerial function is negligently performed. Needless to say, there can be much disagreement as to which category any situation may fall in.

■■■

Quicknotes

MUNICIPAL IMMUNITY Immunity from liability for local government entities.

■■■

Deuser v. Vecera

Deceased (P) v. Federal government (D)

139 F.3d 1190 (8th Cir. 1998).

NATURE OF CASE: Wrongful death suit.

FACT SUMMARY: Deuser's (P) survivors brought suit against the United States (D) under the Federal Tort Claims Act based on the alleged negligence of two park rangers (D) resulting in Deuser's (P) death.

🏛 RULE OF LAW
The federal government is immune from civil liability under the discretionary function exception if the federal government or its employees' conduct involves an element of judgment or choice of the type that the exception was designed to shield.

FACTS: Deuser (P) attended the Veiled Prophet Fair on the grounds of the Jefferson National Expansion Memorial. The memorial is a national park and under the jurisdiction of the National Park Rangers. Rangers Vecera (D) and Bridges (D) observed Deuser (P) grabbing women on the buttocks and urinating in public. They arrested him and turned him over to local police who decided to release him. Deuser (P) was released in a parking lot with no money or transportation. He wandered onto an interstate highway and was struck and killed. Deuser's (P) survivors brought a wrongful death action against the United States (D) under the Federal Tort Claims Act (FTCA) based on the allegedly negligent acts of the park rangers. The claim was dismissed and the survivors (P) appealed.

ISSUE: Is the federal government immune from civil liability under the discretionary function exception if the federal government or its employees' conduct involves an element of judgment or choice of the type that the exception was designed to shield?

HOLDING AND DECISION: (Bowman, J.) Yes. The federal government is immune from civil liability under the discretionary function except if the federal government or its employees' conduct involves an element of judgment or choice of the type that the exception was designed to shield. The FTCA waives the federal government's immunity to civil suit for money damages for injury or loss of property or personal injury or death caused by the negligent or wrongful act or omission of any of its employees acting within the scope of their employment. The federal courts have subject matter jurisdiction over such claims where a private party would be liable to the claimant under the law of the particular placed where the act or omission occurred. There are, however, exceptions where the federal government is not amenable to suit,

such as the discretionary function exception. This exception shields the government from civil liability for claims based on the exercise or performance of a discretionary function or duty on the part of the federal government or its employees, whether or not the discretion involved the abused. The court applies a two-step analysis in determining whether the exception applies. First is whether the conduct was discretionary. This requires there to be an element of judgment or choice. Here the rangers' (D) decision to terminate the arrest requires such element of judgment or choice. The rangers' Standard Operating Procedure (SOP) for an arrest and the VP Fair Operations Handbook did not set forth a policy for terminating an arrest; however, the court concluded that such a determination is similar to the decision to make the arrest in the first place. Such decisions have been held to be in the discretion and judgment of the arresting officers. Thus the termination of Deuser's (P) arrest was a discretionary function. Second it must be determined whether the judgment is of the kind that the discretionary function exception was designed to shield. To avoid liability, the rangers' (D) conduct must be based on the social, economic or political goals of the Handbook's discretionary enforcement guidelines. Here all three were the basis for the rangers' (D) conduct. Affirmed.

▶ ANALYSIS

An immunity relieves a party from liability under any circumstance within the scope of the immunity. The immunity is conferred because of the position of the tortfeasor. While the underlying conduct still constitutes a tort, the particular person is shielded from liability by virtue of his status.

Quicknotes

GOVERNMENTAL IMMUNITY Implied immunity of state and federal governments from taxation by the other.

WRONGFUL DEATH An action brought by the beneficiaries of a deceased person, claiming that the deceased's death was the result of wrongful conduct by the defendant.

Quick Reference Rules of Law

Bussard v. Minimed, Inc.

Car accident victim (P) v. Negligent driver's employer (D)

Cal. Ct. App., 105 Cal. App. 4th 798 (2003).

NATURE OF CASE: Negligence action against a driver's employer under a theory of respondeat superior.

FACT SUMMARY: A company's employee rear-ended a stopped car while driving home after becoming ill at work and going home early for the day.

🏛 RULE OF LAW
An employer can be held liable when an employee leaves work early and foreseeably causes an accident while driving home.

FACTS: Hernandez, an employee of Minimed, Inc. (D), became ill at work after she inhaled fumes from pesticide sprayed at the Minimed (D) facility, at Minimed's (D) request, the night before. Hernandez grew dizzy and left work early, declining the suggestion from one of her supervisors that she see the company doctor. While driving home, Hernandez rear-ended Bussard's (P) car, which was stopped at a red light. Bussard (P) sued Hernandez for negligence and Minimed (D) for vicarious liability as Hernandez's employer, claiming that Hernandez was acting within the scope of her employment when the accident occurred. Minimed (D) eventually responded with a motion for summary judgment based in part on a denial that Hernandez was acting within the scope of her employment when she rear-ended Bussard (P). The trial court granted summary judgment for Minimed (D), and Bussard (P) appealed.

ISSUE: Can an employer be held liable when an employee leaves work early and foreseeably causes an accident while driving home?

HOLDING AND DECISION: (Rubin, J.) Yes. An employer can be held liable when an employee leaves work early and foreseeably causes an accident while driving home. Respondeat superior generally applies to injuries caused by employees who are acting within the scope of their employment because, so the theory goes, a business should be accountable for costs incurred to promote its interests. The definition of "acting within the scope of employment" is broad, but typically not so expansive that it includes an employee's daily commute to and from work. But there is an exception to this going-and-coming rule: When an employee imposes upon others a risk that arose at, or is otherwise related to, work, and the risk was foreseeable, the employer can be held liable for the employee's conduct under the theory of respondeat superior. Foreseeability in this context differs from the foreseeability used in the law of negligence; here the foreseeability analysis asks whether the employee's conduct is so startling that it cannot fairly be attributed to the employer. In this case, Hernandez's unfitness for driving was foreseeable in this manner, and the going-and-coming rule therefore does not preclude judgment against Minimed (D). Hernandez's job at Minimed (D) created a risk that Hernandez then imposed upon Bussard (P). Minimed's (D) diligent inquiries into Hernandez's condition before she left work do nothing to undermine that determinative fact. Whatever weight such arguments might have when the issue is negligence, they are irrelevant when the asserted liability is vicarious. Reversed.

▶ ANALYSIS

Bussard contradicts a key aspect of the casebook's discussion of respondeat superior. The casebook [pp. 660–661] stresses that the "superior" who is held liable "is without any fault of his own." The exception and the foreseeability test applied in *Bussard*, however, are rooted in Minimed's (D) role in both creating the risk and being able to predict its consequences. In this particular case, then, concern for the superior's own fault clearly supports the decision, regardless of whether such a concern fits the hornbook description of respondeat superior.

Quicknotes

FORESEEABLE DANGER A danger that is likely to result from a certain act or failure to act.

NEGLIGENCE Conduct falling below the standard of care that a reasonable person would demonstrate under similar conditions.

RESPONDEAT SUPERIOR Rule that the principal is responsible for tortious acts committed by its agents in the scope of their agency or authority.

SCOPE OF EMPLOYMENT Those duties performed pursuant to a person's occupation or employment.

SUMMARY JUDGMENT Judgment rendered by a court in response to a motion made by one of the parties, claiming that the lack of a question of material fact in respect to an issue warrants disposition of the issue without consideration by the jury.

VICARIOUS LIABILITY The imputed liability of one party for the unlawful acts of another.

O'Shea v. Welch

Car accident victim (P) v. Negligent driver (D) and his employer (D)

350 F.3d 1101 (10th Cir. 2003).

NATURE OF CASE: Suit for negligent driving and for vicarious liability against the driver's employer.

FACT SUMMARY: A store manager drove into another car when, on a whim, he tried to turn his car into a service station to get an estimate on his car. He was en route to his employer's district office to deliver football tickets to other managers when the accident occurred.

🏛 RULE OF LAW
A reasonable juror could conclude that driving a personal car to deliver sports tickets to one's fellow employees during working hours, and turning one's personal car into a service station to get a maintenance estimate while delivering the sports tickets during working hours, are actions within the scope of an employee's employment.

FACTS: Welch (D), a store manager for Osco (D), drove from his store toward Osco's (D) district office to deliver Kansas City Chiefs football tickets to other Osco (D) store managers. Welch (D) suddenly decided to turn his car into a service station to get an estimate on his car, and his car then struck O'Shea's (P). O'Shea (P) sued both Welch (D) and Osco (D), Welch (D) for negligence and Osco (D) for vicarious liability. The parties filed cross-motions for summary judgment. The trial judge ruled for Osco (D) on the issue of vicarious liability, reasoning that, even if Welch's (D) delivery of the tickets was within the scope of his employment, no reasonable juror could conclude that Welch's (D) attempt to get an estimate on his personal car was within the scope of his employment for Osco (D). O'Shea (P) appealed.

ISSUE: Can a reasonable juror conclude that driving a personal car to deliver sports tickets to one's fellow employees during working hours, and turning one's personal car into a service station to get a maintenance estimate while delivering the sports tickets during working hours, are actions within the scope of an employee's employment?

HOLDING AND DECISION: (McKay, J.) Yes. A reasonable juror could conclude that driving a personal car to deliver sports tickets to one's fellow employees during working hours, and turning one's personal car into a service station to get a maintenance estimate while delivering the sports tickets during working hours, are actions within the scope of an employee's employment. Kansas law, which applies in this case, restricts employer liability to injuries caused within the scope of an employee's employment. That limitation can extend to actions reasonably incidental to that employment, to conduct that an employer can fairly be expected to have foreseen based on the kind of employment and its related duties. Kansas courts probably would determine the boundaries of these principles by reference to the "slight deviation" rule. To determine whether an employee acted within the scope of his employment under that rule, courts ask whether the employee was acting on a frolic or a detour. A detour is within that scope, but a frolic is not. The question is whether the employee entirely leaves the employer's business purpose, even for a moment; if such an abandonment occurs, the act is outside the scope of employment and the employer cannot be held liable for any injuries caused by the employee's actions. Under this analysis, whether Welch's (D) attempted turn into the service station was a frolic or a detour is a fact-question for a jury to decide. Several specific fact-questions inform the "slight deviation" analysis: what the employee intended, when and where the deviation occurred, how long the deviation lasted, what the employee's typical work responsibilities were, what incidental actions the employer reasonably expected from the employee, and how much latitude the employee enjoyed in his work. These factors show that a reasonable juror could return a finding for O'Shea (P) in this case. Welch (D) intended to get an estimate for a car that he used for Osco's (D) benefit. The accident happened only a matter of minutes and feet away from the road Welch (D) was driving on to reach Osco's (D) district office. The accident arguably occurred on the main road, since Welch (D) did not complete his turn into the service station, and it is therefore reasonable to conclude that he was still discharging work-related duties for Osco (D) even if the intended trip to the service station was only a personal errand. Any deviation from the employment purpose lasted a very short time. It is also reasonable to conclude that a person in a managerial position, as Welch (D) was, normally had latitude to tend to personal errands during working hours. Thus, seeing the summary-judgment evidence in the light most favorable to O'Shea (P), a reasonable juror could conclude that Welch (D) was acting within the scope of his employment in trying to turn into the service station. Moreover, as the trial judge correctly noted, genuine issues of material fact are present on whether delivering football tickets to one's fellow employees fell within the scope of Welch's (D) employment in

Continued on next page.

the first instance; summary judgment therefore would not be appropriate on that question either. Trial is necessary on both questions. Reversed and remanded.

▶ *ANALYSIS*

Lest this case be seen as offering little more than a dry procedural ruling—on whether a reasonable juror could render a reasonable conclusion on the given questions of fact—consider the next step in this lawsuit. O'Shea (P) has just won the right to proceed to the risky world of trial, where he will have little to lose and everything to gain, and where Osco (D) will have much to lose and nothing to gain. O'Shea's (P) bargaining position in settlement negotiations, in other words, has just increased dramatically. Indeed, O'Shea (P) now *has* a bargaining position, whereas, before the appellate court's decision, he had none. Another key practice point of note in *O'Shea* is the Court's use of evidence in deciding the appeal. Note that the Court does not decide whether Welch's (D) actions were, in fact, within the scope of his employment; it decides only that a juror can point to record evidence (assuming that the evidence before the appellate court is eventually properly admitted at trial) to conclude that Welch (D) was acting within the scope of his employment. The Court can review such evidence before trial solely because O'Shea's (P) counsel put such evidence before the trial court in opposing Osco's (D) motion for summary judgment. The first goal of O'Shea's (P) counsel in opposing summary judgment was to demonstrate genuine issues of material fact, see Fed. R. Civ. P. 56(c), questions whose resolution could go either way and thus require the assistance of a fact-finder to determine which side's interpretation of the evidence is more likely true. O'Shea's (P) counsel succeeded in that objective in this case.

■══■

Quicknotes

QUESTION OF FACT An issue relating to a factual assertion that is disputed at trial and is properly left to the jury to resolve.

SCOPE OF EMPLOYMENT Those duties performed pursuant to a person's occupation or employment.

SUMMARY JUDGMENT Judgment rendered by a court in response to a motion made by one of the parties, claiming that the lack of a question of material fact in respect to an issue warrants disposition of the issue without consideration by the jury.

VICARIOUS LIABILITY The imputed liability of one party for the unlawful acts of another.

■══■

Murrell v. Goertz

Assault victim (P) v. Deliveryman (D) and employer (D)

Okla. Sup. Ct., 597 P.2d 1223 (1979).

NATURE OF CASE: Appeal from dismissal of action for battery.

FACT SUMMARY: The trial court ruled that Goertz (D), a newspaper deliverer, was an independent contractor and thus Oklahoma Publishing Co. (D) was not vicariously liable for his striking a customer (P) on his delivery route.

🏛 RULE OF LAW
An independent contractor is one who performs a service for another, free from control and direction of his employer in all matters connected with the performance of the service, except for the end result.

FACTS: Goertz (D), a newspaper deliverer, got into an argument with Murrell (P), one of his customers. The argument culminated in Goertz (D) striking Murrell (P), allegedly causing her injury. She brought suit for assault and battery against both Goertz (D) and the Oklahoma Publishing Co. (D), publisher of the newspaper which Goertz (D) had been delivering. At trial, the court sustained the motion for summary judgment by Oklahoma Publishing (D), which contended that Goertz (D) was an independent contractor, and thus Oklahoma Publishing (D) could not be charged with vicarious liability for his actions. Murrell (P) appealed the trial court order.

ISSUE: Is one who performs a service for another, free from control and direction of his employer in all matters connected with the performance of the service, save for the end result, an independent contractor?

HOLDING AND DECISION: (Reynolds, J.) Yes. The evidence adduced at trial shows that Oklahoma Publishing (D) had no connection at all with Goertz (D). Instead, it dealt with an independent distributor who hired Goertz (D). It is true that the company placed certain guidelines on the performance of all its distributors and deliverers, including Goertz (D). However, it in no way exercised the requisite control and direction over Goertz' (D) performance necessary to have him classified as an employee. As he was clearly an independent contractor, Oklahoma Publishing (D) could not be held vicariously liable for his torts. Thus, the action was properly dismissed as to the company (D). Affirmed.

▌ *ANALYSIS*

Traditionally, in cases of this kind, the court focused on the performance of the independent contractor/servant, and his freedom from control or lack thereof, in determining his status. However, there has been somewhat of a recent trend focusing on the enterprise involved, and determining which of the parties receives the primary benefit from it. When this approach is taken, it is more likely that an employer-employee relationship will be found, and vicarious liability imposed. See *Konick v. Berke, Moore Co., Inc.*, 355 Mass. 463 (1969).

Quicknotes

BATTERY Unlawful contact with the body of another person.

INDEPENDENT CONTRACTOR A party undertaking a particular assignment for another who retains control over the manner in which it is executed.

MOTION FOR SUMMARY JUDGMENT Judgment rendered by a court in response to a motion by one of the parties, claiming that the lack of a question of material fact in respect to an issue warrants disposition of the issue without consideration of the jury.

VICARIOUS LIABILITY The imputed liability of one party for the unlawful acts of another.

Maloney v. Rath

Injured driver (P) v. Other driver (D)

Cal. Sup. Ct., 69 Cal. 2d 442, 445 P.2d 513 (1968).

NATURE OF CASE: Action for personal injuries.

FACT SUMMARY: Maloney (P) was injured when her car was struck by Rath's (D) due to a negligent overhaul of Rath's (D) brakes by Evanchick, a mechanic.

> ## RULE OF LAW
> An employer who fails to provide specified safeguards or precautions will not be insulated from liability for injuries caused by the negligence of an independent contractor.

FACTS: Maloney (P) was injured when Rath's (D) car ran into hers. She thereupon filed this action to recover damages for the personal injuries so suffered. At trial, it was proved that the accident had resulted from brake failure on Rath's (D) car, that Rath (D) had no idea of the defective condition of his brakes prior to the accident, that Rath (D) had his brakes overhauled by an independent contractor mechanic, Peter Evanchick, only three months before, and that Evanchick's negligent repair effort had been the cause of the accident. The trial court gave judgment to Rath (D) on the ground that he was not liable for the negligence of his independent contractor mechanic. Maloney (P) appealed on the ground that Rath's (D) duty was nondelegable since it was (1) dangerous, and (2) statutorily required by the California Vehicle Code.

ISSUE: Is an employer insulated from liability for the negligence of his independent contractor even when the task entrusted to him is a statutorily mandated, dangerous one?

HOLDING AND DECISION: (Traynor, J.) No. An employer who fails to provide specified safeguards or precautions will not be insulated from liability for injuries caused by the negligence of an independent contractor. Certain duties are nondelegable and the duty involved in the conduct of a dangerous activity, like driving a car or the satisfaction of a statutory duty, like the one here, are such duties. Such a standard is not strict liability but rather a refusal to shift liability to a third party who may not be able to pay. Reversed.

▌ANALYSIS

This case points up the "nondelegable duty" limitation on the independent contractor exception to the doctrine of respondeat superior. Contrast this rule with strict liability since here a tortfeasor may escape liability by showing that he exercised due care in the performance of his "nondelegable" duty. Note, however that the determination of what duties are nondelegable (e.g., compliance with safety codes) is done on an ad hoc basis for largely independent policy reasons in each case.

■═■

Quicknotes

INDEPENDENT CONTRACTOR A party undertaking a particular assignment for another who retains control over the manner in which it is executed.

NEGLIGENCE Conduct falling below the standard of care that a reasonable person would demonstrate under similar conditions.

PERSONAL INJURY Harm to an individual's person or body.

STRICT LIABILITY Liability for all injuries proximately caused by a party's conducting of certain inherently dangerous activities without regard to negligence or fault.

■═■

Popejoy v. Steinle

Accident victim (P) v. Estate representative (D)

Wyo. Sup. Ct., 820 P.2d 545 (1991).

NATURE OF CASE: Appeal from summary judgment dismissing action seeking damages for personal injury.

FACT SUMMARY: Popejoy (P) sought to hold Steinle (D) vicariously liable when Steinle's (D) wife was involved in a car accident while traveling to buy a family pet.

 RULE OF LAW
Vicarious liability will not be imposed on a tortfeasor's spouse for acts arising in a personal context.

FACTS: Steinle's (D) wife, while driving her daughter to buy a calf, was involved in an accident with Popejoy (P). Although the Steinles (D) owned a ranch, the evidence was essentially uncontroverted that the calf was being bought for their daughter to raise as a pet rather than for a commercial purpose. Mrs. Steinle died in the accident. Popejoy (P), whose injuries at first seemed minor, did not make a creditor's claim against her estate. By the time Popejoy (P) filed a suit, the estate had been probated. Popejoy (P) filed a suit against the estate of Mr. Steinle (D), who had since died of unrelated causes, contending that Mr. Steinle (D) had been vicariously liable for his wife's negligence. The trial court granted summary judgment, dismissing the case, and Popejoy (P) appealed.

ISSUE: Will vicarious liability be imposed on a tortfeasor's spouse for acts arising in a personal context?

HOLDING AND DECISION: (Golden, J.) No. Vicarious liability will not be imposed on a tortfeasor's spouse for acts arising in a personal context. Vicarious liability exists among members of a joint enterprise. A joint enterprise involves four elements: (1) an express or implied agreement among members; (2) a common purpose; (3) a common pecuniary interest; and (4) an equal right of control. The third element implies that the enterprise must be for some commercial purpose and that the act giving rise to liability must have been in furtherance of that purpose. A personal act, even if between enterprising members, does not lead to vicarious liability. Here, even though the Steinles owned a commercial ranch, Mrs. Steinle had been on a personal mission at the time of the accident, so Mr. Steinle (D) was not vicariously liable. Affirmed.

ANALYSIS

The imposition of vicarious liability for a joint enterprise is essentially based on notions of fairness. A member of a joint enterprise obtains benefits from other members' acts. Consequently, he should also bear any consequential burdens.

Quicknotes

JOINT ENTERPRISE Venture undertaken based on an express or implied agreement between the members, common purpose and interest, and an equal power of control.

PERSONAL INJURY Harm to an individual's person or body.

SUMMARY JUDGMENT Judgment rendered by a court in response to a motion by one of the parties, claiming that the lack of a question of material fact in respect to an issue warrants disposition of the issue without consideration by the jury.

VICARIOUS LIABILITY The imputed liability of one party for the unlawful acts of another.

Shuck v. Means

Injured passenger (P) v. Rental car driver (D) and agency (D)

Minn. Sup. Ct., 226 N.W.2d 285 (1974).

NATURE OF CASE: Action for personal injuries.

FACT SUMMARY: Shuck (P) was injured when a car he was riding in was negligently struck by one leased by Hertz to Codling but driven by Means (D).

🏛 RULE OF LAW
Owner consent statutes do not require that a vehicle owner necessarily be aware that his car is being driven by a particular person for liability to be imputed to the owner for such driver's negligence.

FACTS: In March 1967, Codling leased a car from Hertz (D). On March 27, Codling permitted Means (D), an uninsured driver, to drive the Hertz car whereupon he negligently caused an accident with another car. Shuck (P), a passenger in this other car, was injured thereby. Shuck (P) thereupon filed this personal injury action against Hertz (D) based upon the Minnesota "owner consent" statute which reads, "whenever any motor vehicle . . . shall be operated upon any public street or highway of this state, by any person other than the owner, with the consent of the owner, express or implied, the operator thereof shall in case of accident, be deemed the agent of the owner of such motor vehicle in the operation thereof." From judgment for Shuck (P), this appeal followed on the question of whether Hertz (D) could escape liability because it had not known that Means (D) would use the car it leased to Codling.

ISSUE: Must a vehicle owner necessarily be aware that his car is being driven by a particular person before a so-called owner consent statute may be employed to impute liability to him for such driver's negligence?

HOLDING AND DECISION: (Kelly, J.) No. Owner consent statutes do not require that a vehicle owner necessarily be aware that his car is being driven by a particular person for liability to be imputed to the owner for such driver's negligence. Such statutes are intended to make the owners liable to those injured by their operation where no such liability would otherwise exist in order to encourage the maintenance of sufficient liability insurance. The gravamen of such liability is consent, express or implied; and here, since Hertz' (D) leasing of the car to Codling was subject only to a minor contractual prohibition against anyone else driving it, implied consent for Means's (D) use can be found. Affirmed.

▶ ANALYSIS

This case points up one way in which states have managed to get around the general rule of no vicarious liability between bailor and bailee—the consent statute. Indeed, many liability insurance policies have adopted identical coverage provisions. Though the finding of consent in Shuck was based on an admittedly loose construction of "consent" (Means's (D) driving was expressly prohibited by the rental agreement), it is well settled that where an owner is present in the car driven by another, consent will always be inferred, were appropriate.

Quicknotes

BAILEE Person holding property in trust for another party.

BAILOR Person who delivers property to be held in trust to a bailee.

NEGLIGENCE Conduct falling below the standard of care that a reasonable person would demonstrate under similar conditions.

PERSONAL INJURY Harm to an individual's person or body.

VICARIOUS LIABILITY The imputed liability of one party for the unlawful acts of another.

Smalich v. Westfall

Passenger's estate (P) v. Driver (D)

Pa. Sup. Ct., 440 Pa. 409, 269 A.2d 476 (1970).

NATURE OF CASE: Actions for wrongful death and for survival.

FACT SUMMARY: The estate (P) of a deceased auto passenger, who was also the passenger in one of two cars in a collision, sued the driver (D) of the other vehicle; the trial court, finding that both drivers were negligent, ruled that the negligence of the driver in whose car the deceased was a passenger precluded recovery by the estate (P).

🏛 RULE OF LAW
A driver's negligence will not be imputed to a passenger, unless the relationship between them is such that the passenger would be vicariously liable as a defendant for the driver's negligent acts.

FACTS: An automobile owned by Smalich, and operated by Westfall (D), collided with a vehicle driven by Blank (D). As a result of the accident, Smalich, a passenger in the automobile operated by Westfall (D), received mortal wounds. Smalich's estate (P) brought a wrongful death action and a survival action against both Westfall (D) and Blank (D) to recover damages. The jury rendered a verdict for Smalich's estate (P) against Blank (D), and also found that Westfall's (D) negligent operation of the Smalich automobile was a proximate cause of the collision. The trial court rendered judgment n.o.v. for Blank (D), ruling that Westfall's (D) negligence must, as a matter of law, be imputed to Smalich as owner of the vehicle, thus precluding recovery by Smalich's estate (P) against Blank (D). The Estate (P) appealed.

ISSUE: Should the doctrine of imputed contributory negligence be applied in all automobile accident cases?

HOLDING AND DECISION: (Eagen, J.) No. A plaintiff ought not to be barred from recovery against a negligent defendant by the contributory negligence of a third person unless the relationship between the plaintiff and the third person is such that the plaintiff would be vicariously liable as a defendant for the negligent acts of the third person. In the context of automobile accident cases, only a master-servant relationship or a finding of joint enterprise will justify the imputation of contributory negligence. It is doubtful whether, in the ordinary situation, the driver and the owner-passenger have reached a mutual understanding that the owner-passenger reserves a right to control over the physical details of driving or that the driver consents to submit himself to the control of a "backseat" driver. More likely, the only mutual understanding reached is that the driver will use care and skill in his operation, subject to the duty of obedience to the wishes of the owner-passenger as to such things as destination. No more than an agency relationship is involved. By its verdict, the jury must have determined that Smalich had relinquished her right to control her automobile to Westfall (D). Reversed.

CONCURRENCE: (Roberts, J.) The imputed contributory negligence doctrine should be entirely repudiated. It is subject to two main criticisms. First, in the real world, a passenger can in no way safely exercise operational control over the vehicle in which he rides, even if he is the owner. Second, mechanical application of the rule to an owner-passenger, regardless of whether he is the plaintiff or the defendant, makes little sense. The only reason to impute a servant's liability to his master is to produce a solvent defendant.

▶ ANALYSIS

Although the doctrine has been virtually abandoned, the passenger himself may still be found contributorily negligent. Thus, a passenger will be barred from recovering for his injuries where he voluntarily rides with a driver whom the passenger knows is incompetent, drunk, or reckless, or neglects, without good reason, to alert the driver to a danger he has discovered. Otherwise, the passenger is free to trust in the ability of the driver, and not watch the road.

■▬■

Quicknotes

IMPUTED CONTRIBUTORY NEGLIGENCE A situation in which the contributory negligence of one person is imputed onto another.

JUDGMENT N.O.V. A judgment entered by the trial judge reversing a jury verdict if the jury's determination has no basis in law or fact.

MASTER-SERVANT RELATIONSHIP Relationship where a particular individual agrees to render his personal services to another for valuable consideration.

NEGLIGENCE Conduct falling below the standard of care that a reasonable person would demonstrate under similar conditions.

VICARIOUS LIABILITY The imputed liability of one party for the unlawful acts of another.

WRONGFUL DEATH An action brought by the beneficiaries of a deceased person, claiming that the deceased's death was the result of wrongful conduct by the defendant.

■▬■

Quick Reference Rules of Law

Rylands v. Fletcher

Flood victim (P) v. Mill owners (D)

In the Exc., [1865] 3 H&C 774, House of Lords, L.R. 3 H.L. 330 (1868).

NATURE OF CASE: Action to recover damages for injury to plaintiff's coal mine.

FACT SUMMARY: Fletcher (D), mill owners, built a reservoir on their land. The water escaped through an abandoned coal mine shaft and flooded an adjoining mine owned by Rylands (P).

RULE OF LAW
A person using his land for a dangerous, non-natural use is strictly liable for any damage to another's property resulting from such non-natural use.

FACTS: Fletcher (D) owned a mill, and built a water reservoir on his land. The water broke through into an abandoned coal mine shaft and flooded along connecting passages into Ryland's (P) adjoining mine. Fletcher (D) himself was not negligent in allowing the reservoir to break, although the independent contractors who did the actual construction on the reservoir may have been at fault. There was no trespass by Fletcher (D), since the flooding was not direct or immediate; nor was there a nuisance (as then defined). Rylands (P) was nevertheless allowed to recover upon an analogy of the strict liability for trespassing cattle, dangerous animals, and "absolute" nuisance. The case went to the Exchequer Chamber, where Justice Blackburn used language often erroneously quoted as the rule of the case, to the effect that a person is strictly liable whenever he brings something dangerous on his land and it escapes and does damage. The case then went to the House of Lords, where Blackburn's broad statement was sharply limited, as discussed below.

ISSUE: Is a person who uses his land for non-natural, dangerous purposes liable for any damages to another's land stemming from such use, even in the absence of negligence?

HOLDING AND DECISION: (Blackburn, J.) Yes. A person using his land for a dangerous, non-natural use is strictly liable for any damage to another's property that results from the non-natural use. A person is strictly liable when he damages another by a thing or activity that is unduly dangerous and inappropriate to character and surroundings of the place where it is maintained. Judgment for plaintiff.

HOLDING: (Lord Cairns, Lord Chancellor) The defendants could have used their reservoir for any ordinary purpose, and Rylands (P) could not have complained if the water then had escaped onto, and damaged, his property from natural causes. In such circumstances, Rylands (P) would have been obligated to protect his property from those accidents caused by nature.

▶ ANALYSIS

This is the leading case from which was developed the doctrine of strict liability for abnormally dangerous activities or conditions. In determining whether a certain activity is a non-natural use, the court looks to the place where the activity occurs, the customs of the community, and the natural fitness or adaptation of the premises for the purpose. By and large, the rule is followed in most states. The Restatement had accepted the principle of Rylands, but has limited it to "ultrahazardous activities," defined as ones which "necessarily involve a risk of serious harm to . . . others which cannot be eliminated by the exercise of the utmost care." Most frequently, in all American courts, the same strict liability is imposed under the name of "nuisance." These nuisance cases generally recognize that the activity's relation to its surroundings is the controlling factor. Thus, "non-natural" use has become "unreasonable" use.

Quicknotes

ABNORMALLY DANGEROUS ACTIVITY An activity, as set forth in Restatement (Second) of Torts § 520, giving rise to strict liability on the part of the actor for damages caused thereby.

NUISANCE An unlawful use of property that interferes with the lawful use of another's property.

STRICT LIABILITY Liability for all injuries proximately caused by a party's conducting of certain inherently dangerous activities without regard to negligence or fault.

Miller v. Civil Constructors, Inc.

Injured (P) v. Gravel pit owners (D)

Ill. Ct. App., 651 N.E.2d 239 (1995).

NATURE OF CASE: Claims sounding in strict liability for injuries sustained during nearby firearm practice.

FACT SUMMARY: A stray bullet injured a man after it ricocheted from a nearby gravel pit during firearm practice by law enforcement officers.

🏛 RULE OF LAW
The use of guns or firearms is not an ultrahazardous activity as required for strict liability.

FACTS: Miller (P) was struck and injured by a stray bullet that ricocheted out of a nearby property, a gravel pit, while law enforcement officers took firing practice there. Miller (P) sued the owners of the gravel pit, Civil Constructors (D), alleging, among other claims, two counts for strict liability. The trial court dismissed those two counts on grounds that shooting a firearm is not an ultrahazardous activity. Miller (P) appealed.

ISSUE: Is using guns or firearms an ultrahazardous activity as required for strict liability?

HOLDING AND DECISION: (Bowman, J.) No. The use of guns or firearms is not an ultrahazardous activity as required for strict liability. The general rule is that the use of guns or firearms is a matter of negligence, not strict liability, and thus the appropriate standard of care in such cases is generally accepted to be that of ordinary care. Miller (P), however, argues that shooting a gun or firearm is an ultrahazardous activity that justifies strict liability. Section 519 of the Restatement of Torts posits six factors to consider in deciding whether an activity is ultrahazardous: a high degree of risk of harm, the likelihood that any harm will be substantial, the futility of exercising reasonable care, the commonness of the activity, the activity's appropriateness for the place where it occurs, and the degree to which the community benefits from the activity outweigh its dangers. Under these factors, the use of a gun or firearm is not an ultrahazardous activity. First, reasonable care will suffice to prevent the dangers. Second, use of guns is common; guns are not inherently dangerous. Third, the Court assumes that the location was appropriate because Miller's (P) complaint alleges no facts to the contrary. Fourth, the firearm practice, allegedly performed by law enforcement officers, provides benefits to the community. Miller's (P) allegations on the strict-liability counts are therefore facially insufficient, and those counts were properly dismissed. Affirmed.

▶ ANALYSIS

The key point in the developed rule of *Rylands*—the appropriateness of the activity to the place—was assumed by the Court in *Miller* [p. 701]. Given the weakness of Miller's (P) claim on the other factors stated in section 519 of the Restatement, though, his argument that guns are ultrahazardous very likely would have failed even if his complaint had alleged that firing practice was not appropriate for a gravel pit.

Quicknotes

NEGLIGENCE Conduct falling below the standard of care that a reasonable person would demonstrate under similar conditions.

ORDINARY CARE The degree of care exercised by a reasonable person when conducting everyday activities or under similar circumstances; synonymous with due care.

STANDARD OF CARE A uniform degree of behavior against which a person's conduct can be measured when determining liability in negligence cases.

STRICT LIABILITY Liability for all injuries proximately caused by a party's conducting of certain inherently dangerous activities without regard to negligence or fault.

ULTRAHAZARDOUS ACTIVITIES Dangerous activities that give rise to strict liability by presenting a risk of serious harm to the community that cannot be removed through any exercise of due care.

Indiana Harbor Belt R.R. Co. v. American Cyanamid Co.

Railroad (P) v. Chemical manufacturer (D)

916 F.2d 1174 (7th Cir. 1990).

NATURE OF CASE: Appeal of damages awarded for injury to property.

FACT SUMMARY: American Cyanamid (D), manufacturer of a dangerous chemical, was held strictly liable when a quantity of it spilled during transportation.

RULE OF LAW
Strict liability will not be imposed against the manufacturer of a toxic chemical for accidents occurring during transportation.

FACTS: American Cyanamid Co. (D), a chemical manufacturer, engaged a railroad car to transport 20,000 gallons of liquid acrylonitrile, a toxic substance, to a processing plant in New Jersey. While the car was sitting in a Chicago railroad yard owned by Indiana Harbor Belt R.R. (P), about 5,000 gallons spilled, which necessitated an evacuation of nearby homes and nearly $1 million in cleanup. Indiana Harbor Belt R.R. (P) filed suit against American Cyanamid (D) to recover the cost of cleanup, contending that the transportation of toxic chemicals was an ultrahazardous activity for which the manufacturer should be strictly liable. A district court, sitting in diversity, agreed and so instructed the jury. A verdict for damages was rendered, and American Cyanamid (D) appealed.

ISSUE: Will strict liability be imposed against the manufacturer of a toxic chemical for accidents occurring during transportation?

HOLDING AND DECISION: (Posner, J.) No. Strict liability will not be imposed against the manufacturer of a toxic chemical for accidents occurring during transportation. The Restatement (Second) of Torts, at § 520, lists six factors to be considered in determining whether an activity is ultrahazardous: (1) great probability of harm; (2) potentially serious level of harm; (3) the activity is not a matter of common usage; (4) harm cannot be prevented by utmost care; (5) the activity is inappropriate for the location; and (6) the social value of the activity is not sufficient to offset the risks. The basic purpose behind the ultrahazardous activity doctrine is to encourage the use of alternative methods when possible. In this case, no alternative exists to transport chemicals other than truck transport, which is not inherently safer. It would not be feasible to reroute the shipment of all hazardous materials around Chicago. Moreover, the negligence regime is perfectly adequate for deterring railway spills. Finally, the ultrahazardous activity doctrine concentrates on the activity, not the subject of the activity. American Cyanamid (D) is not considered to be engaged in an abnormally dangerous activity just because a product it manufactures becomes dangerous when handled. It is the transportation, not the manufacture of the chemical, that is under scrutiny. For these reasons, strict liability is inappropriate in this context. Reversed and remanded.

ANALYSIS

The classic case of ultrahazardous activity is dynamite blasting in an urban area. It entails a great risk of harm, and a less dangerous (albeit more expensive) method building demolition exists—the wrecking ball. The ultrahazardous activity rule will make the demolisher strictly liable if he chooses the more dangerous method.

◼︎▬◼︎

Quicknotes

STRICT LIABILITY Liability for all injuries proximately caused by a party's conducting of certain inherently dangerous activities without regard to negligence or fault.

◼︎▬◼︎

Foster v. Preston Mill Co.

Mink farm owner (P) v. Blasters (D)

Wash. Sup. Ct., 44 Wash. 2d 440, 268 P.2d 645 (1954).

NATURE OF CASE: Action to recover for damages due to blasting operations.

FACT SUMMARY: Mother mink, frightened by blasting, killed their own kittens.

🏛 RULE OF LAW
Strict liability is only imposed for those injuries resulting as the natural consequence of that which makes an activity ultrahazardous.

FACTS: Foster (P) raised mink, which are by nature very nervous creatures. Blasting operations carried out by Preston Mill Co. (D) frightened the mink mothers and caused them to eat their kittens. Foster (P) informed Preston Mill Co. (D) of the effect their blasting was having on his mink, but they kept on blasting. Foster (P) sought to hold Preston Mill Co. (D) strictly liable for his damages, and was awarded $1,953.

ISSUE: Is one who engages in an ultrahazardous activity strictly liable for any and all damages that result?

HOLDING AND DECISION: (Hamley, J.) No. Strict liability is only imposed for those injuries resulting as the natural consequence of that which makes the activity ultrahazardous. One who carries on an ultrahazardous activity is liable to another whose person, land, or chattels the actor should recognize as likely to be harmed by the unpreventable miscarriage of the activity for harm resulting thereto from that which makes the activity ultrahazardous, although the utmost care is exercised to prevent the harm. The risk that mink may eat their young when frightened by the noise is not one of the things that make blasting ultrahazardous. It is the mink's exceedingly nervous disposition, rather than the normal risks inherent in blasting operations that must bear the responsibility for the loss sustained. Reversed.

▶ ANALYSIS

The court in this case limits the application of the doctrine of strict liability. The court bases its decision on the same kind of policy considerations that underlie the doctrine of "proximate cause" in the law of negligence. A defendant cannot be held limitlessly responsible for every consequence flowing from his actions. In strict liability law, the line is drawn at those injuries that result from the very things that cause an activity to be classified as ultrahazardous. Had the mink been killed by flying rocks and debris, for example, strict liability

may have been imposed. Note that the court accepts the policy that strict liability is not designed to protect against harms incident to a plaintiff's extraordinary or unusual use of his land. The court here is applying the principle that the extent to which one man in lawful conduct of his business is liable for injuries to another is an adjustment of conflicting interests. Here, the plaintiff's interests must yield.

Quicknotes

CHATTEL An article of personal property, as distinguished from real property; a thing personal and moveable.

NEGLIGENCE Conduct falling below the standard of care that a reasonable person would demonstrate under similar conditions.

PROXIMATE CAUSE The natural sequence of events without which an injury would not have been sustained.

STRICT LIABILITY Liability for all injuries proximately caused by a party's conducting of certain inherently dangerous activities without regard to negligence or fault.

ULTRAHAZARDOUS ACTIVITIES Dangerous activities that give rise to strict liability by presenting a risk of serious harm to the community that cannot be removed through any exercise of due care.

Golden v. Amory

Flood victim (P) v. Hydroelectric plant owner (D)

Sup. Jud. Ct. of Mass., 329 Mass. 484, 109 N.E.2d 131 (1952).

NATURE OF CASE: Action to recover damages caused by the overflow of a dike.

FACT SUMMARY: A hurricane caused floods, damaging the Golden's land.

> 🏛 **RULE OF LAW**
> The rule of strict liability for the escape of stored water does not apply where the injury results from an act of God, which the owner had no reason to anticipate.

FACTS: Amory (D) owned a hydroelectric plant and built a dike on a river. A hurricane caused the river to overflow, damaging Golden's (P) land. Golden (P) brought an action based on both strict liability and negligence.

ISSUE: Is a person strictly liable for any damage caused by the escape of water stored on his land?

HOLDING AND DECISION: (Lummus, J.) No. The rule of strict liability for the escape of stored water does not apply where the injury results from an act of God, which the owner had no reason to anticipate. In the present case, the flood was plainly beyond the capability of anyone to anticipate, and was clearly an act of God.

▌*ANALYSIS*

This case is an example of the decision to limit strict liability when the harm is caused by acts of God unforeseen by the defendant. In negligence law, the defendant is frequently held liable when the risk he has created is realized through unforeseeable intervening causes. But in strict liability law, the strong current of authority—notwithstanding the Restatement, which is contrary—relieves the defendant of liability in such a case. Thus, act of God is used to mean an unforeseeable, intervening force of nature. In the same manner, the defendant has been relieved from liability by the independent act of a third person, which he could not have foreseen or prevented.

▪═▪

Quicknotes

VIS MAJOR Damages incurred as the result of a natural cause and which could not have been prevented.

▪═▪

Sandy v. Bushey

Horse-kick victim (P) v. Horse owner (D)

Me. Sup. Ct., 128 A. 513 (1925).

NATURE OF CASE: Action to recover damages for injuries sustained when kicked by a horse.

FACT SUMMARY: Sandy (P) was kicked by Bushey's (D) horse when he went into the pasture to feed his own horse.

🏛 RULE OF LAW
The keeper of a vicious domestic animal known to be dangerous cannot interpose contributory negligence as a defense to relieve him of his strict liability as an insurer.

FACTS: Sandy (P) turned his horses out in a neighbor's pasture, where Bushey's (D) horse was also pastured. When Sandy (P) was in the pasture feeding his mare, he was seriously injured when kicked by Bushey's (D) horse, which had previously exhibited vicious tendencies, known to Bushey (D). Sandy (P) brought an action in strict liability for the keeping of a vicious domestic animal. Bushey (D) attempted to plead Sandy's (P) contributory negligence as a defense.

ISSUE: May the keeper of a vicious domestic animal plead contributory negligence as a defense to relieve him of his strict liability as an insurer?

HOLDING AND DECISION: (Sturgis, J.) No. The keeper of a vicious domestic animal known to be dangerous cannot interpose contributory negligence as a defense to relieve him of his strict liability as an insurer. In an action for an injury caused by such an animal, the plaintiff has only to allege and prove the keeping, the vicious propensities, and the scienter. Negligence is not the ground of liability; therefore, contributory negligence cannot be a defense. Something more than slight negligence or want of due care on the part of the injured party must be shown in order to relieve the keeper of a vicious domestic animal known to be such from his liability as an insurer. The owner is only relieved of liability if the injured party voluntarily and knowingly put himself in harm's way, or if he incites the animal and brings the attack on himself.

▶ ANALYSIS

This case illustrates the policy which places the absolute responsibility for preventing harm upon the defendant. A plaintiff who is injured by a defendant's dangerous animal is not barred from recovery by his own lack of ordinary care in failing to discover its presence, or in inadvertently coming in contact with it. He will only be barred from recovery if his own conduct brings the attack on himself.

Quicknotes

CONTRIBUTORY NEGLIGENCE Behavior on the part of an injured plaintiff falling below the standard of ordinary care that contributes to the defendant's negligence, resulting in the plaintiff's injury.

STRICT LIABILITY Liability for all injuries proximately caused by a party's conducting of certain inherently dangerous activities without regard to negligence or fault.

Products Liability

Quick Reference Rules of Law

MacPherson v. Buick Motor Co. (II)

Injured automobile owner (P) v. Automobile manufacturer (D)

N.Y. Ct. of App., 217 N.Y. 382, 111 N.E. 1050 (1916).

NATURE OF CASE: Negligence action.

FACT SUMMARY: MacPherson (P) sued Buick (D) for injuries sustained when a defective wheel in the automobile he purchased collapsed.

🏛 RULE OF LAW
A manufacturer breaches a duty of care to a foreseeable user of its product if the product was likely to cause an injury if negligently made and it places the product on the market without conducting a reasonable inspection.

FACTS: Buick (D), an automobile manufacturer, sold a car to a retail dealer who in turn sold it to MacPherson (P). While MacPherson (P) was in the car it suddenly collapsed due to the wheel being made out of defective wood. While the wheel was not manufactured by Buick (D), there was evidence that a reasonable inspection would have revealed the defects. The supreme court held in favor of MacPherson and the appellate division affirmed. Buick (D) appealed.

ISSUE: Does a manufacturer breach a duty of care to a foreseeable user of its product if the product was likely to cause an injury if negligently made and it places the product on the market without conducting a reasonable inspection?

HOLDING AND DECISION: (Cardozo, J.) Yes. A manufacturer breaches a duty of care to a foreseeable user of its product if the product was likely to cause an injury if negligently made and it places the product on the market without conducting a reasonable inspection. A product is dangerous if it is reasonably certain to place life and limb in peril when negligently made. If the manufacturer knows the item will be used by person other than the purchaser, he is under a duty to manufacture the item carefully. There must be knowledge of a probable danger and that the danger will be borne by others in addition to the buyer in the normal course of events. The proximity or remoteness of the transaction is also to be considered. If the manufacturer of a finished product places it on the market without inspection, then mobility will attach. Buick (D) was not relieved from its duty to inspect because it bought the wheels from a reputable manufacturer. Buick (D) had a duty to inspect the component parts of its automobiles before placing them on the market. Affirmed.

▶ *ANALYSIS*

There was a traditional distinction between cases involving nonfeasance and misfeasance. Nonfeasance was actionable under contract law and resulted where there was a promise and a subsequent breach of that promise. Misfeasance was actionable in tort and existed when the defendant attempted to perform a contract and did so in error.

Quicknotes

DUTY OF CARE A principle of negligence requiring an individual to act in such a manner as to avoid injury to a person to whom he or she owes an obligatory duty.

FORESEEABLE USER A person who is likely to use a certain product or service.

MISFEASANCE The commission of a lawful act in a wrongful manner.

NEGLIGENCE Conduct falling below the standard of care that a reasonable person would demonstrate under similar conditions.

NONFEASANCE The omission, or failure to perform, an obligation.

Baxter v. Ford Motor Co.

Injured car owner (P) v. Car manufacturer (D)

Wash. Sup. Ct., 12 P.2d 409 (1932).

NATURE OF CASE: Action to recover damages for personal injuries, based on breach of warranty in tort.

FACT SUMMARY: Baxter (P), while driving a car whose windshield, according to representations made by Ford Motor Co. (D), was made of nonshatterable glass, suffered injuries when a pebble struck the windshield, causing small pieces of glass to fly into his eyes.

🏛 **RULE OF LAW**
A manufacturer or retailer of a product is responsible in tort for all representations upon which the consumer must rely, regardless of a contractual relationship between plaintiff and defendant.

FACTS: Baxter (P) purchased a car from a dealer, who acquired it in turn from Ford Motor Co. (D). Baxter (P) was injured when a pebble from a passing car struck the windshield of his car, causing small pieces of glass to fly into his eyes, and resulting in loss of his left eye and damage to his right eye. Ford Motor Co. (D) had made misrepresentations through its advertising that the windshields of its automobiles were constructed of nonshatterable glass. Ford Motor Co. (D) contended, however, that there can be no implied or express warranty without privity of contract, and warranties as to personal property do not attach themselves to, and run with, the article sold. The trial court refused to admit in evidence the printed matter containing Ford's (D) misrepresentations, and entered judgment for Ford Motor Co. (D). Baxter (P) appealed.

ISSUE: Can there be an express or implied warranty, based on a manufacturer's representations as to his product, regardless of privity of contract between manufacturer and purchaser?

HOLDING AND DECISION: (Herman, J.) Yes. The purchaser has a right to a remedy against the manufacturer because of damages suffered by reason of a failure of goods to comply with the manufacturer's representations as to the existence of qualities which they did not in fact possess, when the absence of such qualities was not readily discoverable, even though there was no privity of contract between the purchaser and the manufacturer. Here, Ford Motor Co. (D) made representations as to the nonshatterability of its windshields, upon which Baxter (P) was forced to rely, as he as a consumer had no means of testing their truthfulness. Ford (D) was therefore under a duty to ascertain that their representations were true, and it is immaterial that they did not in fact know that the representations were false, or that there was in existence no better make of glass. The trial court erred in excluding evidence of the representations from trial and in taking the case from the jury. The rule which long afforded a remedy, independent of contract, to the purchaser of a dangerous article, such as a drug, against the manufacturer who misrepresents its contents is now extended to all consumer goods. It would be unjust, and against public policy, to permit manufacturers of goods to create a demand for their products by representing that they possess qualities which they in fact, do not possess, and then, because there is no privity of contract existing between the consumer and the manufacturer, deny the consumer the right to recover if damages result from the absence of those qualities, when such absence is not readily noticeable. Reversed.

▶ **ANALYSIS**

The action in Baxter was based on breach of an express warranty, but the effect of the decision was to hold manufacturers and retailers to strict liability for their misrepresentations. See Restatement of Torts, Second, § 402B, which holds the manufacturer liable for physical harm to a consumer caused by the latter's justifiable reliance upon the former's misrepresentations, regardless of contractual relationship, fraud, or negligence. However, in order for there to be strict liability, the representation must be made with the expectation that it will reach the plaintiff, and he, in turn, must actually rely upon the representation in his use of the product. The above case is the leading decision in this area, and has been followed almost without exception.

Quicknotes

EXPRESS WARRANTY An express promise made by one party to a contract that the other party may rely on a fact, relieving that party from the obligation of determining whether the fact is true and indemnifying the other party from liability if that fact is shown to be false.

IMPLIED WARRANTY An implied promise made by one party to a contract that the other party may rely on a fact, relieving that party from the obligation of determining whether the fact is true and indemnifying the other party from liability if that fact is shown to be false.

PRIVITY OF CONTRACT A relationship between the parties to a contract that is required in order to bring an action for breach.

Henningsen v. Bloomfield Motors, Inc.

Injured car owner (P) v. Manufacturer (D) and dealer (D)

N.J. Sup. Ct., 32 N.J. 358, 161 A.2d 69 (1960).

NATURE OF CASE: Action to recover damages for personal injuries based on a theory of implied warranty of merchantability.

FACT SUMMARY: Mrs. Henningsen (P), severely injured when her steering gear malfunctioned and caused her car to crash into a wall, sued the manufacturer, Chrysler (D), and the dealer, Bloomfield (D), from whom her husband purchased the car.

🏛 RULE OF LAW
When a manufacturer and a dealer put a new automobile in the stream of trade and promote its purchase by the public, an implied warranty that it is reasonably suitable for use as such accompanies it into the hands of the ultimate purchaser, despite any contractual provisions to the contrary.

FACTS: Mrs. Henningsen (P) was badly injured when the steering gear in her car malfunctioned, causing her to crash into a wall. The car was a gift from her husband, who purchased it from Bloomfield Motors, Inc. (D), who had, in turn, acquired it from Chrysler Corp. (D). Mr. Henningsen signed a contract for sale, the back of which contained a disclaimer of warranties, express or implied, except for a promise to repair or replace any defective parts within 90 days, or 4,000 miles, after delivery to the original purchaser (whichever came first). This form was standard, not only with Chrysler (D), but with the entire automotive industry. Mrs. Henningsen's (P) claim based on negligence was dismissed, the case went to the jury solely on the issues of an implied warranty of merchantability, and a verdict was returned for Mrs. Henningsen (P). Chrysler Corp. (D) and Bloomfield Motors, Inc. (D) appealed.

ISSUE:
(1) Is privity of contract necessary for an implied warranty of merchantability (fitness for use) to run from the manufacturer of a car to the ultimate purchaser?
(2) Can the implied warranty be nullified by an express contractual agreement?
(3) Is the dealer, as well as the manufacturer, bound by this implied warranty of merchantability?

HOLDING AND DECISION: (Francis, J.)
(1) No. Where the buyer of a product, such as an automobile, has neither the opportunity nor the capacity to inspect or determine its fitness for use, and must rely upon the manufacturer, the law will not limit the latter's responsibility to the bare terms of the contract; rather it will imply a warranty that the product is reasonably fit for its intended use, and extend this warranty for the protection of the ultimate consumer. In this way, the burden of losses consequent upon the use of defective articles is borne by the manufacturer, who is in a position both to minimize the danger through care in construction, and to make an equitable distribution (through insurance and price control) of any losses that do occur.
(2) No. Recognizing the gross inequality of bargaining position between Mr. Henningsen, an individual purchaser, and Chrysler Corp. (D), a large corporation whose practices here are mirrored by the rest of the same industry, public policy implies a warranty of merchantability for the protection of the ultimate consumer, in this case, Mrs. Henningsen (P). Consequently, the law will not allow the protection to be nullified through a contract of adhesion which purports to either limit liability or disclaim any implied warranty. Any such terms will be declared unconscionable and void.
(3) Yes. The principles that establish the obligation of the manufacturer apply with equal force to the retailer, even though there may be no agency relationship between the two. The bargaining position of the dealer is stronger than that of the consumer, and even though the dealer may have only a limited opportunity for inspection of the car, he is in a position to make an equitable distribution of any losses through insurance and price control. Affirmed.

▶ ANALYSIS

Under early common law concepts of contractual liability, only those parties who were parties to the bargain could sue for a breach of it. In this decision, the court took judicial notice of the realities of modern-day mass marketing, particularly of the fact that people do not buy goods strictly for their own consumption or use. The ultimate consumer must therefore be protected. Furthermore, the court, taking notice of the consumer's lack of bargaining power, protected him by implying a warranty and refusing to honor disclaimers to the contrary. However, the value of the "implied warranty of merchantability" as a weapon in the consumer's legal arsenal has been largely superseded by the advent of strict liability in tort.

Greenman v. Yuba Power Products, Inc.

Injured tool user (P) v. Manufacturer (D)

Cal. Sup. Ct., 377 P.2d 897 (1963).

NATURE OF CASE: Action to recover damages for personal breach of warranties and negligence.

FACT SUMMARY: Greenman (P), injured when a piece of wood flew out of a power tool he was using and struck his forehead, sued the manufacturer and retailer of the product.

🏛 RULE OF LAW
When an article is placed on the market by a manufacturer who knows the product will be used without inspection for defects, the manufacturer will be strictly liable in tort for any injury caused by a defect in the product.

FACTS: Greenman (P) was injured when a power tool his wife had given him malfunctioned. Ten and a half months later, Greenman (P) gave the manufacturer, Yuba Power Products, Inc. (D), notice of claimed breaches of the express warranties contained in the latter's brochures. At trial, Greenman (P) introduced substantial evidence that his injuries were caused by the tool's defective design and construction. Yuba (D) contended that Greenman (P) did not give prompt notification of the breach of warranty, as required by state law. After judgment for Greenman (P), Yuba (D) appealed.

ISSUE: Does a consumer's failure to comply with the provisions of a product's warranty bar any recovery of damages for injuries sustained as a result of a defect in the product?

HOLDING AND DECISION: (Traynor, J.) No. The liability of the manufacturer is governed not by the law of contract warranties, but by the law of strict liability in tort. Therefore, the manufacturer, in this case Yuba (D), is held strictly liable for all injuries resulting from defects in its products, regardless of negligence, contractual relationship, or warranties (express or implied), as it placed its product on the market knowing it would be used without inspection. The purpose of such liability is to insure that the costs of injuries resulting from defective products are borne by the manufacturers that put such products on the market, rather than the injured persons who are powerless to protect themselves. Sales warranties serve this purpose fitfully at best. Affirmed.

▌ *ANALYSIS*

In this landmark decision, Justice Traynor reasoned that: (1) since a manufacturer's liability is based on a warranty implied by law, (2) since there need be no privity of contract, and (3) since the law prohibits the manufacturer from limiting his liability disclaimer, the liability has evolved from a contractual basis to that of strict liability. This concept, as stated in § 402A of Second Restatement of Torts, is now accepted and applied by a good majority of American courts. Section 402A applies to damage to the person or property of any user, whether or not the user bought the product from the seller, and it is no longer necessary, of course, to prove negligence on the part of the manufacturer.

■▬■

Quicknotes

CONTRACT WARRANTY An express promise made by one party to a contract that the other party may rely on a fact, relieving that party from the obligation of determining whether the fact is true and indemnifying the other party from liability if that fact is shown to be false.

NEGLIGENCE Conduct falling below the standard of care that a reasonable person would demonstrate under similar conditions.

STRICT LIABILITY Liability for all injuries proximately caused by a party's conducting of certain inherently dangerous activities without regard to negligence or fault.

■▬■

Rix v. General Motors Corp.

Accident victim (P) v. Truck manufacturer (D)

Mont. Sup. Ct., 222 Mont. 318, 723 P.2d 195 (1986).

NATURE OF CASE: Appeal from defense verdict in personal injury action.

FACT SUMMARY: Rix (P) contended that GMC (D) had manufactured a vehicle with a defective braking system.

🏛 RULE OF LAW
A manufacturer will be strictly liable for manufacturing defects.

FACTS: Rix (P) was injured when he was hit from behind by a truck manufactured by General Motors Corporation (D) that failed to brake. Rix (P) filed a personal injury action alleging defective brakes. GMC (D) argued that the brakes had been altered after the truck left its assembly line. A jury returned a defense verdict, and Rix (P) appealed, arguing that the jury instructions regarding strict liability under a manufacturing defect theory were incorrect.

ISSUE: Will a manufacturer be strictly liable for manufacturing defects?

HOLDING AND DECISION: (Weber, J.) Yes. A manufacturer will be strictly liable for manufacturing defects. One who sells any product in a defective condition unreasonably dangerous to the consumer is subject to liability for physical harm thereby caused to the consumer if the product reaches the consumer without substantial change in the condition in which it was sold. In this case, the jury was instructed that Rix (P) must establish three elements in order to recover under a strict liability theory: (1) that GMC (D) manufactured and sold a product in a defective condition; (2) that the product reached the ultimate consumer without substantial change in its condition; and (3) that the defective condition caused Rix's (P) injuries. A manufacturing defect is an imperfection of the type that inevitably occurs in products of a given design as a result of the fallibility of the manufacturing process, where the end result does not match the design. The jury instructions given here were an adequate explanation of the applicable law with regard to strict liability under a manufacturing defect theory. [The verdict was reversed on other, unstated grounds.]

▶ ANALYSIS

Defects come in two types, manufacturing and design. True strict liability exists only in manufacturing defects. Defective design issues involve an analysis of possible alternative designs and a cost-benefit analysis and therefore incorporate elements of negligence.

Quicknotes

DESIGN DEFECT A situation product that is manufactured in accordance with a particular design; however, such design is inherently flawed so that it presents an unreasonable risk of injury.

PERSONAL INJURY Harm to an individual's person or body.

STRICT PRODUCT LIABILITY Liability of a manufacturer or seller of a product for injuries sustained as a result of any defects without the necessity of a showing of negligence.

Prentis v. Yale Mfg. Co.

Forklift operator (P) v. Manufacturer (D)

Mich. Sup. Ct., 421 Mich. 670, 365 N.W.2d 176 (1984).

NATURE OF CASE: Appeal of reversal of denial of damages in products liability action.

FACT SUMMARY: Prentis (P) contended that he had been injured due to a defectively designed forklift manufactured by Yale (D).

> ## 🏛 RULE OF LAW
> Liability for a defectively designed product shall be based on a pure negligence analysis.

FACTS: Prentis (P), operating a forklift manufactured by Yale Manufacturing Co. (D), was injured. He brought a products liability action against Yale (D) on a design defect theory. The trial court in defining "design defect" couched the meaning in terms of negligence. The jury found the forklift not defectively designed and gave a defense verdict. Prentis (P) appealed, contending that the phrase should have been characterized in terms of strict liability. The appellate court reversed. Yale (D) appealed.

ISSUE: Will liability for a defectively designed product be based on a pure negligence analysis?

HOLDING AND DECISION: (Boyle, J.) Yes. Liability for a defectively designed product will be based on a pure negligence analysis. The modern trend in products liability is to focus on the product, not the manufacturer's conduct. When addressing a manufacturing defect, this is proper. However, in a design defect situation, to focus on the product obscures the true inquiry, which is an examination of conscious decisions made by a manufacturer. Incorporated into the analysis is risk-benefit, consumer expectations, and other related concepts. All of these issues come back to the larger question of whether a manufacturer made prudent design choices. For this reason, a design defect analysis is necessarily one of negligence. Moreover, a negligence standard will reward a careful manufacturer, a result to be encouraged. These factors compel the conclusion that the analysis in design defect cases will be negligence. This was the standard used by the trial court, and it was proper. Reversed.

▶ ANALYSIS

Design and manufacturing defects are often lumped under the generic term "products liability." As the present case demonstrates, however, there is much overlap between products liability and general negligence. Several courts besides that writing in this instance have agreed that design defects are properly analyzed in terms of negligence.

Quicknotes

DESIGN DEFECT A situation product that is manufactured in accordance with a particular design; however, such design is inherently flawed so that it presents an unreasonable risk of injury.

NEGLIGENCE Conduct falling below the standard of care that a reasonable person would demonstrate under similar conditions.

PRODUCTS LIABILITY The legal liability of manufacturers and sellers for damages and injuries suffered by buyers, users, and even bystanders because of defects in goods purchased.

STRICT LIABILITY Liability for all injuries proximately caused by a party's conducting of certain inherently dangerous activities without regard to negligence or fault.

■▬■

O'Brien v. Muskin Corp.

Injured diver (P) v. Pool manufacturer (D)

N.J. Sup. Ct., 94 N.J. 169, 463 A.2d 298 (1983).

NATURE OF CASE: Appeal from denial of damages in a products liability action.

FACT SUMMARY: O'Brien (P) contended Muskin (D) manufactured a pool with a design defect rendering it strictly liable for his injuries incurred in diving into it.

🏛 RULE OF LAW
A trial court must permit a jury to consider whether the risks of injury so outweighed the utility of the product's design so as to render it defective.

FACTS: O'Brien (P) was injured when he dove into an above-ground pool manufactured by Muskin (D). He sued, contending the use of vinyl on the pool's bottom constituted a design defect which proximately caused his injury and rendered Muskin (D) strictly liable. The court instructed the jury only to consider whether Muskin (D) had provided adequate warnings of the potential danger of diving in the pool. The jury found O'Brien (P) contributorily negligent, barring his recovery. He appealed, contending the trial court erred in not allowing the jury to consider whether the risk of injury outweighed the utility of using vinyl in the pool to render the design defective. The court of appeals reversed, and Muskin (D) appealed.

ISSUE: Must a trial court in a strict liability case allow the jury to use a risk-utility analysis to determine whether a product was defective?

HOLDING AND DECISION: (Pollock, J.) Yes. A trial court must permit the jury in a products liability case to consider whether the risk of injury so outweighed the utility of the product's design so as to render it defective. By prohibiting the jury from performing this analysis and considering only the sufficiency of the warning, the trial court precluded one of the two necessary elements in a products liability action. The jury could have found the pool defective without regard to the warning provided. O'Brien (P) could have established the existence of a defect without showing the existence of a safer, alternative design. As a result, the trial court erred in withholding this opportunity from the jury. Affirmed.

▶ ANALYSIS

The court further held in this case that evidence of the state of the art was admissible to determine whether the risk of injury from the design outweighed the benefit or utility of the design. It pointed out, however, that such evidence is not necessarily dispositive on the issue of defectiveness. A manufacturer's conformance with state of the art techniques does not ensure that the product will not be found defective.

Quicknotes

CONTRIBUTORY NEGLIGENCE Behavior on the part of an injured plaintiff falling below the standard of ordinary care that contributes to the defendant's negligence, resulting in the plaintiff's injury.

DESIGN DEFECT A defect in a product manufactured according to the intended design, but present because the design of the product itself presents a risk of harm to consumers.

PRODUCT LIABILITY The legal liability of manufacturers and sellers for damages and injuries suffered by buyers, users, and even bystanders because of defects in goods purchased.

STRICT LIABILITY Liability for all injuries proximately caused by a party's conducting of certain inherently dangerous activities without regard to negligence or fault.

Anderson v. Owens-Corning Fiberglas Corp.

Asbestosis victim (P) v. Manufacturer (D)

Cal. Sup. Ct., 810 P.2d 549 (1991).

NATURE OF CASE: Appeal from an order allowing state-of-the-art evidence in a products liability action.

FACT SUMMARY: Owens-Corning (D), an asbestos manufacturer, sought to admit evidence regarding the knowability of the risks of asbestos exposure at the time of the distribution.

🏛 RULE OF LAW
Knowability is a required element of strict liability for failure to warn.

FACTS: Anderson (P) alleged that he contracted asbestosis and other lung ailments through exposure to asbestos while working as an electrician from 1941 to 1976. Anderson (P) filed a strict liability action against Owens-Corning (D), the manufacturer of the asbestos, for failure to warn of the risk of harm. Owens-Corning (D) sought to introduce evidence that the risk was unknowable at the time of the manufacture and distribution of all asbestos products. Anderson (P), asserting that this type of evidence was not relevant in a strict liability action, appealed the decision to allow Owens-Corning (D) to present it at the trial.

ISSUE: Is the knowability of a risk at the time of manufacture or distribution relevant in a strict liability action for failure to warn?

HOLDING AND DECISION: (Panelli, J.) Yes. Knowability is a required element of strict liability for failure to warn. Strict liability was adopted to insure that the costs of injuries resulting from defective products were borne by the manufacturers. The doctrine relieves injured plaintiffs of many of the onerous evidentiary burdens in a negligence action. However, strict liability was not intended to make manufacturers absolutely liable for all injuries. Strict liability seeks to direct the trier of fact's attention to the condition of the product rather than to the conduct of the manufacturer. The admission of state-of-the-art evidence regarding the knowability of risks does infuse negligence concepts into strict liability cases by focusing on the actions of the manufacturer. However, this must be allowed because failure-to-warn actions are significantly different from design defect claims. Strict liability would become absolute liability if manufacturers were required to warn about risks that were unknowable at the time of distribution. Furthermore, the infusion of some negligence features into a strict liability failure-to-warn suit would only require the injured plaintiff to prove that the manufacturer did not warn of a knowable risk rather than to prove that a standard of due care has been breached. Therefore, in a failure-to-warn theory of strict liability, knowability of the risk according to the state-of-the-art evidence at the time of distribution is relevant. Affirmed.

▶ ANALYSIS

In a separate opinion, Justice Mosk advocated that failure-to-warn actions should be maintained only in negligence, given the fact that there was nearly no distinction left after this ruling. This decision is in accord with the majority rule that a fault-based standard is applicable in warnings cases. See *Fibreboard Corp. v. Fenton*, 845 P.2d 1168 (Colo. 1993).

Quicknotes

FAILURE TO WARN The failure of an owner or occupier of land to inform persons present on the property of defects or active operations which may cause injury.

STATE OF THE ART The relevant information available at a particular time.

STRICT LIABILITY Liability for all injuries proximately caused by a party's conducting of certain inherently dangerous activities without regard to negligence or fault.

Friedman v. General Motors Corp.

Runaway-car driver (P) v. Manufacturer (D)

Ohio Sup. Ct., 43 Ohio St. 2d 209, 331 N.E.2d 702 (1975).

NATURE OF CASE: Action to recover damages for personal injuries against car manufacturer.

FACT SUMMARY: Friedman (P) was injured when he started his car and it unexpectedly lept forward; in an action against the car's manufacturer, Friedman (P) was unable to present direct evidence that the ignition system was defectively designed.

> ### 🏛 RULE OF LAW
> A product defect may be proved by circumstantial evidence, where a preponderance of that evidence establishes that an accident was caused by a defect and not other possibilities, although not all other possibilities need be eliminated.

FACTS: Friedman (P), in his complaint against General Motors (D) alleged that he turned the ignition on his 17-month-old 1966 Oldsmobile while the gearshift was in the "drive" position, and that unexpectedly, the car "leaped forward, and so startled [him] that he could not regain control before the automobile ran wild," crashing, and thereby injuring him and his family. At trial, testimony by the car's retailer-dealer and Friedman (P) suggested that the linkages and the adjustments existing at the time of the accident were the original factory set. Friedman (P) and his family testified that the car had always been started in Park, thus affording no opportunity for discovering the alleged defect, that the gear shift indicator and transmission had always operated properly, and that prior to impact the Toronado accelerated. There was also evidence that a Toronado starts only in "neutral" or "park" gear position. However, expert witnesses called by Friedman (P) could only state that the gear shift pointer was probably damaged; they could not point to an identifiable defect. General Motor's (D) expert witness suggested that any damage to the indicator resulted from the accident. The trial court's directed verdict for General Motors (D) was reversed by the intermediate appellate court. General Motors (D) appealed.

ISSUE: May a product defect be proven by circumstantial evidence?

HOLDING AND DECISION: (Brown, J.) Yes. Where a preponderance of that evidence shows that a defect was responsible for the accident, although there possibly may have been other causes, all a plaintiff need present, in terms of evidence, is that the product was defective; that the defect existed at the time the product left the factory; and that the defect

was the direct and proximate cause of the accident and injuries. Since Friedman (P) met this burden, the case should have been left to the jury. Affirmed.

DISSENT: (Stern, J.) While evidence may be sufficient to permit an inference that something was wrong with a car, that alone is not sufficient to establish a defect except, perhaps, in cases analogous to res ipsa loquitur, in which ordinary human experience tells us that the defect could not happen without a defect. The instant case is not such a case, for driver error, failure of some part, accidental or unwitting damage to the car, and other possibilities do provide other explanations.

▶ ANALYSIS

A design defect has been defined as applying to the situation where the product is as intended by the manufacturer, but is designed in such manner as to pose an inherent danger of injury in ordinary usage. Cases involving design defect may usually be argued either on a strict liability or negligence theory, and fall into three main groups: failure to provide a product with safety features; failure to anticipate emergency situations which are foreseeable; and failure to adequately test product before placing it in the stream of commerce.

Quicknotes

CIRCUMSTANTIAL EVIDENCE Evidence that, though not directly observed, supports the inference of principal facts.

DESIGN DEFECT A defect in a product manufactured according to the intended design, but present because the design of the product itself presents a risk of harm to consumers.

Daly v. General Motors Corp.

Driver's survivor (P) v. Car manufacturer (D)

Cal. Sup. Ct., 20 Cal. 3d 725, 575 P.2d 1162 (1978).

NATURE OF CASE: Appeal from denial of damages in products liability action.

FACT SUMMARY: Daly (P), whose decedent was killed in an automobile accident, alleged that a defective door latch caused the death, while GM (D) attributed the death to the driver's failure to use a shoulder harness and his intoxication.

🏛 **RULE OF LAW**
A plaintiff's recovery in a strict products liability action may be reduced according to the extent to which his injury resulted from his own lack of reasonable care.

FACTS: Daly's (P) decedent was killed in an automobile accident. Daly (P) alleged that the door latch of the Opel automobile in question was defective, and that the defect caused the accident. GM (D), the manufacturer of the Opel, alleged that the accident and death were caused by the driver's failure to wear a shoulder harness and by his intoxication at the time of the accident. At trial, the jury gave its verdict for GM (D). Daly (P) appealed.

ISSUE: May a plaintiff's recovery in a strict products liability action be reduced according to the extent to which his injury resulted from his own lack of reasonable care?

HOLDING AND DECISION: (Richardson, J.) Yes. This case presents the question of whether the principles of comparative negligence now in force in this state should be applicable to actions brought under the theory of strict products liability. This court has already recognized that a plaintiff's negligence in such a case comprises a defense when it reaches the level of assumption of risk. Terms such as "assumption of risk" and "comparative negligence" are not exact measurements, and the judicial posture in applying them must be flexible rather than doctrinaire. The purpose and goal of strict products liability is to eliminate problems of proof of negligence. With the application in these cases of the comparative negligence doctrine, proof of negligence is still obviated, but the defendant may show that its negligence caused the injury only to the extent that the plaintiff's own conduct did not. Thus, a plaintiff's recovery in a strict products liability action may be reduced according to the extent to which his injury resulted from his own lack of reasonable care. This moves the law closer to the goal of the equitable allocation of legal responsibility for personal injuries. Reversed.

▶ *ANALYSIS*

There is an important distinction between strict products liability and absolute liability. Absolute liability is imposed where a defendant is held as an insurer of the plaintiff's safety as a matter of social policy. The defendant's use of even the utmost care will not relieve him of absolute liability. These cases usually arise in the context of ultrahazardous activities or the keeping of wild animals and are sometimes referred to as "strict liability" cases, though "absolute liability" is a term better demonstrating the difference between these cases and strict products liability cases. The plaintiff's conduct is irrelevant in absolute liability cases, though some jurisdictions permit assumption of the risk as a defense. In strict products liability cases, however, assumption of risk is always a defense, and under the above case, the comparative negligence of the plaintiff can reduce, if not defeat, his recovery.

Quicknotes

ABSOLUTE LIABILITY Liability for all injuries proximately caused by a party's conducting of certain inherently dangerous activities without regard to negligence or fault.

ASSUMPTION OF RISK DOCTRINE An affirmative defense to a negligence suit by the defendant contending that the plaintiff knowingly and voluntarily subjected himself to the hazardous condition wholly absolving the defendant of liability for injuries incurred.

COMPARATIVE NEGLIGENCE Doctrine whereby the court in assessing the appropriate measure of damages compares the relative fault of the parties and reduces the amount of damages to be collected by the plaintiff in proportion to his degree of fault.

STRICT PRODUCT LIABILITY Liability of a manufacturer or seller of a product for injuries sustained as a result of any defects without the necessity of a showing of negligence.

Ford Motor Co. v. Matthews

Estate administrator (P) v. Tractor manufacturer (D)

Miss. Sup. Ct., 291 So. 2d 169 (1974).

NATURE OF CASE: Action for wrongful death on a theory of strict liability.

FACT SUMMARY: Matthews' Ford (D) tractor was not supposed to start while in gear; while standing alongside it, Matthews turned on the ignition while the tractor was in gear, it started and ran over Matthews, killing him.

🏛 **RULE OF LAW**
Although misuse of a product that causes an injury is normally a bar to strict liability, a manufacturer is liable for injuries resulting from abnormal or unintended use of his product if such use was reasonably foreseeable.

FACTS: Matthews purchased a Ford (D) tractor equipped with a starter safety switch which was designed to prevent the tractor from being started in gear. While the tractor was in gear, Matthews, standing alongside it, started the ignition. Matthews was killed as a result of being run over by the tractor. Matthews's estate (P) sued Ford (D) for wrongful death, contending that the plunger connected with the safety switch was defective, thus allowing the tractor to be started in gear. Ford (D) argued that Matthews' act of standing on the ground and starting the tractor while in gear was a misuse of the product and constituted an absolute limitation on its liability. From judgment for the Estate (P), Ford (D) appealed.

ISSUE: Does a consumer's misuse of a defective product always preclude a strict products liability suit against the manufacturer?

HOLDING AND DECISION: (Rodgers, P.J.) No. The Restatement of Torts, Second, § 402A provides: "A product is not in a defective condition when it is safe for normal handling and consumption. If the injury results from abnormal handling . . . the seller is not liable." However, the cases the institute cites in support of its position either involved no defect, or if a defect was present it played no part in the accident. Here, the failure of the safety gear switch was a cause of the accident. Matthews had neither been warned nor knew of the danger. A manufacturer is free from liability for misuse of his product only when such use is not reasonably foreseeable. Ford (D) could certainly foresee that one day a tractor operator might carelessly crank the engine without first making certain that it was not in gear, especially if he were aware of the purpose of the safety switch system. Affirmed.

▶ **ANALYSIS**

Prosser lists as normal foreseeable uses the following: "standing on a chair, eating coffee, testing heating fixtures, or wearing a cocktail robe in proximity to the kitchen stove. The seller of pork usually has been held to be entitled to expect that it will be cooked to kill trichinae; but where the question has arisen, it has been held that there is a normal use where the pork is cooked to an extent which the buyer erroneously believes to be sufficient." Law of Torts (1971 4th ed.), ch. 17, § 96, p. 648. Thus, the manufacturer's duty to warn the consumer of all reasonably foreseeable dangers has been broadly applied by the courts.

■≡■

Quicknotes

DUTY TO WARN An obligation owed by an owner or occupier of land to persons who come onto the premises, to inform them of defects or active operations which may cause injury.

FORESEEABLE DANGER A danger that is likely to result from a certain act or failure to act.

STRICT LIABILITY Liability for all injuries proximately caused by a party's conducting of certain inherently dangerous activities without regard to negligence or fault.

WRONGFUL DEATH An action brought by the beneficiaries of a deceased person, claiming that the deceased's death was the result of wrongful conduct by the defendant.

■≡■

Medtronic, Inc. v. Lohr

Manufacturer (D) v. Pacemaker recipient (P)

518 U.S. 470 (1996).

NATURE OF CASE: Suit alleging negligence and strict liability.

FACT SUMMARY: Lohr (P) brought suit against Medtronic (D) for negligence and strict liability based on injuries sustained as the result of an alleged defect in its pacemaker.

🏛️ **RULE OF LAW**

An area is preempted by federal law where Congress has weighed the competing interests relevant to the particular requirement, reached an unambiguous conclusion about how these interests should be resolved, and implemented that conclusion in the form of a specific mandate on manufacturers.

FACTS: A Medtronic (D) pacemaker was implanted in Lohr's (P) heart. Three years later it failed, allegedly resulting in a complete heart block requiring emergency surgery. According to her doctor, a defect in the lead was the likely cause of the failure. Lohr (P) filed suit alleging negligence and strict liability. Medtronic (D) removed the suit to federal court and argued that 21 U.S.C. § 360k(a) preempted the state common law claims. The trial judge granted the motion and dismissed. The Eleventh Circuit affirmed in part and reversed in part. Both parties sought review.

ISSUE: Is an area preempted by federal law where Congress has weighed the competing interests relevant to the particular requirement, reached an unambiguous conclusion about how these interests should be resolved, and implemented that conclusion in the form of a specific mandate on manufacturers?

HOLDING AND DECISION: (Stevens, J.) Yes. An area is preempted by federal law where Congress has weighed the competing interests relevant to the particular requirement, reached an unambiguous conclusion about how these interests should be resolved, and implemented that conclusion in the form of a specific mandate on manufacturers. Here § 360k(a) expressly preempts state law. While that means that the court not look beyond the language of the statute to determine the scope of the preemption, the interpretation of the statutory language is subject to two presumptions. First is that the state's police powers are not to be superceded by federal law unless that is the clear and manifest intent of Congress. Second, the scope of the preemption rests primarily on the congressional purpose. This may be determined from both the language of the statute and the statutory scheme surrounding it. Here

Medtronic (D) argued that Congress intended to bar all common law tort claims based on medical devices in enacting the MDA. This argument is erroneous. Since there is no express or implied private cause of action against manufacturers under the MDA, this reading would bar any relief for persons injured by defective medical devices. The legislative history also supports the conclusion that § 360(k) was not intended to preempt most common law claims. The statute and regulations require a careful comparison between the allegedly preempting federal requirement and the allegedly preempted state requirement to determine whether they fall within the intended scope of the preemption. This comparison warrants the conclusion that Lohr's (P) common law claims were not preempted by the MDA. Here the federal state reflects concerns about medical device regulation generally, and not the type of specific concerns that the federal statute intended to protect against conflicting state regulations. Reversed and remanded.

▶ *ANALYSIS*

The MDA was enacted in order to provide for the safety and effectiveness of medical devices intended for human use. In addition, it was intended to apply to the introduction of new medical devices, which was not otherwise regulated by federal law, in response to Congress's concern with respect to the injuries resulting from the failure of these devices.

■■■

Quicknotes

NEGLIGENCE Conduct falling below the standard of care that a reasonable person would demonstrate under similar conditions.

PREEMPTION Judicial preference recognizing the procedure of federal legislation over state legislation of the same subject matter.

STRICT LIABILITY Liability for all injuries proximately caused by a party's conducting of certain inherently dangerous activities without regard to negligence or fault.

■■■

Peterson v. Lou Bachrodt Chevrolet Co.

Pedestrians (P) v. Driver (D), car owner (D) and retailer (D)

Ill. Sup. Ct., 61 Ill. 2d 17, 329 N.E.2d 785 (1975).

NATURE OF CASE: Action to recover damages for wrongful death, and for personal injuries on a theory of strict liability.

FACT SUMMARY: Consumer suit sought to impose strict liability on a used-car dealer (D) who had sold a 1965 Chevrolet which had defective brakes.

🏛 RULE OF LAW
Strict liability does not extend to the seller of a defective used car.

FACTS: Two minors, Mark (P) and Maradean Peterson were struck by a used 1965 Chevrolet automobile while on their way home from school. Maradean suffered mortal wounds, and Mark (P) sustained severe injuries. Mark (P), and Maradean's Estate (P) brought, respectively, an action for personal injuries, and a wrongful death suit against the driver (D) of the used car, its owners (D), and the retailer of the car, Lou Bachrodt Chevrolet Co. (D). The count against Lou Bachrodt (D), which was founded on a theory of strict liability, alleged that at the time the 1965 Chevrolet was sold it was defective, and not reasonably safe for driving in that springs in the braking system were missing, a brake shoe was completely worn out, and a part of the cylinder braking system was missing. The trial court dismissed the count against Lou Bachrodt (D), and Mark (P) and Maradean's Estate (P) appealed. The appellate court reversed.

ISSUE: Is a retailer of a defective used car strictly liable for injuries which are caused by the defect?

HOLDING AND DECISION: (Schaefer, J.) No. Strict liability should not be imposed upon a defendant who is outside the original producing and marketing chain. Imposition of liability upon wholesalers and retailers is justified on the ground that their position in the marketing process enables them to exert pressure on the manufacturer to enhance the safety of the product. The manufacturer is liable on the ground that having created the risk and reaped the profit by placing the product in the stream of commerce, it should bear the loss. However, a used-car dealer, who ordinarily does not create the defects, should not become an insurer against defects which had come into existence after the chain of distribution was completed, and while the product was under the control of one or more consumers. Reversed.

DISSENT: (Goldenhersh, J.) Strict liability has been held applicable to the lessor of a motor vehicle. The same reasoning should extend to a used car dealer who can discover a defect upon reasonable inspection.

▶ ANALYSIS

Most courts, and the Restatement (Second) of Torts § 402 have limited the application of strict product liability to only those individuals who are regularly engaged in the business of selling, leasing, or manufacturing. Thus, the occasional bailor or lessor is, as a rule, not strictly liable for defects in the chattel he loans out. The application of this limitation to used car retailers has been criticized as ignoring the fact that used car dealers are in fact engaged in an ongoing business.

Quicknotes

STRICT LIABILITY Liability for all injuries proximately caused by a party's conducting of certain inherently dangerous activities without regard to negligence or fault.

WRONGFUL DEATH An action brought by the beneficiaries of a deceased person, claiming that the deceased's death was the result of wrongful conduct by the defendant.

Hector v. Cedars-Sinai Medical Ctr.

Patient (P) v. Medical center (D)

Cal. Ct. App., 180 Cal. App. 3d 493 (1986).

NATURE OF CASE: Appeal from dismissal of a personal injury claim.

FACT SUMMARY: Hector (P) sought to bring a strict products liability action against Cedars-Sinai (D), the hospital where her defective pacemaker was implanted.

RULE OF LAW

Since the essence of the relationship between hospitals and patients is for the provision of medical services, hospitals are not liable under strict products liability because they are not engaged in the business of selling products.

FACTS: Hector (P) had a pacemaker, manufactured by American Technology, implanted at Cedars-Sinai Medical Center (D). Hector (P) filed a complaint against Cedars-Sinai (D), alleging personal injuries from a defective pacemaker. The complaint contained causes of action under negligence, strict liability, and breach of warranty theories. Cedars-Sinai (D) moved for the dismissal of the strict liability action, and the trial court granted the motion. Hector (P) appealed.

ISSUE: May hospitals be held liable under a strict products liability theory?

HOLDING AND DECISION: (Spencer, J.) No. Since the essence of the relationship between hospitals and patients is for the provision of medical services, hospitals are not liable under strict products liability because they are not engaged in the business of selling a product. Originally, strict liability was applied to manufacturers who placed a product on the market. Later, strict liability was extended to retailers since they were engaged in the business of distributing goods to the public and were an integral part of the overall enterprise. In other words, every party who plays a vital part in the chain of production and distribution may be held strictly liable. However, strict liability does not apply to a supplier of professional services. Medical personnel furnish services as a healer of illnesses. These services depend upon the skill and judgment derived from specialized training, knowledge, and experience. Doctors who treat patients cannot be construed as selling a product. Similarly, a hospital is not ordinarily engaged in the business of selling any products. The essence of the transaction between a hospital and a patient does not relate essentially to any product. Thus, hospitals may not be held strictly liable for products, such as blood or pacemakers, which it may supply to its patients. Furthermore, the policy considerations behind strict liability, which is based in part on the ability of manufacturers and distributors to protect themselves through testing and promoting safety, would not be served by holding a hospital strictly liable. The hospital is in a poor position to test pacemakers and other medical products. Cedars-Sinai (D) does not ordinarily stock pacemakers and does not recommend, sell, or distribute these devices. In this case, Hector (P) entered the hospital to obtain a course of treatment which included the implantation of the pacemaker. Thus, the essence of the transaction was for the provision of services, and strict liability may not be applied to Cedars-Sinai (D). Affirmed.

ANALYSIS

This court drew a distinction between products and services that is also included in the Uniform Commercial Code and § 402A of the Restatement (Second) of Torts. The rationale behind this distinction is that, in service transactions, there is no mass production, and the risk of loss cannot be easily passed on to consumers. In hybrid transactions, which include both a product and a service, courts usually look to see whether the transaction was predominantly a service or a sale.

Quicknotes

STRICT LIABILITY Liability for all injuries proximately caused by a party's conducting of certain inherently dangerous activities without regard to negligence or fault.

Nuisance

Quick Reference Rules of Law

Philadelphia Electric Co. v. Hercules, Inc.

Polluted-property owner (P) v. Successor (D)

762 F.2d 303 (3d Cir. 1985).

NATURE OF CASE: Appeal from award of damages for nuisance.

FACT SUMMARY: Philadelphia Electric Co. (PECO) (P) contended that Hercules' (D) predecessor created a private nuisance on property purchased by PECO (P), which later had to pay the cost of eliminating the nuisance.

RULE OF LAW
A vendor of real property cannot be held liable in nuisance to the vendee.

FACTS: The Pennsylvania Industrial Chemical Corp. owned property known as the "Chester" site, on which it operated a hydrocarbon resin plant. The property was sold to Gould, who in turn sold it to PECO (P). Hercules (D) then took over all debts of Pennsylvania Industrial and assumed all of its liabilities. It was determined that chemicals used by Pennsylvania Industrial were polluting the Delaware River, and PECO (P) was required to pay $400,000 to clean up the pollution. It sued Hercules (D), contending the condition constituted a nuisance. Hercules (D) defended on the basis that no duty was owed to the vendee of land, and thus PECO (P) had no standing to sue. The jury found for PECO (P), and Hercules (D) appealed.

ISSUE: Can a vendor of real property be held liable in nuisance to the vendee?

HOLDING AND DECISION: (Higginbotham, J.) No. A vendor of real property cannot be held liable in nuisance to the vendee. The relationship between buyer and seller is ruled by the maxim "caveat emptor." The duty not to maintain a nuisance on one's property is owed to the owner or occupiers of adjacent land who would be affected by it. No duty is owed to the vendee in this regard. The vendee's remedies arise out of the sales transaction and any breach therein must be remedied within the contractual area. Similarly, no cause of action for public nuisance exists because PECO suffered no injury distinct from that suffered by the public in general. Reversed.

▶ ANALYSIS

This case illustrates the elements necessary to establish a cause of action for private and public nuisance. A private nuisance incurs damage to an individual while a public nuisance impacts on society generally. A private action for public nuisance requires a showing of distinct injury. See Restatement, Second, Torts § 821 C.

■■■

Quicknotes

CAVEAT EMPTOR Let the buyer beware; doctrine that a buyer purchases something at his own risk.

VENDEE Purchaser.

VENDOR Seller.

■■■

Morgan v. High Penn Oil Co.

Property owner (P) v. Refinery (D)

N.C. Sup. Ct., 77 S.E.2d 682 (1953).

NATURE OF CASE: Action to recover temporary damages for a private nuisance, and to enjoin such nuisance.

FACT SUMMARY: Morgan (P) owned land next to High Penn Oil Co.'s (D) refinery, which emitted nauseating gases and odors.

🏛 RULE OF LAW
A person who intentionally creates or maintains a private nuisance is liable for the resulting injury to others, regardless of the degree of care or skill exercised by him to avoid such injury.

FACTS: Morgan (P) owned a nine-acre tract of land. High Penn Oil Co. (D) owned an adjoining tract on which it operated an oil refinery, 1,000 feet from Morgan's (P) house. A few days each week, the refinery emitted nauseating gases and odors, which invaded Morgan's (P) land and made people sick. High Penn Oil Co. (D) failed to stop the pollution after notice and demand from Morgan (P) to abate it. High Penn Oil Co. (D) contended that the refinery was a modern plant, of a type in general use, and that, since it was not negligent in the plant's operation or maintenance Morgan (P) could not recover.

ISSUE: Must there be proof of negligent operation or construction before an enterprise can be termed a nuisance in fact?

HOLDING AND DECISION: (Ervin, J.) No. A person who intentionally creates or maintains a private nuisance is liable for the resulting damage to others regardless of the degree of care or skill exercised by him to avoid such injury. Nuisances per accidens or in fact are those which become nuisances by reason of their location, or by reason of the manner in which they are constructed, maintained, or operated. A private nuisance in fact may be created or maintained without negligence. Nuisance, as a concept of law, has more than one meaning. The primary meaning does not involve the element of negligence as one of its essential factors. One acts sometimes at one's peril. In such circumstances, the duty to desist is absolute whenever conduct, if persisted in, brings damage to another.

▶ ANALYSIS

This case gives a good discussion of the difference between a nuisance per se or at law and a nuisance per accidens or in fact. A nuisance per se is an act, occupation, or structure that is nuisance at all times under any circumstances, regardless of location or surroundings. Nuisances per accidens or in fact are those which become nuisances by reason of their location, or by reason of the manner in which they are constructed, maintained, or operated. An oil refinery is, obviously, not a nuisance per se since it is a lawful enterprise, lawfully carried on. But the emission of nauseating gases that invade neighboring property make the refinery a nuisance in fact, even if the refinery is carefully operated. Note that the nuisance is a field of tort liability rather than a type of tortious conduct. It has a reference to the interests invaded, to the damage or harm inflicted, and not to any particular kind of act or omission that has led to the invasion. Negligence is merely one type of conduct that may give rise to a nuisance. Liability for nuisance may rest upon an intentional invasion of the plaintiff's interests, or a negligent one, or conduct which is abnormal.

Quicknotes

DICTUM Statement by a judge in a legal opinion that is not necessary for the resolution of the action.

NUISANCE An unlawful use of property that interferes with the lawful use of another's property.

Carpenter v. The Double R Cattle Co., Inc.

Homeowners (P) v. Feedlot owners (D)

Idaho Sup. Ct., 108 Idaho 602, 701 P.2d 222 (1985).

NATURE OF CASE: Appeal from denial of damages for nuisance.

FACT SUMMARY: The court of appeals held that Double R (D) had maintained a nuisance even though the utility of maintaining the feedlot outweighed the harm caused thereby.

RULE OF LAW
No nuisance may be found where the utility of the activity outweighs the gravity of harm.

FACTS: Double R (D) maintained a feedlot for cattle. The lot fed approximately 9,000 cattle. Carpenter (P) and other adjacent homeowners sued in nuisance, contending the accumulation of manure, pollution of the river, odors, and insect infestation caused by the cattle damaged their right to quiet enjoyment of their land. The trial court refused Carpenter's (P) requested jury instructions based on Restatement (Second) Torts § 826, which provided a nuisance could be found even where the gravity of harm was outweighed by the utility of the act, if damages could be paid. The jury found for Double R (D), and Carpenter (P) appealed. The court of appeals reversed, and Double R (D) appealed.

ISSUE: May nuisance be found even where the gravity of harm is outweighed by the utility of activity?

HOLDING AND DECISION: (Bakes, J.) No. A nuisance cannot be found even where the gravity of harm is outweighed by the utility of activity. In modern society, individuals must be willing to accept a certain amount of interference with quiet enjoyment in order to foster coexistence. The balancing test between harm and utility is well suited to this task. As a result, the Restatement does not reflect the law of Idaho, and the trial court did not err in failing to instruct the jury as requested by Carpenter even where the gravity of harm is outweighed by the utility of activity. Reversed.

DISSENT: (Bistline, J.) While community interest is a factor, the blind adherence to ancient antiquated precedent serves to deny a remedy to a clear wrong. Such must be changed due to changes in modern lifestyle.

▶ ANALYSIS

The court relied heavily on the specific factual circumstances in this case in arriving at its decision. It indicated that Idaho is sparsely populated and its economy is based on agribusiness. Thus, because the feed lot promotes this type of economy, it will be sanctioned only if the harm outweighs its utility. It is likely that if this case arose in a nonagricultural state, the utility of the act would be viewed differently, and the result would differ.

Quicknotes

NUISANCE An unlawful use of property that interferes with the lawful use of another's property.

Winget v. Winn-Dixie Stores, Inc.

Homeowners (P) v. Supermarket owner (D)

S.C. Sup. Ct., 242 S.C. 152, 130 S.E.2d 363 (1963).

NATURE OF CASE: Action for damages to land and for an injunction, on a theory of nuisance.

FACT SUMMARY: The Wingets (P), whose home was adjacent to a newly-opened Supermarket (D) sought to enjoin the operation of the Supermarket (D), alleging, among other claims, that it heightened traffic congestion and thereby decreased the market value of their property.

🏛 RULE OF LAW
Acts that are the normal or necessary incidents of a business may not ordinarily be enjoined as a nuisance.

FACTS: Winn-Dixie Stores, Inc. (D) opened a grocery supermarket in an area zoned by the city for retail business and at a location which the local zoning board specifically approved. The Wingets (P), whose home was adjacent to the supermarket, brought an action against Winn-Dixie (D) for damages and to enjoin continued operation of the supermarket as a nuisance because of both its location, and the manner of its operation. In their complaint, the Wingets (P) alleged that: (1) the store had attracted crowds of people and many automobiles which caused noise, fumes, and traffic congestion; (2) trash trucks and street sweepers operated on the premises at late night hours; (3) air conditioning fans blew against their trees and shrubbery causing damage and inconvenience; (4) floodlights cast a bright glare over their property until late at night; and (5) garbage odors, and paper and trash were accumulated. An expert witness for the Wingets (P) testified that the location of the supermarket caused a substantial depreciation in the market value of the Wingets' (P) home. From judgment in the form of damages for the Wingets (P), Winn-Dixie (D) appealed.

ISSUE: May acts that are the normal or necessary incidents of a business ordinarily be enjoined?

HOLDING AND DECISION: (Lewis, J.) No. Acts that are the normal or necessary incidents of a business ordinarily may not be enjoined. People who live in organized communities must of necessity suffer some inconvenience and annoyance from their neighbors and must submit to annoyances consequent upon the reasonable use of property by others. Here, the normal traffic and noise caused by customers going to and from the supermarket cannot constitute a basis for declaring the operation of the business a nuisance since the purpose of the business is to sell merchandise and in doing so to attract to their store as many customers as possible. There was no showing here that there was any mass exodus from or entrance to the store at unreasonable hours. Similarly, the cleaning operations were usual and normal. However, the same cannot be said for the other allegations in the Wingets' (P) complaint; such acts are not normal or necessary incidents of the business. Finally, the testimony of the expert witness was irrelevant. A use of property which does not create a nuisance cannot be enjoined or a lawful structure abated merely because it renders neighboring property less valuable. Reversed and remanded.

▶ ANALYSIS

The approach adopted in the present case, which focuses on the nature of the business and the manner in which it is conducted, represents a compromise of two extreme positions taken by other courts with respect to the effect zoning regulations have on nuisance actions. One group has held that the legislative action preempts the authority of a court to determine whether or not a given activity constitutes a nuisance. The other group has held to the contra, reasoning that it is not the business itself, but its location and nature, which may be a nuisance.

Quicknotes

INJUNCTION A court order requiring a person to do or prohibiting that person from doing a specific act.

NUISANCE An unlawful use of property that interferes with the lawful use of another's property.

Boomer v. Atlantic Cement Co., Inc.

Property owners (P) v. Cement plant (D)

N.Y. Ct. App., 26 N.Y.2d 219, 257 N.E.2d 870 (1970).

NATURE OF CASE: Action for an injunction to enjoin maintenance of a nuisance, and for damages.

FACT SUMMARY: Property owners (P) sued cement plant (D) alleging that pollution emanating from the plant had injured their lands; while the trial court refused an injunction, it did authorize successive actions for damages.

RULE OF LAW
Although a nuisance will be enjoined even when a marked disparity is shown in economic consequence between the effect of the injunction and the effect of the nuisance, if the practical effect of the injunction will be to close a production plant, a court will condition on equitable grounds the continuance of the injunction on the payment of permanent damages.

FACTS: The Atlantic Cement Co., Inc. (D) operated a large cement plant near Albany, New York in which it had invested $45,000,000, and employed over 300 workers. A group of neighboring landowners (P) brought actions for injunction and damages against Atlantic (D) alleging injury to their property from dirt, smoke, and vibration emanating from the plant. The trial court held that a nuisance existed, but denied the issuance of an injunction. Rather, it awarded the landowners (P) damages up to the time of trial, thus permitting them to maintain successive actions at law for damages thereafter as further injury was incurred. Atlantic (D) appealed.

ISSUE: Where the issuance of an injunction to enjoin the maintenance of a manufacturing operation as a nuisance would have the effect of closing the plant, may a court award permanent damages as an alternative?

HOLDING AND DECISION: (Bergan, J.) Yes. Courts should be wary of using a decision in private litigation as a purposeful mechanism to achieve direct public objectives greatly beyond the rights and interests before the court. The judicial establishment is neither equipped in the limited nature of any judgment it can pronounce nor prepared to lay down and implement an effective policy for the elimination of air pollution. This is a problem government alone is to resolve. Although an injunction should not be denied because the damage to a plaintiff is slight as compared to the defendant's expense of abating a nuisance, to follow this rule literally in this case would have the immediately drastic effect of closing the plant. One alternative would be to grant the injunction but postpone its effect to a specified future date to give opportunity for technical advances to permit Atlantic (D) to eliminate the nuisance. However, it is unlikely that Atlantic (D) by itself will be able to eliminate its pollution in the near future. The rate of the research is simply beyond its control. A better alternative would be to grant the injunction unless Atlantic pays the landowners (P) permanent damages as may be fixed by the court. An amount of $185,000 would fairly compensate the landowners (P) for all past and future injury they have and will suffer. Reversed.

DISSENT: (Jasen, J.) The majority has in effect licensed a continuing wrong. Furthermore, once permanent damages are assessed and paid, the incentive to alleviate the wrong would be eliminated. Moreover, Atlantic (D) should not be allowed, as a private party, inverse condemnation; the public is not being benefitted. Finally, the landowners (D) are being forced to accept a servitude on their land for the benefit of a private party.

▌ ANALYSIS

In determining whether or not to enjoin a nuisance, a court "may take into consideration the relative economic hardship which will result to the parties from the granting or denial of the injunction, the good faith or intentional misconduct of each, and the interest of the general public in the continuation of the defendant's enterprise." Prosser, Law of Torts (1971 4th ed.) ch. 15, § 90 to p. 604. Another factor, as this case illustrates, is the financial investment each party has made in his land.

■═■

Quicknotes

INJUNCTION A court order requiring a person to do or prohibiting that person from doing a specific act.

INVERSE CONDEMNATION the taking of private property for public use so as to impair or decrease the value of property near or adjacent to, but not a part of, the property taken.

NUISANCE An unlawful use of property that interferes with the lawful use of another's property.

■═■

Spur Industries, Inc. v. Del E. Webb Development Co.

Retirement community (P) v. Feedlot operator (D)

Ariz. Sup. Ct., 108 Ariz. 178, 494 P.2d 700 (1972).

NATURE OF CASE: Action by developer to enjoin operation of a business as a public nuisance.

FACT SUMMARY: Del Webb (P), developer of Sun City, a residential community which sprang up in a rural area near Spur's (D) cattle feedlot, sought an injunction against Spur (D) on the ground that as a breeder of flies the feedlot constituted a public nuisance.

🏛 RULE OF LAW
Although the operation of a business, lawful in the first instance, which becomes a nuisance by reason of a nearby residential area, may be enjoined in an action brought by the developer of the residential area, the developer must indemnify the business for a reasonable amount of the cost of moving or shutting down.

FACTS: Spur Industries, Inc. (D) maintained a cattle feedlot in an area which had long been devoted to farming. Del Webb (P) began to develop Sun City, a retirement community, originally some distance from Spur (D). However, the development progressed rapidly and expanded, coming within 500 feet of Spur (D). Complaining that the Spur (D) feeding operation was a public nuisance because of the flies and the odor that were being blown over Sun City, Del Webb (P) sought a permanent injunction against Spur's (D) continued operations. State law defined a public nuisance as including "any condition or place in populous areas which constitutes a breeding place" for disease-carrying "flies, rodents, mosquitos, and other insects . . . ." The trial court, finding that some of the citizens of Sun City were unable to enjoy the outdoor living that Del Webb (P) had advertised, and that prospective purchasers were being discouraged, issued the injunction, but denied any compensatory relief for Spur (D) who appealed.

ISSUE:
(1) May a residential tract bring an action to abate a business as a public nuisance if the business was in the area first?
(2) If an injunction is issued, must the developer of the tract indemnify the business?

HOLDING AND DECISION: (Cameron, V.C.J.)
(1) Yes. Under the doctrine of "coming to the nuisance," courts of equity held that a residential landowner may not have relief if he knowingly came into a neighborhood reserved for industrial or agricultural endeavors and has been damaged thereby. The reasoning behind this rule is that a party cannot justly call upon the law to make the place suitable for his residence which was not so when he selected it. However, under our state statute, a business which is not per se a public nuisance may become such by being carried on at a place where the health, comfort, or convenience of a populous neighborhood is affected. Were Del Webb (P) the only injured party, "coming to the nuisance" would be a bar to the relief sought by it. However, since the residents of Sun City are being injured as well, Spur (D) must move, not because of any wrongdoing on its part, but because of the court's concern for the health and safety of the public;

(2) Yes. It does not seem harsh to require a developer, who has taken advantage of the lesser land values in a rural area, as well as the availability of large tracts of land on which to build and develop a new town or city in the area, to indemnify those who are forced to leave as a result. Del Webb (P) must therefore compensate Spur (D) for a reasonable amount of the cost of moving or shutting down. Affirmed in part; reversed in part.

▶ ANALYSIS

Most courts have held that ordinarily plaintiff who purchases land next to a nuisance is not barred from bringing an action by the "coming to the nuisance" doctrine. However, where the equities between the two parties are fairly evenly balanced, the doctrine may be invoked and given controlling weight. The instant case perhaps represents a new trend in balancing the equities by looking to the compensation accorded the defendant were the plaintiff to prevail, and discarding the "coming to the nuisance" doctrine. Note, however, that "public nuisance" is specifically defined by statute in Arizona.

■■■

Quicknotes

COMING TO THE NUISANCE A claim may be weakened when a plaintiff moves to the defendant's established locale.

INDEMNIFY Securing against potential injury; compensation for injury suffered.

PUBLIC NUISANCE An activity that unreasonably interferes with a right common to the overall public.

■■■

Quick Reference Rules of Law

Belli v. Orlando Daily Newspapers, Inc.

Libeled attorney (P) v. Newspaper (D)

389 F.2d 579 (5th Cir. 1967).

NATURE OF CASE: Action for damages for libel and slander.

FACT SUMMARY: A newspaper (D) printed a false story that Belli (P) had charged clothing to his hotel bill and that this had to be paid for by the local bar association.

🏛 RULE OF LAW
If a statement may be interpreted in both a defamatory and nondefamatory manner, it is the province of the jury to determine which one the general public would have taken.

FACTS: Belli (P), a well-known attorney, agreed to aid a local bar association in exchange for his hotel bills. Nine years later, this story was relayed to a local gossip columnist. It was embellished to include allegations that Belli (P) had charged numerous items of clothing to his hotel bill and had taken the local bar association which had to pay the entire bill. This was false, but was published by Orlando Daily Newspapers (D) which failed to verify the story. Belli (P) sued for libel and slander. The court dismissed on the basis that the story had not diminished Belli's (P) reputation and was not defamatory. The court apparently felt that the story would be viewed by the general public in a nondefamatory light and refused to submit the issue to the jury. Belli (P) appealed on the basis that the story had a defamatory connotation in that it held him up to ridicule, hatred, etc.

ISSUE: Is it the jury's province to decide whether a story, capable of two possible interpretations, is defamatory?

HOLDING AND DECISION: (Wisdom, J.) Yes. The court makes the initial decision as to whether a statement is defamatory. If it is legally nondefamatory, the court removes it from the jury. If it is susceptible to two meanings, one defamatory and the other not, the jury must decide the issue. Here, the story might be viewed as a cute tale of how Belli (P) conned the local bar association. It might also be viewed as defamatory in that it exposed Belli (P) to hate, ridicule, etc., and lowered his reputation in the eyes of the community. It should have been submitted to the jury. Reversed.

▌ANALYSIS

Defamation has tended to broaden in scope in recent years. It is a communication that damages reputation, i.e., diminishes the respect, goodwill, confidence or esteem in which he is held. It may also excite adverse or unpleasant feelings about him. It may even include situations where decent citizens would regard him only with pity. Alternative or companion causes of action include intentional infliction of emotional distress and invasion of privacy.

Quicknotes

ACTIONABLE PER SE Language of such an extreme nature that the law will presume that the person who is the subject of the communication has suffered injury and for which proof of damages is not required.

DEFAMATORY Subjecting to hatred, ridicule or injuring one in his occupation or business.

LIBEL A false or malicious publication that subjects a person to scorn, hatred or ridicule, or that injures him in relation to his occupation or business.

SLANDER Defamatory statement communicated orally.

Grant v. Reader's Digest Ass'n

Libeled attorney (P) v. Publisher (D)

151 F.2d 733 (2d Cir. 1945).

NATURE OF CASE: Action to recover damages for libel.

FACT SUMMARY: Reader's Digest Association (D) printed in its publication an article which made reference to the fact that Grant (P) had been a legislative representative for the Massachusetts Communist Party. Grant (P) brings a suit for libel.

🏛 RULE OF LAW
Libel consists of utterances that arouse hatred, contempt, scorn, obloquy, or shame in the minds of people whether or not those persons are "right thinking" people. It is defamatory as a matter of law to say that a person is an agent of the Communist Party.

FACTS: Reader's Digest Association (D) published in a periodical of general circulation (read by lawyers, judges, and the general public) an article which made reference to a Massachusetts lawyer, Sidney S. Grant (P) as having been hired by the Massachusetts Communist party to act as its legislative agent. Sidney S. Grant (P) brought this action against Reader's Digest Association (D) for libel. The complaint in libel was dismissed for insufficiency in law upon its face and Grant (P) appeals.

ISSUE: Is it libelous to write of a lawyer that he has acted as agent of the Communist Party and is a believer in its aims and methods?

HOLDING AND DECISION: (Hand, J.) Yes. The interest at stake in all defamation actions is the reputation of the person assailed. The New York decisions define libel as consisting of utterances which arouse "hatred, contempt, scorn, obloquy or shame" and the like. However, the opinions at the time seem to make it an additional condition that to bring an action for libel, the words must be such as would cause "right thinking" people to be aroused to hatred, contempt, etc., toward the plaintiff. This limitation has been recognized in England, and there is no doubt that there must come a point when words claimed to be defamatory must be defamatory to "right thinking" people. It is argued that "right thinking" people would not have such feelings toward a person who is a member of the Communist party. This court, however, does not believe that it is necessary to say whether "right thinking" people harbor such feelings toward a lawyer who was an agent for the Communist Party. It is enough if there are some persons who feel hatred, contempt, scorn, obloquy, or shame towards the plaintiff even though they would be "wrong thinking" people if they felt that way. Furthermore, it is defamatory as a matter of law to say that a person is an agent for the Communist Party. Reversed and remanded.

▶ ANALYSIS

It has been held in England that communications must tend to defame the plaintiff in the eyes of the community in general, or at least of a reasonable man, rather than in the opinion of any particular group or class. The American courts have taken a more realistic view, recognizing that the plaintiff may suffer real damage if he is lowered in the esteem of any substantial and respectable group, even though it may be quite a small minority. It has sometimes been said that these must be "right thinking" people, but this seems clearly wrong, since the court cannot be called upon to make a definitive pronouncement upon whether the views of different segments of the community are right or wrong, sound, or morally justifiable.

Quicknotes

DEFAMATION An intentional false publication, communicated publicly in either oral or written form, subjecting a person to scorn, hatred or ridicule, or injuring him or her in relation to his or her occupation or business.

LIBEL A false or malicious publication subjecting a person to scorn, hatred or ridicule, or injuring him or her in relation to his or her occupation or business.

MORAL OBLOQUY Blame; reproach; censure.

Kilian v. Doubleday & Co., Inc.

Libeled officer (P) v. Publisher (D)

Pa. Sup. Ct., 367 Pa. 117, 79 A.2d 657 (1951).

NATURE OF CASE: Action for damages based on libel.

FACT SUMMARY: A book was published by Doubleday (D) which contained an article which claimed that Kilian (P), as commander of an army camp and hospital, had mistreated patients.

🏛 RULE OF LAW
To claim truth as a defense, it must be shown that the statements in the article were substantially true, not that other acts of a different nature occurred.

FACTS: Wolfe held a creative writing course for disabled veterans. Wolfe decided to publish the articles of his students in book form. Doubleday (D) agreed to publish it. One article contained an allegedly first-hand account of mistreatment of patients and staff at an army hospital by Kilian (P), the hospital commander. At the end of the article, the editors added a note that Kilian (P) had been reprimanded and fined for his actions. Kilian (P) brought suit for libel. At trial, it was shown that the author of the article had never been at the hospital but was merely relating stories he had heard. Kilian's (P) reprimand had been for neglect of duty in allowing certain punishments to be inflicted on prisoners by his men. Doubleday (D) had three witnesses testify as to actions they had observed at the hospital which showed cruel punishments being inflicted. There was no showing that the lashing recounted in the article had ever occurred or that Kilian (P) had been personally present at any of the incidents. The jury found that Doubleday (D) had shown that similar but different incidents had occurred and found for Doubleday (D).

ISSUE: Is the defense of truth available where other incidents of a similar nature to those described in the story are shown?

HOLDING AND DECISION: (Stern, J.) No. It must be shown that the events related in the story are substantially true. Here, there was no such showing. While misconduct was shown, it was of a different nature. The events were not the same and there was no showing that Kilian (P) was ever present at these "punishments." None of the witnesses testified as to any lashings administered to staff members. It is not enough to show that different offenses occurred, even if they were more serious. Where specific incidents are alleged, they must be proven. The court erred in submitting the case to the jury. Reversed and remanded.

▶ ANALYSIS

While this holding might seem unfair to some liberal readers, it must be borne in mind that the author was reporting hearsay which could have as easily been false. Where a person's reputation is at stake, it seems fair to require a reasonable attempt to verify such facts. Defendant must establish that the statement is substantially true. This means that the basic accusations must be true in a majority of the facts.

Quicknotes

HEARSAY An out-of-court statement made by a person other than the witness testifying at trial that is offered in order to prove the truth of the matter asserted.

LIBEL A false or malicious publication subjecting a person to scorn, hatred or ridicule, or injuring him or her in relation to his or her occupation or business.

Neiman-Marcus v. Lait

Department store owner (P) v. Book (D)

13 F.R.D. 311 (S.D.N.Y. 1952).

NATURE OF CASE: Action to recover damages for libel.

FACT SUMMARY: Lait (D) published a book in which he referred to Neiman-Marcus (P) models (P) and saleswomen (P) as being call girls and which referred to Neiman-Marcus (P) dress and millinery designers (P) as fairies. There are 382 saleswomen (P), 25 salesmen (P) and 9 models (P).

🏛 RULE OF LAW
Where a group or class disparaged is a large one, absent circumstances pointing to a particular plaintiff as the person defamed, no individual member of the group or class has a cause of action. However, where the group or class libeled is small, and each and every member of the group or class is referred to, then any individual member can sue.

FACTS: In their publication entitled "U.S.A. Confidential," the authors (D) of the book stated that some Neiman-Marcus models (P) are call girls. It further stated that Neiman-Marcus salesgirls (P) are also call girls. The article goes on to state that "the nucleus of the Dallas Fairy Colony" is composed of Neiman-Marcus dress and millinery designers (P). At the time of the publication of the book, there were nine models (P) working at Neiman-Marcus. There were 15 individual salesmen, of a total of 25 salesmen, who worked for Neiman-Marcus at the time of publication and who brought this suit on behalf of themselves and the other salesmen. Also, 30 individual saleswomen (P) of a total of 382 saleswomen sued for libel. Lait (D) requests a motion to dismiss all causes of action for failure to state a cause of action.

ISSUE: When a large group is defamed, may the individual members of that group bring an action for libel?

HOLDING AND DECISION: (Kaufman, J.) It depends on the size of the group. Where the group or class libeled is large, none can sue even though the language used is inclusive. However, where the group or class libeled is small, and each and every member of the class or group is referred to, then any individual member can sue. Where the group or class libeled is small and the publication complained of libels some or less than all of the group, the Restatement of Torts § 564 indicates that each member of the group has a cause of action. The court finds that the plaintiff salesmen, of whom it is alleged that "most . . . are fairies" have a cause of action.

However, the saleswomen do not have a cause of action because their group is too large and no reasonable reader of the libelous statement could believe that 382 saleswomen were all call girls. Nonetheless, if any individual plaintiff saleswoman can prove that some particular circumstances point to her as the person defamed then she may recover.

▌ANALYSIS

This plaintiff must sustain the burden of proof, by way of "colloquium," that the defamatory meaning attached to him. Reference to the plaintiff may, of course, be an indirect one, with the identification depending upon circumstances known to the hearers. When a group is defamed the plaintiff must first of all show that he is in fact a member of the class defamed. Beyond this, he must establish some reasonable personal application of the words to himself.

Quicknotes

COLLOQUIUM The connection between the libelous statements of the defendant and the plaintiff in a defamation action.

DEFAMATION An intentional false publication, communicated publicly in either oral or written form, subjecting a person to scorn, hatred or ridicule, or injuring him or her in relation to his or her occupation or business.

LIBEL A false or malicious publication subjecting a person to scorn, hatred or ridicule, or injuring him or her in relation to his or her occupation or business.

Bindrim v. Mitchell

Group therapist (P) v. Author (D)

Cal. Ct. App., Second Dist., 92 Cal. App. 3d 61, 155 Cal. Rptr. 29 (1979).

NATURE OF CASE: Appeal from award of damages for libel.

FACT SUMMARY: Bindrim (P) alleged that he was defamed in a book written by Mitchell (D).

🏛 RULE OF LAW
The test of identification in a libel action is whether a reasonable person, viewing the work, would identify the "fictional" character described therein as the plaintiff.

FACTS: Gwen Davis Mitchell (D), a novelist, enrolled in a nude therapy group, run by Bindrim (P). She claimed to have enrolled for therapeutic reasons only and warranted that she would not write for publication regarding her experiences in the group. Shortly after undergoing the therapy, Mitchell (D) contracted with Doubleday Publishing Co. (D) to write a book based on the nude therapy group. The book, entitled "Touching," went on to become a best-seller. Bindrim (P) brought suit for libel, alleging that certain false representations were made regarding the character in the novel which was based on himself. A jury returned a verdict in Bindrim's (P) favor. The court issued a remittitur. Mitchell (D) appealed, alleging that Bindrim (P) was not readily identifiable as the character in her book. Bindrim (P) also appealed.

ISSUE: Is the test of identification in a libel action whether a reasonable person would know that the person defamed is the plaintiff?

HOLDING AND DECISION: (Kingsley, J.) Yes. Mitchell (D) seems to base her defense on the fact that there were several major distinctions between the character in her novel and Bindrim (P); namely the physical appearance and the professional degree held. Thus, she seeks a ruling that as a matter of law, Bindrim (P) cannot claim to be defamed by her book. However, such a ruling can only be made in certain extreme cases, of which this is not one. The test of identification in a case of this kind is whether a reasonable person, viewing the work would identify the fictional character described therein as being the plaintiff. Given the factual circumstances presented here, it appears there were many similarities between Mitchell's (D) character and Bindrim (P). As such, the jury's finding that Bindrim (P) was identifiable as the character in "Touching" will not be disturbed on appeal. Affirmed.

CONCURRENCE: (Jefferson, J.) The fictional setting does not insure immunity when a reasonable person would understand that the fictional character is a portrayal of the plaintiff. The First Amendment right to comment does not include a right to commit libel.

DISSENT: (Files, J.) In the first instance, Mitchell's (D) book is not defamatory. In the second instance, the leading character cannot be readily identified, except through tortured logic, as Bindrim (P). Accordingly, an action for libel should not lie.

▎ANALYSIS

The Bindrim decision relies upon a long list of cases which hold that a reference to a libel plaintiff need not expressly name him to be actionable. It is enough that it is reasonably understood as referring to him. See, e.g., *Youssopoff v. M.G.M. Pictures*, 99 A.L.R. 864 (1934). Conversely, there will be no defamation if the plaintiff cannot prove that the statement may be reasonably understood as referring to him.

∎▬∎

Quicknotes

DEFAMATION An intentional false publication, communicated publicly in either oral or written form, subjecting a person to scorn, hatred or ridicule, or injuring him or her in relation to his or her occupation or business.

LIBEL A false or malicious publication subjecting a person to scorn, hatred or ridicule, or injuring him or her in relation to his or her occupation or business.

REASONABLE PERSON STANDARD The standard of care exercised by a hypothetical person who possesses the intelligence, education, knowledge, attention, and judgment required by society of its members when governing behavior; the standard applies to a person's judgment when determining breach of a duty under the theory of negligence.

REMITTITUR The authority of the court to reduce the amount of damages awarded by the jury.

∎▬∎

Shor v. Billingsley

Defamed restauranteur (P) v. Master of ceremonies (D)

N.Y. Cty. Sup. Ct., Special Term, 158 N.Y.S.2d 476 (1956).

NATURE OF CASE: Action to recover damages for libel.

FACT SUMMARY: Billingsley (D), while acting as the master of ceremonies of a telecast show, made reference to Shor (P) as being heavily in debt to "everyone." This statement was made while the show was on the air. Shor (P) sues for libel.

RULE OF LAW
Defamation through the media of motion pictures, television, or radio is considered libel, not slander.

FACTS: During a telecast of "The Stork Club Show," the master of ceremonies of the show, Billingsley (D), made reference to the fact that Shor (P) the owner of "The Toots Shor Restaurant" was heavily in debt to "everyone." These statements, along with a picture of Shor (P) were telecast to the watching audience. Also, it is alleged that the telecast was filmed and the film containing the allegedly defamatory statements and display of Shor's (P) picture was displayed at various times to various individuals. Shor (P) brings suit for libel. Billingsley (D) requests a motion to dismiss.

ISSUE: Do statements made in a telecast, radiocast, or movie which are allegedly defamatory sound in libel or in slander?

HOLDING AND DECISION: (Hecht, J.) Libel. The main focus point of the court's decision lies in the range of dissemination of the complained-of material. As the court points out, the primary reason assigned by the courts from time to time to justify the imposition of broader liability for libel than for slander has been the greater capacity for harm that a writing is assumed to have because of the wide range of dissemination consequent upon its permanence in form. The court states that, "Our own courts experience no difficulty in applying the law of libel to the new instrumentality of the motion picture because in the hands of a wrongdoer these devices have untold possibilities toward producing an effective libel." Therefore, as to the film that was made of the telecast, there is no question that if it is determined to be defamatory it will be considered here at least libel. As to the voice part of the telecast, the court uses the same range of dissemination argument basing it upon the fact that so many people will hear and see telecasts of this type that its effect may be just as forcible as any writing. Therefore, any telecast via television, radio or motion pictures which allegedly contains defamatory statements will be considered as libelous rather than slanderous. Motion denied.

ANALYSIS
The unexpected advent of new methods of communication has left the courts struggling with the distinction between libel and slander. They have found no difficulty in holding that the sound in a "talking" picture is libel, since it accompanies and is identified with the film itself. Defamation of radio and television is, however, still a subject of violent debate. It has been held by some courts to be libel, by one slander, by others to be libel if the broadcaster reads from a script, but slander if he does not; while still others apparently have regarded it as having special characteristics halfway between the two. The dispute rages between those who believe that radio and television broadcasting, because of the extensive damage it may inflict, should incur all of the responsibilities of newspaper publication, and those who think it should be favored by the law.

Quicknotes
LIBEL A false or malicious publication that subjects a person to scorn, hatred or ridicule, or that injures him in relation to his occupation or business.

SLANDER Defamatory statement communicated orally.

Terwilliger v. Wands

Slandered party (P) v. Slanderer (D)

N.Y. Ct. App., 17 N.Y. 54, 72 Am. Dec. 420 (1858).

NATURE OF CASE: Action to recover damages for slander.

FACT SUMMARY: Wands (D) said that Terwilliger (P) was having sexual intercourse with Mrs. Fuller, a married woman.

🏛 RULE OF LAW
Words which claim that a man is having extramarital intercourse are not actionable without a demonstration of special damages, since they do not disparage the man's character or reputation.

FACTS: Wands (D) told a third person that Terwilliger (P) was visiting Mrs. Fuller regularly for the purpose of having sexual intercourse with her, and that Terwilliger (P) would do all he could to keep Mrs. Fuller's husband in the penitentiary so that he could have access to her. The damages alleged were that Terwilliger (P) became ill and was unable to work after hearing of the reports circulated by Wands (D). Wands's motion for a nonsuit was sustained.

ISSUE: Are words which claim that a man is having extramarital intercourse actionable as slanderous without a showing of special damages?

HOLDING AND DECISION: (Strong, J.) No. Words which have a natural and immediate tendency to produce injury are actionable per se, and are adjudged to be injurious, though no special loss or damage can be proved. However, words which do not apparently and upon their face impart such defamation as will of course be injurious, are not actionable per se and special damages must be shown. The kind of special damages which must be shown to have resulted from the words are damages produced by, or through, impairing the reputation. The words must be defamatory in nature, and must, in fact, disparage the character, and this disparagement must be evidenced by some positive loss arising therefrom. Hence, words which do not degrade the character do not injure and cannot occasion loss. In this case, Wands's (D) words were defamatory, and it may be assumed that Terwilliger's (P) illness was a result of the words. However, this result does not prove that Terwilliger's (P) character was injured, and so Terwilliger (P) cannot recover for slander. Affirmed.

▎ ANALYSIS

This case demonstrates the difficulty of recovering if the slanderous words do not fall into one of the four categories that do not require the showing of special damages (pecuniary loss). Prosser states that since a plaintiff is seldom able to prove any specific pecuniary loss as a result of slander, the effect of the rule requiring a demonstration of such loss has to deny recovery unless slander fits into one of the four categories. The fourth category added was words which accuse a woman of unchastity. Such words are actionable per se, without a showing of special damages, because of their harmfulness to a woman's reputation. As this case demonstrates, the law reflects society's double standard, and this rule is not applied to men, since such accusations are not as damaging to their reputation.

■▬■

Quicknotes

ACTIONABLE PER SE Language of such an extreme nature that the law will presume that the person who is the subject of the communication has suffered injury and for which proof of damages is not required.

NONSUIT Judgment against a party who fails to make out a case.

SLANDER Defamatory statement communicated orally.

SPECIAL DAMAGES Damages caused by a specific act that are not the usual consequence of that act and which must be specifically pled and proven.

■▬■

Economopoulos v. A.G. Pollard Co.

Defamed party (P) v. Clerk's employer (D)

Mass. Sup. Jud. Ct., 218 Mass. 294, 105 N.E. 896 (1914).

NATURE OF CASE: Action to recover damages for defamation.

FACT SUMMARY: Economomopoulos (P) was told by agents of Pollard Co. (D) that he had stolen a handkerchief. Economopoulos (P) was told this by a clerk in English and it was later repeated to Economopoulos (P) in Greek. There was no evidence that a third party heard the English conversation or understood the Greek conversation.

> 🏛 **RULE OF LAW**
> For a cause of defamation to lie there must be publication to third parties of the defamatory statement in such a manner so as to be understood by those hearing the statement.

FACTS: Economopoulos (P) was told by the agent of Pollard Co. (D) that he had stolen a handkerchief. Economopoulos (P) was told this by a clerk who spoke to him in English. At the time the statement was made in English no one else was present to overhear the statement. The statement was later repeated to Economopoulos (P) in Greek by a Greek clerk of Pollard Co. (D) and although there were others present who could have overheard the statement at that time it was not shown that anyone other than the clerk and Economopoulos (P) could understand Greek.

ISSUE: Was the statement to Economopoulos (P) published?

HOLDING AND DECISION: (Loring, J.) No. The statement to Economopoulos (P) was not published. No one but Economopoulos (P) heard the clerk's statement to Economopoulos (P) in English. The evidence also failed to show that anyone besides Economopoulos (P) who heard the statements in Greek understood those statements. Affirmed.

▮ ANALYSIS

The student up to this time has been exposed to the general categories of defamation, slander, and libel. This case is an extension of all of those categories in that it discusses publication of the defamatory statement. "Publication" is a word of art in defamation case. It does not mean printing, writing, or even publicity, but merely communication of the defamatory words to someone other than the person defamed. It is never enough that the words are spoken to the plaintiff himself, even in the presence of others, if no one overhears them. Therefore, in this case, the crucial point was made that although a potentially defamatory statement was made to the plaintiff, no one else overheard the statement, and that they did not understand it, which is just as effective as if they had not heard the statement to begin with.

Quicknotes

DEFAMATION An intentional false publication, communicated publicly in either oral or written form, subjecting a person to scorn, hatred or ridicule, or injuring him or her in relation to his or her occupation or business.

PUBLICATION The communicating of a defamatory statement to a third party.

Carafano v. Metrosplash.Com, Inc.

Established actress (P) v. Online dating service (D)

339 F.3d 1119 (9th Cir. 2003).

NATURE OF CASE: Appeal from a ruling on summary judgment subjecting an online dating service to liability for publishing false or defamatory information.

FACT SUMMARY: An unknown person pretended to be an established actress and, without her consent, posted sexually suggestive information to an online dating service under her identity.

> 🏛 **RULE OF LAW**
> The immunity provision of the Communications Decency Act, 47 U.S.C. 230(c)(1) (CDA), immunizes an interactive computer service (ICS) from liability for publishing false or defamatory material if another party besides the ICS provides the objectionable material.

FACTS: Matchmaker.com (D), an online dating service, allowed its members to post profiles that included their pictures and written descriptions of themselves. Much of the descriptive information was posted in response to a questionnaire provided by Matchmaker.com (D). The service's policies forbade members from posting their last names and personal contact information in their profiles. Matchmaker.com (D), however, did not review its members' posted written information to ensure compliance with the company's policies. An unknown person purporting to be Carafano (P) posted a free trial profile, under the name of "Chase529," in Matchmaker.com's (D) Los Angeles section. At the time, Carafano (P) was an established film and TV actress whose stage name was Chase Masterson. Pictures of her were readily available on the Internet, and the fake profile contained several of those readily available photos. Her purported responses to the questionnaire included several sexually suggestive comments, mention of two of her films, her home address, and an email address. When people tried to contact Carafano (P) at the listed email address, an automatic reply provided them her home address and telephone number. Carafano (P) herself knew nothing of the posting when it happened and did not consent to it. Within two weeks after the posting, Carafano (P) received sexually explicit voice mail on her home telephone and a threatening, sexually explicit fax whose threats also applied to Carafano's (P) son. She soon took her son and lived away from her home for months. Within two days of Carafano's (P) request, Matchmaker.com (D) deleted her fake profile. Carafano (P) sued Matchmaker.com (D) in several counts in tort in a California state court, but Matchmaker.com (D) had the case removed to federal court. There, the trial judge granted Matchmaker.com's (D) motion for summary judgment, reaching the merits of Carafano's (P) allegations after ruling that the immunity

provisions of the Communications Decency Act, 47 U.S.C. 230(c)(1), did not shield Matchmaker.com (D) from liability. Carafano (P) appealed.

ISSUE: Does the immunity provision of the CDA, 47 U.S.C. 230(c)(1), immunize an ICS from liability for publishing false or defamatory material if another party besides the ICS provides the objectionable material?

HOLDING AND DECISION: (Thomas, J.) Yes. The immunity provision of the CDA, 47 U.S.C. 230(c)(1), immunizes an ICS from liability for publishing false or defamatory material if another party besides the ICS provides the objectionable material. The broad immunity granted to an ICS by the CDA serves two policy objectives: the unfettered dissemination of ideas online and voluntary control of online content. Courts of appeals are reaching a consensus that such immunity shields an ICS from liability when a third party is the primary provider of the objectionable content. Matchmaker.com's (D) questionnaire in this case does not mean that the company provided the objectionable content, and the company therefore is not an "information content provider" under the CDA. Matchmaker.com's (D) questionnaire is similar to the system of customer responses at issue in *Gentry v. eBay, Inc.*, 99 Cal. App. 4th 816 (2002), in which an online service invited users to rate their satisfaction with persons who used the service to sell products via the Internet. Just as in *Gentry,* here too the ICS was not an "information content provider" as required by the CDA: Neither the collecting nor the classifying of information from the third party in this case makes Matchmaker. com (D) the actual provider of the information. Moreover, Matchmaker.com's (D) transmission of the fake profile did not mean that the service provided the specific personal information about Carafano (P). Matchmaker.com (D) is therefore immune from Carafano's (P) suit. Affirmed.

▶ *ANALYSIS*

Carafano illustrates the different standard of liability applied to Internet providers as opposed to that used for traditional media. Embedded within the casebook excerpt, though, is a further key point about the law of defamation. Matchmaker .com (D) removed the fake profile promptly after Carafano (P) complained to the company about the material. At a minimum, counsel for Matchmaker.com (D) could have reasoned that leaving the material online, after the company had reason to doubt its accuracy, could have made Matchmaker.com (D) an "information content provider" no longer shielded from liability by 47 U.S.C. 230(c)(1).

Ogden v. Association of the U.S. Army

Libeled party (P) v. Publisher (D)

177 F. Supp. 498 (D.C. 1959).

NATURE OF CASE: Action to recover damages for libel.

FACT SUMMARY: The Association of the U.S. Army (D) published a book on the Korean war in which it criticized the handling of a platoon which it said Ogden (P) commanded during certain engagements in Korea. Ogden (P) claims that every individual sale of a public gives rise to a new cause of action at the time of sale and, therefore, Ogden (P) claims his action is not barred by the statute of limitations.

🏛 RULE OF LAW
The publication of a book, periodical, or newspaper containing defamatory matter gives rise to but one cause of action for libel, which accrues at the time of the original publication, and the statute of limitations runs from that date.

FACTS: Pursuant to a contract with the United States, the Association of the U.S. Army published a book entitled "Combat Action in Korea." In the publication the handling of a certain platoon was criticized and it was pointed out that Ogden (P) was the leader of the platoon during certain combat actions. Ogden (P) brought a suit for libel and the Association of the U.S. Army (D) moved for summary judgment on the ground, among others, that the action was barred by the one-year statute of limitations. The book was published in November 1955, whereas this action was brought on June 25, 1959.

ISSUE: Does the sale of an individual copy of a publication rise to a cause of action for libel, as well as start the statute of limitations running anew?

HOLDING AND DECISION: (Holtzoff, J.) No. To say that every sale or delivery of a copy of a publication, if it contains defamatory matter, gives rise to a new cause of action may seem logical from a purely technical standpoint, but to adhere to this doctrine would be to sacrifice reality to strict technical logic. Under modern conditions, the original common-law rule would give rise to an unnecessary multiplicity of suits and would practically destroy the statute of limitations as a statute in response to actions for libel. The court states that the technology of today allows for the printing of millions of copies of a publication daily and to adopt any other rule would lead to an impossible situation. The court adopts the prevailing American doctrine that the publication of a book, periodical, or newspaper containing defamatory matter gives rise to but one cause of action for libel, which accrues at the time of the original publication, and that the statute of limitations runs from that date. It is no longer the law that every sale or delivery of a copy of the publication creates a new cause of action. Defendant motion granted.

▶ ANALYSIS

The common law was originally that every sale or delivery of a copy of libelous matter was a new publication and that, therefore, a new cause of action occurred on each occasion. This court disagrees not in principle with the old common-law rule but rather in light of real issues of modern day living. The court points out the tremendous production capabilities of modern publishers and the effect the application of the common-law rule would have on modern courts in light of these capabilities. To apply the common-law rule today would lead to a multiplicity of suits as well as violate the statute of limitations as to libel.

Quicknotes

LIBEL A false or malicious publication subjecting a person to scorn, hatred or ridicule, or injuring him or her in relation to his or her occupation or business.

STATUTE OF LIMITATIONS A law prescribing the period in which a legal action may be commenced.

New York Times Co. v. Sullivan

Police commissioner (P) v. Newspaper publisher (D)

376 U.S. 254 (1964).

NATURE OF CASE: Civil action for damages for libel.

FACT SUMMARY: The New York Times (D) published a full-page advertisement critical of the manner in which the Montgomery, Alabama police, under Commissioner Sullivan (P), responded to civil rights demonstrations.

🏛 RULE OF LAW
A public official may not recover damages for a defamatory falsehood concerning his official conduct unless he can prove that the statement was made with actual malice.

FACTS: On March 29, 1960, the New York Times (D) carried a full page advertisement entitled "Heed Their Rising Voices," placed by several Negro clergymen of Alabama. The advertisement charged that southern Negro students engaged in nonviolent demonstrations were "being met by an unprecedented wave of terror by those who would deny and negate" the U.S. Constitution and Bill of Rights. The advertisement went on to describe certain alleged events in support of this charge, including various actions taken by the police of Montgomery, Alabama. L.B. Sullivan (P), the Police Commissioner of Montgomery, brought a civil libel action against the New York Times (D), claiming that although the advertisement did not mention him by name, it attributed policy misconduct to him by inference. The trial judge instructed the jury that the advertisement was "libelous per se," leaving the New York Times (D) with no defense other than proving the statement true in all respects. Some of the statements were found to be inaccurate descriptions of events which had occurred in Montgomery, and Sullivan (P) was awarded $500,000. The Supreme Court of Alabama affirmed, and the New York Times (D) appealed on grounds of constitutional protection of speech and press.

ISSUE: Does the First Amendment limit the power of a state to award damages in a civil libel action brought by a public official against critics of his official conduct?

HOLDING AND DECISION: (Brennan, J.) Yes. If criticism of a public official's conduct is published without actual malice—that is, without knowledge that it was false and without reckless disregard of whether or not it was false—it is protected by the constitutional guarantees of freedom of speech and press. This qualified privilege to publish defamation of a public office is not limited to comment or opinion, but extends as well to false statements of fact, providing there was no actual malice. Behind this decision is a "profound national commitment to the principle that debate on public issues should be uninhibited, robust and wide-open," and that "right conclusions are more likely to be gathered out of a multitude of tongues, than through any kind of authoritative selection." There would be a pall of fear and timidity imposed upon those who would give voice to pure criticism by any rule that would compel such a critic of official conduct to guarantee the truth of all his factual assertions. In addition, any attempt to transmute criticism of government to personal criticism, and hence potential libel of the officials of whom the government is composed would be unconstitutional. Reversed.

▶ ANALYSIS

Prior to the Sullivan case, there was a general recognition, at common law, of a qualified privilege known as "fair comment." Criticism of public officials' conduct and qualifications was allowed to be published as a matter of public concern—this much was undisputed. But sharp disagreement existed between state courts: the majority holding that the privilege of public discussion was limited to opinion and comment, and a vigorous minority insisting the even false statements of fact were privileged, if made for the public benefit with an honest belief in their truth. The Supreme Court of Alabama was thus following the majority position in the instant case, and the holding of the Supreme Court came as something of a bombshell, termed by Prosser as "unquestionably the greatest victory won by the defendants in the modern history of the law of torts." Since *Sullivan*, the rule has been applied to criminal, as well as civil, libel and has been extended to all public officers and employees, no matter how inferior their position.

Quicknotes

ACTUAL MALICE The issuance of a publication with knowledge of its falsity or with reckless disregard as to its truth.

LIBELOUS PER SE A false or malicious publication that subjects a person to scorn, hatred or ridicule, or that injures him in relation to his occupation or business of such an extreme nature that the law will presume that the person has suffered such injury.

St. Amant v. Thompson

Sheriff (P) v. Defamer (D)

390 U.S. 727 (1968).

NATURE OF CASE: Action for damages for libel.

FACT SUMMARY: In a televised political speech, St. Amant (D) read statements falsely charging Thompson (P), a deputy sheriff, with criminal conduct relating to a union dispute.

🏛 RULE OF LAW
In a defamation suit, a public official must prove the defendant had serious doubts as to the truth of his publication in order to demonstrate actual malice.

FACTS: St. Amant (D) made a televised political speech, during which he read statements made by Albin, a union member, falsely charging Thompson (P), a deputy sheriff, with criminal conduct. Thompson (P) was awarded damages by the trial court in his suit against St. Amant (D) for defamation. The intermediate appellate court reversed the judgment, holding that St. Amant (D) had not acted with the actual malice required by the *New York Times v. Sullivan*, 376 U.S. 254 (1964), rule. The Louisiana Supreme Court reversed the appellate court, finding that St. Amant (D) had acted in "reckless disregard" of the truth, in that he had failed to verify the defamatory information given to him by Albin.

ISSUE: Does defamation of a public official's conduct, made in good faith but without investigation, demonstrate a reckless disregard for truth or falsity?

HOLDING AND DECISION: (White, J.) No. The standard for reckless conduct is different from that of mere negligence. "Reckless conduct is not measured by whether a reasonably prudent man would have published, or would have investigated before publishing. There must be sufficient evidence to permit the conclusion that the defendant in fact entertained serious doubts as to the truth of his publication." Only the proof of publication with such doubts will show a reckless disregard for truth or falsity and thus bear the burden of demonstrating actual malice. However, a defendant in a defamation action cannot insure a favorable verdict merely by testifying that he published with a belief that the allegations were true. The finder of fact must be satisfied that the publication was indeed made in good faith. After reviewing the facts in the record, the Court concluded that "by no proper test of reckless disregard was St. Amant's (D) broadcast a reckless publication about a public officer." There was no evidence to indicate an awareness of probable falsity of Albin's statement about Thompson (P). Failure to investigate does not in itself establish bad faith.

▶ ANALYSIS

The holding in the instant case reiterates a point made by the Court in *New York Times v. Sullivan*, 376 U.S. 254 (1964), in speaking to the evidence that the Times had failed to check the accuracy of the advertisement against the news stories in its own files. The Court held that "evidence against the Times supports at most a finding of negligence in failing to discover the misstatements, and is constitutionally insufficient to show the recklessness that is required for a binding of actual malice." The Supreme Court's retention of the term "malice" has been deplored as "highly unfortunate" by Prosser. In *Henry v. Collins*, 380 U.S. 356 (1965), the Court completely dispensed with the old-fashioned meaning of "malice," holding that actual ill will and a desire to do harm were not sufficient to defeat the constitutional privilege. Yet it chose to cling to the discredited term, though "scienter" would have been more appropriate. The state of mind required by the test of "actual malice" is the same as that required by "scienter" in deceit actions for intentional misrepresentation: actual knowledge of falsity or reckless disregard of the truth. In either instance, where this test is met, liability is established.

■—■

Quicknotes

ACTUAL MALICE The issuance of a publication with knowledge of its falsity or with reckless disregard as to its truth.

DEFAMATION An intentional false publication, communicated publicly in either oral or written form, subjecting a person to scorn, hatred or ridicule, or injuring him or her in relation to his or her occupation or business.

LIBEL A false or malicious publication subjecting a person to scorn, hatred or ridicule, or injuring him or her in relation to his or her occupation or business.

■—■

Harte-Hanks Communications, Inc. v. Connaughton

Newspaper publisher (D) v. Judicial candidate (P)

491 U.S. 657 (1989).

NATURE OF CASE: Suit for libel by a public figure against a newspaper publisher.

FACT SUMMARY: During an election campaign, a newspaper ran a front-page story against the candidate the newspaper opposed. The story quoted a grand-jury witness's testimony that one candidate tried to bribe her and her sister to testify against a former official in the incumbent candidate's office.

🏛 RULE OF LAW
In a defamation suit filed by a public figure, an appellate court must conduct a plenary review of the entire record to confirm whether the plaintiff has shown that the allegedly defamatory statements were made with a reckless disregard for the truth.

FACTS: Connaughton (P) ran for the office of Municipal Judge. The Journal News, a local newspaper owned by Harte-Hanks Communications, Inc. (D), supported Connaughton's (P) opponent, the incumbent in the race. An official in the incumbent judge's office resigned about one month before the election. During a grand-jury investigation of bribery charges filed against the resigned official, one witness testified that Connaughton (P) had tried to bribe her and her sister to testify against the incumbent judge's staff member. One week before the election, the Journal News (D) ran a front-page story quoting the grand-jury testimony on Connaughton's (P) alleged attempt to reward persons for testifying against the incumbent judge. Connaughton (P) lost the election and sued the newspaper (D) for libel. At trial, the jury returned a verdict in Connaughton's (P) favor, the trial judge denied Harte-Hanks's (D) motion for judgment notwithstanding the verdict, and Harte-Hanks (D) appealed. The Court of Appeals affirmed the judgment after considering whether the article was defamatory and false. Harte-Hanks (D) petitioned the U.S. Supreme Court for further review.

ISSUE: In a defamation suit filed by a public figure, must an appellate court conduct a plenary review of the entire record to confirm whether the plaintiff has shown that the allegedly defamatory statements were made with a reckless disregard for the truth?

HOLDING AND DECISION: (Stevens, J.) Yes. In a defamation suit filed by a public figure, an appellate court must conduct a plenary review of the entire record to confirm whether the plaintiff has shown that the allegedly defamatory statements were made with a reckless disregard for the truth. Under *New York Times v. Sullivan,* 376 U.S. 254, 279-280 (1964), a public figure can prevail in a defamation suit only with clear and convincing proof that allegedly false statements against him were "made with 'actual malice'"—either knowingly or recklessly false. Appellate courts review evidence of actual malice for themselves under a plenary standard to ensure that the constitutionally required convincing clarity of proof is present. The Court of Appeals applied the correct standard for determining actual malice in this case; any statements in the Court's opinion about the newspaper's failure to meet journalistic standards of investigation only supported the ultimate conclusion that the newspaper (D) published the false statements against Connaughton (P) with actual malice—that is, either very aware that the claims probably were false, or with great doubts of their truth. The independence of the Court of Appeals' review of the evidence, however, deserves a closer look. The evidence must have convincingly shown not only a failure to investigate but also the higher burden that the newspaper (D) had definite reasons to doubt the accuracy of the grand-jury witness's testimony about Connaughton (P). To establish that fact, the Court of Appeals had to review the evidence in full, for itself, deferring to the jury only on credibility determinations. Here, although the Court of Appeals reached the correct conclusion—that the statements were published with actual malice—its grounds for that conclusion were too speculative. Whereas the Court of Appeals held that the jury "could have" determined that actual malice appears in the record evidence, that conclusion inexorably follows when the jury's findings are placed alongside the undisputed evidence. It is undisputed that five other witnesses besides Connaughton (P) denied the false witness's claims against Connaughton (P). It is also undisputed that the newspaper (D) failed to review Connaughton's (P) audio evidence challenging the published statements or to interview a woman whom the newspaper (D) knew to be a crucial witness. The newspaper therefore likely failed to meet standards of journalistic investigation out of a purposeful avoidance of the truth, a likelihood that defeats the newspaper's (D) First Amendment protections under the exacting *New York Times* standard. Affirmed.

▌ *ANALYSIS*

As the Court observes in *Harte-Hanks,* the constitutional freedom of press is great but not absolute. The demanding burden of proof in public-figure defamation cases accommodates

Continued on next page.

the public's interest in robust reporting while preserving the reputation interest of the individual. The relatively onerous burden of review placed on appellate courts in such cases further ensures that the evidence passes, or does not pass, constitutional muster on such important issues.

■══■

Quicknotes

BURDEN OF PROOF The duty of a party to introduce evidence to support a fact that is in dispute in an action.

DEFAMATION An intentional false publication, communicated publicly in either oral or written form, subjecting a person to scorn, hatred or ridicule, or injuring him in relation to his occupation or business.

FREEDOM OF THE PRESS The right to publish and publicly disseminate one's views.

LIBEL A false or malicious publication subjecting a person to scorn, hatred or ridicule, or injuring him or her in relation to his or her occupation or business.

PLENARY Unlimited and open; as broad as a given situation may require.

■══■

Gertz v. Robert Welch, Inc.

Libeled attorney (P) v. Publisher (D)

418 U.S. 323 (1974).

NATURE OF CASE: Appeal from judgment n.o.v. for the defense in suit for damages for defamation.

FACT SUMMARY: Robert Welch, Inc. (D) published an article accusing Gertz (P) of being a communist in a conspiracy against the police.

 RULE OF LAW:
(1) The standard of liability for a defamation which a publisher or broadcaster publishes about a private individual is set by the states.
(2) The private defamation plaintiff must prove falsity or reckless disregard for the truth to recover any damages other than compensation for actual injury.

FACTS: A policeman shot and killed a youth. The policeman was convicted of second degree murder. The youth's family retained Gertz (P) as their attorney in a civil action against the policeman. Robert Welch, Inc. (D) published an article in its magazine accusing Gertz (P) of being part of a communist conspiracy against the police and of belonging to two Marxist organizations. Gertz (P) sued Robert Welch, Inc. (D) for libel. Robert Welch, Inc. (D) contended that the article was about a matter of public interest, and, therefore, they were entitled to the protection of the *New York Times* rule. The jury awarded Gertz (P) $50,000, but judge agreed with Robert Welch, Inc., and granted its motion for a judgment n.o.v. The Seventh Circuit affirmed, and Gertz (P) appealed.

ISSUE:
(1) Is the standard for defamation against a private individual set by the state?
(2) May the private defamation plaintiff recover other than compensatory damages without proving falsity or reckless disregard for the truth?

HOLDING AND DECISION: (Powell, J.)
(1) Yes. So long as they do not impose liability without fault, the states may define for themselves the appropriate standard of liability for a publisher or broadcaster of defamatory falsehood injurious to a private individual. This rule recognizes the legitimate state interest in compensating private individuals for wrongful injury to reputation, yet shields the press and broadcast media from the rigors of strict liability for defamation.
(2) No. The private defamation plaintiff who establishes liability under a less demanding standard than that stated by the *New York Times* (which requires the proof of falsity

or reckless disregard for the truth) may recover only damages sufficient to compensate him for actual injury. Actual injury is not limited to out-of-pocket loss, it includes impairment of reputation and standing in the community, personal humiliation, and mental anguish and suffering. The evidence showed that Gertz (P) had not achieved general fame or notoriety in the community, and therefore was not a public figure to whom the *New York Times* standard is applicable. Therefore the trial court erred in entering judgment for Robert Welch, Inc. (D). However, since the jury was allowed to presume damages without proof of fault, a new trial is necessary. Reversed and remanded for further proceedings.

▶ **ANALYSIS**

This case appears to overrule the plurality in *Rosenbloom v. Metromedia, Inc.*, 403 U.S. 29 (1970), which had stated that the protection of the *New York Times* privilege should be extended to defamatory falsehoods relating to private persons if the statements concerned matters of general or public interest. The Gertz opinion states: "The 'publication or general interest' test for determining the applicability of the *New York Times* standard to private defamation actions inadequately serves both of the competing values [protection of the individual v. protection of the press] at stake."

Quicknotes

COMPENSATORY DAMAGES Measure of damages necessary to compensate victim for actual injuries suffered.

DEFAMATION An intentional false publication, communicated publicly in either oral or written form, subjecting a person to scorn, hatred or ridicule, or injuring him or her in relation to his or her occupation or business.

JUDGMENT N.O.V. A judgment entered by the trial judge reversing a jury verdict if the jury's determination has no basis in law or fact.

Dun & Bradstreet, Inc. v. Greenmoss Builders, Inc.

Libeled company (P) v. Credit service (D)

472 U.S. 749 (1985).

NATURE OF CASE: Appeal from award of damages for libel.

FACT SUMMARY: Dun & Bradstreet (D) contended that Greenmoss (P) could not recover for libel without a showing of actual malice.

🏛 RULE OF LAW
Recovery may be obtained for libel without a showing of actual malice when the statements do not involve a matter of public concern.

FACTS: Dun & Bradstreet (D), through the negligence of an employee, notified Greenmoss' (P) creditors that it (P) had petitioned for bankruptcy. Greenmoss (P) notified Dun & Bradstreet (D) that such was untrue and demanded a correction. A correction was sent; however, Greenmoss (P) felt it was inadequate and sued for libel. It obtained a judgment for compensatory and punitive damages. Dun & Bradstreet (D) appealed, contending no showing of actual malice was made; thus, recovery could not be had. The Vermont Supreme Court reversed the trial court's grant of Dun's (D) motion for a new trial, and the U.S. Supreme Court granted certiorari.

ISSUE: May recovery be obtained for libel without a showing of actual malice if the defamatory statements do not concern matters of public concern?

HOLDING AND DECISION: (Powell, J.) Yes. Recovery may be obtained for libel without a showing of actual malice if the defamatory statements do not involve matters of public concern. First Amendment protections extend to speech not of public concern; however, the protection is less stringent than for public speech. The state interest in providing adequate remedies for defamation outweighs this protection; thus, recovery is properly awarded. Affirmed.

DISSENT: (Brennan, J.) The First Amendment requires actual malice be shown to recover for libel where the speech is not of public concern.

▶ ANALYSIS

This case represents a synthesis of the historic decisions in *New York Times v. Sullivan*, 376 U.S. 254 (1964), and in *Gertz v. Robert Welch, Inc.*, 418 U.S. 323 (1974). The first decision dealt with a public figure. The second involved a private figure, but dealt with speech concerning public affairs. Here, we are dealing with a nonpublic plaintiff and nonpublic speech. The Court held that the First Amendment would not intrude in this situation with state common law principles.

Quicknotes

ACTUAL MALICE The issuance of a publication with knowledge of its falsity or with reckless disregard as to its truth.

COMPENSATORY DAMAGES Measure of damages necessary to compensate victim for actual injuries suffered.

LIBEL A false or malicious publication subjecting a person to scorn, hatred or ridicule, or injuring him or her in relation to his or her occupation or business.

Philadelphia Newspapers, Inc. v. Hepps

Principal stockholder (P) v. Newspaper (D)

475 U.S. 767 (1986).

NATURE OF CASE: Appeal from denial of damages for defamation.

FACT SUMMARY: The trial court held that the burden of proving the truth of allegations that Hepps (P) was connected to the Mafia fell on Philadelphia Newspapers (D).

RULE OF LAW
A plaintiff may not recover damages for defamation without showing the statements are false.

FACTS: Hepps (P) sued the Philadelphia Newspapers (D) for libel for printing stories linking him and his corporation to organized crime. Hepps (P) requested a jury instruction that the burden of proving the truth of the statements rested with the defendant. Philadelphia Newspapers (D) requested an instruction that the plaintiff bears the burden of proving the statements false. The trial court refused both instructions, and the jury found for Philadelphia (D). The Pennsylvania Supreme Court held Philadelphia (D) bore the burden of providing the truth of the statements. The U.S. Supreme Court granted certiorari.

ISSUE: May a plaintiff recover damages for defamation without showing the statements were false?

HOLDING AND DECISION: (O'Connor, J.) No. A plaintiff may not recover for defamation unless he bears the burden of proving that the statements were false. The common law requirement that the defendant prove the truth of the matter asserted must fall to the constitutional requirement enunciated here. Although the plaintiff in this case is not a public figure, the statements made are of public concern. The burden of proving falsity is no greater than the burden of proving fault and supplies the necessary burden of proof to satisfy the first amendment. Reversed and remanded.

DISSENT: (Stevens, J.) This case overrides the common-law presumption that defamatory speech is false. It gives no weight to the state's interest in protecting the reputation of its citizens.

▶ ANALYSIS

This case focuses on the evidentiary burdens applicable in a defamation case. The Court carefully limited its ruling to the particular facts of this case. It held that the speech must be of public concern for this holding to apply. Thus, a private plaintiff who is defamed on a private matter may still resort to the common law for recovery and evidentiary burdens.

Quicknotes

CERTIORARI A discretionary writ issued by a superior court to an inferior court in order to review the lower court's decisions; the Supreme Court's writ ordering such review.

DEFAMATION An intentional false publication, communicated publicly in either oral or written form, subjecting a person to scorn, hatred or ridicule, or injuring him or her in relation to his or her occupation or business.

Milkovich v. Lorain Journal Co.

Coach (P) v. Publisher (D) and columnist (D)

497 U.S. 1 (1990).

NATURE OF CASE: Appeal from dismissal of a libel action.

FACT SUMMARY: Diadiun (D) wrote a sports column implying that Milkovich (P), a wrestling coach, had lied under oath at a judicial hearing.

RULE OF LAW
Expressions of opinion that imply an assertion of objective fact may be the basis of a libel action.

FACTS: Milkovich (P) was a wrestling coach for a high school in Ohio. In 1974, his team was involved in a fight at a match, and at a subsequent hearing Milkovich (P) was censured for his actions by the athletic association. The order was overturned in a court hearing where Milkovich (P) testified. Diadiun (D), a sports columnist, wrote an article about the situation that stated that Milkovich (P) had lied at the court hearing. Milkovich (P) brought a libel action against Diadiun (D) and the newspaper (D). The Ohio Supreme Court ruled that the column was an opinion and therefore constitutionally protected. Milkovich (P) appealed.

ISSUE: Are expressions of opinion completely protected from libel actions?

HOLDING AND DECISION: (Rehnquist, C.J.) No. Expressions of opinion that imply an assertion of objective fact may be the basis of a libel action. In *Ollman v. Evans*, 750 F.2d 970 (1984), the court of appeals applied four factors to determine whether a statement was fact or opinion: (1) the specific language used; (2) the verifiability of the statement; (3) the general context of the statement; and (4) the broader context in which the article appeared. This test is improper because although defamation requires a false statement of fact in order to be actionable, expressions of opinion often imply an assertion of objective fact. Simply couching a statement in terms of opinion, such as "In my opinion, Jones is a liar," does not dispel the implication that the speaker has facts on which to base the statement. However, additional separate protection for opinion is not required to ensure the freedom of expression guaranteed by the First Amendment. A libel plaintiff must still prove that a statement of public concern is false as part of his prima facie case. Statements that cannot be reasonably interpreted as stating actual facts are not actionable. Furthermore, statements about public figures and officials must be made with actual malice. These protections are adequate to protect the breathing space necessary to allow writers latitude to write about issues of public concern.

Since libel plaintiffs must prove that a statement is false, the verifiability of the statement is the only issue regarding fact and opinion. Diadiun's (D) column carries the connotation that Milkovich (P) committed perjury at the hearing. This is a sufficiently factual statement because it is capable of being proved true or false. Therefore, Milkovich (P) must be allowed to bring a libel action. Reversed.

ANALYSIS

Justice Brennan's dissenting opinion essentially agreed with the majority regarding the standard for determining whether a statement is sufficiently factual to be actionable. However, Brennan argued that Diadiun's (D) column clearly expressed the view that Milkovich (P) had lied given what Diadiun (D) had witnessed at the wrestling match rather than stating that Milkovich (P) had committed perjury.

Quicknotes

LIBEL A false or malicious publication subjecting a person to scorn, hatred or ridicule, or injuring him or her in relation to his or her occupation or business.

Sindorf v. Jacron Sales Co., Inc.

Salesman (P) v. Previous employer (D)

Md. Ct. Special App., 27 Md. App. 53, 341 A.2d 856 (1975).

NATURE OF CASE: Action for damages in slander.

FACT SUMMARY: An officer of Jacron Sales (D) called Sindorf's (P) new employer and advised them that Sindorf (P) might be a thief.

🏛 RULE OF LAW
A conditional privilege may be lost where the person who utters the defamation acts with malice or in utter disregard of the truth.

FACTS: Sindorf (P) was employed by Jacron Sales (D) as a salesman. A dispute arose between them and Sindorf (P) quit. Sindorf (P) retained some of his inventory as security for commissions due him. Sindorf (P) wrote Jacron (D) that these items would be returned when his commission was paid. Sindorf (P) went to work for Tool Box. Fridkis, a vice-president of Jacron (D), called Brose, Tool Box's president. In the course of conversation as to whether Sindorf (P) had worked for Tool Box prior to resigning, Fridkis said that Sindorf (P) had been fired and was a thief. Sindorf (P) sued for slander and Jacron (D) defended on the basis of privilege. The court directed a verdict for Jacron (D) based on privilege. Sindorf (P) contended that even if the privilege had existed, it was lost based on Fridkis' malice or total disregard of the truth.

ISSUE: May a conditional privilege be lost through a reckless disregard of the truth or malice?

HOLDING AND DECISION: (Orth, C.J.) Yes. Privilege is a defense the law allows to defamation actions. It may be absolute or qualified. If the privilege has relatively little social or public significance, it is conditional. Communications between an ex-employer and the new one are conditionally privileged if conducted for a legitimate business or social purpose. Here, Brose and Fridkis were friends and Fridkis had a business purpose for the call. However, even though a conditional privilege exists, it may be lost if the utterance was made with malice or with a total disregard for truth. Here, Fridkis found out early in the conversation that Sindorf (P) had not worked for Tool Box while employed by Jacron (D). He then gratuitously volunteered that Sindorf (P) had been fired and that money and inventory were missing. These statements were false, were not made in response to questions, and appear to have been made to force Sindorf (P) into immediately returning the inventory. The question of malice should have been submitted to the jury. Reversed.

▶ ANALYSIS

An absolute privilege cannot be lost. Most privileges, however, are conditional. If Fridkis (D) had made his statements in response to Tool Box's inquiries, the case might have been decided differently. This would be especially true if there was no spite motive and no attempt to pressure Sindorf (P). It is the socially undesirable motive that destroys the conditional privilege.

Quicknotes

CONDITIONAL PRIVILEGE Immunity from liability for libelous or slanderous statements communicated in the execution of a political, judicial, social or personal obligation, unless it is demonstrated that the statement was made with actual malice and knowledge of its falsity.

DEFAMATION An intentional false publication, communicated publicly in either oral or written form, subjecting a person to scorn, hatred or ridicule, or injuring him or her in relation to his or her occupation or business.

MALICE The intention to commit an unlawful act without justification or excuse.

SLANDER Defamatory statement communicated orally.

Quick Reference Rules of Law

Joe Dickerson & Associates, LLC v. Dittmar

Private investigator (D) v. Convicted felon (P)

Colo. Sup. Ct., 34 P.3d 995 (2001).

NATURE OF CASE: Suit for invasion of privacy by appropriation of another's name or likeness.

FACT SUMMARY: A private investigator published an article about, and a photograph of, a convicted felon in the newsletter the investigator used to promote his services.

🏛 RULE OF LAW
A claim for invasion of privacy by appropriation in Colorado does not require proof of the value of the plaintiff's name or likeness, and an appropriation claim will not lie against a self-promotional article on another person's felony conviction where the defendant asserts a First Amendment privilege.

FACTS: Joe Dickerson (D), a private investigator, investigated Rosanne Dittmar (P) during a divorce case. Dickerson's (D) investigation revealed improprieties in Dittmar's (P) conduct, and Dickerson (D) reported Dittmar (P) to law enforcement officials. Eventually Dittmar (P) was convicted of felony theft for taking bonds from clients of the brokerage firm where she worked. After Dittmar (P) was convicted, Dickerson (D) published an article on her conviction, along with a photograph of her, in the promotional newsletter that Dickerson (D) used to market his investigation service. Dittmar (P) sued Dickerson (D) on several grounds, including invasion of privacy by appropriation of another's name or likeness. Dickerson (D) prevailed in the trial court by summary judgment on all counts of Dittmar's (P) complaint. On the appropriation count, the trial court reasoned that, even if Colorado recognized the tort of appropriation, Dittmar (P) had failed to come forward with evidence on the value of her name or likeness. Dittmar (P) appealed. On the appropriation count, Colorado's intermediate appellate court reasoned that a plaintiff must prove that her name or likeness has value, but that court concluded that Dittmar (P) had shown genuine issues of material fact on other elements of appropriation; accordingly, the intermediate court reversed the trial court's judgment. Dickerson (D) sought further review in the Colorado Supreme Court.

ISSUE: Does a claim for invasion of privacy by appropriation in Colorado require proof of the value of the plaintiff's name or likeness, and will an appropriation claim lie against a self-promotional article on another person's felony conviction where the defendant asserts a First Amendment privilege?

HOLDING AND DECISION: (Bender, J.) No. A claim for invasion of privacy by appropriation in Colorado does not require proof of the value of the plaintiff's name or likeness, and an appropriation claim will not lie against a self-promotional article on another person's felony conviction where the defendant asserts a First Amendment privilege. Invasion of privacy by appropriation is a cognizable claim in Colorado. Unlike section 652C of the Second Restatement of Torts and the jurisdictions that follow that section of the Restatement, Colorado does not require a showing that the plaintiff's name or likeness has value; a property-oriented analysis that focuses on value diminishes the more logical focus on the mental anguish that all plaintiffs allegedly experience in claims sounding in appropriation. Accordingly, the elements of appropriation in Colorado are (1) use of the plaintiff's name or likeness by the defendant (2) to benefit the defendant (3) in a way that plaintiff suffered damages (4) caused by the defendant. Dittmar's (P) complaint here is therefore facially sufficient even though it does not allege value. On the other hand, Dickerson's (D) use of Dittmar's (P) name and photograph in his newsletter was privileged, and therefore insulated from suit, because his article was primarily non-commercial speech on an issue of legitimate public concern. See *Cox Broadcasting Co. v. Cohn,* 420 U.S. 469, 492 (1975). The publication of the article and photograph in a newsletter is irrelevant to determining whether the publication was primarily commercial or non-commercial; so is Dickerson's (D) profit motive for publishing the newsletter. Thus, although Dickerson's (D) use of Dittmar's (P) name and likeness clearly had both commercial and non-commercial purposes, the use was primarily non-commercial. Accordingly, the publication was privileged under the First Amendment, and Dittmar's (P) claim for appropriation must fail. Reversed with instructions to reinstate the trial court's entry of judgment for Dickerson (D).

▶ ANALYSIS

In hindsight, the appropriation claim in *Dickerson* seems ill-advised. Dickerson's (D) mixture of commercial and non-commercial purposes is obvious, and the article just as obviously fails to satisfy the narrow definition of commercial speech. See *Central Hudson Gas & Electric Corp. v. Public Service Commn. of New York,* 447 U.S. 557, 561 (1980) ("expression related solely to the economic interests of the

Continued on next page.

speaker and its audience"); *Virginia State Bd. of Pharmacy v. Virginia Citizens Consumer Council*, 425 U.S. 748, 761 (1975) ("no more than propose a commercial transaction"). On the other hand, although Dittmar (P) lost on the merits in *Dickerson*, she and her counsel succeeded in persuading the Colorado Supreme Court to recognize an entirely new cause of action. That is no mean feat, but it also points up the radical redefinition of "success" that the practice of law requires. Note also that attorneys representing clients on similarly weak facts in future cases will have more difficulty discharging their professional responsibilities under, for example, Model Rule of Professional Conduct 3.1 (requiring "meritorious claims and contentions").

■═■

Quicknotes

APPROPRIATION The act of making something one's own or making use of something to serve one's own interest.

INVASION OF PRIVACY The violation of an individual's right to be protected against unwarranted interference in his personal affairs, falling into one of four categories: (1) appropriating the individual's likeness or name for commercial benefit; (2) intrusion into the individual's seclusion; (3) public disclosure of private facts regarding the individual; and (4) disclosure of facts placing the individual in a false light.

SUMMARY JUDGMENT Judgment rendered by a court in response to a motion made by one of the parties, claiming that the lack of a question of material fact in respect to an issue warrants disposition of the issue without consideration by the jury.

■═■

Sanders v. American Broadcasting Companies, Inc. et al.

Telepsychic (P) v. Undercover reporter (D)

Cal. Sup. Ct., 978 P.2d 67 (1999).

NATURE OF CASE: Suit for invasion of privacy by intrusion.

FACT SUMMARY: A television journalist posed as a telepsychic and used a hidden videocamera and microphone to do an undercover story on a business that gave psychic readings to people who called the company's 900 number.

🏛 **RULE OF LAW**
An employee has a limited expectation of privacy in conversations at his workplace against a reporter's secret videotaping even if coworkers could have seen or heard the conversations.

FACTS: Mark Sanders (P) worked as a telepsychic in the Los Angeles office of Psychic Marketing Group (PMG). As a telepsychic, he performed psychic readings for people who called PMG's 900 number. Several relatively private aspects marked Sanders's (P) workplace: cubicles enclosed on three sides by partitions standing five feet high, a lunchroom apart from the workspace itself, and separate offices for supervisory staff. PMG's policy prohibited access to the workplace by nonemployees unless they had permission to enter. Stacy Lescht (D), a reporter for American Broadcasting Companies (ABC) (D), secured a job as a telepsychic with PMG so that she could do an undercover story on the company. While she worked as a telepsychic for PMG, she easily heard conversations from nearby cubicles and walkways in the office. Without her coworkers' knowledge or consent, Lescht (D) recorded her conversations with them, including two with Sanders (P), while using a hidden videorecorder and microphone. Sanders (P) sued Lescht (D) and ABC (D), alleging one count under section 632 of the California Penal Code and a second count for invasion of privacy by intrusion. The jury found for the defendants on the Penal Code count because workers at PMG could reasonably have expected their conversations not to be private. The defendants then moved to dismiss the claim for intrusion on the same ground. The trial judge denied that motion, reasoning that Sanders (P) had a limited right to privacy against secret videotaping, and the jury returned a verdict against the defendants. The defendants appealed, and the California Court of Appeal reversed, ruling that the findings on the Penal Code count precluded judgment for the plaintiff on the intrusion count as a matter of law. On Sanders's (P) petition for further review, the California Supreme Court ordered the issues confined to determining whether there can be a limited expectation of privacy in a busy workplace.

ISSUE: Does an employee have a limited expectation of privacy in conversations at his workplace against a reporter's secret videotaping even if coworkers could have seen or heard the conversations?

HOLDING AND DECISION: (Werdergar, J.) Yes. An employee does have a limited expectation of privacy in conversations at his workplace against a reporter's secret videotaping even if coworkers could have seen or heard the conversations. In California, the tort of invasion of privacy by intrusion has two elements: (1) intrusion into a place, conversation, or matter that is private, and (2) the intrusion must highly offend a reasonable person. This Court has never stated that the expectation of privacy in the law of intrusion must be complete or absolute; indeed, this Court's recent decision in *Shulman v. Group W Productions, Inc.*, 18 Cal. 4th 200 (1998), suggested that privacy exists on a sliding scale rather than as an all-or-nothing absolute. Thus, there can be a legitimate expectation of limited privacy, as in workplace conversations overheard by coworkers. Defendants' "complete expectation of privacy" argument therefore fails under caselaw and in the standard, everyday sense of privacy, even in the workplace. With reference to both senses of privacy, an assessment of privacy in an intrusion analysis must evaluate who is doing the intruding and how they are doing it. Further, the principal cases relied on by defendants, exemplified by *Desnick v. American Broadcasting Companies, Inc.*, 44 F.3d 1345 (7th Cir. 1995), are inapposite. The doctor-patient interaction in *Desnick* cannot control when the conversations occur between coworkers and among the different expectations that such conversations bring. Therefore, the reasonableness of an expectation of privacy in conversations, in workplaces as anywhere else, involves not only the presence of others who could have seen or heard the conversations but also the alleged intruder's identity and the purpose of the alleged intrusion. This holding does not create an automatic expectation of privacy in the workplace; on the contrary, the fact-sensitive rule announced today requires an analysis that will vary from case to case. Furthermore, a media defendant still has every right to try to defeat the offensiveness element of intrusion with reference to the media's legitimate newsgathering function. Reversed and remanded.

Continued on next page.

▶ *ANALYSIS*

Sanders ends with a lesson in legal analysis straight out of the first semester of law school. This case substantially increases plaintiffs' prospects on intrusion claims against undercover reporting by weakening a strong defense on one element of intrusion (privacy). At the same time, as the Court notes at both the beginning and the end of its opinion, media defendants can adjust their trial strategy to negate the other element of intrusion (offensiveness). Plaintiffs prevail only by meeting their burden on *all* essential elements of a claim—a point worth remembering in any area of the law.

Quicknotes

INTRUSION   The unlawful entering on to or the taking of possession of another's property.

INVASION OF PRIVACY   The violation of an individual's right to be protected against unwarranted interference in his personal affairs, falling into one of four categories: (1) appropriating the individual's likeness or name for commercial benefit; (2) intrusion into the individual's seclusion; (3) public disclosure of private facts regarding the individual; and (4) disclosure of facts placing the individual in a false light.

REASONABLE EXPECTATION OF PRIVACY   In order to invoke the Fourth Amendment's protection against unreasonable searches and seizures, an individual must have a reasonable expectation of privacy in respect to the location searched or thing seized.

Hall v. Post

Daughter and adoptive mother (P) v. Newspaper and reporter (D)

N.C. Sup. Ct., 372 S.E.2d 711 (1988).

NATURE OF CASE: Suit for invasion of privacy by public disclosure of private facts.

FACT SUMMARY: A biological mother returned to the county where she had abandoned her daughter seventeen years before. The local newspaper ran stories on the mother's search and on the subsequent contact between the biological mother and the girl's adoptive mother.

> ### 🏛 RULE OF LAW
> A plaintiff cannot sue for invasion of privacy by public disclosure of private facts in North Carolina.

FACTS: Rose Post (D) wrote and published an article in The Salisbury Post (D) about an ex-carnival worker who was trying to find the biological daughter she had abandoned seventeen years earlier. The story related various details from the biological mother's life: her marriage seventeen years earlier to another carnival worker, the birth and abandonment of their daughter, the father's arrangements seventeen years earlier to leave the child with a babysitter named Mary Hall (P), and the father's later statements that he had formally consented to the child's adoption. The article included a plea to contact the biological mother, who was then staying in the area. The biological mother soon learned the child's name and location. The newspaper then ran a second story by Post (D) two days after her first. The second story identified the child as Susie Hall (P) and Mary Hall (P) as her adoptive mother. The Halls (P) sued Post (D) and the newspaper (D) for invasion of privacy by public disclosure of private facts. Their complaint alleged, in part, that they had fled their home to escape the resulting publicity, and that they both had undergone psychiatric counseling in the stories' wake. [The trial court entered summary judgment for the defendants, and the North Carolina Court of Appeals reversed.] Defendants petitioned for review in the North Carolina Supreme Court.

ISSUE: Can a plaintiff sue for invasion of privacy by public disclosure of private facts in North Carolina?

HOLDING AND DECISION: (Mitchell, J.) No. A plaintiff cannot sue for invasion of privacy by public disclosure of private facts in North Carolina. The Restatement (Second) of Torts recognizes a tort for public disclosure of private facts that has four elements: (1) publicity, (2) private facts, (3) offensiveness, and (4) illegitimate public concern. This Court now declines to adopt such a tort in North Carolina for the same reasons articulated in *Renwick v. News and Observer,* 312 S.E.2d 405 (N.C. 1984), where the Court declined to adopt the false-light privacy tort. False-light claims duplicate other

causes of action; so do claims for public disclosure of private facts. Moreover, adopting the disclosure tort would only increase the tension between tort law and the First Amendment without returning an appreciable benefit to anyone. Further, the U.S. Supreme Court has held that even false statements are entitled to some leeway when assessing potential liability. See, e.g., *Hustler Magazine v. Falwell,* 485 U.S. 46 (1988). It is therefore eminently reasonable to conclude that publication of true statements, such as the statements here, should receive at least the constitutional protection to which false statements are entitled. Reversed.

CONCURRENCE: (Frye, J.) The majority reached the correct result but for the wrong reasons. This Court should adopt a tort theory that permits non-public figures to recover for wrongful, highly offensive publication of private facts that serve no legitimate public purpose. The U.S. Supreme Court has taken affirmative steps not to decide whether such a tort exists, but the proper resolution of the tension between this new tort and the First Amendment is the middle ground of a "newsworthiness" or "public interest" standard for determining whether private-fact disclosures are constitutionally protected. To minimize any chilling effect from this tort, the threshold question of the legitimacy of the public interest is a question of law for the court. The legitimacy should be measured by the Restatement's standard, which focuses on avoiding "a morbid and sensational prying into private lives for its own sake." In this case, no reasonable juror could find such a prying into the Halls' (P) lives in the challenged stories because the matters clearly were legitimate public issues. Thus, though the private-facts tort should be cognizable in North Carolina, the plaintiffs have failed to meet their evidentiary burden on summary judgment. The majority therefore correctly reverses the court of appeals.

▶ ANALYSIS

If consistency in the law on a country's most fundamental values is a virtue, then the majority's focus on First Amendment issues is clearly the sounder of the two positions in *Hall*. Publication of true statements, in and of itself, should not form a basis for liability in a country in which false statements are protected under the highest court's interpretation of the country's most fundamental law. Under such a rationale, it is at least arguable that the mere adoption of the private-facts tort is a per se violation of the minimum federal standards established by the U.S. Supreme Court's First Amendment jurisprudence.

Cantrell v. Forest City Publishing Co.

Wife of accident victim (P) v. Publishing company (D) and Reporter (D)

419 U.S. 245 (1974).

NATURE OF CASE: Action for damages for invasion of privacy.

FACT SUMMARY: Eszterhas (D), a reporter, did a follow-up story on the effects of a bridge collapse on the survivors of those who had died.

🏛 RULE OF LAW
A reckless disregard of the truth will expose a publisher to liability in an action for invasion of privacy.

FACTS: Cantrell's (P) husband died in a bridge collapse. Forest City Publishing (D) decided to do a follow-up story on the disaster. Eszterhas (D), a reporter, decided to interview the Cantrells (P) to determine the effect that Mr. Cantrell's death had on the family. Eszterhas (D) went to the Cantrell (P) home and interviewed and took pictures of the children. Mrs. Cantrell (P) was not at home. The story, when published, contained many inaccuracies including a so-called interview with and description of Mrs. Cantrell (P). She sued for invasions of privacy in that she and her children were cast in a false light and were exposed to ridicule and pity. The court dismissed the punitive damage issue on the basis that there was no showing of actual malice. It declined to dismiss the entire action and instructed the jury that liability could be found for reckless disregard of the truth. The jury found for Cantrell (P), but was reversed by the appellate court. It felt that the district court's dismissal of the punitive damage issue through a showing of no actual malice was dispositive of the issue since this was necessary for recovery.

ISSUE: Will a reckless disregard of the truth expose a publisher to liability for invasion of privacy?

HOLDING AND DECISION: (Stewart, J.) Yes. It is obvious from the facts that the district court was using "malice" in its common-law meaning when the punitive damage issue was dismissed. The jury was properly instructed that they could find liability for a reckless falsehood or a knowing disregard of the truth. The record contains adequate facts upon which to find that Eszterhas (D) knew that a portion of his story was false and published it in reckless disregard of the truth. For this, both he and Forest City Publishing (D) are liable. Reversed.

▶ ANALYSIS

This case should be compared with *Gobin* and *Cohn*. In *Cantrell*, the newsworthy value and interest in the story were stale. The embellishments in the story were knowingly false.

They were included to make the feature more interesting. Such knowingly false attempts to sensationalize a story abrogate the conditional privilege to inform the public. It would appear that simple negligence would not be sufficient to establish liability. Malice is necessary.

Quicknotes

ACTUAL MALICE The issuance of a publication with knowledge of its falsity or with reckless disregard as to its truth.

INVASION OF PRIVACY The violation of an individual's right to be protected against unwarranted interference in his personal affairs, falling into one of four categories: (1) appropriating the individual's likeness or name for commercial benefit; (2) intrusion into the individual's seclusion; (3) public disclosure of private facts regarding the individual; and (4) disclosure of facts placing the individual in a false light.

PUNITIVE DAMAGES Damages exceeding the actual injury suffered for the purposes of punishment, deterrence and comfort to plaintiff.

Hustler Magazine v. Falwell

Televangelist (P) v. Publisher (D)

485 U.S. 46 (1988).

NATURE OF CASE: Appeal from an award of damages for emotional distress.

FACT SUMMARY: Falwell (P) contended that he could recover for emotional distress caused by a Hustler (D) cartoon, even though actual malice had not been shown.

RULE OF LAW
Public figures may not recover for infliction of emotional distress due to an allegedly defamatory act unless actual malice is shown.

FACTS: Hustler (D), an adult magazine, printed an ad parody, labeled as such, depicting Falwell (P), a televangelist, as having had sex with his mother and being drunk. Falwell (P) sued for defamation and intentional infliction of emotional distress. The district court directed a verdict for Hustler (D) on a privacy invasion count, and the jury found for Hustler (D) on the libel count. It awarded Falwell (P) $200,000 for infliction of emotional distress. The court of appeals affirmed, holding actual malice standards need not be shown to recover an emotional distress theory. The Supreme Court granted certiorari.

ISSUE: May public figures recover for infliction of emotional distress in a defamation context without showing actual malice?

HOLDING AND DECISION: (Rehnquist, C.J.) No. Public figures may not recover for infliction of emotional distress due to an allegedly defamatory act unless actual malice is shown. The state common law tort of infliction of emotional distress illustrates a legitimate state interest in the protection of its residents, however, such protection cannot impair First Amendment rights. To allow a recovery for emotional distress in this context would allow first amendment freedoms to be subverted. Because no actual malice was shown, no recovery could be had. Reversed.

CONCURRENCE: (White, J.) Penalizing publication of parody precludes the free exercise of freedom of press.

ANALYSIS

Actual malice, in the constitutional context of defamation, means the knowledge of the falsity of a statement or a reckless disregard for its truth. In the area of parody, this seems to be inapplicable. No assertion of fact exists to determine whether such was true. However, in the other areas of defamation, this case will have a widespread effect.

Quicknotes

ACTUAL MALICE The issuance of a publication with knowledge of its falsity or with reckless disregard as to its truth.

DEFAMATION An intentional false publication, communicated publicly in either oral or written form, subjecting a person to scorn, hatred or ridicule, or injuring him or her in relation to his or her occupation or business.

CHAPTER 19

Civil Rights

Quick Reference Rules of Law

Ashby v. White

Frustrated voter (P) v. Elections officer (D)

K.B., 2 Ld. Raym. 938, 92 Eng. Rep. 126 (1702).

NATURE OF CASE: Action for having right to exercise the right to vote.

FACT SUMMARY: Ashby (P) was refused the right to vote in an election by White (D).

🏛 RULE OF LAW
A party may recover for wrongfully being denied his right to vote.

FACTS: White (D), an elections official, wrongfully denied Ashby (P) his right to vote in an election. Ashby (P) brought suit against White (D) alleging that he had been damaged. No statutory or common law cause of action could be found which provided a remedy in such a situation. However, a jury found in favor of Ashby (P). White (D) appealed.

ISSUE: May a party recover for wrongfully being denied his right to vote?

HOLDING AND DECISION: (Holt, C.J.) Yes. Ashby (P) had the right to vote. White (D) wrongfully deprived Ashby (P) of his franchise. An injury of this nature damages a party. While no statutory penalty exists, a wrong has been committed. A right without a remedy is no right at all. There must be some method of sanction to enforce the right. For this reason, recovery should be granted to Ashby (P). In no other way can we compensate him for his loss of franchise, and such a decision is necessary to prevent future abuses. [Holt's opinion notwithstanding, a majority of the Court of King's Bench reversed the jury verdict for Ashby (P). Holt was vindicated, however, when the House of Lords subsequently took his side, over turned the King's Bench judgment, and awarded damages to Ashby (P).]

▶ ANALYSIS

A similar rationale to that in *Ashby* was the basis for the passage of the Civil Rights Act of 1964. Where the state refuses to accord rights of citizenship to its citizens, another remedy must be provided. Viewed pragmatically, what remedy does Ashby (P) have? He can't be allowed to vote in an election that is already over. He could seek an injunction to prevent future abuse, but this is hardly an adequate remedy for past misconduct. What damages has Ashby (P) suffered which can be recompensed by money damages? Evidently, White (D) was not terminated from his position. Therefore, Ashby (P) could only sue for punitive damages or seek criminal sanctions.

Quicknotes

CIVIL RIGHTS ACT OF 1964 42 U.S.C. § 2000-2(a) § 703(a) makes it an unlawful employment practice to here or to discharge anyone on the basis of race, color religion, sex, or national origin.

PUNITIVE DAMAGES Damages exceeding the actual injury suffered for the purposes of punishment, deterrence and comfort to plaintiff.

Camp v. Gregory

Aunt (P) v. Caseworker (D)

67 F.3d 1286 (7th Cir. 1995).

NATURE OF CASE: Suit claiming deprivation of liberty in violation of the Fourteenth Amendment.

FACT SUMMARY: Camp (P) brought suit against her nephew's caseworker, Gregory (D), claiming Anthony's substantive due process rights were violated by Gregory's (D) failure to ensure that he was placed in a safe living environment.

> **RULE OF LAW**
> A child placed in the guardianship of the state has a due process right not to be placed with a custodian whom the state knows will fail to exercise the requisite degree of supervision over the child.

FACTS: Camp (P) assumed guardianship of Anthony from his mother, who was unable to care for him. She immediately sought appointment of another guardian since she could not provide him with the highly structured care he needed. The state court appointed the DFCS as guardian and Gregory (D) was assigned as Anthony's caseworker. Despite knowledge that Anthony needed a highly structured environment, Gregory (D) returned him to Camp's (P) care. He failed to make any recommendations for an education or guidance program or to follow up on Anthony's progress. In addition he falsely represented to the state court under oath that Anthony was doing fine. Anthony died and Camp (P) brought suit claiming Gregory (D) denied Anthony substantive due process by failing to ensure that he was placed in a safe living environment. The district court dismissed and Camp (P) appealed.

ISSUE: Does a child placed in the guardianship of the state have a due process right not to be placed with a custodian whom the state knows will fail to exercise the requisite degree of supervision over the child?

HOLDING AND DECISION: (Posner, J.) Yes. A child placed in the guardianship of the state has a due process right not to be placed with a custodian whom the state knows will fail to exercise the requisite degree of supervision over the child. There are two issues presented here. First is whether the DCFS and Gregory (D) owed a duty to protect Anthony and, second, whether that duty extended to dangers beyond the home. In *DeShaney v. Winnebago County Dept. of Social Services*, 489 U.S. 189 (1989), the Supreme Court held that due process does not require the state to protect a child from abuse by his parents. Gregory (D) argues that *DeShaney* stands for the proposition that he had no duty to protect Anthony from

a danger that he nor he state had no role is creating. The fact that the DCFS had been appointed Anthony's guardian, however, is a key distinction from the *DeShaney* case. The DCFS had a cognizable duty to protect Anthony as his guardian. Many jurisdictions have held government officials liable for placing minors in foster homes in which they suffered abuse or neglect. Likewise, other circuits have recognized that public officials may be held liable for damages when they place a child in a foster home knowing or having reason to know the child is likely to suffer harm. Camp (P) moves one step beyond these holdings, claiming that Gregory (D) denied Anthony due process by knowingly returning him to a home that could not guide and supervise him properly. A child placed in the guardianship of the state has a due process right not to be placed with a custodian whom the state knows will fail to exercise the requisite degree of supervision over the child. While the cases acknowledge a difference between the state placing a child with a relative and placing him in a foster home, such distinction is not implicated here. Camp (P) sought the termination of her guardianship because she believed that she was unable to provide Anthony adequate care and supervision. Gregory's (D) and the DCFS's duty to Anthony did not terminate upon the return of Anthony to the Camp (P) household. Thus, the allegd danger Anthony encountered as a result of Camp's (P) failure to properly care for him is properly attributable to Gregory (D). Another issue here is whether Gregory's (D) duty extended to dangers outside the Camp (P) household. Since a parent owes a duty to his child to supervise the child's activities outside the home, the state also has a duty not to place one of its wards with an adult that it knows will not or cannot exercise such supervision. When a DFCS caseworker places a child in a home knowing that the caretaker cannot provide reasonable supervision, and such failure results in injury to the child, the caseworker may he held liable for a deprivation of liberty under the circumstances of the particular case. However, a public official who has deprived someone of their constitutional right is entitled to immunity from an action for civil damages if his actions were objectively reasonable and his conduct does not violate clearly established statutory or constitutional rights of which a reasonable person would have known. While Camp's (P) complaint sufficiently stated a claim for deprivation of substantive due process, Gregory (D) was entitled to qualified immunity. Affirmed.

Continued on next page.

▶ *ANALYSIS*

The court articulated a narrow range of circumstances under which a DCFS caseworker will be held liable for injuries sustained outside of the home as a result of placing a child with a guardian who it has reason to know will not provide adequate supervision. Such factors to be considered include the following: (1) the caseworker must have failed to exercise a bona fide professional judgment; (2) the guardian is only expected to provide reasonable supervision; (3) the harm sustained must be reasonably foreseeable; and (4) there must be sufficient causation between the failure to supervise and the resultant injury.

Quicknotes

DUE PROCESS CLAUSE   Clauses found in the Fifth and Fourteenth Amendments to the United States Constitution providing that no person shall be deprived of "life, liberty, or property, without due process of law."

DUTY TO PROTECT/AID   A moral duty and not one imposed by law; no liability attaches to those persons who fail to undertake a rescue or otherwise aid a person in need absent a special relationship between them.

REASONABLE PERSON STANDARD   The standard of care exercised by a hypothetical person who possesses the intelligence, education, knowledge, attention, and judgment required by society of its members when governing behavior; the standard applies to a person's judgment when determining breach of a duty under the theory of negligence.

Memphis Community School Dist. v. Stachura

Suspended teacher (P) v. School board (D)

477 U.S. 299 (1986).

NATURE OF CASE: Appeal from award of damages for violation of civil rights.

FACT SUMMARY: The court of appeals held the jury could award Stachura (P) damages for the importance of the constitutional right violated, as well as compensatory and punitive damages.

🏛 **RULE OF LAW**
Damages for deprivation of constitutional rights may not be awarded merely for the importance of the rights themselves.

FACTS: Stachura (P) was suspended from teaching by Memphis (D), based on his teaching methods. He sued, contending his constitutional rights had been violated. The district court instructed the jury on punitive and compensatory damages, and instructed it that damages could be awarded based on the importance of the constitutional rights violated. The jury awarded compensatory and punitive damages, the court of appeals affirmed, and the Supreme Court granted certiorari.

ISSUE: May damages for deprivation of constitutional rights be awarded merely for the importance of the rights themselves?

HOLDING AND DECISION: (Powell, J.) No. Damages for deprivation of constitutional rights may not be awarded merely for the importance of the rights themselves. Compensatory damages are awarded to compensate. They include out-of-pocket losses as well as intangible losses. The jurors here were asked to put a price on constitutional rights as an abstract concept. This differs from compensation for a deprivation of such right. As a result, the instruction was erroneous. Reversed.

CONCURRENCE: (Marshall, J.) The majority opinion opens the door to interpretation that damages in a § 1983 case are limited to out-of-pocket injuries. This is not so.

▶ *ANALYSIS*

The Court rejected Stachura's (P) argument that some constitutional rights are stronger than others. So-called substantive rights, such as freedom of speech, would be given greater importance. The Court declined the invitation to set up a hierarchy of rights which it believed would cause more problems than it would solve.

Quicknotes

COMPENSATORY DAMAGES Measure of damages necessary to compensate victim for actual injuries suffered.

CONSTITUTIONAL TORT Federal law providing a cause of action to any person who under the color of state law is deprived of their constitutional rights.

CHAPTER 20

Misuse of Legal Procedure

Quick Reference Rules of Law

Texas Skaggs Inc. v. Graves

Hot check writer (P) v. Store (D)

Tex. Ct. Civ. App., 582 S.W.2d 863 (1979).

NATURE OF CASE: Appeal from award of damages for malicious prosecution.

FACT SUMMARY: Skaggs (D) contended that it was not liable to Graves (P) for malicious prosecution because the criminal charge did not adequately terminate in her favor, there was sufficient probable cause to bring charges, and no malice was shown.

RULE OF LAW
In order to establish a cause of action for malicious prosecution, a favorable termination of the underlying action must be shown, as well as lack of probable cause to institute the prosecution and malice.

FACTS: Graves (P) left signed blank checks for her husband. Two of the checks were cashed at Skaggs (D) and returned dishonored. Graves (P) paid the checks, yet Skaggs (D) alerted the police. The police arrested Graves (P), but released her after verifying she had paid the checks. Skaggs (D) demanded the charges be filed, but the case was dismissed because the prosecution could not produce the checks as evidence. Graves (P) then sued for malicious prosecution and received an award of $20,000. Skaggs (D) appealed, contending the dismissal did not constitute a favorable termination, it had probable cause to press charges, and insufficient evidence of malice was shown.

ISSUE: In order to establish a cause of action for malicious prosecution, is it necessary to show a favorable termination, lack of probable cause, and malice?

HOLDING AND DECISION: (Ray, J.) Yes. In order to establish a cause of action for malicious prosecution, a favorable termination of the underlying action must be shown, as well as lack of probable cause to institute the prosecution and malice. In this case, the criminal action was dismissed for lack of sufficient evidence. Clearly, this constitutes a favorable termination of the case. The jury found that Graves (P) did not know the checks would be negotiated, and that Skaggs (D) had no evidence showing the lack of funds to be knowing or intentional. Malice was found by the jury based upon the insistence to prosecute even after the checks were paid. Affirmed.

► ANALYSIS

Malicious prosecution can be charged in cases where the underlying matter was civil or criminal in nature. Because it has a chilling effect on people in having their rights adjudicated, this tort is disfavored in the law. If one element is found lacking, the action will fail. For example, if probable cause to sue or charge the person criminally exists, it matters not that malice is shown, or that the proceeding terminated in favor of the malicious prosecution plaintiff.

Quicknotes

MALICE The intention to commit an unlawful act without justification or excuse.

MALICIOUS PROSECUTION The unlawful civil or criminal prosecution of a party without probable cause.

PROBABLE CAUSE A reasonable basis for believing that a crime has been committed.

Friedman v. Dozorc

Physician (P) v. Adversarial attorney (D)

Mich. Sup. Ct., 412 Mich. 1, 312 N.W.2d 585 (1981).

NATURE OF CASE: Appeal from summary judgment denying damages for malicious prosecution.

FACT SUMMARY: Friedman (P) contended that Dozorc (D), an attorney who previously sued him, owed a duty of care not to bring suit until reasonable investigation revealed some basis for liability.

🏛 RULE OF LAW
An attorney owes no actionable duty of care to an adverse party.

FACTS: Friedman (P) treated Serafin for an urological problem and performed surgery on her. During surgery, Serafin hemorrhaged due to an unknown blood disease. After she died, Dozorc (D) sued him for malpractice on behalf of Serafin's family. Dozorc (D), as plaintiff's attorney, tried the case, presenting no expert testimony that Friedman (P) was negligent. Friedman (P) prevailed and then sued Dozorc (D), contending that he breached a duty owed to Friedman (P) to reasonably investigate the case before bringing suit. Dozorc (D) successfully moved for summary judgment, but the court of appeals reinstated the cause of action for malicious prosecution. Both sides appealed.

ISSUE: Does an attorney owe an actionable duty of care to an adverse party?

HOLDING AND DECISION: (Levin, J.) No. An attorney owes no actionable duty of care to an adverse party. Imposing a duty of this nature would interfere with the attorney's duty to his own client. This would create a conflict of interest which could not be overcome. Further, Friedman (P) showed no special injury which would have allowed a suit for malicious prosecution. To abandon the special injury requirement would open malicious prosecution to any former defendant. As a result, no cause of action was stated. Reversed.

CONCURRENCE: (Levin, J.) The court should fashion a rule that allows successful litigants to recover all costs of litigation and thus lighten the load of wrongful litigation.

▶ ANALYSIS

The English Rule holds that a person must plead and prove special injury, such as to his reputation or person, or an arrest or seizure in order to recover for malicious prosecution. The American Rule does not require a showing of special injury. In this case, no special injury was pled and, thus, because Michigan follows the English Rule, no recovery could be had.

Quicknotes

ABUSE OF PROCESS The unlawful use of the legal process after it has been granted.

DUTY OF CARE A principle of negligence requiring an individual to act in such a manner as to avoid injury to a person to whom he or she owes an obligatory duty.

MALPRACTICE A failure to perform one's professional duties during the course of a client relationship, either intentionally or negligently, or the poor or improper discharge of one's professional obligations.

Grainger v. Hill

Owner of mortgaged vessel (P) v. Lender (D)

Ct. of Common Pleas, 4 Bing. N.C. 212, 132 Eng. Rep. 769 (1838).

NATURE OF CASE: Action for abuse of process.

FACT SUMMARY: Hill (D) contended that Grainger (P) failed to state a cause of action for abuse of process because he failed to allege the underlying arrest had been terminated.

RULE OF LAW
An action for abuse of process is not based upon a favorable termination of the underlying proceeding.

FACTS: Grainger (P) owned a boat which he mortgaged to Hill (D). He continued to operate the vessel under the loan agreement. In breach of such agreement, Hill (D) demanded early repayment of the debt. Grainger (P) refused, and Hill (D) had him arrested and held until he gave up possession of the ship. Grainger (P) sued for abuse of process, and a jury verdict was returned in his favor. Hill (D) sought entry of a nonsuit on the basis that Grainger (P) failed to plead and prove that the prosecution had terminated.

ISSUE: Is an action for abuse of process based upon a favorable termination of the underlying action?

HOLDING AND DECISION: (Tindal, C.J.) No. An action for abuse of process is not based upon a termination of the underlying action. The tort rests upon the improper invocation of legal process for an ulterior motive. It matters not what or whether the disposition of the underlying was achieved. Judgment for Grainger (P).

ANALYSIS

This early case illustrates the fundamental difference between the tort of malicious prosecution and abuse of process. Malicious prosecution requires a favorable termination of the underlying case. Abuse of process is available for interlocutory actions which may or may not end the case.

━━━

QUICKNOTES

ABUSE OF PROCESS The unlawful use of the legal process after it has been granted.

INTERLOCUTORY Intervening; temporary; refers to an issue that is determined during the course of a proceeding and which does not constitute a final judgment on the merits.

MALICIOUS PROSECUTION The unlawful civil or criminal prosecution of a party without probable cause.

━━━

Misrepresentation

Quick Reference Rules of Law

Swinton v. Whitinsville Savings Bank

Home buyer (P) v. Seller (D)

Mass. Sup. Jud. Ct., 42 N.E.2d 808 (1942).

NATURE OF CASE: Action to recover damages for fraudulent concealment.

FACT SUMMARY: Swinton (P) purchased a dwelling house from Whitinsville Savings Bank (D) which was infested with termites. Whitinsville Savings Bank (D) through its salesman knew of the termites and did not disclose this information to Swinton (P) nor were they asked for any such information by Swinton (P).

RULE OF LAW
There is no liability for bare nondisclosure.

FACTS: Swinton (P) purchased a dwelling house from Whitinsville Savings Bank (D). Swinton (P) alleges that Whitinsville Savings Bank (D) knew that the home was infested with termites at the time of sale to Swinton (P) and that he had no idea nor any reasonable way at the time to tell whether termites were present or not. Swinton (P) made no allegation of any false statement or representation, or of the uttering of a half-truth which may be tantamount to a falsehood. There was no intimation that the Whitinsville Savings Bank (D) by any means prevented Swinton (P) from acquiring information as to the condition of the house. There was nothing to show any fiduciary relation between the parties. Based upon these facts, the trial court sustained a demurrer in favor of Whitinsville Savings Bank (D). Swinton (P) appeals.

ISSUE: Is there any duty to disclose facts when not requested to do so?

HOLDING AND DECISION: (Qua, J.) No. There is no liability for bare nondisclosure. Whitinsville Sav. Bank (D) was to be found liable on these facts, every seller would be liable who fails to disclose any nonapparent defect known to him in the subject of the sale which materially reduces its value and which the buyer fails to discover. Similarly, it would seem that every buyer would be liable who fails to disclose any nonapparent virtue known to him in the subject of the purchase which materially enhances its value and of which the seller is ignorant. The law has not yet reached the point of imposing upon the frailties of human nature a standard so idealistic as this. Affirmed.

▶ ANALYSIS

This case may be considered a modern one which is based upon very old case law. The rule set down in this case although still very much operable and in use today, has been eroded from the severity seen here to much more acceptable applications by numerous exceptions which have been created. This case does not represent the modern-day trend, which is toward more of a duty to disclose known material facts. Many states have specific statutes dealing with the subject of concealment in many fields, including that of real estate.

Quicknotes

DEMURRER The assertion that the opposing party's pleadings are insufficient and that the demurring party should not be made to answer.

DUTY TO DISCLOSE The duty owed by a fiduciary to reveal those facts that have a material effect on the interests of the party that must be informed.

FIDUCIARY Person holding a legal obligation to act for the benefit of another.

FRAUDULENT CONCEALMENT The concealing of a material fact which a party is under an obligation to disclose.

Griffith v. Byers Constr. Co. of Kansas, Inc.

Home buyers (P) v. Developer (D)

Kan. Sup. Ct., 212 Kan. 65, 510 P.2d 198 (1973).

NATURE OF CASE: Action by purchasers of new homes to recover damages against real estate developer on theories of implied warranties and fraud.

FACT SUMMARY: Purchasers (P) of new homes in a tract sued developer (D) of home sites when they discovered that their lots, because of high saline content, could not be landscaped; the homes had been bought not from the developer (D), but from the building contractor.

> ## RULE OF LAW
> A purchaser who has bought a home on a lot that contains sterile soil may recover on a fraud theory from the developer of the lot, even though, in its strict sense, there is a lack of privity between them.

FACTS: Purchasers of new homes (P), who bought from the builder, discovered that the lots on which the homes rested contained a high saline soil content, thus making it impossible to landscape the homesites. The saline content did not affect the structural qualities of the homes. Byers Constr. Co. of Kansas, Inc. (D), the developer of the lots, had sold the homesites directly to the builder; who in turn had constructed homes on them and sold them to the purchasers (P). These purchasers (P) sued Byers (D) to recover damages on alternate theories of breach of an implied warranty of fitness, and fraud in the concealment of a material matter. Their complaint alleged that Byers (D) had developed and advertised the lots as a choice residential area, that it knew of the soil's saline condition, and that it purposely graded the homesites to prevent them from discovering the presence of salt. The trial court granted summary judgment in favor of Byers (D) on the implied warranty count. It also dismissed the fraud count on the ground that no privity existed between Byers (D) and the purchasers (P). The purchasers (P) appealed.

ISSUE: May a purchaser of a new home bring a fraud action against the lot developer for nondisclosure of defects in the homesite's soil?

HOLDING AND DECISION: (Fromme, J.) Yes. [The court initially holds that the trial court was correct in dismissing the implied warranty count because a real estate developer by subdividing and offering lots for sale as choice residential homesites does not by implication warrant the fertility of the soil of said lots.] This court has already held that where a vendor has knowledge of a defect in property that is not within the fair and reasonable reach of the vendee and that

he could not discover by the exercise of reasonable diligence, the silence and failure of the vendor to disclose the defect in the property constitutes actionable fraudulent concealment. There is no reason why this rule should not be extended to a developer of residential lots. The complaint in the present case satisfies the elements of this rule. Furthermore, the fraudulent concealment here is material. A prospective purchaser of a residential buildingsite would consider the soil condition a material factor in choosing a lot on which to build his home since this factor affects the value and acceptability of the homesite. Finally, the lack of strict privity is immaterial. Liability for fraudulent misrepresentation or concealment extends to the persons or class of persons whom the maker intends or has reason to expect to act or to refrain from action in reliance upon the misrepresentation or concealment. Here, the fact that title was first taken in the name of the builder did not change the identity of those who would be ultimately affected by the fraud—the purchasers (P). The builder was merely acting as a conduit for the passage of title. Reversed as to the dismissal of the fraud count.

▌ANALYSIS

Where the fraud action is predicated on intentional tort theory, and the misrepresentation is in the nature of a "continuous deception," the plaintiff need not show that he belongs to a class of persons whom the defendant intended to rely on his assertions. Where a negligent misrepresentation is alleged, the plaintiff must show that he was in that class of persons which was reasonably foreseeable or intended by the defendant to rely. In strict liability cases, no scienter on the part of the defendant need be proved.

Quicknotes

FRAUD A false representation of facts with the intent that another will rely on the misrepresentation to his detriment.

IMPLIED WARRANTY An implied promise made by one party to a contract that the other party may rely on a fact, relieving that party from the obligation of determining whether the fact is true and indemnifying the other party from liability if that fact is shown to be false.

NONDISCLOSURE The failure to communicate certain facts to another person.

PRIVITY Commonality of rights or interests between parties.

Derry v. Peek

Investor (P) v. Company chairman (D)

House of Lords, 14 App. Cas. 337 (1889).

NATURE OF CASE: Action on the case for damages for deceit.

FACT SUMMARY: Peek (P) had purchased shares in Derry's (D) tramway company, which folded after its use of steam and mechanical power was refused by the Board of Trade.

🏛 RULE OF LAW
An action in deceit will not lie for a false representation made with an honest belief in its truth.

FACTS: Derry (D) and other directors of a tramway company issued a prospectus, representing their company as authorized by the Board of Trade to use steam or other mechanical power. Peek (P) purchased shares in the company, relying upon the directors' further representation that a considerable savings would result from this technological innovation. The Board of Trade had not, in fact, consented to the use of steam or mechanical power by the company, and refused to do so. "In consequence, the company was wound up" and Peek (P) sued Derry (D). The trial court came to the conclusion that the directors had all believed that the company had the authorization as stated in the prospectus, and that their belief was not unreasonable. On appeal by Peek (P) to the court of appeals, the judgment was reversed on the ground that "while the defendants honestly believed that the statements in the prospectus were true, the statements were made without any reasonable grounds for believing them." Derry (D) appealed to the House of Lords.

ISSUE: Will an action for deceit lie for a false representation honestly believed though on insufficient grounds?

HOLDING AND DECISION: (Herschell, J.) It is important to distinguish this action for deceit from a suit for rescission of a contract. Rescission requires proof only of misrepresentation; deceit requires more. Specifically, an action of deceit requires proof of fraud: a misrepresentation made (1) knowingly, or (2) without belief in the statement's truth, or (3) recklessly. Belief in a false statement's truth, as the defendants claim here, always defeats an allegation of fraud. The alleged belief in the truth of a false statement can be tested by examining whether the belief had reasonable grounds and how the witness acquired his alleged belief. This application of the reasonable man standard thus permits a way to assess the witness's state of mind on this point. Reversed.

▶ ANALYSIS

Prior to *Derry v. Peek*, it was generally assumed, by the early text writers at least, that negligent misrepresentation would find a remedy in deceit. But in 1889, the House of Lords clearly identified the action of deceit with intentional misrepresentation, and left merely negligent misrepresentation to be dealt with by an action for rescission of a contract. Although this decision has been condemned as a backward step in the law, the majority of American courts still purport to accept it. In reality, however, most have devised fictions which do allow recovery in deceit for misrepresentation made with less than an actual intent to deceive. It is generally agreed that a wrong motive, as distinguished from a fraudulent intent, is not essential to the tort of deceit.

Quicknotes

DECEIT A false statement made ether knowingly or with reckless disregard as to its truth and which is intended to induce the plaintiff to act in reliance thereon to his detriment.

RESCISSION The canceling of an agreement and the return of the parties to their positions prior to the formation of the contract.

International Products Co. v. Erie R.R. Co.

Importer (P) v. Railroad (D)

N.Y. Ct. App., 244 N.Y. 331, 155 N.E. 662 (1927).

NATURE OF CASE: Action for damages for negligent misrepresentation.

FACT SUMMARY: International Products (P) insured its imported goods, relying upon Erie Railroad's (D) misinformation that they were located at Dock F; the goods were later destroyed by fire at Dock D.

🏛 RULE OF LAW
An action for damages for negligent misrepresentation will lie where the speaker owes a duty to give correct information.

FACTS: International Products (P), an importer, was expecting a shipment of goods and made arrangements with Erie R.R. Co. (D) to receive and store the goods. International Products (P) desired to insure the shipment after its arrival, and giving this reason for its question, it inquired of Erie (D) where the goods would be stored. Erie (D) replied that the goods were docked at Dock F, from which International (P) inferred that they were already received and stored, and obtained its insurance on this basis. The goods arrived later and were stored at Dock D. They were subsequently destroyed by fire, and International (P) was unable to collect any insurance because of Erie's (D) misdescription. In a suit to recover its loss, International (P) received judgment from the trial court, which was affirmed by the appellate court. Erie (D) again appeals.

ISSUE: Does a cause of action arise from a negligent misrepresentation where the speaker owes a duty to give correct information?

HOLDING AND DECISION: (Andrew, J.) Yes. Although the English rule, since *Derry v. Peek*, was that no cause of action would lie "unless the statement be false to the knowledge of the person making it," the court spoke of New York as already committed to the American, as distinguished from the English, rule. It cited two earlier cases where recovery was allowed on the basis of a negligent statement, but here limited the rule to where a duty exists, if one speaks at all, to give the correct information. To determine whether there is such a duty, there must be knowledge that: (1) the information is desired for a serious purpose; (2) that the person to whom it is given intends to rely and act upon it; and (3) that if false or erroneous, he will be injured in person or property. In addition, "the relationship of the parties, arising out of contract or otherwise, must be such that in morals and good conscience the one has

the right to rely upon the other for information, and the other giving the information owes a duty to give it with care." The court concluded that in such a proper case, words negligently spoken may justify the recovery of proximate damages caused by faith in their accuracy. After discounting as "immaterial" the fact that Erie's (D) negligent answer was not given to serve its own purposes, the court determined that International (P) was entitled to such recovery. Affirmed.

▶ ANALYSIS

Only a minority of American courts have refused to accept *Derry v. Peek*, House of Lords, 14 App. Cas. 337 (1889), holding instead that an action for deceit will lie for negligent statements. The prevailing majority have preferred to limit the historical action of deceit and have instead based liability on the negligence action. The instant case was one of the first to carry over negligence from tangible injuries to such economic loss as caused by a negligent misrepresentation. It is generally agreed today that the negligence action is equally appropriate to either type of damage.

━■━■

Quicknotes

DECEIT A false statement made ether knowingly or with reckless disregard as to its truth and which is intended to induce the plaintiff to act in reliance thereon to his detriment.

NEGLIGENT MISREPRESENTATION A misrepresentation that is made pursuant to a business relationship, in violation of an obligation owed, upon which the plaintiff relies to his detriment.

━■━■

Winter v. G.P. Putnam's Sons

Mushroom eater (P) v. Publisher (D)

938 F.2d 1033 (9th Cir. 1991).

NATURE OF CASE: Appeal from summary judgment in a products liability action.

FACT SUMMARY: Winter (P) relied on a book on mushrooms published by Putnam (D) and became critically ill after eating a poisonous mushroom.

🏛 RULE OF LAW
Strict products liability is not applicable to the expressions contained within a book.

FACTS: Winter (P) purchased *The Encyclopedia of Mushrooms*, a book published by Putnam (D), to help in collecting and eating wild mushrooms. In 1988, Winter (P), relying on descriptions in the book, ate some wild mushrooms which turned out to be poisonous. Winter (P) became so ill he required a liver transplant. He brought a strict products liability action against Putnam (D), alleging that the book contained erroneous and misleading information that caused his injury. Putnam (D) responded that the information in the book was not a product for purposes of strict products liability, and the trial court granted its motion for summary judgment. The trial court also rejected Winter's (P) actions for negligence and misrepresentation. Winter (P) appealed.

ISSUE: Is strict products liability applicable to the expressions contained within a book?

HOLDING AND DECISION: (Sneed, J.) No. Strict products liability is not applicable to the expressions contained within a book. Products liability is geared toward tangible objects. The expression of ideas is governed by copyright, libel, and misrepresentation laws. The Restatement (Second) of Torts lists examples of the items that are covered by §402A strict liability. All are tangible items, such as tires or automobiles. There is no indication that the doctrine should be expanded beyond this area. Furthermore, there is a strong public interest in the unfettered exchange of ideas. The threat of liability without fault could seriously inhibit persons who wish to share thoughts and ideas with others. Although some courts have held that aeronautical charts are products for purposes of strict liability, these charts are highly technical tools which resemble compasses. The Encyclopedia of Mushrooms, published by Putnam (D), is a book of pure thought and expression and therefore does not constitute a product for purposes of strict liability. Additionally, publishers do not owe a duty to investigate the contents of books that they distribute. Therefore, a negligence action may not be maintained by Winter (P) against Putnam (D). Affirmed.

▶ ANALYSIS

This decision is in accord with the rulings in most jurisdictions. See *Alm v. Nostrand Reinhold Co., Inc.*, 480 N.E.2d 1263 (Ill. 1985). The court also stated that since the publisher is not a guarantor of the accuracy of an author's statements, an action for negligent misrepresentation could not be maintained. The elements of negligent misrepresentation are stated in § 311 of the Restatement (Second) of Torts.

Quicknotes

NEGLIGENT MISREPRESENTATION A misrepresentation that is made pursuant to a business relationship, in violation of an obligation owed, upon which the plaintiff relies to his detriment.

STRICT LIABILITY Liability for all injuries proximately caused by a party's conducting of certain inherently dangerous activities without regard to negligence or fault.

SUMMARY JUDGMENT Judgment rendered by a court in response to a motion by one of the parties, claiming that the lack of a question of material fact in respect to an issue warrants disposition of the issue without consideration by the jury.

Hanberry v. Hearst Corp.

Consumer (P) v. Publisher (D)

Cal. Ct. App., 276 Cal. App. 2d 680 (1969).

NATURE OF CASE: Action against publishing company for negligently recommending a product.

FACT SUMMARY: Good Housekeeping (D) issued its seal of approval to a pair of slippers which Hanberry (P) claimed were defective.

🏛 RULE OF LAW
A party who endorses a product for its own economic gain, and for the purpose of inducing the public to buy it, may be liable to purchasers who, relying on the endorsement, purchase the product and are injured by it.

FACTS: Hanberry (P) purchased a pair of slippers manufactured by Handal (D). While wearing them, Hanberry (P) slipped on her kitchen floor. Hanberry sued Handal (D) for negligent manufacturing. Hanberry (P) also sued Hearst Corp. (D), publishers of Good Housekeeping, which had given its seal of approval for the slippers. Hanberry (P) alleged that Hearst (D) had either not tested the slippers or had been negligent in conducting such tests. Hanberry (P) claimed that she had relied upon the endorsement, that it had been given for the purpose of inducing the public to purchase the product and for the economic gain of Hearst (D). Hearst (D) demurred and the court dismissed the complaint against it.

ISSUE: Is an endorser potentially liable for its negligent misrepresentation of a product?

HOLDING AND DECISION: (Ault, A.J.) Yes. The issue is triable. Hearst (D) awarded its Good Housekeeping seal of approval. Consumers rely upon such representations by reputable allegedly disinterested parties. Hearst (D) issues such seals of approval for its own economic gain. Hearst (D) owes a duty to the public to use proper testing procedures before issuing its seal. These do not represent mere statements of opinion. Hearst (D) held itself out as possessing superior knowledge and special information concerning the slippers. Under such circumstances, Hearst (D) may be liable for negligent misrepresentation if Hanberry's (P) allegations concerning the testing procedure are correct. In any event, the issue is best decided by the trier of fact, not on the pleadings. Hanberry's (P) allegations concerning strict liability and express and implied warranty cannot be maintained since they are only reserved for manufacturers or suppliers to the public. Summary judgment was properly granted as to them. Reversed.

▶ ANALYSIS

Before liability can be found in such cases, it must be alleged and proved that there was reliance on the endorsement. It must have been a significant factor in inducing the purchase. The endorsement must be reasonably specific. In some instances, a products liability theory may be used against an endorser. Hearst's (D) alleged special knowledge is the key point. A mere recommendation would not be actionable unless other special circumstances exist.

Quicknotes

EXPRESS WARRANTY An express promise made by one party to a contract that the other party may rely on a fact, relieving that party from the obligation of determining whether the fact is true and indemnifying the other party from liability if that fact is shown to be false.

NEGLIGENT MISREPRESENTATION A misrepresentation that is made pursuant to a business relationship, in violation of an obligation owed, upon which the plaintiff relies to his detriment.

RELIANCE Dependence on a fact that causes a party to act or refrain from acting.

STRICT LIABILITY Liability for all injuries proximately caused by a party's conducting of certain inherently dangerous activities without regard to negligence or fault.

Richard v. A. Waldman and Sons, Inc.

Homeowner (P) v. Developer (D)

Conn. Sup. Ct., 155 Conn. 343, 232 A.2d 307 (1967).

NATURE OF CASE: Action to recover damages for alleged false representations in connection with the sale of land.

FACT SUMMARY: Real estate developer (D) "innocently" misrepresented to a purchaser of a lot that a structure on the lot was in accordance with local zoning regulations.

🏛 **RULE OF LAW**
An innocent misrepresentation may be actionable if the declarant has the means of knowing, ought to know, or has the duty of knowing, the truth.

FACTS: At the closing date for a real estate transaction, A. Waldman and Sons (D), a real estate developer who had contracted with Richard (P) to prepare plans for and construct a house with an attached garage for Richard's (P) use, delivered to Richard (P) a plot plan. This plan showed a sideyard of 20 feet as required by local zoning laws. Subsequently, local authorities issued to Richard (P) a certificate of occupancy based on Waldman's (D) survey. Four months later, Richard (P) discovered that the actual sideyard of the lot he had purchased was less than 3 feet away from his neighbor's boundary line, and that the house's location was in violation of zoning laws. In an action by Richard (P) against Waldman (D) to recover damages for false representation, Waldman (D) claimed that the misrepresentation as to the width of the sideyard was innocently made. The trial court found that Waldman (D) had falsely and recklessly represented to Richard (P), for the purpose of inducing action, that the premises' sideyard was 20 feet and that there was no violation of the zoning regulations. The court further found Richard (P) was induced to rely on these representations which were mistaken, but not innocent. Richard (P) was awarded the difference between the actual value of the property and its value had it been as represented. Waldman (D) appealed.

ISSUE: Is an innocent misrepresentation ever actionable?

HOLDING AND DECISION: (Cotter, J.) Yes. An innocent misrepresentation may be actionable if the declarant has the means of knowing, ought to know, or has the duty of knowing the truth. Here, Waldman (D), a real estate developer, had special means of knowing the location of the lot's structure, such being a matter peculiarly relating to its business and one on which Richard (P) was entitled to rely. Neither actual knowledge of the falsity, nor fraud or bad faith need be alleged. Furthermore, it is immaterial whether the wrong which can be legally inferred from these facts arises in tort or in contract. Richard (P) may retain the property and recover damages. The misrepresentation here was in the nature of a warranty entitling Richard (P) to a recovery under the contract as for a breach of warranty. Affirmed.

▶ *ANALYSIS*

There are two important limitations on liability for negligent, or "innocent" misrepresentations. First, most jurisdictions require that the maker of the representation be in the business of providing others with information to guide them in certain business transactions. Second, while in a deceit action, the maker will be charged with intending the reliance of all persons who would probably receive the information, in a negligent misrepresentation suit, the maker is liable only if he could have anticipated reliance by the particular plaintiff.

■■■

Quicknotes

BREACH OF WARRANTY The breach of a promise made by one party to a contract that the other party may rely on a fact, relieving that party from the obligation of determining whether the fact is true and indemnifying the other party from liability if that fact is shown to be false.

CERTIFICATE OF OCCUPANCY A certificate issued by local government stating that a building is in accordance with local law.

MISREPRESENTATION A statement or conduct by one party to another that constitutes a false representation of fact.

RELIANCE Dependence on a fact that causes a party to act or refrain from acting.

■■■

Credit Alliance Corp. v. Arthur Andersen & Co.

Client's lender (P) v. Auditors (D)

N.Y. Ct. App., 483 N.E.2d 110, 493 N.Y.S.2d 435 (1985).

NATURE OF CASE: Appeal from denial of motion to dismiss action for negligence.

FACT SUMMARY: Andersen (D) contended it could not be found liable for negligently preparing financial statements relied upon by Credit Alliance (P), as they lacked privity.

🏛 RULE OF LAW
Accountants may be liable to persons not in privity for negligently preparing financial reports if the accountant knew the report would be relied on for a specific purpose by a known party.

FACTS: Andersen (D), accountants, prepared various financial reports outlining the financial situation of L.B. Smith, Inc. Credit Alliance (P), which lent money to Smith based on such reports, sued Andersen (D), contending that the reports were negligently prepared. Andersen (D) moved to dismiss, arguing in the absence of privity no actionable negligence occurred. The court denied the motion, and Andersen (D) appealed.

ISSUE: May accountants be held liable to persons not in privity for negligently preparing financial reports if the accountant knew the report would be relied upon by that party for a particular purpose?

HOLDING AND DECISION: (Jasen, J.) Yes. Accountants may be held liable to persons without privity for the negligent preparation of financial documents if they knew the report would be relied upon by a person for a specific purpose. In this type of situation, the accountant has a type of relationship with the person that approaches privity. Thus, the duty is recognized. In this case, no evidence was presented indicating Andersen (D) prepared the reports for a specific purpose or that Credit Alliance (P) was to use them. Thus, no duty of care was owed, and no recovery may be had. Reversed.

▶ ANALYSIS

This case was a companion case to *European American Bank & Trust Co. v. Strahs & Kaye*, which was decided at the same time. This decision is an extension of *Ultramares Corp. v. Touche*, 179 N.E. 441 (N.Y. 1931), an opinion by Justice Cardozo. The decision became the seminal case in the area holding that no accountant's liability exists absent privity. As privity became more flexible, it deteriorated as a required element of proof.

Quicknotes

DUTY OF CARE A principle of negligence requiring an individual to act in such a manner as to avoid injury to a person to whom he or she owes a duty.

NEGLIGENCE Conduct falling below the standard of care that a reasonable person would demonstrate under similar conditions.

PRIVITY Commonality of rights or interests between parties.

Citizens State Bank v. Timm, Schmidt & Co.

Bank (P) v. Accounting firm (D)

Wis. Sup. Ct., 113 Wis. 2d 376, 335 N.W.2d 361 (1983).

NATURE OF CASE: Appeal from summary judgment denying damages for misrepresentation.

FACT SUMMARY: Timm (D) contended that Citizens (P) could not recover from them as accountants because no privity existed when the reports upon which Citizens (P) relied were negligently prepared.

🏛 RULE OF LAW
Accountants may be held liable for the negligent preparation of audit reports to a third party not in privity who relies on the report.

FACTS: Timm (D), certified public accountants, prepared audit reports on and for Clintonville Fire Apparatus, Inc. The report negligently failed to accurately reflect C.F.A.'s financial position. Prior to discovery of the problem, Citizens (P) relied upon the reports in lending C.F.A. money. After the errors were revealed, C.F.A. went bankrupt. Citizens (P) sued Timm (D) to recover the outstanding balance on the C.F.A. debt. Timm (D) successfully moved for summary judgment on the basis that an accountant cannot be held liable to a third party without privity. Citizens (P) appealed.

ISSUE: May accountants be held liable for the negligent preparation of audit reports to a third party not in privity who relies thereon?

HOLDING AND DECISION: (Day, J.) Yes. Accountants may be held liable for the negligent preparation of audit reports to a third party not in privity who relies thereon. Third parties must be able to rely upon financial statements in order to facilitate commerce. It is reasonably foreseeable that a third party would use reports to gauge a company's financial condition preparatory to lending money. In this case, whether the harm caused was reasonably foreseeable was a factual question, and summary judgment was improperly granted. Reversed.

▶ ANALYSIS

The seminal case in this area is *Ultramares v. Touche*, 174 N.E. 441 (N.Y. 1931). In that case, Judge Benjamin Cardozo held that no liability could attach in this type of case because of the lack of determination in amount, time, and class of liability. Gradually, this case was rejected as the potential plaintiffs became known to the accountant.

Quicknotes

LIABILITY Any obligation or responsibility.

NEGLIGENCE Conduct falling below the standard of care that a reasonable person would demonstrate under similar conditions.

PRIVITY Commonality of rights or interests between parties.

SUMMARY JUDGMENT Judgment rendered by a court in response to a motion made by one of the parties, claiming that the lack of a question of material fact in respect to an issue warrants disposition of the issue without consideration by the jury.

Ultramares Corp. v. Touche, Nivens & Co.

Lender (P) v. Public accounting firm (D)

N.Y. Ct. App., 255 N.Y. 170, 174 N.E. 441 (1931).

NATURE OF CASE: Appeal from denial of damages for fraudulent misrepresentation.

FACT SUMMARY: In reliance upon an audit of Fred Stern & Co. prepared by Touche, Nivens & Co. (D), Ultamares Corp. (P) made several loans to Fred Stern & Co. The audit showed Fred Stern & Co. to be worth $1,000,000, when the company was actually insolvent.

RULE OF LAW
Negligent words are not actionable unless they are uttered directly, with knowledge or notice that they will be acted on, to one to whom the speaker is bound by some relation of duty, arising out of public calling, contract, or otherwise.

FACTS: Touche, Nivens & Co. (D), a firm of public accountants, were employed by Fred Stern & Co. to prepare a balance sheet indicating the condition of the business. Touche (D) had been so employed by Stern for the previous three years. Touche (D) knew that the balance sheet would be shown by Stern to banks, creditors, stockholder's purchasers, or sellers in the course of business as a basis of financial dealings. Touche (D) also knew that to finance its business, Stern borrowed large sums of money. When the sheet was completed, Touche (D) provided Stern with 32 certified copies. It was not shown that Touche (D) knew that Ultramares Corp. (P) would be shown the balance sheet. Touche's (D) audit showed Stern's net worth to be $1,000,000. Stern asked Ultramares Corp. (P) for a loan, and showed it the balance sheet certified by Touche (D). On the faith of Touche's (D) balance sheet, Ultramares (P) made several loans to Stern amounting to over $165,000. Stern went bankrupt, and it was found that at the time Touche (D) prepared its audit, Stern was insolvent. Ultramares (P) brought two cases of action against Touche (D). One was for negligent misrepresentation. The second was for fraudulent misrepresentation.

ISSUE: Can a defendant be held liable for negligent misrepresentation to one with whom the defendant did not have a contract?

HOLDING AND DECISION: (Cardozo, C.J.) No. If there has been neither reckless misstatement nor insincere expression of an opinion, but only honest blunder, the ensuing liability for negligence is bounded by the contract and is to be enforced between the parties to the contract. The court distinguishes *Glanzer v. Shepard*, 233 N.Y. 236, 135 N.E. 275 (1922), on the ground that there the transmission of the weigher's receipt to the plaintiff was not "merely one possibility among many" but "the end and aim of the transmission." It distinguishes *International Products Co. v. Erie R.R. Co.*, 244 N.Y. 331, 155 N.E. 662 (1927), on the ground that there existed a determinative relation of bailor and bailee. Of course, negligence may still be evidence from which fraud might be inferred. Even an opinion, especially an expert's opinion, may be found to be fraudulent if the grounds supporting it are so flimsy as to lead to the conclusion that there was no genuine belief in it. But negligence alone is not a substitute for fraud. The court feels that if the distinction between the willful or reckless representation essential to an action at law for deceit and the misrepresentation, innocent or negligent, that is sufficient for rescission in equity is to be abolished, such a change should be made by the legislature. The court will not extend liability for a negligent misrepresentation beyond the contract. In this case, Touche (D) owed a duty to creditors and investors to whom Stern showed the balance sheet, a duty to prepare it without fraud. However, it did not owe them a duty which would make it liable for negligence. To hold otherwise might expose accountants to a liability in an indeterminate amount, for an indeterminate time to an indeterminate class. Ultramares Corp. (P) should be given a new trial as to its second cause of action for fraud.

ANALYSIS

The basis for the court's decision in this case seemed to have been the prospect of "a liability in an indeterminate amount for an indeterminate time to an indeterminate class," and of a huge and crushing burden of liability out of all proportion to a defendant's fault. This case demonstrates the more restrictive rule in cases involving invasion of intangible economic interests by negligent misrepresentation.

Quicknotes

BAILEE Person holding property in trust for another party.

BAILOR Person who delivers property to be held in trust to a bailee.

BALANCE SHEET A financial statement reflecting the assets and liabilities of a company on a particular date.

FRAUDULENT MISREPRESENTATION A statement or conduct by one party to another that constitutes a false representation of fact.

NEGLIGENT MISREPRESENTATION A misrepresentation that is made pursuant to a business relationship, in violation of an obligation owed, upon which the plaintiff relies to his detriment.

Williams v. Rank & Son Buick, Inc.

Buyer (P) v. Used-car dealer (D)

Wis. Sup. Ct., 44 Wis. 2d 239, 170 N.W.2d 807 (1969).

NATURE OF CASE: Action to recover damages for fraud.

FACT SUMMARY: Williams (P) bought what he thought was an air-conditioned car from Rank & Son Buick, Inc. Later, he found it was not air conditioned.

🏛 RULE OF LAW
A plaintiff cannot recover for misrepresentation unless his reliance upon the misrepresentation was justifiable.

FACTS: Williams (P) was looking for an air-conditioned car and went to Rank & Son Buick, Inc. (D). A salesman showed him a car and told him it was air conditioned. Williams (P) also testified that particular car had been so described in an advertisement on which he relied. However, the evidence was that the advertisement was first published after Williams (P) bought the car. Williams (P) was allowed to take the car for 1½-hour test drive, and he did so. He testified, however, that it was not until several days later that he discovered that the car was not air conditioned. Williams (P) was a high school graduate, capable of reading and writing, who operated his own business. Williams (P) bought an action for fraud and was awarded $150.

ISSUE: Can a plaintiff who had opportunity, by the exercise of ordinary observation, to discover the falsity of a misrepresentation recover for damages resulting from his reliance on such misrepresentations?

HOLDING AND DECISION: (Hanly, J.) No. A plaintiff may not recover where, under the circumstances, his reliance was not justified. Courts will refuse to act for the relief of one claiming to have been misled by another's statements, who had opportunity, by the exercise of ordinary observation, to have known of their falsity. Of course, the obviousness of a statement's falsity negates reliance since no one can rely on a known falsity. The intelligence and experience of the plaintiff and the relationship between the parties are factors to be considered in deciding whether the falsity of the statement could have been discovered through ordinary care. Here, Williams (P) was a high school graduate capable of operating his own business. Rank & Son Buick's (D) salesman allowed him to drive and examine the car for a considerable length of time. No great search was required to discover that the car was not air conditioned, and if, as Williams (P) testified, that was of primary importance to him it would seem reasonable for him to have tried the air conditioner. Reversed.

DISSENT: (Wilkie, J.) The falsity of the representation was not so obvious that it could be held as a matter of law that Williams (P) had no right to rely on it.

▶ ANALYSIS

This case demonstrates that in an action for misrepresentation not only must there be reliance, but the reliance must be found to be justifiable under the circumstances. The plaintiff's conduct must not be so unreasonable, in light of information available to him, that the law may say his loss was his own responsibility.

Quicknotes

FRAUD A false representation of facts with the intent that another will rely on the misrepresentation to his detriment.

MISREPRESENTATION A statement or conduct by one party to another that constitutes a false representation of fact.

RELIANCE Dependence on a fact that causes a party to act or refrain from acting.

Saxby v. Southern Land Co.

Buyer (P) v. Seller (D)

Va. Sup. Ct. App., 109 Va. 196, 63 S.E. 423 (1909).

NATURE OF CASE: Appeal from a dismissal of action for land fraud.

FACT SUMMARY: Saxby (P) contended that Southern (D) misrepresented the acreage of the farm he bought.

RULE OF LAW
Actionable misrepresentation must be of an existing fact, not a statement of opinion.

FACTS: Southern (D) indicated to Saxby (P), the buyer, that the farm being sold had approximately 150 acres of pine timber, of which about 20 acres had been burned over. Saxby (P) purchased the farm and discovered that there were actually 120 acres in timber, 60 acres of which were burned over. Saxby (P) sued for misrepresentation, but Southern's (D) demurrer was sustained on the basis the statement by Southern (D) was opinion and not actionable. Saxby (P) appealed.

ISSUE: Must actionable misrepresentation be of an existing fact, not a statement of opinion?

HOLDING AND DECISION: (Harrison, J.) Yes. Actionable misrepresentation must be of an existing fact, not a statement of opinion. Opinion is not substantial enough for one to reasonably rely upon. Only statements of fact will induce a reasonable person to rely, and, thus, only misstatements of fact are actionable. In this case, the statement of the approximation of total acreage and burned acreage was an opinion, not a statement of fact. Thus, no actionable misrepresentation occurred. Affirmed.

▶ ANALYSIS

It would appear that in this case a factual determination was made regarding the interpretation of the acreage estimate. A more clearly stated estimate may have given rise to a different result. Commentators point out that all opinions are based upon factual assumptions. Thus, if these assumptions are misrepresented, a cause of action may exist.

■■■■

Quicknotes

DEMURRER The assertion that the opposing party's pleadings are insufficient and that the demurring party should not be made to answer.

FRAUD A false representation of facts with the intent that another will rely on the misrepresentation to his detriment.

MISREPRESENTATION A statement or conduct by one party to another that constitutes a false representation of fact.

RELIANCE Dependence on a fact that causes a party to act or refrain from acting.

■■■■

Vulcan Metals Co. v. Simmons Mfg. Co.

Buyer (P) v. Manufacturer (D)

248 Fed. 853 (2d Cir. 1918).

NATURE OF CASE: Action for deceit, on appeal.

FACT SUMMARY: Simmons Manufacturing (D) sold vacuum cleaner manufacturing machines to Vulcan Metals (P) claiming that they were (inter alia) "perfect," and that the vacuum cleaners had never been marketed before.

> ## 🏛 RULE OF LAW
> An opinion is a fact, and when parties are so situated that a buyer may reasonably rely upon the expression of a seller's opinion, the fact that it is an opinion is not a defense to an action in deceit; but, there are some statements that no sensible man takes seriously.

FACTS: Simmons Mfg. Co. (D) sold Vulcan Metals (P) machinery for the manufacture of vacuum cleaners. Representations, now challenged by Vulcan (P), were made to the effect that: (1) the vacuum cleaners were "perfect in even the smallest detail," "most economical," "everyone could afford one," "guaranteed perfect satisfaction" etc., and (2) that the vacuum cleaner had never before been put on the market. Vulcan (P) now sues for deceit, charging the representations above were false. Simmons (D) contended that both statements were mere opinion and, therefore, not actionable and they were substantively true since only 60 machines had ever been sold. The trial court directed a verdict for Simmons Mfg. (D) on each count. Vulcan (P) appealed.

ISSUE: May an action for deceit (misrepresentation) lie where the representations challenged involve mere opinions as well as misrepresentations about a product sold?

HOLDING AND DECISION: (Hand, J.) Yes. An opinion is a fact, and when parties are so situated that a buyer may reasonably rely upon the expression of a seller's opinion, the fact that it is an opinion is not a defense to an action in deceit; but, there are some statements that no sensible person takes seriously. Much depends on the relative equality of the parties involved in terms of their ability to know whether a statement is mere "dealer's talk" opinion, or fact statement (the ability to examine merchandise is but one factor in considering this question). Some statements are so patently "dealer's talk" that no sensible person would take them seriously. Here, the statements about the quality of the machines are clearly such "dealer's talk." No sensible person expects anything to be perfect. This is not true of the statement about previous sales, however. There, only the seller has reason to know the relative

truth of such statements. Here, the misrepresentation is sufficiently material (to the salability of the vacuum cleaners) to be actionable. The judgment is reversed, with instructions to permit a new trial in the action of deceit.

▶ ANALYSIS

This case points up the general relationship between opinion and misrepresentation or deceit. Note the comparison made by Learned Hand. A political campaign manager or a politician will often make claims that no one really believes (e.g., "I will balance the budget," "I will eradicate poverty"). Such "puffing up" talk is done to show the candidate's intentions; it is not meant to be taken literally. No sensible person would ever rely upon it.

▄▬▄

Quicknotes

DECEIT A false statement made ether knowingly or with reckless disregard as to its truth and which is intended to induce the plaintiff to act in reliance thereon to his detriment.

MISREPRESENTATION A statement or conduct by one party to another that constitutes a false representation of fact.

PUFFING The communication of an opinion not intended as a representation of fact and upon which an action for fraud or misrepresentation cannot be based.

RELIANCE Dependence on a fact that causes a party to act or refrain from acting.

▄▬▄

Sorenson v. Gardner

Home buyer (P) v. Seller (D)

Or. Sup. Ct., 215 Or. 255, 334 P.2d 471 (1959).

NATURE OF CASE: Action for deceit, on appeal.

FACT SUMMARY: Gardner (D) made false representations about the code violation status of a house which Sorenson (P) was buying.

🏛 RULE OF LAW
If a representation as to a matter of law is a representation of fact, the recipient is entitled to rely upon it to the same extent as if it were a representation of any other fact; and, an action for deceit will lie if it proves to be false.

FACTS: Before Sorenson (P) bought his house, Gardner (D) had represented to Sorenson (P) that the house had met all code requirements, with respect to electric wiring, plumbing septic tank, and sewage disposal, and that it was generally well constructed. These representations, which in part induced Sorenson (P) to buy the house, proved to be false. Sorenson (P) sued for deceit. Upon judgment for him, Gardner (D) appeals contending that the representations he made were as to matters of law and/or opinion and are not actionable thereby.

ISSUE: May an action for deceit ever lie where representations involved were related to matters of law?

HOLDING AND DECISION: (Lusk, J.) Yes. If a representation as to a matter of law is a representation of fact, the recipient is entitled to rely upon it to the same extent as if it were a representation of any other fact, and, an action for deceit will lie if it proves to be false. On the other hand, if a representation as to a matter of law is a representation of opinion as to the legal consequences of facts known to or assumed by both the speaker and the recipient, the recipient is entitled to rely upon it only to the same extent as if it were a representation of any other opinion, and, an action for deceit will not lie no matter how false it proves to be. The general rule that misrepresentations of law are not actionable deceit, applies only to the latter case (i.e., misrepresentations about legal consequences). Here, the misrepresentation involved was of the "fact" of meeting code requirements. This "fact" was not the basis of a mere opinion either, since, (by the rule above) it was neither known nor assumed by either of the two parties. The judgment must be affirmed as to these points. [Reversed on other grounds.}

▶ ANALYSIS

This case points up the application of the general fact/opinion dichotomy in "misrepresentation" to expressions of law. It is generally stated that misrepresentations of law are never actionable. This is true only if misrepresentations of law are limited to legal opinions about the law, where the recipient ought to know that the representation is one of opinion. It is not the status as a representation of law that makes such an expression not actionable, but its status as an opinion. Essentially, therefore, representations of law are no different than any other representations, subject merely to the standard fact/opinion dichotomy. Though most courts tend to give lip service to the general statement above, the overwhelming trend of authority is that it is virtually useless.

Quicknotes

DECEIT A false statement made either knowingly or with reckless disregard as to its truth and which is intended to induce the plaintiff to act in reliance thereon to his detriment.

MISREPRESENTATION A statement or conduct by one party to another that constitutes a false representation of fact.

RELIANCE Dependence on a fact that causes a party to act or refrain from acting.

McElrath v. Electric Investment Co.

Hotel lessee (P) v. Hotel owner

Minn. Sup. Ct., 114 Minn. 358, 131 N.W. 380 (1911).

NATURE OF CASE: Appeal of an order overruling a demurrer to a deceit complaint.

FACT SUMMARY: Electric Investment Co. (D) induced McElrath (P) to lease property on assurances that an electric car line would be constructed on it.

🏛 RULE OF LAW
Deceit, to be actionable, requires the misrepresentation of some material "existing" (past or present) fact, not mere prediction of future facts; but, if in making said predictions the speaker intends to create in the mind of the recipient, this impression that the intention to complete that future act is a present fact in the mind of some party, that is actionable as well.

FACTS: Electric Investment (D) leased property to McElrath (P) for a term of years. In order to induce the lease, Electric Investment (D) had represented to McElrath (P) that: (1) the Minneapolis, St. Paul, Rochester and Dubuque Electric Traction Co. would complete and operate an electric railway through the area of said property, (2) which would make said property an important resort area, and (3) that McElrath (P) would surely make $1500 per annum from the resort business. McElrath (P) sued claiming deceit. Electric Investment (D) demurred on the grounds that the representations were mere nonactionable predictions of future facts. Upon an overruling of this demurrer, Electric Investment (D) appeals.

ISSUE: Will an action for deceit lie for misrepresentations of future facts (predictions)?

HOLDING AND DECISION: (Brown, J.) No. Deceit, to be actionable, requires the misrepresentation of some material "existing" (past or present) fact, not mere prediction of future facts; but, if in making said predictions the speaker intends to create in the mind of the recipient, the impression that the intention to complete the future act is a present fact in the mind of some party, that is actionable as well. In such cases, an existing fact (present intention) has been misrepresented. Here, the general rule applies only to the representation about the area becoming an important resort area, such was a mere prediction, and the demurrer must be granted to that part of the complaint. On the other hand, the representations about the construction of a railway are actionable since they may have misrepresented (this is yet to be proven at trial) the existing fact of the Railroad Co.'s intent to build an electric railroad there. Such is a proper subject for deceit. Affirmed.

▶ ANALYSIS

This case points up the material element in deceit (or misrepresentation) of a "material past or present fact." Only such a fact may be the proper subject of a deceit action. The seeming "exception" above is really no exception at all. Predictions may never be a proper subject for deceit. Misrepresentations, implicit or express, of present intents may always be, however. Ordinarily, a prediction as to events occurring in the future is considered mere opinion. No action will lie for such statements, since it is impossible to "warrant" something which does not exist. An intention, however, does "exist." It may be guaranteed or warranted. As such, it is actionable.

Quicknotes

DECEIT A false statement made ether knowingly or with reckless disregard as to its truth and which is intended to induce the plaintiff to act in reliance thereon to his detriment.

DEMURRER The assertion that the opposing party's pleadings are insufficient and that the demurring party should not be made to answer.

MISREPRESENTATION A statement or conduct by one party to another that constitutes a false representation of fact.

Burgdorfer v. Thieleman

Property buyer (P) v. Seller (D)

Or. Sup. Ct., 153 Or. 354, 55 P.2d 1122 (1936).

NATURE OF CASE: Action for deceit, on appeal.

FACT SUMMARY: Thieleman (D) induced Burgdorfer (P) to transfer a lot upon which there was a mortgage to him, partially on the promise to pay off that mortgage.

🏛 RULE OF LAW
Deceit requires a misstatement of an existing fact, but the promise to do something, with the present intent to do the contrary, is as clear a case of misrepresentation or fraud as can be made, and the proof of such fraud will not be precluded by the statute of frauds (even though the promise involved cannot be performed within one year).

FACTS: Thieleman (D) owned "Collins View" (certain property), on which there was a $500 mortgage. He induced Burgdorfer (P) to buy the land from him (for a $2,000 secured note and 2 unsecured notes) partially upon his, Thieleman's (D), promise to pay off that mortgage himself (made orally). Burgdorfer (P) sued for deceit on the ground that Thieleman (D) never intended to carry out that promise. Upon judgment in Burgdorfer's (P) favor, Thieleman (D) appeals on the grounds that the promise was not actionable deceit: (1) as a future fact, and (2) as within the statute of frauds provision that any promise not to be performed within one year (as the mortgage payment evidently could not be) must be reduced to writing to be valid.

ISSUE: Is a promise a "future fact" not actionable as deceit, necessarily?

HOLDING AND DECISION: (Kelly, J.) No. Deceit requires a misstatement of an existing fact, but the promise to do something, with the present intent to do the contrary, is as clear a case of misrepresentation or fraud as can be made, and the proof of such fraud will not be precluded by the statute of frauds (even though the promise involved cannot be performed within one year). The purpose of the statute of frauds is to avoid the use of fraud in proving the existence of an agreement (i.e., must be in writing if not to be performed within one year). The proof here, however, goes to the existence of fraud not the existence of an agreement, and, as such, is not blocked by the statute. As for the misrepresentation involved, the state of a man's mind is as much a fact as the state of his digestion. Here, the misrepresentation of the fact of the intent to pay off the mortgage was no less actionable because that present fact related to a future fact. The fraud was actionable. The judgment must stand.

⏸ ANALYSIS

This case points up the general rule for differentiating between actionable opinion and nonactionable opinion. Where a promise is involved, it is not the failure to perform a future act, but the present act of misrepresentation of intent which is actionable. In such cases, the intent is a fact. A mere prediction, however, carries no present misrepresented mental state. It is not actionable.

Quicknotes

ACTIONABLE OPINION An opinion based on which an action will lie.

DECEIT A false statement made ether knowingly or with reckless disregard as to its truth and which is intended to induce the plaintiff to act in reliance thereon to his detriment.

PROMISE The expression of an intention to act, or to forbear from acting, granting a right to the promisee to expect and enforce its performance.

STATUTE OF FRAUDS A statute stating that certain contracts must be evidenced by a writing signed by the party against whom enforcement is sought, or an agent thereof, in order to be enforceable.

Hinkle v. Rockville Motor Co., Inc.

Car buyer (P) v. Dealership (D)

Md. Ct. App., 262 Md. 502, 278 A.2d 42 (1971).

NATURE OF CASE: Action for damages for misrepresentation of a new car.

FACT SUMMARY: Rockville Motor Co. (D) sold, as a new car, a vehicle which had been previously wrecked.

🏛 **RULE OF LAW**
A defrauded plaintiff should be allowed to claim out-of-pocket expenses. If the defendant is morally culpable, the representations definite, and the present value ascertainable, then plaintiff should be permitted to sue for the benefit of the bargain.

FACTS: Hinkle (P) purchased an allegedly new car from Rockville Motor Co. (D). Hinkle (P) discovered that the car actually had 2,000 miles on its speedometer. Rockville (D) reduced the purchase price to compensate Hinkle (P). Some 4 months later, Hinkle (P) found out that the car had been involved in an accident some months before he purchased it. Hinkle (P) brought suit for breach of warranty and misrepresentation. Hinkle (P) alleged that it would cost $800 to return the car to its warranted condition. At the close of testimony, Rockville (D) moved for a directed verdict since Hinkle (P) had failed to produce evidence as to value of the automobile at the time of sale. Therefore, the jury had no facts upon which to render a verdict for damages. The directed verdict was granted. Hinkle (P) appealed on the basis that he was entitled to out-of-pocket expenses for the misrepresentation and that the $800 repair cost was a sufficient showing of value to sustain a jury verdict.

ISSUE: Can a plaintiff recover for misrepresentation only if the value of the misrepresented chattel is proven?

HOLDING AND DECISION: (Barnes, J.) No. A majority of states allow recovery for the "benefit of the bargain" if sufficiently proved in order to compensate a plaintiff as though the transaction had been carried out as represented. Other states restrict plaintiff to his "out-of-pocket expenses" to recoup his actual losses. Maryland is a middle-of-the-road state. If the fraudulent representation also amounted to a warranty, plaintiff may recover for the loss of the bargain because a fraud accompanied by a broken promise should cost the wrongdoer as much as the latter alone. Where damages under the benefit-of-the-bargain rule are proved with sufficient certainty, that rule will be employed. Here, the $800 figure to repair the automobile was sufficiently explicit to allow a jury to find that this was the amount of damages sustained and that the car was worth $800 less than the purchase price. Judgment reversed.

▶ **ANALYSIS**

This case outlines the problems associated with establishing damages. A plaintiff may recover his actual loss based on the misrepresentation (out-of-pocket damages) or, if warranted to be of a certain value, then his benefit of the bargain, i.e., the difference between the value of the property and that as represented. In addition, the plaintiff may plead and prove consequential damages. These are losses which are based upon the misrepresentation. Therefore, in *Vezina v. Souliere*, 103 Vt. 190 (1931), the plaintiff was allowed to recover when a supposedly gentle horse kicked him.

▬▭▬

Quicknotes

BENEFIT OF THE BARGAIN Calculation of assessing damages in actions for breach of contract measured as the difference between the actual value and the purported value of the goods being bought.

CONSEQUENTIAL DAMAGES Monetary compensation that may be recovered in order to compensate for injuries or losses sustained as a result of damages that are not the direct or foreseeable result of the act of a party, but that nevertheless are the consequence of such act and which must be specifically pled and demonstrated.

MISREPRESENTATION A statement or conduct by one party to another that constitutes a false representation of fact.

▬▭▬

Quick Reference Rules of Law

Ratcliffe v. Evans

Business owner (P) v. Publisher (D)

2 Q.B. 524 (1892).

NATURE OF CASE: Action for injury based on a published falsehood.

FACT SUMMARY: Evans (D) published injurious and false words regarding Ratcliffe's (P) business.

RULE OF LAW
An action for malicious interference with business, based on a published falsehood, will lie even though special damages are not proven.

FACTS: Ratcliffe (P) had carried on a business with his father. Upon his father's death, he continued to operate the business. However, Evans (D), publisher of the County Herald, falsely printed an article stating that the business had ceased existence. Ratcliffe (P) brought suit for damages based on the false and malicious publication and received a judgment. Evans (D) appealed, contending that a judgment could not lie since Ratcliffe (P) was unable to prove special damages.

ISSUE: May an action for malicious interference with business, based on a published falsehood, lie even though special damages are not proven?

HOLDING AND DECISION: (Bowen, J.) Yes. By the very nature of the tort, the plaintiff will often only be able to show general damages. For this reason, an allegation of general damages is sufficient to support the analogous tort of libel. The same should be true where, as here, a false publication is maliciously intended to cause, and actually does cause, damage to the plaintiff. In such a case, proof of general damages will suffice to support the action. Affirmed.

ANALYSIS

The principle of "injurious falsehood," established in the *Ratcliffe* case, is now deemed to include a wide variety of more specific torts arising out of false and malicious statements resulting in a pecuniary loss to another. Some of these torts may still be referred to by other titles, such as trade libel or slander of title.

Quicknotes

INJURIOUS FALSEHOOD A defamatory statement that inflicts actual damage.

LIBEL A false or malicious publication that subjects a person to scorn, hatred or ridicule, or that injures him in relation to his occupation or business.

SLANDER Defamatory statement communicated orally.

SPECIAL DAMAGES Damages caused by a specific act that are not the usual consequence of that act and which must be specifically pled and proven.

Horning v. Hardy

Putative property owners (P) v. Sellers (D)

Md. Ct. Spec. App., 36 Md. App. 419, 373 A.2d 1273 (1977).

NATURE OF CASE: Appeal from nonsuit to injurious falsehood counterclaim.

FACT SUMMARY: The trial court found that the Hardys (P) were privileged to make their damaging assertion regarding their belief that they owned property which the Hornings (D) sought to sell to a third party, thereby breaking off the deal.

🏛 RULE OF LAW
The conditional privilege to make a damaging statement when necessary to protect one's own economic interests may only be overcome by a showing of constitutional or common-law malice.

FACTS: The Hardys (P) claimed they were the true owners of property which the Hornings (D) were in the process of selling. As such, they filed suit for trespass and ejectment and informed the potential purchasers of the property of their claim. The Hornings (D), in turn, filed a counterclaim based on slander of title and interference with a contract (the purchasers backed out of the deal after being apprised of the Hardys' [P] claim to the property). The trial court found for the Hornings (D) on the original suit, holding that the Hardys (P) had produced no evidence demonstrating their ownership of the property. It additionally found for the Hardys (P) on the counterclaim, holding that they were privileged to protect their asserted interest by informing the prospective purchasers of their claim. The Hornings (D) appealed the adverse judgment on the counterclaim.

ISSUE: In the absence of malice, is a party privileged to make damaging statements, if necessary to protect its economic or property interests?

HOLDING AND DECISION: (Liss, J.) Yes. The tort complained of by the Hornings (D) has been combined and reclassified as the tort of injurious falsehood. It is similar to the tort of defamation, although it differs in that actual damages must be proved in all cases for an action to lie. However, other rules derived from the law of defamation also apply to the tort of injurious falsehood. As such, a true statement, though injurious, is privileged. Furthermore, a plaintiff must show that the false, injurious statement, was made negligently by the defendant. Finally, a plaintiff in such an action has a conditional privilege to make a statement, even though it is false and injurious, if he does so to protect an economic interest, such as property ownership, unless he does so with malice, either constitutional (as defined by the *New York Times*

case) or common law (spite or ill will). Thus, in the instant case, the Hardys (P) were privileged to assert their ownership claim, although false and injurious to the Hornings' (D) claim, unless it is shown they did so maliciously. The Hornings (D) have not made such a showing, and on the basis of the record, they cannot. Mere failure to properly investigate, as is alleged, does not reach the level of such reckless disregard of the truth as to constitute malice. Affirmed.

▮ ANALYSIS

The law of injurious falsehood in Maryland, applied in the *Horning* case, was defined by Judge Barnes, in the case of *Beane v. McMullen*, 291 A.2d 37 (Md. 1972), as follows: "Injurious falsehood or disparagement . . . consist[s] of the publication of matter derogatory to the plaintiff's title to his property, or its quality, or to his business in general . . . of a kind calculated to prevent others from dealing with him, or otherwise to interfere with his relations with others."

Quicknotes

DEFAMATION An intentional false publication, communicated publicly in either oral or written form, subjecting a person to scorn, hatred or ridicule, or injuring him or her in relation to his or her occupation or business.

DEFENSE OF CONDITION PRIVILEGE A defense to an action for libel or slander asserting immunity from liability for libelous or slanderous statements communicated in the execution of a political, judicial, social or personal obligation, unless it is demonstrated that the statement was made with actual malice and knowledge of its falsity.

INJURIOUS FALSEHOOD A defamatory statement that inflicts actual damage.

NONSUIT Judgment against a party who fails to make out a case.

SLANDER OF TITLE A defamatory statement made with the intent to disparage a party's title to real or personal property.

Testing Systems, Inc. v. Magnaflux Corp.

Equipment manufacturer (P) v. Competitor (D)

251 F. Supp. 286 (E.D. Pa. 1966).

NATURE OF CASE: Action to recover damages for disparagement of property.

FACT SUMMARY: Testing Systems, Inc. (P) and Magnaflux Corp. (D) were competing manufacturers of the same product. Testing Systems, Inc. (P) alleged that Magnaflux Corp. (D) falsely informed Testing Systems, Inc.'s (P) customers that the U.S. Government had found that Testing Systems, Inc.'s (P) products were 40 percent as effective as Magnaflux Corp's (D).

🏛 RULE OF LAW
While statements which make an unfavorable comparison of products are privileged, statements which contain specific assertions of unfavorable facts are not privileged and are actionable.

FACTS: Testing Systems, Inc. (P) and Magnaflux Corp. (D) were competing manufacturers of industrial and commercial testing equipment, devices, and systems. Testing Systems, Inc. (P) alleged that Magnaflux Corp. (D) distributed a false report to Testing Systems, Inc.'s (P) current and prospective customers. The report stated that the U.S. Government had tested Testing Systems, Inc.'s (P) product and found it to be 40 percent as effective as Magnaflux Corp.'s (D). It was also alleged that Magnaflux Corp.'s (D) agent said that Testing Systems, Inc.'s (P) "stuff is no good" and that "the government is throwing them out." Magnaflux Corp. (D) contends that it did no more than make an unfavorable comparison of Testing Systems, Inc.'s (P) product with its own.

ISSUE: Is a statement which contains specific assertions of unfavorable facts about a competitor's product protected by the privilege to make statements of unfavorable comparisons of products?

HOLDING AND DECISION: (Lord, J.) No. A statement which makes an unfavorable comparison of products, or which "puffs" or exaggerates the quality of one's own product is not usually actionable. However, there is a difference between saying that one's product is better than another's and asserting specific unfavorable facts. The latter, being an assertion of fact, implies that the party making the statement is fortified with the substantive facts necessary to make it. In this case, Magnaflux Corp. (D) admitted the truth of the allegations. Statements of unfavorable comparison merely express an opinion, the truth or falsity of which is difficult or impossible to ascertain. Magnaflux Corp.'s (D) statement is an assertion of a specific fact, and hence is not privileged. Further,

Magnaflux Corp. (D) gave added authenticity to its statements by invoking the authority of the U.S. Government. Such statements and its statement that the government was throwing out Testing Systems, Inc.'s (P) products are not mere comparison and are not protected.

▶ ANALYSIS

As this case demonstrates, general statements of comparison stating that the defendant's products are better than the plaintiff's are privileged so long as they contain no specific assertions of unfavorable facts about the plaintiff's product. The basis for this rule is that the practice of sellers to "puff," boast, or exaggerate as to the excellence of their product over rival products is so well known that purchasers attach little or no importance to such assertions, and so they usually can do no serious harm.

Quicknotes

DISPARAGEMENT OF PROPERTY An untrue statement regarding certain property which denigrates such property and for which an action may lie.

PUFFING The communication of an opinion not intended as a representation of fact and upon which an action for fraud or misrepresentation cannot be based.

Lumley v. Gye

Theatre manager (P) v. Interferer (D)

Queen's Bench, 2 El. & Bl. 216, 118 Eng. Rep. 749 (1853).

NATURE OF CASE: Action to recover damages for interference with a contract.

FACT SUMMARY: Wagner had a contract with Lumley (P) to sing exclusively at his theater for a period of time. Gye (D) knew the conditions of the contract. For the purpose of injuring Lumley (P), Gye (D) enticed Wagner to refuse to perform.

RULE OF LAW
A person who procures a breach of another's contract is liable for damages due to his interference.

FACTS: Lumley (P) and Wagner had contracted that she would perform in Lumley's (P) theater for a period of time during which she would not perform elsewhere without Lumley's (P) consent. Gye (D) knew the conditions of this contract. During the time the agreement was in force, and with the intention of injuring Lumley (P), Gye (D) enticed and procured Wagner to refuse to perform. Due to this enticement and procurement, Wagner did wrongly refuse to perform in Lumley's (P) theater.

ISSUE: Is one who procures the breach of a contract liable for damages caused by his interference?

HOLDING AND DECISION: (Erle, J.) Yes. It is clear that an action will lie by a master against a person who procures that a servant should unlawfully leave his service. The master's right of action arises from the wrongful act of putting an end to the relation of employer and employed by the procuring of the servant to break his contract. The same principle is applicable in this case, since the cause of action arises from the procurement of the violation of a right. When this principle is applied to a violation of a right arising out of an employment contract, the nature of the service contracted for is immaterial. In this case, Gye's (D) enticement and procurement of Wagner which caused her to breach her contract with Lumley (P) was a violation of Lumley's (P) right for which Gye (D) should be held liable. It is immaterial that Gye (D) did not act unlawfully in procuring the breach of the contract. His malicious interference with Lumley's (P) rights makes him liable.

▶ ANALYSIS

Lumley v. Gye is the leading modern case allowing recovery in tort for the interference with a contract. It and subsequent cases emphasized that the existence of the contract

is something of a property interest in the plaintiff. Interference with such an interest gives rise to a cause of action. Although American courts were reluctant to accept the doctrine in the beginning, now decisions which rejected it have been for the most part overruled. The tort is recognized everywhere except in Louisiana which continues to hold that there is no action for inducing the breach of a contract unless means unlawful in themselves are used. Elsewhere, the tort is recognized as to any contract, regardless of its character.

Quicknotes

INTERFERENCE WITH CONTRACTUAL RELATIONS An intentional tort whereby a defendant intentionally elicits the breach of a valid contract resulting in damages.

Bacon v. St. Paul Union Stockyards Co.

Livestock dealer (P) v. Stockyard owner (D)

Minn. Sup. Ct., 161 Minn. 522, 201 N.W. 326 (1924).

NATURE OF CASE: Appeal from demurrer to action for damages for interference with business relations.

FACT SUMMARY: Bacon (P) contended that St. Paul (D) had wrongfully barred him from the stockyards, and had deprived him of his means of livelihood.

🏛 RULE OF LAW
The wrongful interference with the contract relations of others causing a breach is a tort.

FACTS: Bacon (P) contended that he was employed by the Drover Livestock Commission Co., engaged in buying, selling, and dealing in livestock in St. Paul's (D) stockyards, but that St. Paul (D) had wrongfully, unlawfully, and willfully excluded him from its stockyards, and had further barred and prevented him from carrying on his occupation, and had further forbade any person, firm, or corporation from employing him in or near the stockyards. After St. Paul's (D) demurrer to the complaint was sustained by the trial court, Bacon (P) appealed.

ISSUE: Does the wrongful interference with the contract relations of others causing a breach constitute a tort?

HOLDING AND DECISION: (Per curiam) Yes. The wrongful interference with the contract relations of others causing a breach is a tort. Here, the complaint states a cause of action for wrongful interference with Bacon's (P) employment. It appears that Bacon (P) had steady employment, and that St. Paul (D) wrongfully, willfully, and unlawfully prevented him from continuing in that employment. Such conduct is in violation of Bacon's (P) rights. Reversed.

▶ ANALYSIS

As this case indicates, the action of barring an employee from his place of employment may constitute an actionable tort. Related acts which may result in tort liability include restricting the sales of a person's employee, fraudulently inducing a person to breach a contract, and depriving a person of necessary labor.

■━■

Quicknotes

DEMURRER The assertion that the opposing party's pleadings are insufficient and that the demurring party should not be made to answer.

INTERFERENCE WITH CONTRACTUAL RELATIONS An intentional tort whereby a defendant intentionally elicits the breach of a valid contract resulting in damages.

■━■

Della Penna v. Toyota Motor Sales, U.S.A., Inc.

Automobile wholesaler (P) v. Automobile manufacturer (D)

Sup. Ct. of Cal., 11 Cal. 4th 376, 902 P.2d 740 (1995).

NATURE OF CASE: Appeal from reversal of verdict for defendant in claim for interference with prospective economic advantage.

FACT SUMMARY: Della Penna (P), an auto wholesaler who exported cars to Japan for resale, brought action against Toyota (D) when it took steps to prevent him from conducting his business.

RULE OF LAW

A plaintiff seeking to recover for interference with prospective economic advantage has the burden of proving that the defendant's interference was wrongful by some measure beyond the fact of the interference itself.

FACTS: Della Penna (P) had a lucrative business in which he bought Lexus cars from U.S. retailers at near retail prices and then exported them to Japan for resale. Toyota (D), the maker of Lexus, wanted to prevent imported U.S. Lexus cars from being re-exported to Japan. To try to curb this practice, Toyota (D) compiled a list of offending auto brokers and warned its dealers that those who did business with them faced possible sanctions. As a result, Della Penna's (P) supply of cars dried up. Della Penna (P) brought suit for interference of prospective economic advantage. The judge gave the jury instructions that Della Penna (P) had the burden of showing that Toyota's (D) interference was wrongful "by some measure beyond the fact of the interference itself." The jury returned a verdict for Toyota (D), but the court of appeals reversed, finding that the judge erred in placing the burden on Della Penna (P). The Supreme Court of California granted review.

ISSUE: Is it unfair to charge a plaintiff seeking to recover for interference with prospective economic advantage with the burden of proving that the defendant's interference was wrongful by "some measure beyond the fact of the interference itself?"

HOLDING AND DECISION: (Arabian, J.) No. A plaintiff seeking to recover for interference with prospective economic advantage has the burden of proving that the defendant's interference was wrongful by some measure beyond the fact of the interference itself. There is an important distinction between the disruption of an existing contract and the interference with a prospective contract or economic relationship. Courts should firmly distinguish these differences and acknowledge that relationships short of a contract have

inherent risks. Della Penna's (P) business, although lucrative, was inherently risky because it was entirely speculative. Della Penna (P) did not have contracts with the dealers he bought from. Therefore, the instruction given by the trial court, that Della Penna (P) had the burden of proving that Toyota's (D) actions were wrongful beyond the fact of the interference, was proper under the circumstances. The judgment of the court of appeals should be reversed, and the trial court's judgment for Toyota (D) should be reinstated. Reversed.

CONCURRENCE: (Mosk, J.) The majority's reversal of the court of appeals was correct although the rationale was not. The tort of interference with prospective economic advantage can be proven by showing other tortious conduct such as defamation, fraud, or deceit. The majority was wrong in accepting that the instruction given to the jury by the trial court was proper. The formulation of an instruction should not include any reference to motive. However, this error was not prejudicial.

ANALYSIS

Courts faced with cases of interference with prospective economic advantage have developed numerous formulas and tests for determining liability. The Restatement (Second) of Torts § 766B identified a seven-factor balancing test which the California court declined to apply. These factors include: (1) the nature of the actor's conduct; (2) the actor's motive; (3) the interests of the other with which the actor's conduct interferes; (4) the interests sought to be advanced by the actor; (5) the social interests in protecting the freedom of action of the actor and the contractual interests of the other; (6) the proximity or remoteness of the actor's conduct to the interference; and (7) the relations between the parties.

Quicknotes

INTERFERENCE WITH PROSPECTIVE ADVANTAGE An intentional tort whereby a defendant intentionally interferes with a valid business expectancy, resulting in the termination of the expectancy and damages.

Adler, Barish, Daniels, Levin and Creskoff v. Epstein

Law firm (P) v. Former associate (D)

Pa. Sup. Ct., 482 Pa. 416, 393 A.2d 1175 (1978).

NATURE OF CASE: Appeal from dismissal of action for interference with business relations.

FACT SUMMARY: Adler (P), a law firm, contended that Epstein (D), a former associate of the firm, had tortiously interfered with its business relations by soliciting its clients to change firms.

🏛 RULE OF LAW
One has the right to pursue his business relations free from interference on the part of third parties, unless such interference is justified or constitutes the exercise of an absolute right.

FACTS: Adler (P), a law firm, brought suit against Epstein (D), a former associate of the firm, contending that Epstein (D) had tortiously interfered with the firm's business relations by contacting Adler's (P) clients, advising them that he was leaving the firm, and telling them that they could choose to be represented by him, Adler (P), or any other firm or attorney. Epstein (D) mailed clients form letters which could be used to discharge Adler (P) as counsel, name Epstein (D) as the client's new counsel and create a contingent fee agreement. After the superior court dissolved an injunction granted by the court of common pleas, and dismissed the action, Adler (P) brought this appeal.

ISSUE: Does one have the right to pursue his business relations free from interference on the part of third parties, unless such interference is justified or constitutes the exercise of an absolute right?

HOLDING AND DECISION: (Roberts, J.) Yes. One has the right to pursue his business relations free from interference on the part of third parties, unless such interference is justified or constitutes the exercise of an absolute right. One who intentionally and improperly interferes with the performance of a contract, except a contract to marry, between another and a third person by inducing or otherwise causing the third person not to perform the contract, is subject to liability to the other for the pecuniary loss resulting to the other from the third person's failure to perform the contract. Here, there is no doubt that Epstein (D) intentionally sought to interfere with the performance of the contractual relations between Adler (P) and its clients. While still at Adler (P), Epstein's (D) behavior, particularly the use of expected fees from Adler's (P) clients' cases, indicates Epstein's (D) desire to gain a segment of the firm's business. Epstein (D) was actively attempting to induce the clients to change law firms in the middle of their active cases. Reversed.

▶ ANALYSIS

The court additionally found in this case that Epstein (D) and other defendants who had taken similar actions had violated the Code of Professional Responsibility, DR 2-103 (A). That rule provides that: "A lawyer shall not recommend employment, as a private practitioner, of himself, his partner, or associate to a nonlawyer who has not sought his advice regarding employment of a lawyer."

Quicknotes

TORTIOUS INTERFERENCE WITH BUSINESS RELATIONS An intentional tort whereby a defendant intentionally elicits the breach of a valid contract resulting in damages.

Brimelow v. Casson

Troupe owners (P) v. Actors' union (D)

Chancery Division, 1923, 1 Ch. 302 (1924).

NATURE OF CASE: Action to recover damages for interference with a contract.

FACT SUMMARY: Arnold, the manager of a theater group, underpaid the women in the group, causing them to supplement their income by prostitution. The actors' association (D) persuaded theater owners to cancel their contracts with Arnold unless he paid higher wages.

🏛 RULE OF LAW
A reasonable and disinterested motive for the protection of other individuals or the public will justify intentional interference with contract.

FACTS: Arnold was the manager of a theater group. He underpaid the women in the group, and they supplemented their incomes by prostitution. The court was quite appalled and upset by the fact that one of the women was living in immorality with a dwarf. An officer of the actors' association (D), Lugg, intervened on behalf of the women and persuaded theater owners to cancel their contracts with Arnold unless higher wages were paid. Brimelow (P), the owner of the group, brought this action against the representative of the union, Casson (D), to enjoin them from inducing such breaches of contract.

ISSUE: Is a person justified in inducing the breach of a contract when he does so out of a legitimate concern for another or for the public?

HOLDING AND DECISION: (Russell, J.) Yes. Prima facie interference with a person's contractual rights is actionable. However, such interference may be justified. In this case, the actors' association (D) had found by experience that paying women less than a living wage causes them to supplement their income by prostitution. Such activity ruins their morals and brings discredit on the theater business. The actors' association (D) found that Brimelow (P) was paying far less than a living wage. In the interest of the theatrical profession and its members, the actors' association (D) wanted to stop this underpayment. The only way open to them to do that was to persuade theater owners to cancel or not enter into contracts with Brimelow (P). In light of the circumstances and the actor's association's (D) motives, the inducement to breach contracts was justified. Brimelow's (P) action for such interference is dismissed.

▶ ANALYSIS

This case demonstrates the importance of a defendant's motive in an action for interference with contract. As demonstrated here, an impersonal and reasonable motive may justify a defendant's interference. This is especially true if the defendant is seeking to protect one toward whom he stands in a relation of responsibility such as a parent/child, employer/employee, agent/principal or school official/student. The justification also exists, as shown here, where the motive is to protect the public health morals.

■=■

Quicknotes

A FORTIORI A method of reasoning whereby if one fact is true then a lesser fact, which is necessarily encompassed by the greater fact, must also be true.

INTERFERENCE WITH CONTRACTUAL RELATIONS An intentional tort whereby a defendant intentionally elicits the breach of a valid contract resulting in damages.

MOTIVE Reason or other impetus inciting one to action.

■=■

Harmon v. Harmon

Disappointed son (P) v. Brother (D)

The Sup. Jud. Ct., 404 A.2d 1020 (1979).

NATURE OF CASE: Appeal from dismissal of action for interference with business relations.

FACT SUMMARY: Richard Harmon (P) contended that his brother and sister-in-law (D) had conspired to have him disinherited.

🏛 RULE OF LAW
The expectancy of future contractual relations is protected from wrongful interference.

FACTS: In his complaint, Richard Harmon (P) asserted that his brother and sister-in-law, Harold C. Harmon (D) and Virginia S. Harmon (D), had by fraud and undue influence induced Richard's (P) mother, Josephine F. Harmon, while she was 87 years old and in ill health, to transfer her property to them, effectively disinheriting Richard (P). By her 1976 will and by her more recent statements, Josephine had indicated her intention that Richard (P) should receive at least a one-half interest in the property. The mother was still living when the action was brought. The superior court dismissed the complaint on the grounds that it failed to state a cause of action, and that Richard (P) lacked standing to bring suit. Richard (P) appealed.

ISSUE: Is the expectancy of future contractual relations protected from wrongful interference?

HOLDING AND DECISION: (Nichols, J.) Yes. The expectancy of future contractual relations is protected from wrongful interference. The issue in such cases is not whether the interest is vested or expectant; rather, the issue is whether it is legally protected so that intentional and wrongful interference causing damage to the plaintiff gives rise to liability in tort. Where a person can prove that, but for the tortious interference of another, he would in all likelihood have received a gift or a specific profit from a transaction, he is entitled to recover for the damages thereby done to him. Reversed and remanded.

▶ ANALYSIS

In discussing actions based upon the loss of an expectancy interest, Dean Prosser states: "There is no essential reason for refusing to protect such noncommercial expectancies, at least where there is a strong probability that they would have been realized . . . The problem appears in reality to be one of satisfactory proof that the loss has been suffered, instead of the existence of a ground to tort liability." W. Prosser, Law of Torts 950-951 (4th ed. 1971).

Quicknotes

JUSTICIABLE INTEREST An actual controversy that is capable of resolution by the court.

LEGATEE A person who is granted a legacy or bequest pursuant to a will.

STANDING Whether a party possesses the right to commence suit against another party by having a personal stake in the resolution of the controversy.

Neibuhr v. Gage

Shareholder (P) v. Corporate officer (D)

Minn. Sup. Ct., 99 Minn. 149, 108 N.W. 884 (1906).

NATURE OF CASE: Appeal from order for new trial.

FACT SUMMARY: Neibuhr (P) contended that he should be allowed to bring suit in tort for Gage's (D) actions in compelling him to transfer stock.

RULE OF LAW
A party who his been injured by duress is entitled to the same remedies which are available in cases of deceit.

FACTS: Neibuhr (P) possessed 91 shares of stock in Gage, Hayden & Co, with a face value of $9,100. Gage (D) accused Neibuhr (P) of grand larceny and threatened to have him convicted unless he transferred the shares to Gage (D). Neibuhr (P) contended that he was innocent, but that Gage (D) had led him to believe that Gage (D) would produce perjured testimony against him in support of the accusation. Under threat of immediate arrest and imprisonment and without opportunity for consultation, Neibuhr (P) transferred the shares. He then brought this action to recover damages which he suffered by reason of being required to transfer those shares under duress. After the trial judge granted a motion for new trial, both parties appealed.

ISSUE: Is a party who has been injured by duress entitled to the same remedies which are available in cases of deceit?

HOLDING AND DECISION: (Elliot, J.) Yes. A party who has been injured by duress is entitled to the same remedies which are available in cases of deceit. As commonly understood, fraud is a wrong accomplished by deception, but duress is a species of fraud in which compulsion in some form takes the place of deception in accomplishing the injury. In both cases, the wrongdoer accomplishes the same wrong and does it with the same bad intent. Reversed; judgment ordered for Neibuhr (P).

ANALYSIS

The remedy of restitution is usually available to victims of conduct which could be labeled duress, fraud, or deception. Restitution will allow the victim to recover any unjust enrichment obtained by the party exercising the duress over the victim. It will also invalidate certain otherwise available defenses, such as consent.

Freeman & Mills, Inc. v. Belcher Oil Company

Accounting firm (P) v. Client (D)

Cal. Sup. Ct., 11 Cal. 4th 85, 900 P.2d 669 (1995).

NATURE OF CASE: Grant of review.

FACT SUMMARY: Freeman (P) sued Belcher (D) for money owed pursuant to Freeman's (P) providing of accounting services to Belcher (D). Pursuant to litigation, he asserted breach of contract, bad faith denial of contract, and quantum meruit bases for recovery.

RULE OF LAW
There is no tort cause of action for bad faith denial of a contract.

FACTS: Belcher (D) retained the Morgan firm to defend it in a Florida lawsuit. Pursuant to a letter of understanding, Belcher (D) was obligated to pay for costs, including accountant fees. Morgan hired Freeman (P) to provide financial analysis and litigation support for Belcher (D) in the suit. Morgan was subsequently discharged and asked for a summary of the work performed by Freeman (P). Freeman (P) was also asked to terminate its work for Belcher (D). Freeman's (P) final statement was for fees of $70,042.50, plus $7,495.63 for costs. Freeman (P) billed Belcher (D) who refused payment. Freeman (P) filed suit against Belcher (D) alleging breach of contract, bad faith denial of contract, and quantum meruit. The jury concluded that Belcher (D) was in breach of contract and denied the existence of the contract. Belcher (D) appealed from the court's corrected judgment. The court of appeals found that no special relationship existed between the parties to justify a tort theory of recovery for bad faith denial of the contract. The court remanded for a retrial limited to the issue of damages under the breach of contract cause of action. This court granted review to resolve confusion regarding its holding in *Seaman's*, 36 Cal. 3d 752, 686 P.2d 1158 (1984), recognizing a tort cause of action for bad faith denial of a contract.

ISSUE: Is there a tort cause of action for bad faith denial of a contract?

HOLDING AND DECISION: (Lucas, C.J.) No. There is no tort cause of action for bad faith denial of a contract. In Seaman's, this court established the tort of bad faith denial of contract. Subsequent decisions indicated a reluctance to allow tort recovery for noninsurance contract breaches. The Seaman's decision left a number of questions unresolved and resulted in inconsistent decisions. Many court of appeals decisions recognized compelling policy reasons to preclude tort remedies for breaches of contract outside the insurance context. In Harris, the court set forth the following reasons for denying tort recovery in breach of contract cases: (1) the different objectives of tort and contract law; (2) the importance of predictability and stability in contractual dealings; (3) the danger of tort liability (including punitive damages) for every breach of contract; and (4) deference to legislation in making decisions regarding the appropriate remedies. Based on these reasons, Seaman's is overruled. Affirmed.

ANALYSIS

There is no tort liability on a party for interference with its own contract. Rather, there must be an independent tort upon which to base liability.

■═■

Quicknotes

BAD FAITH Conduct that is intentionally misleading or deceptive.

BREACH OF CONTRACT Unlawful failure by a party to perform its obligations pursuant to contract.

CAUSE OF ACTION A fact or set of facts the occurrence of which entitles a party to seek judicial relief.

LIABILITY Any obligation or responsibility.

QUANTUM MERUIT Equitable doctrine allowing recovery for labor and materials provided by one party, even though no contract was entered into, in order to avoid unjust enrichment by the benefited party.

■═■

Nash v. Baker

Wronged wife (P) v. The other woman (D)

Okla. Ct. App., 522 P.2d 1335 (1974).

NATURE OF CASE: Action by wife and minor children for alienation of affection.

FACT SUMMARY: The court dismissed the action of Mrs. Nash's (P) minor children against the woman (D) who enticed their father from the marriage.

🏛 RULE OF LAW
Children do not have a cause of action for any losses sustained through the efforts of a third party to break up the marriage.

FACTS: Mr. Nash had an affair with Baker (D). Mr. Nash left his family for Baker (D) and Mrs. Nash (P) sued for alienation of affection, loss of consortium, adultery, etc. on her own behalf and for her minor children. The children's action was dismissed and a judgment was rendered against Mrs. Nash (P) for her own cause of action. She appealed.

ISSUE: Do minor children have any cause of action for their father's adultery and the breakup of the marriage?

HOLDING AND DECISION: (Romang, J.) No. Neither the Constitution nor statute gives any right to children in this area. They have no cause of action for alienation of affection, loss of future income, adultery, loss of consortium, etc. Unless specifically authorized by statute, they may not recover. The court correctly dismissed their action. Judgment affirmed.

▶ ANALYSIS

Nash has several interesting facets. First, the law may not provide a remedy for every wrong. It must be granted by the legislature (statutory), the common law (previous judicial decisions which have not been abrogated by statute), or by the creation of new judicial causes of action. Secondly, the case illustrates an attempt to extend the coverage of existing law to cover claims by the children. In most such situations, courts are hesitant to enter into a quasilegislative area and prefer to defer to a decision by the legislature if the law is to be changed.

■=■

Quicknotes

ALIENATION OF AFFECTIONS A cause of action arising from the willful and malicious interference with a marital relationship.

LOSS OF CONSORTIUM An action brought based on willful interference with the marital relationship.

■=■

Torts in the Age of Statutes

Quick Reference Rules of Law

Burnette v. Wahl

Children (P) v. Their mothers (D)

Or. Sup. Ct., 284 Or. 705, 588 P.2d 1105 (1978).

NATURE OF CASE: Appeal from dismissal of action for damages for breach of parental duties.

FACT SUMMARY: Five minor children (P) sought damages from their mothers (D) for emotional and psychological injury caused by abandonment and failure to perform parental duties.

 RULE OF LAW
No action lies in tort for breach of parental duties.

FACTS: Burnette (P), as guardian, brought suit on behalf of five minor children, aged two to eight, against their mothers (D) for emotional and psychological injury caused by the failure of the mothers (D) to perform their parental duties towards the children. Among the allegations in the action were claims for violation of an Oregon criminal statute for failure to maintain them, abandonment, and neglect. After the trial court entered orders of dismissal after sustaining demurrers to the complaint, Burnette (P) appealed.

ISSUE: Does an action lie in tort for breach of parental duties?

HOLDING AND DECISION: (Holman, J.) No. No action lies in tort for breach of parental duties. There is a strong state policy, as evidenced by the state criminal statute, of requiring the kind of parental nurturing, support, and physical care of children which the mothers (D) here are alleged to have denied their children. However, it does not follow that it would be wise or judicious to vindicate that policy by a tort action for damages by children against their mothers. If there is ever a field in which juries and general trial courts are ill equipped to do social engineering, it is in the realm of the emotional relationship between mother and child. Affirmed.

CONCURRENCE: (Tongue, J.) The doctrine of intrafamily tort immunity should not be abandoned with respect to intrafamily torts resulting in mental and emotional injuries.

CONCURRENCE AND DISSENT: (Lent, J.) In view of the costs, both tangible and intangible, to society for caring for these dependent children who have well been termed the "orphans of the living," and the character of the mothers' conduct, the mothers should shoulder as much of the financial burden as their resources permit.

DISSENT: (Linde, J.) It is incongruous to hold that the legislature provided for a felony prosecution of parents who egregiously violate a duty toward their children, but that it meant to exclude civil actions on behalf of the maliciously abandoned children for fear of impairing the family unit.

▶ ANALYSIS

The majority opinion in this case was grounded upon the state legislature's actions in creating remedies for the type of conduct involved in this case, and the reluctance of the court to permit judicial interference with the family unit. As the court noted, the legislature had never established a cause of action for a parent's refusal to provide parental services.

Quicknotes

ALIENATION OF AFFECTIONS A cause of action arising from the willful and malicious interference with a marital relationship.

INTRAFAMILY TORT IMMUNITY The immunity of family members from tort liability in actions brought by another member of the family.

OREGON CHILD PROTECTION LAWS The Oregon legislature enacted an array of laws for the purpose of protecting or vindicating children's rights.

Nearing v. Weaver

Spousal abuse victim (P) v. Police officers (D)

Or. Sup. Ct., 295 Or. 702, 670 P.2d 137 (1983).

NATURE OF CASE: Suit to recover damages for physical and emotional injuries.

FACT SUMMARY: Nearing (P) brought suit against St. Helen's police officers (D) for injuries allegedly sustained as a result of their failure to arrest her husband for violation of a restraining order.

🏛 **RULE OF LAW**
A police officer who knowingly fails to enforce a judicial order may be held liable for resulting psychological and physical harm to the intended beneficiaries of the order, over the defenses of official discretion and official immunity.

FACTS: Henrietta (P) separated from her husband. Several months later, the husband entered her home without her permission and struck her. Henrietta (P) reported the incident to police officer Weaver (D) and her husband was arrested and charged with assault. The following day a court issued an order restraining the husband from bothering Henrietta (P) or her children (P) and from entering their home. The husband continued to enter the home. Henrietta (P) reported the incidents to Weaver (D) and asked him to arrest her husband. He declined on the basis that he had not seen the husband on the premises. The husband repeatedly continued to enter the home and to assault Henrietta's (P) friend. The police department continued to be unresponsive to Henrietta's (P) reports. She brought suit alleging that she suffered severe emotion distress and physical injuries as a proximate result of the police officers' (D) failure to arrest her husband and that her children (P) suffered acute emotional distress and psychological impairment. The officers (D) denied the allegations and pleaded the affirmative defenses of immunity and discretion. Henrietta (P) appealed and moved to strike the affirmative defenses and assigned denial of the motion as error.

ISSUE: May a police officer who knowingly fails to enforce a judicial order be held liable for resulting psychological and physical harm to the intended beneficiaries of the order, over the defenses of official discretion and official immunity?

HOLDING AND DECISION: (Linde, J.) Yes. A police officer who knowingly fails to enforce a judicial order may be held liable for resulting psychological and physical harm to the intended beneficiaries of the order, over the defenses of official discretion and official immunity. Weaver (D) argued that Oregon does not allow recovery of damages for negligent infliction of emotional distress. The plaintiffs responded that the law does allow recovery of damages for psychic or emotional harm when the defendant's conduct infringes a legal right independent of an ordinary negligence claim. The plaintiff's argument is correct. The issue then is whether the plaintiffs asserted the infringement of a legal right independent of a negligence action, which they did. The duty the officers (D) are alleged to have neglected is not the ordinary common law duty of care but a specific duty imposed by statute to enforce court orders. The act clearly established a duty on the part of the officers (D) towards the plaintiffs and mandates that the officers (D) arrest and take into custody without a warrant persons whom the officer has probable cause to believe have violated a restraining order that has been served and filed by the court. The act was passed specifically in response to the failure of police officers to remove persons involved in cases of domestic violence, such as here, to allow the victim to escape immediate danger. The officers (D) claimed that a determination of probable cause is a discretionary function immune from liability. Discretion, however, exists only where responsibility has been delegated to the officer. Here the act negates any discretionary function on the part of the officer by mandating enforcement of the restraining order. The officers' (D) claim of immunity also fails since it provides for a shield against liability for a good faith arrest, not for the failure to do so. Reversed and remanded.

CONCURRENCE: (Linde, J.) The court should reject the creation of a new, strict liability tort based on the violation of the statute implicated here. This is a negligence case and the conduct of the officers (D) does not warrant the imposition of liability for mental distress damages absent physical injury.

▶ **ANALYSIS**

The majority responds to both the dissent and the concurrence in its opinion. In response to the claim that it imposes strict liability, the majority answers that it does not impose liability without fault. The statute simply mandates that the officers respond to the court order. It also rejects the concurrence's contention that damages may not be recovered for mental injuries absent physical injuries since the officers (D) owed a specific duty toward the plaintiff under the statute.

■—■

Bivens v. Six Unknown Named Agents of Federal Bureau of Narcotics

Suspect (P) v. Federal agents (D)

403 U.S. 388 (1971).

NATURE OF CASE: Violation of Fourth Amendment rights.

FACT SUMMARY: Bivens (P), who had been the victim of an unwarranted search for narcotics, brought an action for damages directly under the Fourth Amendment to the United States Constitution.

RULE OF LAW
Monetary damages may be recovered for violations of the Fourth Amendment by federal officials.

FACTS: Bivens (P) brought suit, seeking damages for violation of his Fourth Amendment rights to be free from unreasonable searches and seizures. His complaint stated that several agents of the Federal Bureau of Narcotics (D), acting under claim of federal authority, entered his apartment and arrested him for alleged narcotics violations. The agents manacled Bivens (P) in front of his wife and children and threatened to arrest the entire family. A thorough search of the family residence was then conducted. Bivens (P) stated that the arrest and search were effected without a warrant, and that unreasonable force was employed in making the arrest, and that he had suffered great humiliation, embarrassment, and mental suffering as the result of the agents' unlawful conduct. After the court of appeals affirmed the district court's dismissal of the action, Bivens (P) appealed.

ISSUE: May monetary damages be recovered for violations of the Fourth Amendment by federal officials?

HOLDING AND DECISION: (Brennan, J.) Yes. Monetary damages may be recovered for violations of the Fourth Amendment by federal officials. The Fourth Amendment operates as a limitation upon the exercise of federal power regardless of whether the state in whose jurisdiction that power is exercised would prohibit or penalize the identical act if engaged in by a private citizen. Historically, damages have been regarded as the ordinary remedy for an invasion of personal interests in liberty. Bivens (P) is entitled to recover money damages for any injuries he has suffered as a result of the agents' violation of the Fourth Amendment. Reversed and remanded.

CONCURRENCE: (Harlan, J.) It is entirely proper that these injuries be compensable according to uniform rules of federal law, especially in light of the very large element of federal law which must control the scope of official defenses to liability.

DISSENT: (Burger, C.J.) Legislation is the business of the Congress, and it has the facilities and competence for that task, which the courts do not.

DISSENT: (Black, J.) Neither Congress nor the State of New York has enacted legislation creating such a right of action. For the court to do so is an unconstitutional exercise of power.

ANALYSIS

This case, a landmark decision, is generally recognized as the first case in which the Supreme Court implied a cause of action arising directly from a constitutional provision. The nature of Bivens's (P) action, though, is nearly identical to that which may be asserted against state officials under the federal civil rights statute, 42 U.S.C. § 1983.

Quicknotes

FOURTH AMENDMENT Provides that persons be secure as to their person and private belongings against unreasonable searches and seizures.

Alexander v. Sandoval

Director of public safety (D) v. Driver's license examinee (P)

532 U.S. 275 (2001).

NATURE OF CASE: Suit to enjoin enforcement of a state policy requiring English-only driver's license examinations.

FACT SUMMARY: A state department of public safety adopted a policy requiring driver's licenses to be administered only in English. A non-English-speaking driver's license examinee sued under Title VI of the Civil Rights Act to enjoin the state department from enforcing the policy.

> 🏛 **RULE OF LAW**
> A private individual cannot sue to enforce regulations promulgated under Title VI of the Civil Rights Act.

FACTS: The Alabama Department of Public Safety, whose director was Alexander (D), accepted federal funds and thus was required to comply with Title VI of the federal Civil Rights Act, 42 U.S.C. 2000d et seq. Section 601 of the statute prohibited the department from discriminating against persons on the basis of race, color, or national origin. Section 602 authorized federal agencies to adopt and promulgate rules to carry out § 601's prohibition on discrimination. The U.S. Department of Justice (DOJ) adopted and promulgated such a rule, proscribing policies that had even the effect of such discrimination. The Alabama Department of Public Safety then adopted a policy requiring all driver's license examinations to be administered in English. Sandoval (P), who did not speak English, filed suit to enjoin enforcement of the English-only policy; he claimed that the DOJ's rule, promulgated pursuant to § 602, created a right for him to sue to enforce the regulation's requirements. The trial court agreed, and it also agreed with Sandoval (P) on the merits of his request for injunctive relief, enjoining Alexander (D) from enforcing the English-only policy. The Eleventh Circuit Court of Appeals affirmed the trial court. Alexander (D) petitioned for review in the U.S. Supreme Court.

ISSUE: Can a private individual sue to enforce regulations promulgated under Title VI of the Civil Rights Act?

HOLDING AND DECISION: (Scalia, J.) No. A private individual cannot sue to enforce regulations promulgated under Title VI of the Civil Rights Act. The Court may take three aspects of Title VI as given for purposes of this appeal. First, § 601 does create a private right of action. Second, the only discrimination prohibited by § 601 is intentional. Third, the Court will assume in this case that regulations pro-

mulgated pursuant to § 602 can apply to groups. Against that backdrop, it is clear that § 601's private right of action cannot include a similar right in the DOJ's regulations promulgated under § 602 because the regulations prohibit conduct allowed by § 601. Thus, if a private right of action exists in the DOJ's regulations, it must derive from § 602. To determine whether § 602 implies a private right to sue, it is improper to refer to the law of implied rights as it existed when Title VI was enacted in 1964. That understanding was superseded, without deviation in the interim, in *Cort v. Ash,* 422 U.S. 66, 78 (1975). Further, the "contemporary legal context" is no more than possible support for the statutory text itself. In this case, the text of § 602 ends the inquiry: It has no rights-creating language, limits federal agencies to "effectuating" § 601, and applies only to the regulated recipients of federal funds, not to the individuals who are protected by § 601. Section 602's methods of enforcement also fail to demonstrate Congressional intent to create a private right of action. Sandoval (P) and the Government next would find the private right in the DOJ's regulations themselves, but regulations cannot create rights of action where Congress not first done so in the empowering statute. Nor have the two most recent amendments to Title VI implicitly "ratified" this Court's implied-rights decisions. Indeed, no case has found the implied right that is essential to Sandoval's (P) argument. Further, the implicit-ratification argument is fundamentally flawed anyway because Congress's inaction on specific portions of a statutory scheme means only that Congress took no action in those areas. It does not mean that Congress has affirmatively approved any of this Court's decisions. Reversed.

▶ *ANALYSIS*

Sandoval is part of a distinct trend in the Supreme Court to limit judicial recognition of new implied rights of action. A fruitful question to ponder, especially when weighing the possibility of bringing suit under a statutory scheme that does not directly express a right of action, is whether that trend is grounded in the law or in something even more intangible and personal. Justice Stevens, writing in dissent in the 5-4 decision in *Sandoval*, concluded that "today's decision is the unconscious product of the majority's profound distaste for implied causes of action rather than an attempt to discern the intent of the Congress that enacted Title VI of the Civil Rights Act of 1964." 532 U.S. at 317.

De Falco v. Bernas

Land developers (P) v. Local government racketeers (D)

244 F.3d 286 (2d Cir. 2001).

NATURE OF CASE: Appeal from a trial court's order vacating a civil jury's award of damages on violations of the federal Racketeer Influenced and Corrupt Organization Act (RICO).

FACT SUMMARY: Local government officials, and people influencing them, conditioned the local government's approval of a land-development project upon the developers' surrender of property and their employment of certain persons.

🏛 RULE OF LAW
A private individual cannot successfully enforce the federal criminal RICO statute, 18 U.S.C. 1962(c), unless he proves that the prohibited racketeering conduct was both the factual and proximate cause of his injuries.

FACTS: De Falco and others (P) bought land in Delaware Township, Sullivan County, New York to develop the land. Dirie (D), the Town of Delaware's supervisor and a member of the Town's legislative body, expressly conditioned the Town's approval of the planned development on De Falco (P) allowing Dirie's (D) son to harvest timber on the property. When De Falco (P) entered a logging contract with an out-of-state logging company for the project, Dirie (D) demanded that De Falco (P) dissolve the contract and threatened De Falco (P) with the prospect of losing the approval of the Town's planning board. The Bernas defendants (D) also threatened De Falco (P) with the local government's disapproval of the development project even though they were not officially members of the local government. The Bernas defendants (D), who operated a road-construction business, withdrew gravel from De Falco's (P) property and demanded that De Falco (P) transfer shares in the proposed new business to the Bernas defendants (D). After about seven months, De Falco (P) eventually complied with the demand, but the Bernas defendants (D) escalated their demands by requiring expanded rights to the property's gravel pit, threatening to close down the entire development project if De Falco (P) resisted. De Falco (P) sued. The jury found a violation of the federal RICO statute, 18 U.S.C. 1962(c), and awarded De Falco (P) $1.6 million, as well as $1,000.00 for truck wheels and tires that Dirie (D) had extorted from De Falco (P) for Dirie's (D) son. The trial judge vacated the $1.6 million award, finding that the evidence failed to show sufficient causation between the RICO violations and De Falco's (P) injuries, but the trial judge left the $1,000.00 award intact. De Falco (P) appealed.

ISSUE: Can a private individual successfully enforce the federal criminal RICO statute, 18 U.S.C. 1962(c), if he fails to prove that the prohibited racketeering conduct was both the factual and proximate cause of his injuries?

HOLDING AND DECISION: (Underhill, Dist. J.) No. A private individual cannot successfully enforce the federal criminal RICO statute, 18 U.S.C. 1962(c), unless he proves that the prohibited racketeering conduct was both the factual and proximate cause of his injuries. The evidence at trial established that Dirie (D) and the Bernas defendants (D) did violate 18 U.S.C. 1962(c). That provision of the RICO Act requires that a defendant committed at least two instances of racketeering activity; that the defendants participated in an enterprise, either directly or indirectly; and that the defendants' activities affected interstate or foreign commerce. De Falco (P) met its burden on these essential elements of a RICO claim. First, the Town and the defendants were distinct, as 18 U.S.C. 1962(c) requires. The defendants here were separate and distinct from the Town but used their power to adversely affect De Falco's (P) ability to secure the Town's approval of the development project. As this Court has held, see *United States v. Angelilli*, 660 F.2d 23, 30-35 (2d Cir. 1981), the enterprise contemplated by RICO includes governmental units: The statutory language is broad enough to include governments, the Act's substantive goals of combating bribery and extortion are peculiarly applicable to governments, and the legislative history shows that Congress expressly intended for the statutory scheme that contains RICO to apply to governments. Further, Dirie's (D) challenge to RICO's interstate-commerce requirement has no merit because his conduct forced De Falco (P) to break a contract with an out-of-state logging company and because the Town's business regularly touched interstate commerce. De Falco (P) also showed that both Dirie (D) and the Bernas defendants (D) participated in the RICO enterprise. Dirie (D) directly participated in the Town's affairs, and he used his positions to impose extortionate demands upon De Falco (P). The Bernas defendants' (D) participation in the Town's operations was shown by their threats to close down De Falco's (P) project altogether and by a Town official's written reference to the need for the Bernas defendants' (D) approval of the project. The evidence also established that Dirie (D) and the Bernas defendants (D) each engaged in racketeering activity at least

Continued on next page.

twice within a ten-year period. The five acts of extortion allegedly committed by Dirie (D) need not have involved fear of force or violence; fear of economic injury is enough, and the evidence meets that element of extortion here. Further, the Bernas defendants (D) engaged in a pattern of open-ended continuity sufficient to constitute a pattern of racketeering activity. The other way to prove a racketeering pattern, as closed-ended continuity, has always required a period of at least two years in this Court. The Bernas defendants' (D) extortions of De Falco (P) over the latter half of 1989 fail to satisfy that requirement; even viewing the evidence most favorably to De Falco (P), which yields a period of eighteen months for the racketeering activities of the Bernas defendants (D), De Falco (P) still has failed to show closed-ended continuity. De Falco (P) has shown open-ended continuity, however, because there was a threat that the Bernas defendants' (D) criminal activities would continue after their proven racketeering activities occurred. Although De Falco (P) thus established a violation of 18 U.S.C. 1962(c), the evidence fails to satisfy RICO's remedies provision, 18 U.S.C. 1964(c). Under that provision's "by reason of" requirement, a defendant's violative conduct must be both the factual and the proximate cause of De Falco's (P) injuries. In this case, De Falco (P) therefore needed to prove that it complied with all requirements for approval of its lots and that no other cause besides the racketeering activities burdened De Falco's (P) sale of the lots. The record contains no such evidence. Accordingly, the trial court correctly vacated the $1.6 million award but incorrectly left the $1,000.00 award intact. Affirmed in part, vacated in part.

▌ANALYSIS

The plaintiffs in *De Falco* might easily have grounded their complaint on a common-law claim such as intentional interference with a business or economic relationship, particularly with respect to the contract with the out-of-state logging company. A common-law claim, though, would not have included the treble-damages incentives provided under the federal RICO statute. Students should note, though, that civil RICO claims can be temptations that exact a sharp price upon attorneys themselves. The strength of the evidence here on the defendants' violations of 18 U.S.C. 1962(c) minimizes the absence of evidence on causation. It is all too possible, however, for counsel's failure to determine an adequate foundation for civil RICO claims, certainly before filing a complaint, to cause courts to impose strict penalties upon such professionally delinquent attorneys themselves. See, e.g., *Byrne v. Nezhat*, 261 F.3d 1075, 1115 (11th Cir. 2001) ("[p]articularly with regard to civil RICO claims, plaintiffs must *stop and think* before filing them") (quoting *Pelletier v. Zweifel*, 921 F.2d 1465, 1522 (11th Cir. 1991)) (emphasis in original).

Quicknotes

BRIBERY The offering, giving, receiving, or soliciting of something of value for the purpose of influencing the action of an official in the discharge of his public or legal duties.

BURDEN OF PROOF The duty of a party to introduce evidence to support a fact that is in dispute in an action.

CAUSE IN FACT The event without which an injury would not have been incurred.

EXTORTION The unlawful taking of property of another by threats of force.

PROXIMATE CAUSE The natural sequence of events without which an injury would not have been sustained.

RICO Racketeer Influenced and Corrupt Organization laws; federal and state statutes enacted for the purpose of prosecuting organized crime.

TORTIOUS INTERFERENCE WITH CONTRACTUAL RELATIONSHIP An intentional tort whereby a defendant intentionally elicits the breach of a valid contract resulting in damages.

■▬■

Pulliam v. Coastal Emergency Svcs.

Estate of medical patient (P) v. Hospital (D)

Va. Sup. Ct., 257 Va. 1, 509 S.E.2d 307 (1999).

NATURE OF CASE: Appeal on the constitutionality of a statutorily proscribed damages cap on recovery for medical malpractice.

FACT SUMMARY: An emergency room patient dies after being misdiagnosed, but the damage award recovered by her estate is reduced based on a damages cap mandated by statute.

🏛 RULE OF LAW
The doctrine of stare decisis does not compel a court to follow a prior decision where there has been error or mistake in that decision.

FACTS: Mrs. Pulliam (P) was admitted to the hospital (D) complaining of pain in her legs. She was examined by Dr. DiGiovanna (D) in the emergency room, and discharged after being prescribed a muscle relaxant. Mrs. Pulliam (P) returned later, complaining of weakness in her extremities. She was admitted for further examination, and her condition subsequently worsened, whereupon she was transferred to the intensive care unit. Mrs. Pulliam (P) died, and an autopsy revealed the cause of death as pneumonia and bacterial infection. Her husband (P), executor of her estate, brought suit for malpractice against Dr. DiGiovanna (D) and the hospital (D) vicariously. At trial, Pulliam (P) was awarded a verdict of $2.05 million, which the trial court judge later reduced to $1 million based on a statutorily imposed cap on damages for medical malpractice. Mr. Pulliam (P) filed an appeal, asserting that the trial court committed error by failing to recognize that such a cap was unconstitutional.

ISSUE: Does the doctrine of stare decisis compel a court to follow a prior decision where there has been error in that decision?

HOLDING AND DESCISION: (Carrico, C.J.) No. The doctrine of stare decisis does not compel a court to follow a prior decision where there has been error in that decision. The present case requires this court to reaffirm the holding of the court in *Etheridge v. Medical Center Hospitals*, 237 Va. 87, 376 S.E.2d 525 (Va. 1989), a case of similar facts dealing with the consitutionality of a malpractice cap. In *Etheridge*, the court concluded that a medical malpractice cap does not violate any constitutional guarantees. Where flagrant error or mistake existed in the *Etheridge* decision, this court cannot follow its precedent as an aforementioned violation of the doctrine of stare decisis. Pulliam's estate (P) contends that such error does indeed exist, and this court should not be deterred from ignoring the doctrine of stare decisis and reversing *Etheridge* on several independent grounds. We address Pulliam's (P) contention on all grounds and find no merit in plaintiff's (P) arguments that any error existed in *Etheridge* as decided. First, a damages cap is appropriate after a plaintiff has had the proper benefit of a jury trial, contrary to Pulliam's (P) assertion that a new trial is necessary first. Pulliam (P) contends that the cap applied in *Etheridge* was impermissible special legislation. However, the cap as applied in *Etheridge* bears a reasonable and substantial relation to the legislature's objective in protecting the public's health, safety, and welfare. Pulliam (P) next argues that a damages cap is an unconstitutional taking of a plaintiff's property, and the failure of the *Etheridge* court to find such a cap unconstitutional is error. We disagree; a taking only results when the right has vested or accrued to the plaintiff first, which is not the case with malpractice damages. Pulliam (P) asserts that an intermediate level of scrutiny should have been applied in *Etheridge*, rather than the lower-level rational basis test. However, no fundamental right or suspect classification has been implicated in the affirmation of the damages cap as applied in *Etheridge*, which enunciated the correct level of scrutiny. Finally, Pulliam (P) asserts that the damages cap in *Etheridge* violates separation of powers by invading the province of the judiciary. However, we have consistently ruled that the legislature has the power to provide, modify, or repeal a remedy. The court therefore rejects all of Pulliam's (P) arguments. Affirmed.

CONCURRENCE: (Kinser, J.) Without addressing the issue of stare decisis, I agree that a medical malpractice cap creates unnecessary injustice, since it operates to disadvantage those persons who are the most severely injured by negligent health care providers.

▎ *ANALYSIS*

A cap on damages is a common tool for state tort reform, to limit the windfall recovered by plaintiffs for various policy reasons. In this case, separation of powers is only briefly implicated, but plays a larger role contextually since it is the province of the legislature to vindicate public policy, often avoiding a damages cap to limit the defendant's ability to subsequently calculate how much it could potentially pay and thereby avoid other remedial measures that might be more costly.

■=∎

Compensation Systems as Substitutes for Tort Law

Quick Reference Rules of Law

Blankenship v. Cincinnati Milacron Chemicals, Inc.

Employees (P) v. Chemical manufacturer (D)

Ohio Sup. Ct., 69 Ohio St. 2d 608, 433 N.E.2d 572 (1982).

NATURE OF CASE: Appeal from dismissal of action for work-related injuries.

FACT SUMMARY: Blankenship (P) contended the workers compensation system did not bar his suit against his employer Cincinnati Milacron (D) (Milacron) for intentional tortious conduct.

🏛 RULE OF LAW
The workers compensation system does not bar direct employee suits against employers for intentional torts.

FACTS: Blankenship (P) and other employees of Milacron (D) brought suit against Milacron (D) for intentionally failing to warn them of the harmful effects of their exposure to certain chemicals while on the job. The trial court dismissed on the basis that the workers compensation system provided the only remedy for such work-related injuries. Blankenship (P) appealed, contending the system did not bar suit for intentional conduct. The court of appeals affirmed, and the Ohio Supreme Court granted a hearing.

ISSUE: Does the workers compensation system bar employee suits for the employer's intentional tortious conduct?

HOLDING AND DECISION: (Brown, J.) No. The workers compensation system does not bar employee suits for the employer's intentional conduct. The risk of intentional tort is not part of the usual risk occasioned by employment. Intentional tortious conduct cannot be considered to be in the course and scope of the employment relationship. Thus, it falls outside the workers compensation system. Reversed.

▶ ANALYSIS

Most states, Ohio now included, have made allowances for employer intentional conduct within their workers compensation systems. Thus, while actual civil suits may not be brought, increased compensation benefits are paid for the intentional conduct of the employer.

■■■■

Quicknotes

WORKER'S COMPENSATION ACT The statutory right of an employee to claim fixed benefits (primarily loss of earnings and medical expenses) from her employer for injury or disease arising out of and in the course of employment.

■■■■

Common Latin Words and Phrases Encountered in the Law

A FORTIORI: Because one fact exists or has been proven, therefore a second fact that is related to the first fact must also exist.

A PRIORI: From the cause to the effect. A term of logic used to denote that when one generally accepted truth is shown to be a cause, another particular effect must necessarily follow.

AB INITIO: From the beginning; a condition which has existed throughout, as in a marriage which was void ab initio.

ACTUS REUS: The wrongful act; in criminal law, such action sufficient to trigger criminal liability.

AD VALOREM: According to value; an ad valorem tax is imposed upon an item located within the taxing jurisdiction calculated by the value of such item.

AMICUS CURIAE: Friend of the court. Its most common usage takes the form of an amicus curiae brief, filed by a person who is not a party to an action but is nonetheless allowed to offer an argument supporting his legal interests.

ARGUENDO: In arguing. A statement, possibly hypothetical, made for the purpose of argument, is one made arguendo.

BILL QUIA TIMET: A bill to quiet title (establish ownership) to real property.

BONA FIDE: True, honest, or genuine. May refer to a person's legal position based on good faith or lacking notice of fraud (such as a bona fide purchaser for value) or to the authenticity of a particular document (such as a bona fide last will and testament).

CAUSA MORTIS: With approaching death in mind. A gift causa mortis is a gift given by a party who feels certain that death is imminent.

CAVEAT EMPTOR: Let the buyer beware. This maxim is reflected in the rule of law that a buyer purchases at his own risk because it is his responsibility to examine, judge, test, and otherwise inspect what he is buying.

CERTIORARI: A writ of review. Petitions for review of a case by the United States Supreme Court are most often done by means of a writ of certiorari.

CONTRA: On the other hand. Opposite. Contrary to.

CORAM NOBIS: Before us; writs of error directed to the court that originally rendered the judgment.

CORAM VOBIS: Before you; writs of error directed by an appellate court to a lower court to correct a factual error.

CORPUS DELICTI: The body of the crime; the requisite elements of a crime amounting to objective proof that a crime has been committed.

CUM TESTAMENTO ANNEXO, ADMINISTRATOR (ADMINISTRATOR C.T.A.): With will annexed; an administrator c.t.a. settles an estate pursuant to a will in which he is not appointed.

DE BONIS NON, ADMINISTRATOR (ADMINISTRATOR D.B.N.): Of goods not administered; an administrator d.b.n. settles a partially settled estate.

DE FACTO: In fact; in reality; actually. Existing in fact but not officially approved or engendered.

DE JURE: By right; lawful. Describes a condition that is legitimate "as a matter of law," in contrast to the term "de facto," which connotes something existing in fact but not legally sanctioned or authorized. For example, de facto segregation refers to segregation brought about by housing patterns, etc., whereas de jure segregation refers to segregation created by law.

DE MINIMUS: Of minimal importance; insignificant; a trifle; not worth bothering about.

DE NOVO: Anew; a second time; afresh. A trial de novo is a new trial held at the appellate level as if the case originated there and the trial at a lower level had not taken place.

DICTA: Generally used as an abbreviated form of obiter dicta, a term describing those portions of a judicial opinion incidental or not necessary to resolution of the specific question before the court. Such nonessential statements and remarks are not considered to be binding precedent.

DUCES TECUM: Refers to a particular type of writ or subpoena requesting a party or organization to produce certain documents in their possession.

EN BANC: Full bench. Where a court sits with all justices present rather than the usual quorum.

EX PARTE: For one side or one party only. An ex parte proceeding is one undertaken for the benefit of only one party, without notice to, or an appearance by, an adverse party.

EX POST FACTO: After the fact. An ex post facto law is a law that retroactively changes the consequences of a prior act.

EX REL.: Abbreviated form of the term ex relatione, meaning, upon relation or information. When the state brings an action in which it has no interest against an individual at the instigation of one who has a private interest in the matter.

FORUM NON CONVENIENS: Inconvenient forum. Although a court may have jurisdiction over the case, the action should be tried in a more conveniently located court, one to which parties and witnesses may more easily travel, for example.

GUARDIAN AD LITEM: A guardian of an infant as to litigation, appointed to represent the infant and pursue his/her rights.

HABEAS CORPUS: You have the body. The modern writ of habeas corpus is a writ directing that a person (body) being detained (such as a prisoner) be brought before the court so that the legality of his detention can be judicially ascertained.

IN CAMERA: In private, in chambers. When a hearing is held before a judge in his chambers or when all spectators are excluded from the courtroom.

IN FORMA PAUPERIS: In the manner of a pauper. A party who proceeds in forma pauperis because of his poverty is one who is allowed to bring suit without liability for costs.

INFRA: Below, under. A word referring the reader to a later part of a book. (The opposite of supra.)

IN LOCO PARENTIS: In the place of a parent.

IN PARI DELICTO: Equally wrong; a court of equity will not grant requested relief to an applicant who is in pari delicto, or as much at fault in the transactions giving rise to the controversy as is the opponent of the applicant.

IN PARI MATERIA: On like subject matter or upon the same matter. Statutes relating to the same person or things are said to be in pari materia. It is a general rule of statutory construction that such statutes should be construed together, i.e., looked at as if they together constituted one law.

IN PERSONAM: Against the person. Jurisdiction over the person of an individual.

IN RE: In the matter of. Used to designate a proceeding involving an estate or other property.

IN REM: A term that signifies an action against the res, or thing. An action in rem is basically one that is taken directly against property, as distinguished from an action in personam, i.e., against the person.

INTER ALIA: Among other things. Used to show that the whole of a statement, pleading, list, statute, etc., has not been set forth in its entirety.

INTER PARTES: Between the parties. May refer to contracts, conveyances or other transactions having legal significance.

INTER VIVOS: Between the living. An inter vivos gift is a gift made by a living grantor, as distinguished from bequests contained in a will, which pass upon the death of the testator.

IPSO FACTO: By the mere fact itself.

JUS: Law or the entire body of law.

LEX LOCI: The law of the place; the notion that the rights of parties to a legal proceeding are governed by the law of the place where those rights arose.

MALUM IN SE: Evil or wrong in and of itself; inherently wrong. This term describes an act that is wrong by its very nature, as opposed to one which would not be wrong but for the fact that there is a specific legal prohibition against it (malum prohibitum).

MALUM PROHIBITUM: Wrong because prohibited, but not inherently evil. Used to describe something that is wrong because it is expressly forbidden by law but that is not in and of itself evil, e.g., speeding.

MANDAMUS: We command. A writ directing an official to take a certain action.

MENS REA: A guilty mind; a criminal intent. A term used to signify the mental state that accompanies a crime or other prohibited act. Some crimes require only a general mens rea (general intent to do the prohibited act), but others, like assault with intent to murder, require the existence of a specific mens rea.

MODUS OPERANDI: Method of operating; generally refers to the manner or style of a criminal in committing crimes, admissible in appropriate cases as evidence of the identity of a defendant.

NEXUS: A connection to.

NISI PRIUS: A court of first impression. A nisi prius court is one where issues of fact are tried before a judge or jury.

N.O.V. (NON OBSTANTE VEREDICTO): Not withstanding the verdict. A judgment n.o.v. is a judgment given in favor of one party despite the fact that a verdict was returned in favor of the other party, the justification being that the verdict either had no reasonable support in fact or was contrary to law.

NUNC PRO TUNC: Now for then. This phrase refers to actions that may be taken and will then have full retroactive effect.

PENDENTE LITE: Pending the suit; pending litigation underway.

PER CAPITA: By head; beneficiaries of an estate, if they take in equal shares, take per capita.

PER CURIAM: By the court; signifies an opinion ostensibly written "by the whole court" and with no identified author.

PER SE: By itself, in itself; inherently.

PER STIRPES: By representation. Used primarily in the law of wills to describe the method of distribution where a person, generally because of death, is unable to take that which is left to him by the will of another, and therefore his heirs divide such property between them rather than take under the will individually.

PRIMA FACIE: On its face, at first sight. A prima facie case is one that is sufficient on its face, meaning that the evidence supporting it is adequate to establish the case until contradicted or overcome by other evidence.

PRO TANTO: For so much; as far as it goes. Often used in eminent domain cases when a property owner receives partial payment for his land without prejudice to his right to bring suit for the full amount he claims his land to be worth.

QUANTUM MERUIT: As much as he deserves. Refers to recovery based on the doctrine of unjust enrichment in those cases in which a party has rendered valuable services or furnished materials that were accepted and enjoyed by another under circumstances that would reasonably notify the recipient that the rendering party expected to be paid. In essence, the law implies a contract to pay the reasonable value of the services or materials furnished.

QUASI: Almost like; as if; nearly. This term is essentially used to signify that one subject or thing is almost analogous to another but that material differences between them do exist. For example, a quasi-criminal proceeding is one that is not strictly criminal but shares enough of the same characteristics to require some of the same safeguards (e.g., procedural due process must be followed in a parole hearing).

QUID PRO QUO: Something for something. In contract law, the consideration, something of value, passed between the parties to render the contract binding.

RES GESTAE: Things done. In evidence law, this principle justifies the admission of a statement that would otherwise be hearsay when it is made so closely to the event in question as to be said to be a part of it, or with such spontaneity as not to have the possibility of falsehood.

RES IPSA LOQUITUR: The thing speaks for itself. This doctrine gives rise to a rebuttable presumption of negligence when the instrumentality causing the injury was within the exclusive control of the defendant, and the injury was one that does not normally occur unless a person has been negligent.

RES JUDICATA: A matter adjudged. Doctrine which provides that once a court of competent jurisdiction has rendered a final judgment or decree on the merits, that judgment or decree is conclusive upon the parties to the case and prevents them from engaging in any other litigation on the points and issues determined therein.

RESPONDEAT SUPERIOR: Let the master reply. This doctrine holds the master liable for the wrongful acts of his servant (or the principal for his agent) in those cases in which the servant (or agent) was acting within the scope of his authority at the time of the injury.

STARE DECISIS: To stand by or adhere to that which has been decided. The common law doctrine of stare decisis attempts to give security and certainty to the law by following the policy that once a principle of law as applicable to a certain set of facts has been set forth in a decision, it forms a precedent that will subsequently be followed, even though a different decision might be made were it the first time the question had arisen. Of course, stare decisis is not an inviolable principle and is departed from in instances where there is good cause (e.g., considerations of public policy led the Supreme Court to disregard prior decisions sanctioning segregation).

SUPRA: Above. A word referring a reader to an earlier part of a book.

ULTRA VIRES: Beyond the power. This phrase is most commonly used to refer to actions taken by a corporation that are beyond the power or legal authority of the corporation.

Addendum of French Derivatives

IN PAIS: Not pursuant to legal proceedings.

CHATTEL: Tangible personal property.

CY PRES: Doctrine permitting courts to apply trust funds to purposes not expressed in the trust but necessary to carry out the settlor's intent.

PER AUTRE VIE: For another's life; during another's life. In property law, an estate may be granted that will terminate upon the death of someone other than the grantee.

PROFIT A PRENDRE: A license to remove minerals or other produce from land.

VOIR DIRE: Process of questioning jurors as to their predispositions about the case or parties to a proceeding in order to identify those jurors displaying bias or prejudice.

Casenote Legal Briefs